THE SHAKESPEARE COMPANY,
1594–1642

This is the first complete history of the theatre company, created in 1594, which in 1603 became the King's Men. Shakespeare was at the heart of the team of players, who with their successors ran an operation that lasted until the theatres closed in 1642. During those forty-eight years they staged all of Shakespeare's plays, a number of Ben Jonson's, most of Thomas Middleton and John Webster, and almost all of the Beaumont and Fletcher canon. Andrew Gurr provides a comprehensive history of the company's activities. A chapter on their finances explains the unique management system they adopted and two chapters study the fashions in their repertory and the complex relationship with their royal patrons. The six appendixes identify the 99 players who worked in the company and the 168 plays they are known to have owned and performed, as well as the key documents from the company's history.

ANDREW GURR is Professor Emeritus at the University of Reading. His many books include *The Shakespearean Stage 1574–1642* (Cambridge), now in its third edition, *Writers in Exile, Playgoing in Shakespeare's London* (Cambridge), also about to appear in a third edition, *The Shakespearian Playing Companies*, and (with Mariko Ichikawa) *Staging in Shakespeare's Theatres*.

THE SHAKESPEARE COMPANY,
1594–1642

ANDREW GURR

PUBLISHED BY THE PRESS SYNDICATE OF THE UNIVERSITY OF CAMBRIDGE
The Pitt Building, Trumpington Street, Cambridge, United Kingdom

CAMBRIDGE UNIVERSITY PRESS
The Edinburgh Building, Cambridge, CB2 2RU, UK
40 West 20th Street, New York, NY 10011–4211, USA
477 Williamstown Road, Port Melbourne, VIC 3207, Australia
Ruiz de Alarcón 13, 28014 Madrid, Spain
Dock House, The Waterfront, Cape Town 8001, South Africa

http://www.cambridge.org

First published 2004
Reprinted 2005

Printed in the United Kingdom at the University Press, Cambridge

Typeface Adobe Garamond 11/12.5 pt.   *System* LATEX 2ε [TB]

A catalogue record for this book is available from the British Library

Library of Congress Cataloguing in Publication data
Gurr, Andrew.
The Shakespeare Company, 1594–1642 / Andrew Gurr.
p.   cm.
Includes bibliographical references and index.
ISBN 0 521 80730 1
1. Shakespeare, William, 1564–1616 – Stage history – to 1625.   2. Shakespeare, William, 1564–1616 –
Stage history – 1625–1800.   3. Shakespeare, William, 1564–1616 – Relations with actors.
4. Theatrical companies – England–London – History – 17th century.   5. Theatrical companies –
England–London – History – 16th century.   6. Repertory theatre – England–London – History –
17th century.   7. Repertory theatre – England–London – History – 16th century.
8. Chamberlain's Men (Theatre company).   9. King's Men (Theatre company).   1. Title.
PR3095.G86   2004
792′.09421 – dc22   2003055895

ISBN 0 521 80730 1 hardback

Thy Muses sugred dainties seeme to us
Like the fam'd Apples of old Tantalus:
For we (admiring) see and heare thy straines,
But none I see or heare, those sweets attaines.
(Thomas Bancroft, *Two Bookes of Epigrammes*
and Epitaphs, 1639, Epigram 118, 'To *Shakespeare*')

Contents

Illustrations

My thanks are due to the Folger Shakespeare Library for permission to reproduce illustrations 1, 17, 18, 19, and 20; to John Kenelm Wingfield Digby for illustration 2; to the National Portrait Gallery for illustrations 3, 9, 21, and 22; to the British Library for illustrations 4 and 16; to the Mellon Foundation, Yale, for illustration 5; to the Guildhall Library, Corporation of London, for illustration 6; to the Royal Library, Stockholm, for illustration 7; to Worcester College Oxford, for illustration 8; to the Records of Early English Drama, Toronto, for illustrations 10 and 15; to the Record Office for Leicestershire, Leicester and Rutland for illustrations 11 and 14; to the International Shakespeare Globe Centre for illustration 12; to the Wilton House Archive for illustration 13; to the Trustees of Dulwich Picture Gallery for illustrations 23, 24, and 26; to the Ashmolean Museum for illustration 25; and to the Marquess of Bath for 27.

Preface

An acting company conceived an idea in 1594 that it realized in 1608 and that helped it to run for forty-eight years as the unrivalled leader of its time. In 1599 the company conceived a management system that made its actors their own managers and financiers, creating the only effective democracy of its time in totalitarian England. For us now the plays of Shakespeare have made the company he worked for into part of the ceremonial regalia commonly paraded in the acts of worship by Shakespeare-lovers. This book is about the company which made the icon so many of us worship.

Shakespeare became what he made Henry V call himself, a gentleman of a company, though the king's was not quite the same as the player's. It seems right to call the company he helped to found, which officially had four different names in the near half-century it did business, by his name. The label 'Shakespearean' is now of course a praise word. I have used it before to point to my subject's first cause, but the eponymity in the title of this book has a more distinct justification. Shakespeare and his plays were gathered up in May 1594 to form an essential component of a new company set up by Henry Carey, the Lord Chamberlain. Carey was the queen's cousin and as Chamberlain he was the official responsible for plays and for entertaining the queen with them. In that month, in alliance with his son-in-law Charles Howard, the Lord Admiral, he set up two new companies to serve his official purpose. A single company had been established eleven years before as the Queen's Men, but it had lost its hegemony. Setting up two companies was a sounder policy than having just one, since it gave better insurance against any future loss of the capacity to entertain royalty. London's two leading actors, Edward Alleyn and Richard Burbage, were each allocated a company of fellow-players and a playhouse belonging to someone in their family, and each company was given a set of already famous plays. One secured Marlowe's, the other Shakespeare's. In its repertoire, if nowhere else, at its creation in 1594 the Lord Chamberlain's Men was the Shakespeare company.

It served several patrons, was subject to no impresarios, and came to own its two playhouses. The first official title was the Lord Chamberlain's Men. When Henry Carey died in July 1596, his son George, the second Lord Hunsdon, became their patron, so that for the next few months they were the second Lord Hunsdon's Men. The new Lord Chamberlain was Lord Cobham. He died less than eight months later and when George Carey succeeded him as Lord Chamberlain the company resumed its original title. Then in 1603 when King James VI of Scotland became King James I of England he took the leading company for himself, later giving the others to his son and his queen. Through the next thirty-nine years it was the King's Men, James's son Charles taking them over at his accession in 1625 when James died. All the professional acting companies playing in London under the early Stuarts were royal property, so in September 1642 with Charles fled and the country at war, Charles's opponent, Parliament, laid a ban on playing. The company and all its competitors died. None were resurrected until a new monarch arrived eighteen years later. Through the forty-eight years of its life under its four different titles the company stayed remarkably the same, so the one name, the Shakespeare company, is the clearest description.

Conditioned as we are to start the study of this period with Shakespeare, it is easy to forget that it was not the author but the company that controlled everything to do with his plays. The company bought the play from the author and did with it whatever they pleased. Indeed, apart from the very few plays that survive in manuscript as the 'allowed book' licensed for staging, it is likely that most of the play-texts we read are only approximations of the texts that the company chose to stage. There is strong evidence to show that even Shakespeare, himself a company co-owner and a performer of his own scripts, never expected his texts to be transferred to the stage as he wrote them. The company did what it pleased with its scripts, as on more than one occasion Jonson, Webster, and other writers lamented. Every play had its first publication on stage by the company. Printed texts came later and rarely show exactly what playgoers to the Globe or Blackfriars saw and heard. The company was the real author of the 168 plays that have survived from its long reign, but its first publications only survive residually in the printed texts.

Besides justifying close study of the companies, that regrettable fact sets up a massive and intangible barrier between then and now. Of the 168 Shakespeare company play-texts still extant, no more than four or five come close to the company's product, and one of those, Q1 *Henry V*, is not the Shakespeare we are used to seeing and reading. The company's 'allowed books' with the Master of the Revels's signature on their final page authorizing them for performance were its most treasured assets. Such unique manuscripts were never handed to a printer because they would never be returned in usable form. Only two of the company's manuscripts with that precious signature survive. All the others are at some remove from the staged versions, printed or copied from authorial or scribal manuscripts with no great authority as performed texts. The Shakespeare company mined its allowed books for its performances, and thought of the manuscript and print copies made for reading as a secondary form of publication, a residue that they remoulded on stage. From the company's more than ten thousand performances (roughly two hundred a year for forty-eight years), we have reliable scripts for fewer than one-fifth of their plays. The deficiency of the available texts is the prime reason for writing about the company ambience that first put them on stage, in the hope that it may assist modern attempts at translating the texts into comprehensible forms.

As a companion to the surviving plays this book is really an extended footnote. Nearly a quarter of the survivors are by Shakespeare, which does not make easy the need to choose what to include and what to omit. My assumption is that readers will have some acquaintance if not close friendship with the Shakespeare plays, so I have gone into detail on them only where they say something special about the company's practices. If this history seems to take more note of the other writers and of features like the company finances and the players' personalities, that is because they are less familiar. That is the price of the Shakespeare presence. It gives value to the context that brought the plays into being.

A number of the names, or rather their spelling, used here are worth a note. Most people use the spelling 'Bolingbroke' for the character in *Richard II* who becomes King Henry IV. That was the eighteenth century's version. Shakespeare himself wrote it as 'Bullingbrook', or 'Bullingbrooke', following Holinshed's spelling in order to open up the image of the usurper as water wetting the hot head of sun-king Richard. I follow Shakespeare's orthography in this case, as in the New Cambridge edition of the play, because it reproduces the phonetic spelling, and therefore what people would have heard on stage in the early performances. 'Fluellen', however, is here rendered as the modern 'Llewellyn', again as in the New Cambridge text. Otherwise the quotations from Shakespeare copy the Norton Shakespeare in this and in act, scene, and line numbering. The Norton is a version of the Oxford edition of *The Complete Works*, but restoring Falstaff's name in place of the Oxford's Oldcastle.

A multitude of people deserve special thanks for this work. In particular I should like to thank those giants Alan Dessen, Bill Ingram, Scott McMillin, Robert Weimann, and Ros Knutson, the 'rival' of my watch. Sally-Beth MacLean and her Records of Early English Drama (REED) organization have been wonderfully generous in checking my notes of the company's travels and in providing the two maps of where they toured. Others have given help both in matters of detail and in the overview. For such uplifts I would like to thank Melissa Aaron, Michela Calore, Janette Dillon, Reg Foakes, Brian Gibbons, Peter Holland, Mark Hutchings, Mariko Ichikawa, Grace Ioppolo, David Kathman, Ron Knowles, Tiffany Stern, Robin Headlam Wells, Charles Whitney, Christopher Wilson, and those labourers in my graduate vineyard at the University of Connecticut, Storrs, in 2001. And there are always the librarians, at that most rewarding resort the Folger Shakespeare Library, at the beautiful new British Library and at my university, Reading. They all have my warmest thanks for their constant readiness to help. Above and behind all, of course, is Sarah Stanton, the quietest, strongest, and most positive underpinner of Shakespeare studies in the business.

CHAPTER I

The plan of 1594

THE LAW OF WRIT AND TAKING LIBERTIES

One drama playing constantly in Shakespeare's time was the liberty people took with the law. In May 1594 staging plays in London, until then a fairly lawless activity attacked by the Lord Mayor but defended by the Privy Council, started for the first time to play an institutionalized role in London. The Lord Chamberlain, Henry Carey, first Baron Hunsdon, serving on the Privy Council as protector of the queen's access to professionally mounted plays, introduced a new idea. It fulfilled the Chamberlain's chief duty by setting up two new companies, each of them with a quasi-monopoly of playing in London. The duopoly's membership was drawn from the best available resources, and Carey licensed a specific playhouse for each of them to use. He made himself patron of one company while his fellow Privy Councillor, his son-in-law Charles Howard, the Lord Admiral, took on the second. Howard, having spent the four years after his appointment as Lord Admiral in 1584 cracking bureaucratic heads together to get the English navy into a shape that could outface the Spanish Armada, knew what had to be done, and was probably the chief deviser of the idea. Each of the new companies got half of the best players and plays then available. Each was allocated to a specified suburban playhouse, Carey's to the Theatre north of the city, owned by the chief player's father, and Howard's to the Rose in the south on Bankside, owned by its chief player's father-in-law. They knew what they were doing, because the Theatre's owner, James Burbage, had worn Carey's livery for the last twelve or more years, and the son-in-law of the Rose's owner, Edward Alleyn, had worn Howard's for nearly as long. The Lord Mayor was appeased by a ban on players using city inns. Now plays could be confined to the two counties north and south of the city where Howard controlled the local magistrates.[1] That little drama started

---

[1] For a more detailed study of the duopoly idea, and Howard's position in Surrey and Middlesex, see Gurr, 'Privy Councillors as Theatre Patrons', in *Shakespeare and Theatrical Patronage in Early*

the two companies on the longest careers that any players enjoyed up to the 1642 closure and the Civil War.

Creating this new scheme meant taking liberties with official writ. Whether Carey and Howard knowingly contrived their drastic bending of the *status quo ante* we cannot be sure, but the delicate precision with which the new set-up was established does suggest they were both working to appease the anger of the city fathers against the players, and had seen how in the face of that the Lord Chamberlain might continue enacting his office's most sensitive duty, providing the queen with her Christmas shows. The crucial novelty in the idea was to allocate each company to a suburban playhouse, and with it ban the players from using any of the inns inside the city.

The two companies set up to run as a duopoly of playing in London were given similarly strong repertoires of plays, Shakespeare to the one and Marlowe to the other, but their ideas about the playhouses allocated to them proved markedly different. While Howard's men were content to play at their open-air Rose all the year round, Carey's almost immediately started looking for somewhere indoors to use through winter. That meant returning inside the city to the inns, in spite of Carey's plan that they would vacate the city for the suburbs. The Shakespeare company ran for forty-eight years, inspired by a scheme that its members conceived within the first months of its existence to circumvent in winter the new ban on plays being staged inside the city. Co-supreme from the outset as one of London's only two sets of licensed players, its status grew largely thanks to its first and best author, Shakespeare, but what secured its lasting fame was in large part the company's decision to evade Carey's ban on playing inside the city.

Carey, showing some inconsistency, gave his own support to the first attempt at circumventing the new plan within five months of setting it up. On 8 October 1594, as winter approached, he wrote a letter to the Lord Mayor asking him to allow 'my nowe companie of Players' to perform indoors inside the city for the winter, at the Cross Keys Inn in Gracechurch Street. Invoking the old story of the need to serve the queen, he wrote asking if they could be permitted 'to plaie this winter time within the Citie at the Crosse kayes in Gracious street'.[2] Gracious (Gracechurch) Street was

---

Modern England, ed. Paul Whitfield White and Suzanne Westfall, Cambridge University Press, 2002, pp. 221–45. No papers about the 1594 deal survive, but the Privy Council reaffirmed its policy in 1598 and in 1600 (the orders are quoted in Appendix 2.7 and 2.13), when the Globe and Fortune replaced the Theatre and the Rose as the licensed playhouses.

[2] See Appendix 2.3.

1. An engraving of Henry Carey, first Baron Hunsdon, Lord Chamberlain 1584–96, first patron of the Shakespeare company.

in the heart of the city. Since the incoming Lord Mayor, John Spencer, who began his rule on 29 October, was known to be deeply hostile to any playing, Carey cannot have seriously expected to have such a request granted so soon after he had agreed to ban playing at city inns. His letter took a liberty with the new law he had himself just set up. The Lord Chamberlain never, before or after, made such a request of the Lord Mayor. The duopoly's monopolizing predecessor, the Queen's Men, had performed at several city inns, notably the Bull and the Bel Savage, as well as at the playhouses, the suburban Theatre and Curtain. After 1594 the only inns used for playing, the suburban Boar's Head and Red Bull, had to be converted from inns to full-time playhouses. Carey was trying to flout his own new agreement with the Lord Mayor. The letter's recipient, the stand-in Lord Mayor Sir Richard Martin, gave no formal reply, but Spencer's understandable response was a letter objecting to plays anywhere.[3]

So the next winter Carey gave his support to a revised plan, to build a winter playhouse inside a city liberty where the Lord Mayor had no power. That was the company's liberty with the new law. Like the St Paul's church-yard, site of the city's only other indoor playhouse, the Blackfriars was a free precinct in the city centre a mere couple of hundred yards south-west of the cathedral. An earlier playhouse had run there for fourteen years. Building a new playhouse in the Blackfriars was a brilliantly original idea. The concept was radical, and was almost certainly the idea of the owner of the playhouse now licensed for the Chamberlain's, James Burbage. He would bypass the Lord Mayor entirely and get his patron to back a replace-ment for the wintertime inns in the form of a permanent indoor playhouse located outside the Lord Mayor's control. Playing indoors inside the city would attract the wealthier clientele of gentry and lawyers at the adjacent Inns of Court who occupied the financial heights in winter, becoming a supplement to the open-air Theatre. Burbage was probably self-assured enough to expect he could keep the Theatre open after its lease expired and run both playhouses, one for the summer and one for the winter, as the company finally did twelve years later.

Shakespeare may have laid the company's golden eggs, but James Burbage built the goose's nest. He was a Londoner deeply experienced in playing and in playhouse management (Appendix 2.1). His thinking was progressive and adventurous. He may even have felt that the day of the larger-capacity amphitheatres was passing and that the brighter future of theatre lay

---

[3] Charles Whitney has documented the exchanges between the Privy Council and Spencer in 1594–5. For a summary of Spencer's anti-theatre activities, plus the likelihood that Dekker attacked him with *The Shoemaker's Holiday*, setting lavish Simon Eyre against his harshly class-conscious predecessor as Mayor, see Whitney, 'The Devil his Due: Mayor John Spencer, Elizabethan Civic Antitheatricalism, and *The Shoemaker's Holiday*', *Medieval and Renaissance Drama in England* 14 (2001), 168–85. Only five days after his inauguration in 1594 Spencer wrote to the Council renewing the call to suppress all public plays. He picked out the Swan, then being built without the sort of licence that the nearby Rose had just gained. His next letter in September 1595 was uncompromising in its demand 'for the present stay & finall suppressing' of all playing, 'aswell at the Theator & Bankside as in all other places about the Cytie' (Appendix 2.4). Spencer renewed the attack two years later in July 1597 on behalf of the new Mayor Henry Billingsley, copying verbatim from the earlier letters. That was the last letter from the mayors over playing, so some tacit accord must have been reached in that year. Dekker's mockery of the bad Lord Mayor in *The Shoemaker's Holiday* in 1599 has a distinct air of triumphalism.

indoors. By 1594 he was thoroughly familiar with the difficulties of running an open-air playhouse through the London winter. Most likely, as Carey's letter requesting access to the Cross Keys indicates, he just wanted a smaller winter venue for the company to augment his existing outdoor playhouse. At least the Blackfriars would be available if he failed to renew the Theatre's lease when it expired in April 1597. The site owner, Giles Allen, had already told him that he would refuse any extension.

Either way, Burbage certainly saw the future of playing exclusively as a London business. Whereas the previous monopoly company, the Queen's Men, had routinely toured the whole country, playing at a variety of city venues including city inns and the Theatre, each of the new duopoly companies did little touring after 1594 except in summer. The Chamberlain's hardly toured at all, and when they did they mainly visited grandees at their country houses, with a few towns on the way. The new licences for the London venues meant forsaking the touring from which the adult companies grew and setting their now-licensed feet permanently in London.

Judging by a letter of 9 January 1596 from Carey, who lived in the Blackfriars, Burbage's new plan had at least his tacit backing.[4] With Carey's support Burbage took over the two properties that were to make the space for his new playhouse in a deed of sale dated 4 February 1596. He got part of an old stone-built hall in the Blackfriars precinct, knocked down the partitions making the fencing-school and tenements that then filled it, and built his new playhouse inside. That cost him £600, and the rest of his financial resources went into stripping it all out and building the tiring house, stage, and three levels of curved galleries. It was not on the same site as the early Blackfriars theatre, and it gave him a grander space: seven upper rooms, 'sometyme being one great and entire room', reached by a winding stair at one end from the yard outside, with a series of other small rooms in adjacent spaces. The playhouse with its curved galleries was constructed inside a hall measuring 66 feet by 46 with a stone floor and a high roof. It had been the upper frater of the original Dominican Friary, built at the end of the thirteenth century and big enough to be used for meetings of Parliament in Richard II's time. If Carey and Burbage had got their plan through in 1596 the Globe might never have been built, and London playing would have moved indoors far earlier than it did.

---

[4] *Malone Society Collections* II.i, 1913, p. 123. Carey wrote to the seller, 'understanding that you have all redie parted with part of your howse to somme that meanes to make a playe howse in yt'.

The plan failed because on 22 July Henry Carey died. As Thomas Nashe wryly reported a little later, the players had great hopes while he lived, but 'however in their old Lords tyme they thought there state setled, it is now so uncertayne they cannot build upon it'. They were already building on it, and the plan misfired with horrible effects on the Burbage finances and therefore the company's backing. Carey's son George, who as the second Lord Hunsdon became the company's new patron, had less reason than his father to back this new venture, because he lived literally next door to it. The Blackfriars was a wealthy neighbourhood, with the social slice of residents displayed in Jonson's *Alchemist*, from Sir Epicure Mammon to Dapper, Drugger, and the Puritan brethren. Enough of them were hostile to professional players and a playhouse in their neighbourhood to stop Burbage's plan in its tracks.

In November 1596 'the inhabitants of the precinct of the Blackfryers, London' drew up a petition, which they presented to 'the right honorable the Lords and others of her Majesties most honorable Privy Councell'. It declared

that whereas one Burbage hath lately bought certaine roomes in the same precinct neere adjoyning unto the dwelling houses of the right honorable the Lord Chamberlaine and the Lord of Hunsdon, which romes the said Burbage is now altering and meaneth very shortly to convert and turne the same into a comon playhouse, which will grow to be a very great annoyance and trouble, not only to all the noblemen and gentlemen thereabout inhabiting, but allso a generall inconvenience to all the inhabitants of the same precinct, both by reason of the great resort and gathering togeather of all manner of vagrant and lewde persons that, under cullor of resorting to the playes, will come thither and worke all manner of mischeefe, and allso to the great pestring and filling up of the same precinct, yf it should please God to send any visitation of sickness as heretofore hath been, for that the same precinct is allready growne very populous; and besides, that the same playhouse is so neere the Church that the noyse of the drummes and trumpetts will greatly disturbe and hinder both the ministers and parishioners in tyme of devine service and sermons . . . now all players being banished by the Lord Mayor from playing within the Cittie by reason of the great inconveniences and ill rule that followeth them, they now thincke to plant them selves in liberties.[5]

Thirty-one residents signed it. The first was the dowager Lady Elizabeth Russell, a well-known pillar of the local church, whose vicar, Stephen Egerton, was another signatory. Lady Russell, widow of the Thomas Hoby who translated Castiglione's *Courtier*, was sister-in-law to William Cecil, who chaired the Privy Council. The second signature was 'G. Hunsdon',

---

[5] Chambers, *Elizabethan Stage*, IV.319–20. For a full quotation, see Appendix 2.5.

2. The second figure from the left at the front, looking back, is the white-bearded Earl of Nottingham, Charles Howard. Next to him, carrying the white rod of the Chamberlain's office in his right hand, is George Carey, Lord Chamberlain, second Lord Hunsdon and second patron of the Shakespeare company.[6]

the company's new patron. Another was Richard Field, formerly from Stratford, the printer of Shakespeare's *Venus and Adonis* and *The Rape of Lucrece*. They made a strong pressure group. With Henry Carey's death the plan lost its only substantial supporter.

The Chamberlain appointed to replace Carey was Lord Cobham, who had little reason to feel benevolent to the ex-Lord Chamberlain's Men, since they had recently staged to great acclaim a play which made fun of his ancestor, Sir John Oldcastle. Cobham forced them to change the name to Falstaff. Although not a Privy Councillor, Cobham could have voiced an opinion about the petition to the Council since it affected the official policy about licensing playhouses. He was certainly a lot less likely than his predecessor to support the Burbage plans, although the award to the new Lord Hunsdon's Men of all the six plays at court that Christmas may have been some sort of official compensation.[7] So the Council upheld the

[6] Most of this information comes from an article by the Earl of Ilchester in *The Walpole Society* IX (1920). The painting is in the possession of Lord Sherborne.

[7] An account of Cobham's short rule as Chamberlain, with a letter protesting about his mistreatment of another courtier during the performance of a play by Hunsdon's at court on 27 December 1596, is

petition, and Burbage lost the hope he had built on. Now the Burbage finances were locked up in a useless property. That was a true disaster for the company, because the Theatre's 21-year lease expired in April 1597, and the landlord rejected all pleas to renew it (Appendix 2.6). James Burbage himself made no attempt to retrieve the Theatre's timbers, to which he had a doubtful claim. He died in February 1597, three months after the Blackfriars petition was upheld and two before the Theatre's lease expired, leaving his sons the problem of getting a renewal of the Theatre's lease and no time to do anything about it. So in April the company lost the second of their possible venues. The Theatre was left, as Everard Guilpin mournfully put it later that year, in 'darke silence and vast solitude', and the company's secure basis in London was gone.

A company of Elizabethan players had to work as a team, and it is misleading to pick out individual members as the key creative forces, but two in particular need special note. One of course was Shakespeare, who as a team member from the outset seems to have supported and perhaps promoted the company's thinking beyond his direct contribution of plays and playing.[8] The other was their sponsor and landlord James Burbage. He did far more for the company than father its first leading player and provide its first playhouse. It was almost certainly his plan that ultimately guaranteed the company its supremacy. Builder of the Theatre in 1576, he had already been Henry Carey's man for a dozen years when the duopoly companies were established. The team's life, following a policy Burbage laid down, depended on and can be traced most clearly through its most material assets, its playhouses. Its patrons changed, and all of them impacted on the company's policies, but it was Burbage's plan to use two playhouses seasonally that finally guaranteed its premier place in London.

The next patron, Carey's son George, did much less for the company than his father. He was not at first made Lord Chamberlain in succession to his father, so during Cobham's seven months in office they were Hunsdon's Men. The company retrieved its original name when Cobham died in March 1597 and George was quickly made Lord Chamberlain. He remained patron till 1603 when King James took the company under his gilded wing barely two weeks after coming to his new treasure, London, a striking

in Paul Whitfield White, 'Shakespeare, the Cobhams, and the Dynamics of Theatrical Patronage', in *Shakespeare and Theatrical Patronage in Early Modern England*, pp. 64–89. Cobham died on 5 March 1597 and was quickly replaced by George Carey.

[8] Identifying any distinctive contribution by Shakespeare to the company's ethos, apart from his tangible contributions of money, plays, and performing, is speculative, but he cannot have argued with the policies he helped finance, and he must have mediated several times through a dozen years over the company's relations with the stormy Jonson.

3. King James I, the Shakespeare company's third patron, by an unknown artist (NPG 549).

mark of his priorities in his new regime.[9] The king's support was the best insurance any company could hope for. Through James's twenty-two years and the seventeen of his son Charles the company stood supreme in England as the King's Men.

In 1596 with Henry Carey's death and the collapse of the Blackfriars scheme the company had little time to make new plans. Old Burbage's

---

[9] Carey was ill through the last years of Elizabeth's reign, and in 1601 Sir John Stanhope was made Vice-Chamberlain to carry out his official duties. James was quick to take over his company, and seems to have been so closely engaged with making his own choice that he gave them as an extra sharer a favoured player from Edinburgh, Lawrence Fletcher. See entry in Appendix 1.

will in 1597 bequeathed his outdoor playhouse to his elder son Cuthbert, who eventually demolished it, giving its timbers and fittings to make the frame of its replacement, the Globe (Appendix 2.10), and his new indoor playhouse to Richard. Not for another eleven years could the two Burbage sons add the Blackfriars to the Globe and at last realize their father's plan to give the company two playhouses for alternating summer and winter use.

When ejected from the old Theatre in April 1597 the company moved to its only slightly younger open-air neighbour the Curtain. Renting the Curtain was a company expense that gave the Burbage sons, now the company's only backers, none of the income they needed to get a new playhouse of their own. For twenty months, while the company enjoyed some of its greatest successes on stage,[10] Cuthbert struggled to secure a fresh lease of the Theatre from Giles Allen, without success. So the brothers made the litigious decision to pull the playhouse down and re-erect it elsewhere (Appendix 2.10, 2.11). By mid-1599 the company was playing at the Globe, built from the Theatre's framing timbers in Southwark next to the Rose and open to the winter air.

The years at the Globe from 1599 to 1608 brought the company a great rise in status. In that rich time two major innovations strengthened the original two-playhouse plan. The first was the king's patronage. The second was the new financial system, explained at length in chapter 3, where five company sharers joined with two Burbages to become co-owners of the company's rebuilt playhouse. By 1608 the Burbages could give the Globe's co-owners, the holders of shares in the playhouse whom Chambers calls 'housekeepers', a matching number of shares in the Blackfriars so that their rental income could be sustained while their outdoor playhouse was not in use. In August 1608, with the previous winter when the Thames froze for six weeks still in mind, the company was able to repossess the Blackfriars. All playhouses were closed for plague at the time, and their occupiers financially worried, but the company was the King's Men. James gave them £40 to help them through the lengthy plague closure while they reorganized. For the next thirty-four years they played seasonally, in the summer at the open-air Globe and through each winter at the roofed Blackfriars, in belated accomplishment of the plan James Burbage first conceived in the summer of 1594. Rebuilding the Globe after the fire of 1613, for all its needless extravagance, was the company's renewal of the original Burbage plan to change playhouses with the seasons.

[10] Falstaff was an instant hit late in 1596; *Romeo and Juliet* was being quoted by Inns of Court students, according to Marston, in 1597, and in 1598 Francis Meres listed twelve of Shakespeare's plays as evidence for England's excellence in drama (Appendix 2.9).

The acquisition of the Blackfriars altered company practices quite drastically. One reason was the prevalence of women in Blackfriars audiences compared with the Globe. Commentators began to write more and more about the women in the audiences, and the plays written for the new repertory started providing a woman-centred perspective. One of John Fletcher's first plays for them was *The Tamer Tamed*, his sequel to *The Taming of the Shrew*, staged for a Blackfriars audience in 1612.[11] In 1614 *Bonduca* took up the subject of a woman ruler and her daughters in war, adding a strong female component to the open-air playhouse tradition of war histories. All Fletcher's plays were strongly woman-centred. The Cockpit, opening as an indoor rival to the Blackfriars in 1617, and the Salisbury Court in 1629 both affirmed the need to accommodate ladies as well as gentry in the city's playhouses. The commercial advantage of imitating the King's Men at Blackfriars became a strong incentive to impresarios, though they never tried to copy the King's system of collaborative management. Beeston of the Cockpit and Gunnell of the Salisbury Court both started as players, the former as a Chamberlain's boy, but they managed their playhouses like impresarios. Other players tried to copy the King's by buying shares in their playhouses, notably the Fortune company in 1618, but never with much success.

With audiences so different in financial resource, a lord's room at the Globe worth only the price of the cheapest place in an upper gallery at the Blackfriars, it would be surprising if the company managers did not rethink their choice of repertory for the indoor winter venue and the outdoor Globe in summer. Yet while the Blackfriars became the principal location for new plays, the evidence for any marked separation of plays chosen for the Blackfriars from Globe plays is much less obvious. The audiences at the Blackfriars were smaller and more affluent, but the Blackfriars playgoers still attended the Globe in summer when they were in town. The ambassador of Venice thought the Globe a suitable venue for a party of dignitaries to go to *Pericles* in 1607 or so – summer was a good time for such parties. Caroline gentry like Sir Humphrey Mildmay went to the Globe as well as

---

[11] Julia Briggs claims that 'in the development from *The Taming of the Shrew* (1592) to Fletcher's *The Woman's Prize, or the Tamer Tamed* (1612), where Petruchio's second wife more than pays back the wrongs done to the first, as well as in the strong heroines of Shakespeare, Middleton (*The Roaring Girl*; the Lady in *The Second Maiden's Tragedy*, both 1611), and Webster, women's points of view determined how a play was to be written and acted'. 'The epilogues to *2 Henry IV*, *As You Like It*, and *Henry VIII* appeal specifically to "the merciful construction of good women (l.10)", assuming that if the women applauded, then the men in the audience would follow their example.' (Julia Briggs, *This Stage-Play World: English Literature and its Background, 1580–1625*, Oxford University Press, 1983, pp. 261–2).

the Blackfriars. The two most scandalous Globe plays, *A Game at Chess* in 1624 and *The Late Lancashire Witches* in 1634, were both attended by large numbers of gentry. The company was always a stronger draw than its playhouse.

It took a decade and more for playgoing at the Blackfriars to gain absolute eminence over the Globe and other playhouses, but by the time James died its social status and its repertory were supreme. The Caroline company ran far more of Fletcher and his imitators than it did of Shakespeare. By the 1630s Shakespeare's plays were still a staple commodity but new plays building on what he established had long overtopped their pleasures. In 1630–1 the sixteen King's Men's plays staged at court included one new play, *The Inconstant Lady*, ten from the Beaumont and Fletcher stable,[12] two by Jonson (*Volpone* and *Every Man in his Humour*), one by Webster (*The Duchess of Malfi*), *The Merry Devil of Edmonton*, and only one, *A Midsummer Night's Dream*, by Shakespeare. If we include the Webster with the Beaumont and Fletchers as new plays in about 1615, only four of the oldest plays were still in demand by 1630. The female component in the Blackfriars audiences, allied with the careful conservatism of company policy under Charles, put Fletcher's radical and pro-feminist plays at the forefront of the repertory. Between 1625, when Fletcher's work concluded with his death from plague, and 1642 when all playing stopped, twenty-nine Beaumont and Fletcher titles were staged at court compared with eleven of Shakespeare's. This was the time when the Fortune and the Red Bull, the two open-air playhouses that played all year round unlike the Globe, came to be known as 'citizen playhouses', their various occupants hanging on to the old-fashioned repertory of war plays, including *The Spanish Tragedy* and *Tamburlaine*, none of which were ever chosen for performance at the court. Under Charles the repertory in those two playhouses openly aimed at the more masculine tastes, with battles and jigs. By then they were a minority interest, unimportant on the social scale compared with the preferences of Blackfriars audiences. Where that left the plays staged every summer at the Globe is matter for chapter 4.

THE TEAM

Teams develop their own chemistry, and a chemical solution grows out of the different elements in the team. That solution includes, even emphasizes,

---

[12] They were *The Custom of the Country*, *The Mad Lover*, *The Beggar's Bush*, *The Maid's Tragedy*, *Philaster*, *The Scornful Lady*, *The Chances*, *The Fatal Dowry*, *A King and No King*, and *Rollo*.

the bubbling individuality of single elements. Richard Burbage had authority from the start as his father's heir. He worked with his older brother to maintain the properties his father had left them, but always in the company's interest, not for personal gain. Unlike his peer Edward Alleyn, who headed the other duopoly company of 1594, he was not a dominating team-leader. The 'better than £300 land' which John Chamberlain reported Burbage leaving at his death was a lot less than that of other players in the team, notably John Heminges and Shakespeare, and far smaller than Alleyn's wealth, which endowed Dulwich College. His decision to allocate shares in the Blackfriars to the Globe housekeepers without exacting payment shows him a team-player. His power was that of company landlord and player of the leading parts, but he used it in distinctly limited ways. It was Heminges who took control of the day-to-day finances and served as tapster and 'grocer' when the land and buildings by the Globe let them add playhouse services to their income.

At the outset the Chamberlain's seems to have been led by eight sharers, the standard number for the time, each holding (and paying for) one full share. In later years it became possible to buy part-shares, and several later sharers such as Henry Condell bought their way in, part-share by part-share. We can be sure of seven of the original eight: George Bryan, Richard Burbage, John Heminges, Will Kemp, Augustine Phillips, Thomas Pope, and Will Shakespeare. The eighth was almost certainly Will Sly. George Bryan only lasted a few years. Henry Condell bought his way in during the first years and may have replaced Bryan as a sharer as early as 1597. Bryan moved off to a court sinecure, probably before the company lost the Theatre in 1597 since Jonson does not name him among the players of *Every Man in his Humour*, and the clown Will Kemp also struck out on an individualist path in 1599. But their replacements, Condell and Richard Cowley, were already working their way up in the team.[13] The only evidence for any major discord in the whole forty-eight years was Kemp's departure (he rather sourly testified that 'I have daunst my selfe out of the world' with his bet that he could jig all the way from London to Norwich),[14] and a dispute in 1635 between some of the newer company sharers and another clown, John Shanks, over shares in the two playhouses.[15]

---

[13] Variable as the spelling of so many names was, I adopt here the forms preferred by E. K. Chambers.

[14] See the entry for Kemp in Appendix 1. The first list of company players to appear was for 1598, listed in Jonson's 1616 Folio edition of *Every Man in his Humour*, Appendix 2.8.

[15] Shanks's acquisitions raised jealousy in three younger company sharers, in a dispute which produced the 'Sharers' Papers' (Appendix 3).

Shakespeare's contribution was in part his reliability, more as writer than as a player of what John Davies of Hereford called 'kingly parts'.[16] As a writer he supplied Burbage with the kind of role that gave best recognition to his skills as a 'character' actor, the art of 'personation' that became the company's most lasting credential. Writing plays that competed with Alleyn's use of 'Marlowe's mighty line' through Hal's, Brutus's, and Hamlet's self-searching was effective team-work. Shakespeare seems to have been most notable to the rest of the team as a willing oversupplier of words, never, as Jonson complained, bothering to blot a line of what he wrote. The first quarto of *Henry V*, half the length of the Folio version, shows what the company could do to their fellow's scripts when preparing them for the stage.[17] The three extant versions of *Hamlet*, plus the ur-*Hamlet* that Thomas Lodge reported hearing at the Theatre in 1596, show how ready they were to shorten their 'allowed book'. That manuscript was the company's prize asset and most valued commodity. It was uniquely important because it contained the crucial licence from the Master of the Revels with his signature authorizing them to perform the play in London and everywhere else in the country.[18] The 'allowed books' were so valuable that almost none of them survive. Most of the playbooks we know are authorial variants of the scripts, not the scripts licensed for performance. Shakespeare himself seems never to have valued his scripts as highly as his poems. He sold them to the company, which did with them whatever the team decided, with little sign of the author himself contributing. The extended versions that found their way into print mislead us about what Elizabethans saw on stage. Most of Shakespeare's printed texts are versions set from manuscripts preceding the 'maximal' allowed books that the company reworked for their slimmer stage scripts (see chapter 4). Shakespeare's readiness to accept such changes seems to mark him as a safe team-player.

Sadly, although the team's skills are evident in their capacity to stage a different play every afternoon, as the Admiral's did on the evidence of

---

[16] *The Scourge of Folly* [1611], Epigram 159.

[17] I stuck my neck out over the company origin of the 1600 quarto of *Henry V* in my edition for the New Cambridge Shakespeare Quartos, 2000, and have yet to be decapitated. It seems certain that it was the company that made the cuts and alterations and sold their copy to the printer. They eliminated all the Choruses and the opening scene where the Archbishop says he will bribe Henry to go to war. They shortened all Henry's speeches, cutting 'Once more unto the breach' altogether, in order to make a slicker play emphasizing Agincourt at the price of Harfleur and removing questions about Henry's conduct. Why Shakespeare did not intercede in the slimming-down we do not know. Perhaps it was the routine practice over his too-long texts, and he expected it.

[18] See also Gurr, 'Maximal and Minimal Texts: Shakespeare v. the Globe', *Shakespeare Survey* 52 (1999), 68–87. Lukas Erne, 'Shakespeare and the Publication of His Plays', *Shakespeare Quarterly* 53 (2002), 1–20, argues for Shakespeare's hand in the publication of the early quartos, but he ignores the fact that it was the company, not the author, who owned the playscripts.

Henslowe's records, we know almost nothing of who originally played which parts. We know some of Burbage's and his successor Joseph Taylor's parts. We know that John Lowin had taken on Falstaff by the 1630s. Not many others can be identified, except when plays surviving in manuscript and occasionally in print record the players' names, and they usually note only the minor parts. Names for who was playing what in about 1612 in *The Alchemist* and other plays survive in a copy of Jonson's 1616 Folio.[19] Otherwise we can only guess at them, and wonder at the team commitment that kept everyone confident that they would all be available for playing duty every day.

The intensity of the need to stage a different play every day argues for type-casting at least among the sharers. This assumption led T. W. Baldwin in 1927 to ascribe every speaking part to a particular player with an overconfident detailing that took a long time to unpack.[20] Lowin played Falstaff, for instance, but he did not join the company until seven years after the part was invented, and probably did not start to play it until he was much older. Still, Burbage is known to have taken almost all the leading roles till 1619, and players known for their specific skills as blunt soldier or sly counsellor or the sort of 'kingly part' that John Davies of Hereford said was Shakespeare's would have been the obvious candidates when the company read through a new play and started to allocate the parts. Staid John Heminges might well have played the original Polonius. If so, judging from Burbage's joke in *Hamlet*, he would also have been Julius Caesar in the previous year's play. But there is not much evidence to back such speculations.

The company's first six years as half of the duopoly supplying London with its two plays each afternoon settled a number of their practices. Besides the fearsome speed of turnover in the plays they staged, essential in London to keep the same playgoers attending, they got to know their audiences more intimately than companies have ever done before or since. In 1596 Prince Hal addressed his 'I know you all' soliloquy to faces he had been seeing almost daily in the same playhouse for the last two years. Such familiarity helped to generate the sort of metatheatrical alertness that the company exploited when Hamlet/Burbage joked to Polonius about his taking the part of Julius Caesar and being murdered by himself as Brutus/Burbage. Although Burbage was praised for the strength of his 'personation' in

---

[19] See James A. Riddell, 'Some Actors in Ben Jonson's Plays', *Shakespeare Studies* 5 (1969), 285–98.
[20] Thomas Whitfield Baldwin, *The Organization and Personnel of the Shakespearean Company*, Princeton University Press, 1927. See Skiles Howard, 'A Re-examination of Baldwin's Theory of Acting Lines', *Theatre Survey* 26 (1985), 1–20.

character, the rapid turnover of plays and the familiarity between players and audience inhibited truly individualistic characterizations. Playing
as a team, too, meant keeping to a pattern of acting that was sufficiently
standardized to accommodate whatever deviations other players might fall
into, so that when a player lost his place he could be picked up and the
story-line restored. No team working together for so many years to familiar
audiences could have introduced radically divergent techniques. It was in
the nature of the team that its practices were always careful, familiar, and
conservative. When James Wright in his retrospective *Historia Histrionica*
called them 'Men of grave and sober Behaviour'[21] he praised not only their
awareness of their social standing but the conservatism of thinking that the
team lived by.

   Nobody can doubt that the audiences knew the players well by name and
fame. The Induction to the 1604 *Malcontent*, 'with the Additions played by
the Kings Majesties servants',[22] was written so that it started with Sly and
John Sincler coming on stage dressed as gallants demanding to meet 'Harry
Condell, Dick Burbage, and Will Sly'. Condell, Burbage, and Lowin join
them on stage, and Sly, after doing an Osric act to Burbage with his hat,
claims never to have studied 'the art of memory'. Sly demanding to meet
himself was an in-joke that could only work if the audiences were thoroughly familiar with the players and their real names. The same familiarity
is behind Manningham's joke about William the Conqueror getting to the
citizen's wife before Richard the Third.[23] Performances were a community experience, a game of the mind free from the subjection to cinematic
realism that blinkers modern eyes.

   The mentality of the Elizabethan player was quite distinct from that of
modern actors. The duopoly period, when Philip Henslowe's *Diary* gives
his day-by-day record of what one of the two companies did, called for
different skills and a different attitude to work from those required of
a modern actor, who thinks about character before dialogue, relies on a
film set as background rather than a bare stage, and acts from behind a
picture-frame instead of in the middle of a visible and energized crowd.
Playing a different script every day for six days a week with no break
until Lent laid intense demands on memory and teamwork. If one of your

---

[21] *Historia Histrionica*, 1699, B3.
[22] From the augmented title page, where Webster is credited with the Induction. It claims that the
   company staged it in reprisal for the boy company's theft of one of their plays, the Induction filling
   in the time originally taken by the boy company's musical overture.
[23] *The Diary of John Manningham*, ed. Robert Parker Sorlien, University Press of New England,
   Hanover, 1976, p.75.

fellows forgot his lines you had to help him. If you entered by the wrong door when you were meant to encounter your exiting fellow on the way, you had to adjust very smartly. Such demands left little time for tricks of characterization. In such a fast-moving repertory you could not afford to sink deeply into thoughts about your character. Comic improvisation must have been a standard resort when such problems were the norm. Such energized readiness demanded metatheatrical alertness in all the players. Their best help was the self-confidence that could turn a crisis to advantage.

The need for good teamwork made a star system difficult. Burbage as the leading player with the longest parts would normally not double his roles, and he evidently became adept at taking non-stereotyped roles day by day, as he moved from playing Hamlet to Othello or Lear, or Ferdinand in *The Duchess of Malfi*. That must have helped his new art of personation wonderfully. Almost everyone else, however, played several parts in each play. The only surviving text containing comprehensive evidence about doubling, the 'plot' for the Admiral's *Battle of Alcazar*, allocates up to four speaking parts to each major player other than Alleyn himself, who played the lead. Such versatility meant very tight teamwork as well as an audience who knew that a change of garb meant a change of character. Telling who was a new character and who was an old one in disguise must have challenged audiences.

Of the eight men we know were the company's founding sharers in 1594 the biggest enigma is Richard Burbage. We cannot be sure how positive a leader he was. His status and family certainly made him one in 1594, and his later reputation as a player endorses it, but he never became an impresario like Alleyn. Aged twenty-five in 1594, three years younger than Alleyn and Heminges, five years younger than Shakespeare, his talent as the company's leading player is attested by the many praises heaped on him through his working life. His personality is on record in his defence of his father's playhouse in 1591 with a belligerent broomstick. Yet while Alleyn left playing for management in 1601 aged thirty-five and Heminges at forty-four, Burbage continued playing till his death at fifty. It is easy to think of the player for whom the part of Hamlet was written as a leader, yet the biggest asset his inclusion brought the company in 1594 was not his acting but his father's Theatre, the largest as well as the oldest of the custom-built London playhouses.

These reservations do not mean that Burbage lacked the qualities of a team-leader. Most likely he joined the company having first led a group formed at his father's Theatre after his broomstick act in 1591. It ran under the patronage of the Earl of Pembroke, but 'broke' in late summer of the plague year 1593, re-forming under the Earl of Sussex, who died in early 1594. Burbage was popular with his fellows, since he had been partnered in his two former companies by others who joined the Chamberlain's in 1594, notably Sly, Shakespeare, and some hired men. John Sincler and John Holland were two of the new company's hired men who we know played with Burbage in Pembroke's before the Chamberlain's was formed.[24] Echoes of various Pembroke's plays such as *Edward II* and *Edward III*, as well as the survival of names later found in the Chamberlain's plays in Pembroke's *2* and *3 Henry VI*, support the case for a core of Pembroke's joining the Chamberlain's. There is no other easy explanation for the links between these and other early Pembroke's plays and the plays and players found in the new company. The sequence of companies listed on the title page of the 1594 and 1600 quartos of *Titus Andronicus*, Strange's, Pembroke's, Sussex's, and finally the Chamberlain's (Appendix 2.2), most likely marks the track of the companies that Burbage and others followed. When the Chamberlain's began Burbage had been acting with some of the new company for at least three years, and with others before that.

Altogether four of the new company's sharers came directly from Strange's, which became Derby's when Ferdinando Stanley's elder brother died in September 1593, but were bereft of their patron seven months later when Strange, now the new earl, also died. They were George Bryan, Will Kemp, Augustine Phillips, and Thomas Pope.[25] It was a reunion of sorts. Bryan, Kemp, Phillips, and Pope, along with Burbage, Sly, Holland, and Sincler are all named in the 'plot' of *2 Seven Deadly Sins*, a play usually ascribed to Strange's in about 1590.[26] Almost every member of the two teams who made up the 1594 duopoly of Chamberlain's and Admiral's Men

[24] The evidence for these individual allegiances, including the Lord Chamberlain's to Lord Strange, who became the Earl of Derby, is given in Gurr, *The Shakespearian Playing Companies*, Oxford University Press, 1996, pp. 70–4. A rather heavy-handed assessment of the cross-linkages is supplied by Roslyn Lander Knutson, *Playing Companies and Commerce in Shakespeare's Time*, Cambridge University Press, 2001, pp. 24–30, as part of her claim that acting companies followed the model of city guilds in their collaborative organization and allegiances.

[25] Burbage's presence in Strange's up to 1591, on the evidence of his name in the plot for *2 The Seven Deadly Sins* (if that date is correct: see note 25) may help to explain why four others from that group came to the Chamberlain's in 1594. Heminges, if he joined direct from the Queen's, may have been acquired because he could bring the new company at least five good plays. Shakespeare may have known Heminges from his time in the Queen's early on, as is conjectured. The conjunction of these spirits so quickly making themselves into a tight team may have been expected by their new patrons, or by Tilney their adviser. Their reunion in the Chamberlain's is likely to have been more than just a lucky coincidence.

[26] David Kathman, 'Reconsidering *The Seven Deadly Sins*', *Early Theatre* 7 (2004), makes a case for it as a Chamberlain's 'plot' from 1597–8, slipping into the Henslowe papers via the younger William Cartwright. This does not explain the presence in the 'plot' of players like Robert Gough who were in the Admiral's at that time.

had previous experience acting together in different formations.[27] The only newcomer to these groups of former Strange's and Pembroke's players was John Heminges. While he may have been a Strange's man at some point, he more likely joined the new company directly from the Queen's along with several of their playbooks. Connections between the Queen's and Sussex's existed in April 1594 when both companies shared playing at the Rose. The Queen's plays used in the first days of the company's work may be due to the presence of Heminges as the only outsider.

As a team, the Chamberlain's had the advantage of being close in age and experience, and most of them, if not actually Londoners, had worked there for some years already. The word 'company' tells us what the essence of any Elizabethan playing group was, nothing like that of a modern limited liability company. Its obligations were unlimited, as were its liabilities. Originally a 'company' meant an assembly of people, a community. When Augustine Phillips presented the company's excuses for performing *Richard II* on the afternoon before the attempted Essex coup, he explained that they were reluctant to do the conspirators' bidding because 'they should have small or no company at it'. An Elizabethan company was a gathering of like-minded people, a theatre audience or a group of players conjoined to produce a play. Such a term accurately describes those workers who toured the country or set up in London to get money from their combined skills. The durability of this word for the ensembles who produce any live play certifies it as the right signifier for a collective working as a team.

Teamwork was the basic feature of company playing from long before 1594. The author of the Character 'A Common Player' in 1614 called them a 'Brother-hood'.[28] Impresario control came later, and was never adopted by the King's Men. Like any team, the players were interdependent. They shared the processes of play selection, rehearsal, and performance, and any absentee let the team down. This sharing led eventually to the Chamberlain's company's shared playhouse-owning that became its greatest security from 1599. Even when playhouse shares passed away from the company's sharers through deaths and inheritance the corporate feeling usually overrode the divisiveness of individual share-owning.

---

[27] The clown John Shanks may have been in Pembroke's and then the Queen's through this period. His petition of 1635 over shares in the King's Men's playhouses (Appendix 3) says that he was first a servant of Lord Pembroke and then of the queen. He did not join Burbage's company until 1613. Possibly the presence of Will Kemp from Strange's/Derby's precluded Shanks from joining the new group in 1594.

[28] Probably written by an Inns of Court student, John Cocke, it appeared in 1615 among a collection called *Satyricall Essayes and Characters* by John Stephens, another lawyer.

The company set up in 1594 proved a quite remarkable assembly of collaborative talents. Most companies had one or two dominant figures who provincial records named as the leaders or who the royal accountants named as payees. Like other groups, the Chamberlain's usually specified at least two sharers entitled to claim payments, but up to 1600 their payees varied more than most. The names set down in the Chamber accounts for payment in 1595 were 'William Kempe William Shakespeare & Richarde Burbage'. In the next year they were 'John Hemynge and George Bryan'. The third listing was 'Thomas Pope & John Hemynges', and the fourth was 'John Heminges and Thomas Pope'. The fifth was the same, the sixth 'John Hemynge' on his own, and the seventh, in 1601, was 'John Hemynges and Richarde Cowley'.[29] Seven different payees in an eight-year period indicates a wider range of responsible bodies than ever again, even if one of the seven, John Heminges, was named five times. Over the next twenty years it was he who came to serve the company as its chief financial controller, but it still took eight years before his probity as controller of the company's receipts was accepted.

The team became a well-knit community. Intermarriage was a feature of most groups working together, but the Chamberlain's/King's linkages, like the company, were longer-lasting than most. John Lowin joined the company in 1603, and was still playing forty-five years later along with other ex-King's Men during the Commonwealth period. Marriages inside the company started early. Heminges, who had married the widow of William Knell, the chief tragedian of the Queen's, after Knell died in a duel with a fellow-player (touring together could be a peculiarly intense version of family life), gave his daughter Thomasine Heminges to the company's William Ostler. Richard Sharpe married Cowley's daughter, and their son may have been one of John Shanks's boys in the 1630s. Richard Robinson married Richard Burbage's widow. Robert Gough married Augustine Phillips's sister. John Underwood named his second son Burbadge Underwood. Thomas Pope's will in 1603 records that John Holland was a lodger at his house. In 1612 William and Thomasine (Heminges) Ostler's son was baptized 'Beaumont', presumably after the company's poet, and senior sharers like Heminges and Condell served as witnesses or executors of their fellow-players' wills. Company members usually lived close by one another in the vicinity of their playhouses.

Such cross-linkages help to explain the deal which brought five of the sharers in on the Globe in 1599 and the Blackfriars in 1608, making the

---

[29] Chambers, *Elizabethan Stage*, IV.164–6.

housekeeping syndicate a distinctive feature of the team's togetherness. Other syndicates had helped finance the old Theatre, the Rose, and the Fortune, and some of those financiers were linked by marriage. But the Globe syndicate was the first to be made up from a majority of the team who planned to work in their new property. The intimate management system evoked by the Burbage brothers' lack of cash in 1599 sustained the company to the end.

The 'family' aspect of the company meant keeping boy players housed with their masters and teachers, as the boys formally apprenticed to members of London's livery companies were. Players who belonged to the Grocers, Goldsmiths, and others could register boys of twelve or thirteen as their apprentices, even though the official starting age in London for apprentices was seventeen, by which time their voices would have broken. Through his long career Heminges registered ten boys, most of whose names appear in the company lists.[30] Training boys, though, did not necessarily require players to be freemen of the livery guilds. Pope and Phillips, the first dying in 1603 and the second in 1605, have not been identified as freemen of the city, although they bequeathed their working gear to the boys they trained. Pope gave 'my wering aparell and all my armes' to Robert Gough and John Edmonds, to be divided equally between them.[31] Besides giving sums of money to his 'fellows' Shakespeare and Condell (30 shillings each), and Lawrence Fletcher, Armin, Cook, Tooley, and Cowley (20 shillings each), Phillips bequeathed Samuel Gilbourne a larger sum, along with 'my mouse Colloured velvit hose and a white Taffety dublet A blacke Taffety sute my purple Cloke sword and dagger And my base viall', calling him 'my Late Aprentice'. To his current boy James Sands he gave the same sum and 'a Citterne a Bandore and a Lute'.[32] Gilbourne had evidently grown big enough to wear Phillips's richest clothing on stage, whereas Sands only received instruments for his professional work. Both will-makers had swords as well as gentleman's clothing for use on stage (neither was a gentleman, so they could not wear them in the street), while Phillips's musical instruments indicate that he had trained his boys to use them. He affirmed the team principle by assigning Heminges, Richard Burbage, and Will Sly as alternative executors of his will, should his wife, the sole executor,

[30] David Kathman has identified many players who registered apprentices from the Livery Company records. See his 'Freemen and Apprentices in the Elizabethan Theater', *Shakespeare Quaterly* 55 (2004).

[31] *Playhouse wills, 1558–1642. An edition of wills by Shakespeare and his contemporaries in the London theatre*, ed. E. A. J. Honigmann and Susan Brock, Manchester University Press, 1993, p. 70.

[32] *Ibid.*, p. 73.

remarry, as she did two years later.[33] Besides the sums to the other sharers, he also gave £5 to be divided amongst the 'hyred men of the Company, which I am of'. Another mark of the close-knit working community, and the sharers' growing wealth, appeared when Sly died in 1608. He bequeathed Phillips's former boy James Sands £40, and his gentleman's sword and hat to Cuthbert Burbage.

Loyalty as well as profit from company membership is evident in the length of time that sharers stayed, and in their legacies. Besides Lowin's thirty-nine years and Heminges's thirty-six stand testaments such as John Underwood's. In October 1624 he wrote a wordy codicil to his will dividing all his holdings, house and chattels, and his share in the company's playhouses equally amongst his five children for their upbringing and education. The most substantial of his assets was his property share 'within the Blackfryers London or in the Companie of his Majesties Servantes my loving and kinde fellows in theire house there or att the Globe on the Bankside', along with a share in the Curtain. The will's executors were Condell, Heminges, and Lowin, then the premier figures in the company, along with two non-company men. The company's men would see to the Underwood children's future. It was not just a working but a familial community. In her will in 1635 Elizabeth Condell gifted Elizabeth Burbage, Cuthbert's wife, a silver fork and a golden purse.[34]

The women were not a minor element in the team. Condell's own will, drawn up in December 1627, made his wife 'the full and sole Executrixe', with help as 'Overseers' from Heminges, Cuthbert Burbage, and his son-in-law, each of whom got £5 to buy a plate in his memory. The will also gives 'unto my old servant Elizabeth Wheaton a mourninge gowne and Forty shillings in money and that place or priviledge which she nowe exerciseth and enjoyeth in the houses of the Blackfriers London and the Globe on the Banckside for and during all the terme of her naturall life'.[35] This is the only indication that sharers secured their friends regular access to a 'place' at the King's Men's playhouses, though the bequest was more likely a job than a seat in the audience. Condell's widow Elizabeth in her own will in 1635 left the widow Wheaton £20 and 'the gatheringe Place at the Globe during my Lease'.[36] She seems to have been a company gatherer, not an idle spectator.

---

[33] She kept her remarriage secret for a while, but the truth emerged, and later led to a lawsuit over ownership of Phillips's playhouse share when her second husband tried to deny the will's proviso.
[34] *Playhouse Wills*, p. 184.   [35] *Ibid.*, p. 159.
[36] Gerald Eades Bentley, *The Jacobean and Caroline Stage*, 7 vols., Oxford University Press, 1941–68, II.616–17.

Team loyalty lasted beyond the closure in 1642, when a body of the company's sharers followed the king to Oxford to entertain him and some of the younger members joined the king's army. Even Eliart Swanston, the most independent of all the sharers, instigator of the complaint by three of the company sharers to get John Shanks to part with his housekeeping shares in 1635, and the only sharer to join the parliamentary side after 1642,[37] was still close enough to his former fellows in 1647 to add his name to the Beaumont and Fletcher Folio.

The sharers also secured a striking level of loyalty from their paid helpers. As Peter Thomson puts it, 'Loyalty and genuine affection play a part in the history of the Chamberlain's Men in a way that we can neither ignore nor adequately measure. Even among some of the hired men, there is evidence of a commitment beyond the normal limits of a working relationship.'[38] Charles Hart, who became a pillar of the post-Restoration King's Men, started as a boy in the King's living with the sharer Richard Robinson, who himself had begun as a boy player with Richard Burbage. Boys who grew to become sharers included Nicholas Tooley (another of Richard Burbage's boys), Underwood, and Ostler.[39] Alexander Cook, who died young in 1614, when his wife was expecting their third child, asked 'my master hennings' and Condell to look after his money till his children came to maturity. Heminges and Cuthbert Burbage along with John Shanks and the composer Thomas Ravenscroft witnessed Cowley's will in 1618. Richard Burbage's will was witnessed by his brother Cuthbert and two of his former boys still with the company, Tooley and Robinson, the latter subsequently marrying his widow. When Tooley wrote his will in 1623 he made Condell and Cuthbert Burbage his executors, and was resident in the Burbage house at his death that June.[40] His will gave £10 to the sister of 'my late Master Richard Burbadge deceased', along with a debt of nearly £30 owed him by Robinson, to be given to Burbage's daughter Sara. He also gave £10 to his daughter and £5 to Condell's wife 'as a remembrance of my love'. Finally he remitted the debts owed him by Taylor, Underwood, and Eccleston.

One factor underpinning that loyalty must have been the consistent level of good income that the company was able to maintain, which is set

---

[37] Shanks said he was the most 'violent' of the three complainants (Appendix 3(d)).
[38] *Shakespeare's Theatre*, second edition, Routledge, London, 1992, p. 8.
[39] W. R. Streitberger, 'Personnel and Professionalization', in *A New History of Early English Drama*, ed. John D. Cox and David Scott Kastan, Columbia University Press, New York, 1997, pp. 337–55, p. 350.
[40] *Playhouse wills*, p. 234.

out (necessarily in fairly hypothetical form) in chapter 3. It was certainly enough to allow them to survive without regular playing or touring during the appalling plague epidemics. As their wealth grew after the first years of running the Globe, several of the more senior sharers acquired properties outside London. At least one allowed them to stay together as a company while they sheltered from plague in the city – Augustine Phillips acquired a house in Mortlake some time before he died in 1605, and the company was summoned from there to entertain the court at Wilton in December 1603. By his death in 1627 Henry Condell was living in the village of Fulham, six miles from the city. Shakespeare was investing in Stratford properties from 1597. It was their affluence that caused the only major quarrels. By 1635 income from the property shares in the two playhouses was high enough to upset the newer company sharers who had none. Precipitated by three of the younger men, Eliart Swanston, Robert Benfield, and Thomas Pollard, their claims set them against the older leaders Joseph Taylor and Lowin, and the heirs of the first 'housekeepers', Richard Burbage's widow Winifred, her son William and husband Richard Robinson, the widow Condell, and the enduring Cuthbert Burbage. The old player/sharer John Shanks had quietly acquired from Heminges's son shares in both 'houses'. The younger men wanted part of his holding, on the grounds that the income from the two playhouses now far outstripped the take from a company share. The rent from the two playhouses threw the equal sharing of company income out of balance.

Essentially the trouble of 1635, set out in the papers quoted in Appendix 3, came from the fact that the company had run for so long that shares in the playhouses were now in different hands from the players' shares, which always belonged to the active team members. The playhouse holdings were material pieces of property, and some descendants of the first sharers who became 'housekeepers' had sold their inheritance. The three rebels wanted to redress this imbalance in the sharing process, though ironically they hoped to do so by dispossessing another sharer, John Shanks, of his acquisitions in the playhouses. As company sharers they wanted to become housekeepers like Taylor and Lowin by forcing Shanks to redistribute what he had bought from young Heminges's inheritance. Trying to gain a share from the rents, the belligerent Swanston led the two others into petitioning the Lord Chamberlain, Philip Herbert, fourth Earl of Pembroke. In the end he persuaded Shanks to sell a portion of his gains to the three, though Shanks conceded it with great reluctance, as the petitions in Appendix 3 show.

Heminges was exceptional in the team of eight players comprising the first sharers. A Queen's man in 1588 when he married Knell's widow,[41] he probably remained with the Queen's on their travels until summoned to join the new company in May 1594. He may have been included in the duopoly as a token presence from the old monopoly, since he was almost the only new Chamberlain's sharer who had not been in Strange's in 1591. There is nothing else to say why he joined, unless perhaps he had made friends with Shakespeare while in the Queen's Men. He was a middle-England man, from Worcester, and the theory that Shakespeare may have left Stratford with Heminges and the Queen's in 1587 when they lost Knell carries some weight.[42] The most tangible reason for Heminges to be taken into the new Lord Chamberlain's was because he could bring them several of the Queen's Men's plays. At least five (*King Leir, Hamlet, The Troublesome Reign of King John, Hester and Ahasuerus,* and *The Famous Victories of Henry V*) somehow came into their possession in 1594. Shakespeare rewrote four of them for the new company, ignoring only the biblical tale.

As teamwork developed and specific individuals began to take on the more specialized functions, particular skills emerged, such as Heminges's with the company's finances. He was quick to cut in on the new deal over the Globe in 1599. Several grey clouds surround this famous deal, however, one of which relates particularly to Heminges as the company's financial controller. He appears to have been the sharer who ran the Globe's tap-house, an integral part of the complex built in 1599 to produce the ale sold to playgoers. Nothing in the records says whether that was Heminges's personal enterprise from which he took all the profits for himself, whether it belonged to the housekeepers owning the complex who shared the income, or whether its profits went to the company sharers. If the concept of the company as a team has much validity, the odds are on the money being shared, most probably by the landlord–housekeepers. Heminges's reputation as an honest broker, plus the respect he had from everyone up to his death, support the direction of that flight into the clouds of speculation.

When Heminges left off regular playing, probably around 1608, he stayed at the heart of the company's operations. He was certainly present at the Globe in July 1613 when it burned down, since he was described as being traumatized by the sight and stuttering (possibly for the sake of the rhyme)

[41] See Mark Eccles, *Shakespeare in Warwickshire*, University of Wisconsin Press, Madison, 1961, pp. 82–3.
[42] The case for Shakespeare as a Queen's man has been argued most cogently by Scott McMillin and Sally-Beth MacLean, *The Queen's Men and their Plays*, Cambridge University Press, 1998, pp. 160–6.

like a drunken Fleming.[43] He and Condell kept full control of the company after Richard Burbage died in 1619, setting up publication of the first Shakespeare Folio in 1622. Condell died in 1627 and Heminges in 1630. Thereafter their managerial roles were taken by the long-serving Lowin and Joseph Taylor, who had joined the company in 1619 when Burbage died and took over his main parts. After Heminges died Taylor and Lowin were always named together in the court accounts as the chief payees. For the last twelve years they ran the company as joint playing leaders, not as impresarios like other playhouse-owners. In James Wright's memory of the pre-Commonwealth period, it was Taylor and Lowin who stood on the peak of player dignity. As men of 'grave and sober Behaviour' they 'Liv'd in Reputation'.[44]

Heminges was technically a gentleman, having followed Shakespeare in acquiring a coat of arms. Oddly, though, while his fellow Henry Condell called him 'gent' in his will of 1627, his own will, executed in 1630, declared that he was a 'Citizen and Grocer of London'. He found freeman status as a member of a livery guild useful when he took up boy players as ostensible apprentices, though most likely it was his function as company tapster that required him to pay his dues to the Grocers. A grocer gave Henslowe half the cost of building the Rose in 1587 in return for the right to sell food and drink there. Unlike Condell and other sharers, Heminges kept his citizen status, continuing to live in Aldermanbury, and never acquired property outside London. His first concern in his will, to gather up his assets and settle his debts before identifying legacies to his dependants and friends, sorts with his long experience as the company's financial manager. His choice of burial-place and the gift of forty shillings (£2) to the poor marked his senior citizen status as, like Condell, a churchwarden of St Mary's Aldermanbury in the city. His assets, which included a quarter of the Blackfriars and the Globe, he notes brought in 'good yeerely proffitt'. In his bequests he gave ten shillings to 'every of my fellowes and sharers' to buy rings in his memory. The recipients were Taylor, Lowin, Swanston, Shanks, Benfield, Sharpe, Pollard, John Thompson, John Honyman, Alexander Gough, Antony Smith, and Richard Baxter. The will's executor was his son William, and the overseers were Cuthbert Burbage and John Rice, who had been Heminges's boy with the King's from before 1607 until 1610, and a King's man from before 1619. He acknowledged his long-standing affection for Rice with a gift of twenty shillings.

---

[43] In a verse about the burning of the Globe and its alehouse, quoted in Chambers, *Elizabethan Stage*, II.412.

[44] James Wright, *Historia Histrionica*, sig. B3.

A full list of all the sharers, hired men, musicians, and boys known to have belonged to the company at any point between 1594 and 1642 appears in Appendix 1. Richard Burbage's role in the company has been considered already. Another figure worth special note is his brother Cuthbert. Four years older than Richard, at first Cuthbert worked outside the family business. In 1591 he was serving Sir Walter Cope, gentleman usher to Elizabeth's chief minister Lord Burghley, and builder of Cope Castle, later Holland House, in Kensington. Cuthbert seems to have continued working for him over at least a decade. A letter by Cope to Burghley's son and successor Robert Cecil, about plays at court for the Christmas season 1604–5, refers to a 'Burbage' waiting to take a message to the players, which might have been either brother (Appendix 2.18). Cuthbert first started helping with the company business when their father died in February 1597, since the Theatre, the immediate business concern, was bequeathed to him. It was Cuthbert who ran the endless negotiations and litigation over renewing the lease with Giles Allen. After that frustrating stint he inevitably joined the consortium that built the Globe out of the Theatre's timbers. Technically these timbers, the two Burbages' contribution to the cost of construction, were his, not Richard's, but the two were true brothers in their financial dealings. Cuthbert's willingness to regard the Theatre as a shared family resource became Richard's attitude later when he retrieved his own inheritance, the Blackfriars, and apportioned it among the Globe housekeepers with an equal share for Cuthbert. From 1599 Cuthbert was a participating housekeeper. He maintained a close and careful watch over his and the company's two most material resources for the next thirty-seven years.

A particularly intriguing case of an early sharer shows up in the fragments of evidence about Will Sly. Like Richard Burbage, he appears among the names of players in the 'plot' for Strange's *2 Seven Deadly Sins*. The absence of any other mention of him or Burbage in the Henslowe–Alleyn papers probably means that with some others they helped to set up the new Pembroke's in mid-1591, after the famous quarrel at the Theatre between the Alleyns and James Burbage. When Pembroke's 'broke' in August 1593 Sly must have gone with Burbage into Sussex's and then into the new Lord Chamberlain's. He blended well into the new company. What roles he played we do not know, although the Induction added to *The Malcontent* for its first appearance at the Globe gave Sly Osric's words to Burbage/Hamlet over why he would not put his hat back on his head.

Of the later eminences, unquestionably the most distinguished was John Lowin with his thirty-nine and more years of service to the company. Apprenticed to a goldsmith in 1593, he left the trade to act with Worcester's

4. John Lowin on stage as Falstaff, as remembered by an unknown engraver, probably John Chantry. 'Clause' is a character from Fletcher's *The Beggar's Bush*. A detail from the frontispiece of Francis Kirkman's book of drolls, *The Wits* (1661).

players at the Rose before joining the neighbouring Chamberlain's in 1603. In 1607 he published a solemn little pamphlet, *Conclusions upon Dances*, full of examples of dances good and bad taken from the Bible. It was a curiously narrow set of examples, making no mention of the song-and-dance jigs that usually ended stage performances. The pamphlet's brevity, and perhaps its conceived importance, was acknowledged by its republication two years later, retitled '*Brief* Conclusions of Dancers and Dancing'. The moral disputes about dancing were affecting the popularity on stage of what Dekker later called 'nasty, bawdy jigs', a practice the company seems to have abandoned by its composition in 1606. Lowin was quietly doing his bit for the company's reputation. A burly man, it is likely that the engraving of the figure labelled Falstaff in *The Wits* (1661) was of him.

Joseph Taylor took over most of Burbage's roles, apparently brought into the company in March 1619 to do precisely that. In the event he was the only leading actor of the company to take on company management, linked with Lowin and, in the last years, Eliart Swanston as the named payee at court. It was Taylor who brought the company most closely under the

5. The second Globe, a drawing by Wenceslas Hollar from the tower of Southwark Cathedral in the 1630s in preparation for his engraved 'Long View' of London.

royal wing when Charles came to the throne. In 1632 he coached Henrietta Maria's ladies for their roles in Walter Montague's pastoral at court, and was rumoured to have been promised a knighthood for it. He was praised similarly for resurrecting Fletcher's long-dead *Faithful Shepherdess*, a revival that was popular enough to be given a rare repeat performance in the 1635–6 season of plays staged at court.

THE SOCIAL EMINENCE OF THE BLACKFRIARS

The clearest revelation of the company's policy and its thinking came with the loss of the Globe by fire in 1613 (Appendix 2.22). After retrieving its prime commodities, costumes and playbooks, rescued thanks to the fact that the fire started during a performance rather than in the emptiness of night as did the Fortune's in December 1621, the company transferred to the Blackfriars. They could have made that a permanent shift of venue. Their tenure of the Blackfriars through winter had already shown that it brought in more money than the outdoor playhouse. Instead of taking such a sensible and practical option, they drew on their housekeepers' resources and raised £1,400 to rebuild the Globe. On 30 June 1614 John Chamberlain wrote to Alice Carleton about not seeing 'your sister Williams' despite two calls on her, because 'The first time she was at a neighbours house at Cards, and the next she was gon to the new Globe . . . which is saide to be the fayrest that ever was in England.'[45] Jonson wrote that the first Globe had been 'the Glory of the *Banke*', and that the fire left nothing of it but 'the piles, . . . and wit since to cover it with tiles'.[46] But it cannot have been just the wish to replace thatch with fire-resistant tiles that opened the housekeepers' purses. Rebuilding was a sign of the corporate thinking uniting housekeepers and sharers. Outsiders expected them not to renew the luxury of two playhouses for the one company. Henslowe showed that expectation when he contracted to build the Hope near the Globe site within a month of the fire. The rebuilding marks the housekeepers' commitment to their old plan of 1594. Every penny put into the second Globe was an expense the housekeepers could have ignored, and it was not a unanimous decision. Three years after the fire Shakespeare made no mention of any Globe or Blackfriars shares in his will, so he must have been one of the two housekeepers who opted against the new extravagance and sold his commitment.[47] The other nay-sayer was the inheritor of Augustine Phillips's share, who sold it to Heminges. It was the working members of the team, the company sharers like Heminges who were also housekeepers, who chose to renew their two-playhouse resource whatever the price. This decision was the company's ultimate tribute to James Burbage's vision of 1594.

As a concept it reverted to pre-1594 practices, used as players then were to performing at whatever venue was to hand and of finding places to play in winter which put a roof over their heads. The smaller capacity of the winter venues was compensated by higher prices. The most radical feature of the Blackfriars was that it reversed the Theatre's and the Globe's auditorium priorities entirely. With seating for everyone, it could not accommodate much more than one-sixth of the Globe's numbers, but its superior comfort justified prices well over six times what the Globe charged. Most significantly it reversed the open-air playhouse's prioritization of the poorest people, who

[45] *The Letters of John Chamberlain*, ed. N. E. McClure, 2 vols., American Philosophical Society, Philadelphia, 1939, I.544.

[46] In his poem 'An Execration upon Vulcan', *Works*, ed. P. and H. Simpson and C. H. Herford, 11 vols., Clarendon Press, Oxford, 1925–52, VIII.209.

[47] In 1613 he paid off his mortgage on the Blackfriars gatehouse for roughly the same price each housekeeper paid to rebuild the Globe. The gatehouse went to his daughter in his will.

stood closest to the stage as they did at marketplace performances, while the wealthier folk paid for their comforts – seats and a roof – by being marginalized. The Blackfriars was the theatre of the future, where the more you paid the more privileged was your position in relation to the stage and the players. While the Theatre and the Globe surrounded their stage with standing customers, the Blackfriars allowed gallants to walk out of the tiring house onto the stage itself and sit on stools behind the players. That reversed the company's own priorities, from playing at the groundlings, the crowds they were used to in country marketplaces, to playing among gallants on stools and in the adjacent boxes.

THE BASIS FOR SUCCESS

This account leaves understated the company's real achievement through these years. The crisis of 1599 says more than does the Blackfriars story about the collective judgements that perpetuated the two-playhouse system. Through most of 1597 and all 1598 both of the Burbage-owned playhouses were empty. Renting the Curtain, close to and similar in design to the now-silenced Theatre, meant a serious reduction in income for the Burbage sons, no secure storage for the company properties, and no Privy Council licence to use their rented playhouse. What the two Burbage sons then did is a unique testimony to them and to their company. It was unique, in the authoritarianism of Elizabethan–Jacobean times, as a collaborative and egalitarian effort, though almost certainly it was also an act of desperation. The company sharers pitched in to help achieve what their first three years of prosperity had shown was a London-based company's basic need, a licensed place of their own. Losing the Theatre and the Blackfriars pushed the Burbage sons into a radically novel management structure. All the earlier playhouses had been built by entrepreneurs. James Burbage himself was one, with his two innovations in 1576 and 1596, the Theatre and the Blackfriars. Now, driven by their lack of cash and their company's need, his sons invented a new system of management and control for play-acting that lasted the company for the remaining forty-three years of its life and proved an enviable model for later companies.

   In December 1598 the Burbages paid a carpenter, Peter Streete, and twelve workmen to dismantle the oak framing timbers and fittings of the old Theatre and re-erect them on another site as the skeleton of a new playhouse across the river, barely fifty yards from the Admiral's Rose. That skeleton of oak timbers and decorative carvings – worth £800 according to Giles Allen, who promptly sued for the loss, which he called theft – was the

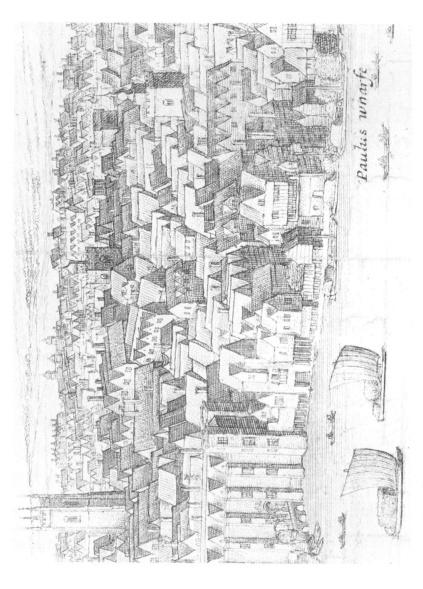

Paulus wharfe

6. The roof of the building containing the Blackfriars playhouse, a detail from Wenceslas Hollar, the 'Long View' of London, 1647. It is the long-ridged roof pierced by two narrow chimneys on the left, below and to the right of St Bride's tall church tower.

7. The first Globe, from the engraving by John Norden, *Civitas Londini*, 1600. The hexagonal roof of the polygon is marked by a single-gable hut projecting over the stage, with a tall black flagpole rising from behind it.

only capital the Burbages had left to bestow on the company as their part in the new deal.[48] Five of the other sharers each paid £100 to make up the additional cost of filling in the skeleton walls of timber with lath and plaster, buying Baltic deal for the seating and cladding, and paying the thatchers and painters who finished the structure. A majority of company members thus became owners of what the Privy Council soon made the company's officially licensed London playhouse, the Globe. Six company sharers out of the total of eight (five when Will Kemp sold out) plus Cuthbert Burbage could now take half the income from the galleries, the company's rent, to augment the money from their company shares. These company sharers were both landlords and tenants.

That deal was and continued to be a unique testimony to the team spirit of the Lord Chamberlain's sharers. It made the company secure as no

[48] In 1600, probably to help pay off the debts incurred building the Globe, Richard Burbage leased the Blackfriars to a new company of boy players. Playing only once a week, they did not attract the hostility of the adults with their daily drums and trumpets. Their activities were mentioned in 1600 in *Hamlet* probably as a discreet advertisement to boost their status and hence their landlord's income.

other company could be. There is nothing to say directly how Alleyn and Henslowe reacted to the cheek or bravado that made the Burbages lease a site for the new Globe so close to the Rose, but they made the best of it and within a year had employed the same builder to move in the opposite direction, building the Fortune in a northern suburb not far from where the Theatre had been. The Privy Council quickly approved both new sites (Appendix 2.13).

The speed of the switch from Shoreditch to the Bankside after five years at the Theatre and Curtain is striking, as was the decision to site themselves so near the Rose and the Bear Garden. While his lease of the Rose lasted Henslowe gave it to a third company, allotting them plays critical of the Chamberlain's repertory, notably *1 Sir John Oldcastle*, to rub in the error over Falstaff's name that still hung over *1 Henry IV*. When the Rose finally closed in 1603 Henslowe kept his bear-baiting interests on Bankside.[49] It is notable that less than a month after the Globe burned down in 1613 he contracted to replace the old Bear Garden nearby with a combined baiting and playhouse, the Hope. Roslyn Knutson sees the two companies as bonded together by their shared interests, like a livery company.[50] I think the relationship was more competitive and opportunistic than that.

The deal set up in 1599 lasted for ten years while the company prospered at the Globe. There were a few changes as sharers and co-owners died and new ones bought in, but the system must have worked to everyone's satisfaction. That was proved by the Burbages' renewal of the sharing process when the Blackfriars came back to them. In August 1608, soon after a lengthy closure for plague had begun, the impresario who had used it since 2 September 1600 surrendered his lease. Richard Burbage promptly extended the Globe-owning system to include the indoor playhouse. Each holder of a share in the Globe received an equivalent share in the Blackfriars.

What Burbage did was a strikingly generous act, only limited in its largesse by the decision that went with it, to run the company at both playhouses as his father intended when he built the Blackfriars in 1596. That halved the potential rental income at each playhouse, so the rent from shares in the Blackfriars was necessary to compensate the housekeepers for

---

[49] He may have run companies there too, if the Lady Elizabeth company's 'Complaint' of 1613 (Chambers, *Elizabethan Stage*, II.248–50) has any basis in truth.

[50] This is the basic argument in her *Playing Companies and Commerce in Shakespeare's Time*. Rejecting the concept of 'rival' companies, she uses the only dubiously parallel example of the city's guilds to argue for a tradition of collaboration rather than competition between the companies.

the loss of half their Globe income. It was costly to the Burbages, but it was in the company's greater interest, and perhaps a proper memorial to father Burbage's plan. A testimony of 1635 from Cuthbert Burbage says that the seven Globe sharers, the two Burbages, Heminges, Condell, Shakespeare, Sly, and a nominee of the Henry Evans who surrendered the boy company lease, had their shares in the Blackfriars 'of us for nothing' (Appendix 3). The model was the desperate Globe deal set up in 1599, and the number of housekeepers was the same, even though the total of company sharers had increased from eight to ten. That still left a clear majority of playing sharers among the housekeepers. Since the interests of the players as tenants and the housekeepers as landlords were co-extensive, the new set-up affirmed and strengthened the deal of 1599.

The Blackfriars was a triumphant gain for the King's Men, and in 1608 there was little opposition to its use. The impresario Henry Evans had regularly staged boy company shows there for the previous eight years, so the precinct's animosity had to be muted. In fact the deal was made just as the king ceded the Blackfriars precinct to the city, giving away its status as a liberty in return for a large loan. But being the King's Men made them immune to the locals, and in any case the precinct had quite a few newcomers. The company's second patron and Blackfriars resident, George Carey, had died in 1603. By 1607 Ben Jonson was living there, as was the owner of the Mermaid tavern which Francis Beaumont celebrated in his poem of 1612 as the great meeting-place for wits. The principal signatory of the 1596 petition, Lady Russell, was still there, not dying till 1616, but once the company started playing at the Blackfriars several of the sharers bought properties there. Being King's Men and Grooms of the royal Chamber gave them a social clout that the Blackfriars residents did not resist. In 1613 four of them bought into the area: Heminges, both Burbages, and Shakespeare, who acquired rooms in the Blackfriars gatehouse.

Richard Burbage's act of 1608 was not simple generosity. Behind it lay the plan to use both playhouses and to keep one empty while the other was in use. Yet however neatly it reverted to pre-1594 habits, the decision in 1608 proved uniquely grandiose. *The Taming of the Shrew*, written pre-1594, was set as a travelling-company play staged indoors at a tavern. Joining the Blackfriars to the Globe renewed the old practice, with the added attraction that the players themselves now owned the tavern. This whiff of nostalgia for the older ways meant performing inside the city and indoors through the winter weather, when the law courts were in session and the court was in town, and outdoors to much larger numbers through the summer. The financial sharing among senior members of the company that began in 1599 was extended in 1608 and it kept the company dominant in London until the closure. The most conspicuous feature of the company's new grandeur was its display of absolute pre-eminence, a company with seasonal playhouses that could afford to keep one of them shut for half of each year, at a time when other companies were seriously short of places to perform at. It came at a time when the king's two younger children were given their own new companies to add to the existing King's, Prince Henry's, and the Queen's, and there were no playhouses available for them. The deal of 1608 made the company unique. Deciding to run two playhouses was the most hegemonic act of all its forty-eight years.

I have maintained elsewhere that co-owning a company's playhouses proved a system enviable enough for later companies such as the heirs of the duopoly Admiral's, the Prince's/Palatine's Men at the Fortune, to try replicating it.[51] Added to that is the equally tenable view that continuing with the Globe in summer kept the company's clientele demotic enough to save them from the fate that Christopher Beeston and his Cockpit, built in imitation of the Blackfriars, suffered in 1617. When Beeston took the open-air Red Bull company's plays over to his new indoor playhouse in Drury Lane, apprentices ganged up to smash it in revenge for his transferring their favourite plays there away from the cheaper northern playhouse. The King's company evidently liked their audiences at the Globe, in view of their massive financial outlay to replace it in 1614. The second Globe was unnecessary. The housekeepers' reason for rebuilding the Globe must have been partly a continuing nostalgia for the old ways that had prompted the 1608 deal, partly the loyalty to their customers that Beeston ignored, and perhaps a wish to maintain the prime status of being the only company to have two playhouses when other companies were desperate for just one.

The company began their indoor playing after the plague in late 1609. Jonson was commissioned to write for the new venue and its richer clientele (he gave them *The Alchemist*, set 'her in the Friers'), and they probably acquired Beaumont and Fletcher, who had written six or seven plays for the boys at Blackfriars already, for the same reason. We cannot be sure how confidently they expected audiences which had enjoyed the satirical and sensational plays of the Blackfriars Boys to accept their own repertory, but they evidently felt they needed writers used to catering for the richer appetites. Perhaps most notably the King's acquired the services of the famous

51 See Gurr, *The Shakespearian Playing Companies*, p. 246.

musicians of the Blackfriars, a consort that offered as much as an hour's instrumental music before the show and played during the pauses between the acts. While the playhouses were closed for plague they converted the Globe's stage balcony into a music room so that the Blackfriars consort could also play at the summer venue. Shakespeare's *The Tempest* utilized its musicians.

In the longer term the seasonal interchange of playhouses and plays at the two venues had a huge effect. At first the indoor character of the Blackfriars and its much smaller stage area clogged with gallants sitting on stools seems to have been acknowledged only by limiting the performance there of plays calling for battles and gunshots.[52] Duels were still possible, though the much less free floorspace of the Blackfriars stage must have inhibited Hamlet when he fought Laertes. The chief long-term effect was that the Blackfriars became the prize place for high society to show itself. There, playgoing became not just respectable but fashionable. In summer the lawcourts were out of session and the privileged left for their country estates to remove themselves from the danger of plague. High society wintered in London. From about 1615 onwards the Blackfriars became society's showplace. The Lord Chamberlain himself kept a key to a box flanking the stage in the 1630s, and Henrietta Maria graced it with her person four times, the first visits by any member of a royal family to a common playhouse. The Blackfriars was the company's ultimate security. It tied them to their royal patrons and courtly interests, and when royalty fell they did too.

I will conclude this survey of the company's history with a colourfully gruesome though quite trivial story taken from a pamphlet written in the 1620s about a visit to a King's play at the Blackfriars. *The Life of a Satyrical Puppy called Nim* says a lot about the kind of stripling who chose to sit on a stool on the Blackfriars stage, more eager for his advancement than his entertainment.[53] Gentlemen could not work for money without imperilling their social status, so a penniless youth's struggle to use his sexual attractions to make money was a popular subject for pamphlet anecdotes and the indoor plays. Nim's tale is about his attempt to use the Blackfriars to make his fortune. It describes the stool-sitters on the stage standing up to flaunt their charms at each interact break, the obtuseness of a country gentleman sitting on the stage who takes the fiction he sees for fact, and most pointedly the playhouse's unquestioned role as the place for romantic encounters. Not

---

[52] For a more detailed account of the variations between the Globe and Blackfriars, see Gurr, 'Playing in Amphitheatres and Playing in Hall Theatres', *Elizabethan Theatre* 13 (1993), 27–62.

[53] Appendix 2.36 reports a quarrel between a gallant on the stage and the occupants of a box behind him.

published till 1657, by 'T.M.', implausibly thought to be the Thomas May
who wrote plays in the 1620s, it certainly belongs to the time when the
Blackfriars was London society's showplace. I make no apology for quoting
this chapter from Nim's adventures in full.[54]

First prepare to admire my Capacity, for thy knowledge never owned such a parlous
Plot before. Which was, that I should go to see a Play in *Black-Fryars*: and there
(by all necessary consequences, or rather inspired assurance) some rich Lady would
cast her Eie on me, and the same night me on her. Be not thou astonish'd Reader,
neither suppose it impossible that Nature can be so opulent, or he that is mortall,
possesse such a strong Brain. For (alas Man!) heretofore I was as full of these
learned-Stratagems, as an Egge is full of meat.

Fifty pounds accroutred me from Top to Toe: having been very thrifty in laying
out my Money, and carefull to refuse *Bunges* [his servant's] advice, for he brought
me a *Taylor*, whom Custome had made to steale from himself. A Slave that the
Devill durst not trust with his old Clothers; no, though he might gaine his Soul
in lue of the Theft.

Thus like a true *English-man* (who wears his Mother too much in his Aparell)
I entered the *Theater*, and sat upon the Stage: making low Congies to divers
Gentlemen; not that I knew them, but I was confident, they would requite me in
the same kinde: which made the Spectators suppose us of very olde, and familiar
acquaintance. Besides (that I might appear no *Novice*) I observ'd all fashionable
Customes; As delivering my Sute to a more apparent view, by hanging the Cloak
upon one shoulder: or letting it fall (as it were) by chance. I stood up also at
the end of every *Act*, to salute those, whom I never saw before. Two *Acts* were
finished before I could discover any thing, either for my Comfort then, or worth
my relation now. Unlesse it were *punycall* absurdity in a Country-Gentleman: who
was so caught with the naturall action of a Youth (that represented a ravish'd Lady),
as he swore alowd, he would not sleep untill he had killed her ravisher: and how
'twas not fit such Rogues should live in a Common-wealth. This made me laugh,
but not merry.

Anon after, I spied a Gentlewomans Eie, fix'd full upon me. Hope and Despaire
threw me into such Distractions, that I was about to bid a Boy (who personated
Cupid in the play) to shoot at her with his counterfeit Arrow. But she presently
disclaimed me her Object: and with the like inconstancy gaz'd upon another.
About the beginning of the Fourth *Act*, my Face withstood a fresh encounter,
given me by a Ladies Eie, whose Seate opposed mine. She look'd stedfast on me,
till the Play ended; seeming to survey my Limbs with amorous curiosity: whilst

[54] Thomas May, born in 1595, dying in 1650, wrote a play, *The Heir*, published in 1622, translated
Virgil, Lucan, and other classics, and after 1642, when Secretary to the Long Parliament, wrote *The
History of the Parliament of England which began Nov 3, 1640*, taking it up to the Battle of Newbury
in 1643, the period when he was Secretary. The misattribution of Nim's pamphlet to him dates from
the 1650s.

I advanced them all, to encounter her approbation. A great desire I had to see her Face: which she discovered, by unmasquing it to take her leave of a Gentleman. But if I ever beheld one so ill-favour'd? do thou abhorre my Book. She look'd like *December*, in the midst of *April*, old and crabbed in her Youth. Her Nose stood towards the *South-East* point: and *Snot* had fretted a preposterous *Channell* in the most remote corner of her Lip. Sure she was chast, *chast* because *deformed*: and her *deformitie* (repugnant to the common course of *Nature*) might beget that *Chastitie*: but in whom? in others, not in her selfe; unlesse *Necessitie* did force it. For no doubt she would be as leacherous as the Mountaine-*Goate*, had not Natures qualmishnesse proved a strong contradiction to her desire: who heaved the Gorge, at her *imperfect* perfecting: therefore had no Stomach to make a Man fitting her embracements. Yet she wore *Jewells*, for the which I could willingly have kiss'd her in the *dark*. And perhaps too (by guilded provocation) supplied the Office of a Husband.

Her uglinesse made me suppose that nothing could be too base for her acceptance: therefore I (following her down the Staires) resolved to discover a good-will to her, either by a wanton gesture of my Body, or whispering in her Ear just as she came forth into the Street, (her Usher being step'd aside to complement with parting Company) I proffer'd my service to attend her home, if she missed any of her Friends. She suspecting that I thought her to be a Whore, told me aloud I was much mistaken. Her Brother (unknown to me) stood behind us, and asked her; what the matter was? *Marry* (quoth she) this Gentleman takes me for some common Creature. He with all violent dexterity strucke me in the Face; and afterwards went about to draw his Sword. But I slunk through the presse of people, and very *tamely* conveied my selfe home. My man *Bunge* (who attended there all the Play-time, to save charges) saw this: and heard the *Young-Gallant* swear (after I was gone) if ever he met me, he would make my Heart the *Scabbard* of his Sword. These woful tydings hee brought to my Chamber, so that my costly *Experiment* was now concluded, and my glorious Garments altogether uselesse. For I durst not visit *Theaters* any more, lest I should meete with him, or Women elsewhere, as fearfull of the like entertainment.'[55]

A feature of such tales is the need for their incidental detailing to appear familiar and plausible. Repulsively though Nim describes the lady he was trying to seduce, his whole account – his lack of interest in the play, his eventual humiliation by sword-waving, even the country gentleman's naïve exclamation – were stock features of the stool-sitters at Blackfriars in the 1620s and 1630s.[56] Commenting out loud during the performance was no more unusual than viewing it from a stool on stage. Being there to be seen

[55] T.M., *The Life of a Satyrical Puppy called Nim*, 1657, pp. 102–7 (sig. H3v–H6).
[56] Fletcher's *A Wife for a Month* has a ravished lady and Cupid, although she is only threatened with rape. Two of Fletcher's other plays and Arthur Wilson's *The Swisser* present rapes, but lack a Cupid.

as much as to see was a feature of the Blackfriars days, one that Jonson used with the gossips he set to chat during the interacts of *The Staple of News*. What the puppy's story says most clearly is that going to plays at the Blackfriars in the 1620s and 1630s had become the best means of self-display for anyone in gentle society. That was the company's most obvious strength and the chief cause of its conservatism through its last years.

CHAPTER 2

The company's work

VOICES

Success in the seventeenth century and fame in the twenty-first have submerged a lot of questions about the team for which all the plays were written, and its practices. What accent, for instance, did the players use on stage? Most of the early team were Londoners, but at least two, Heminges and Shakespeare, came from the Midlands or mid-west of England. None of them ever went to university, although over the years several sharers claimed gentlemanly status. Did they all adopt a similar accent on stage, or did they keep their native regional forms? Did they polish their voices when playing gentlemanly, noble, or regal parts, and did they do what modern actors do, use dialect forms when playing comics? Regional accents were likely to have been more distinctive then, when travel was much less usual and more arduous, than they need be now. And how regional, considering that Raleigh was mocked for his Devon accent, was the class divide in dialect? The longstanding English and upper-class prejudice against non-metropolitan voices is apparent in nineteenth-century jokes about rolling your 'r's and Polonius being stabbed through the arras. The fact that such anti-American and anti-Irish jokes came into existence fairly late may mean that rhotic accents[1] were more standard in Tudor speech than later, and were routine in the speech of Shakespeare's company. But that can only be an assumption. Rhotic speech almost never shows up in the written English that Dobson and other scholars of early modern pronunciation have to rely on in distinguishing speech forms.[2]

We do have reason to suspect that educated and socially superior Elizabethans were impelled towards a centralized form of speech reflecting

[1] A wonderfully mishearable term, the rhotic accent emphasizes the preconsonantal 'r'.
[2] E. J. Dobson, *English Pronunciation 1500–1700*, 2 vols., Clarendon Press, Oxford, 1957, and Fausto Cercignani, *Shakespeare's Works and Elizabethan Pronunciation*, Clarendon Press, Oxford, 1981.

education and high social status. This must mean that the more rhotic accents of areas like the west of England, Ireland, and Scotland (and modern North America) were recognizably not popular with upper-class Londoners. The advice that George Puttenham gave to would-be poets in *The Arte of Englishe Poesie*, 1589, sets out early thinking about the most 'correct' form of spoken English. It is remarkably like the class-based prejudice about good speech which was still predominant when the BBC was founded in 1926. Puttenham identified the proper language that poetry should be written in by citing the analogy of spoken accents and spellings, chiefly warning against the danger of using local idioms as distinct from the language of the court and London, which he reckoned was the only correct form of the mother tongue.[3]

When I say language, I meane the speach wherein the Poet or maker writeth be it Greek or Latine or as our case is the vulgar English, & when it is peculiar unto a countrey it is called the mother speach of that people . . . This part in our maker or Poet must be heedyly looked unto, that it be naturall, pure, and the most usuall of all his countrey: and for the same purpose rather that which is spoken in the kings Court, or in the good townes and Cities within the land, then in the marches and frontiers, or in port townes, where straungers haunt for traffike sake, or yet in Universities where Schollers use much peevish affectation of words out of the primative languages, or finally, in any uplandish village or corner of a Realme, where is no resort but of poore rusticall or uncivill people: neither shall he follow the speach of a craftes man or carter, or other of the inferiour sort, though he be inhabitant or bred in the best towne and Citie in this Realme, for such persons do abuse good speaches by strange accents or ill shapen soundes, and false ortographie . . . Neither shall he take the termes of Northern-men, such as they use in dayly talke, whether they be noble men or gentlemen, or of their best clarkes all is a matter: nor in effect any speach used beyond the river of Trent, though no man can deny but that theirs is the purer English Saxon at this day, yet it is not so Courtly nor so currant as our Southerne English is, no more is the far Westerne mans speach: ye shall therfore take the usuall speach of the Court, and that of London and the shires lying about London within lx. myles, and not much above. I say not this but that in every shyre of England there be gentlemen and others that speake but specially write as good Southerne as we of Middlesex or Surrey do, but not the common people of every shire, to whom the gentlemen, and also their learned clarkes do for the most part condescend.[4]

---

[3] Guilio Lepschy, 'Mother Tongues and Literary Languages', MHRA Presidential Address, 16 March 2001 (Modern Humanities Research Association, 2002), provides a delicate analysis of what this term signifies.

[4] Quoted from the original, fol. 120–1. A modernized version appears in *The Arte of English Poesie*, by George Puttenham, edited by Gladys Doidge Willcock and Alice Walker, Cambridge University Press, 1936, pp. 144–5.

The assumption that the only 'correct' accent is spoken within sixty miles of London has been one of English society's more durable cultural prejudices.

Did such a 'Southerne' prejudice affect the players? As seasoned travellers – far more familiar with regional accents than most of their contemporaries – they well knew the distinctive speech-forms of the rest of the country. Did they, like modern actors, make fun of west country speech-forms when playing rude mechanicals? That may be what Samuel Rowlands meant when he wrote that Pope and Singer of the duopoly companies spoke 'so boorish, when / They counterfaite the clownes upon the Stage'.[5] While Falstaff, as a knight and gentleman, spoke 'good Southerne', would Bardolph, Nym, and the others have spoken 'boorish', or was that only for country clowns like Bottom, or William in *As You Like It*? Did they speak a lower-class London? If accent was regularly used to distinguish social rank and hence to identify comic characters, were all three of the non-English captains in *Henry V* intended to be comic? Llewellyn certainly was, with his reiterated phrases like 'looke you', multiplied in the company's quarto version, and his pluralizing of nouns. Not just Welsh catchphrases but his voice rhythms ('as magnanimous as Agamemnon') are there in the distinctive prose Shakespeare wrote for him. English Gower reproves Pistol for underrating Llewellyn 'because he could not speak English in the native garb', as Gower himself did. Were Macmorris and Jamy equally comic to London ears if the company chose to keep them in their playing text (they were cut from the quarto version)? Exactly what was the 'native garb' used when speaking the serious verse of the gentry and nobility?

Much of our difficulty with early speech forms comes from the limited evidence that the written word can supply. Fletcher, for instance, is commonly identified as chief author of the fifty or so collaborated texts of the 'Beaumont and Fletcher' plays by his recurrent use of the weak 'ye' for the strong 'you' in the sections he is thought to have written. Did Fletcher use 'ye' in his normal speech? When he copied out *Bonduca* the company scribe 'Jhon' altered 162 instances of Fletcher's 'ye' to 'you'. All that the authorities on the history of pronunciation can say about 'ye' is that it was generally a dialect form used by Welsh-speakers and other westerners.[6] Fletcher, born and raised in London, is hardly likely to have used it as a dialectal feature in his own speech. It featured strongly in his orthography, but did it in his voice? And would the players have followed his orthography

---

[5] Samuel Rowlands, *The letting of humors blood in the head-vaine*, 1600, sat.4.
[6] Dobson, *English Pronunciation 1500–1700*, II.468.

when they learned their parts and used 'ye' instead of 'you' wherever his hand was in the text? Did the scribe's corrections reflect the company's standard pronunciation? Was the distinctive orthography that identified Llewellyn's idiosyncratic form of speaking in *Henry V* copied from how the player in the role was expected to speak his lines, or was it the author's own note for how he wanted them pronounced? We have only soft and speculative answers to such questions.

I think we must assume that the company normally used speech-forms that came close to Puttenham's prescription of upper-class London speech, though probably that was more rhotic than received pronunciation in modern England. We can get some inklings of the Southwark dialect from a small book, *The English Primrose*. It was published in 1644, the year the Globe was pulled down, by a Southwark teacher to help his schoolboys spell more correctly by relating the written form of words to their pronunciation of them. But the Shakespeare company is unlikely to have spoken in distinctively Southwark forms, especially when they were addressing the gentles and court dignitaries in the lords' rooms and pretending to be courtiers and kings. In *As You Like It*, Orlando in the forest tells the disguised Rosalind 'Your accent is something finer than you could purchase in so removed a dwelling.' He heard educated speech-forms in Ganymede's voice, like the 'native garb' that Gower and Pistol spoke, however much Pistol elevated his own with Marlovianisms. The boy player of Rosalind must have used the 'good Southerne' spoken within the sixty-mile radius of London that encompassed Oxford and Cambridge. Otherwise the use by specific characters of accents from different parts of the country to mark different social levels would make no sense.

The company did use a Devonshire accent for some of the characters in *The London Prodigal*. The play's orthography indicates that this came close to the early kind of rhotic mummerset[7] used by Poor Tom in *King Lear*. There is nothing to say that they used it for *The Fair Maid of Bristow*, set though it was among the people of Somerset apart from some gentry and King Richard I. An early Mummerset would certainly have affirmed some urban/rural distinctions. On the other hand we might give some thought to the awesome possibility that for *Macbeth* in 1606 the company all adopted Scottish accents. That ponderous and reflective speech of Macbeth's when he says the blood on his hands will 'The multitudinous seas incarnadine, /

---

[7] The orthography denoting west-country accents is remarkably uniform. According to the special forms given them in different plays, characters from Cornwall, Devon, and Somerset all had the same broad accent, an early version of the 'mummerset' still favoured by companies today for rustic roles. Shanks in *The Soddered Citizen* (1630) played the countryman Hodge with a Mummerset accent.

Making the green, one red', truly relishes its 'r's. Some of the Blackfriars company boys certainly used northern voices in the same year as *Macbeth* for *The Isle of Gulls*, a sharp satire on the Scottish presence at the English court, of which Thomas Edmondes reported, 'all men's parts were acted of two diverse nations'.[8] London was full of Scottish accents in 1606. If boys could copy it, the professionals, well-travelled through most of the country, and always alert to local accents, surely could too.

STAGE PRACTICES AND DRESS

Another matter awaiting more study is the staging practices that the company used, and the iconic forms of dress, especially of the boys playing women, and related items of attire. How often did the boys use masks when portraying courtly ladies on stage? At Windsor in July 1603 Dudley Carleton commented on Queen Anne's arrival from Edinburgh that 'in all this journey she hath worn no mask', choosing to show her face to her new subjects at the risk of browning her white complexion. Women outdoors who chose not to wear the black velvet masks that protected ladies against the hated sun paid a price. Sunburn was not good for a lady's face: 'for her favour she hath done it some wrong', said Carleton.[9] So the boys playing ladies on the Globe's stage, which could equally represent an indoor or an outdoor location, and still more at the indoor Blackfriars where they were confronted with Nim's lady, might routinely have worn masks. Isabella in *Measure for Measure* appears to have been dressed as a lady wearing or carrying a mask when she first calls on Angelo, since he refers to it.[10] The ladies in audiences were said to conceal their smiles behind a mask or fan. Such gestures would also suit the King's Men's ladies on stage, from Princess Katherine in *Henry V* to the Duchess Sophia in *Rollo*. Distinctive features of female dress like these must have helped the boys in their women's roles.

Equally potent, but with less evidence to support it, was the dressing of the stage. The Induction to *A Warning for Fair Women*, published in 1599, tells us that 'the stage is hung with blacke', and the audience thus prepared for a tragedy. Through the company's first years, black stage hangings were as precise a signal to the audience of what they were to expect as the

---

[8] The letter is dated February 1606, so the boys' play preceded the first staging of *Macbeth*. It is quoted in *The Court and Times of James I*, ed. Thomas Birch, 2 vols., London, 1848, 1.60–1.

[9] *Dudley Carleton to John Chamberlain 1603–1624*, ed. Maurice Lee Jr, Rutgers University Press, New Brunswick, 1972, p. 35.

[10] See Gurr, '*Measure for Measure*'s Hoods and Masks: the Duke, Isabella, and Liberty', *English Literary Renaissance* 27 (1997), 89–105.

generic name 'tragedy' on a playbill. But this tradition of signalling how a play would end seems to have vanished when tragicomedy entered the repertory. Several writers, Shakespeare in *1 Henry VI*, and Marston and Dekker up to 1608,[11] make references to black hangings, but none after that. Given that *Pericles* introduced tragicomedy to the Globe in 1607, it was logical. *The Winter's Tale* makes fun of the standard definition of the genre, that such plays are half a tragedy, half a comedy, by making its first half tragic and its second comic, and highlighting the transition. Fletcher's plays, starting with *Philaster* at the Globe in 1609, depended on their ability to hold the audience in suspense until the surprise revelation of the ending. *The Winter's Tale* is the only play in all Shakespeare to surprise its audience with Hermione's living statue, as *Philaster* surprises its audience with the boy page who turns out to be a woman. Such a form of drama could not admit black hangings.

The question what were the company's norms for staging and performance reaches far beyond the scope of this book. It is, though, relevant to the company's central concerns and, in the absence of more play-texts in their 'allowed book' form, some of the standard practices, however inferential they are, need a mention here. Above all, given the likelihood that the company shortened the allowed playbooks, there is the question what was the usual time and length of a performance, and whether it changed over the years. Some indications suggest that in the earlier years different companies chose to start their plays at different times in the afternoon. The Admiral's Men at the Fortune seem to have started at 3 pm, whereas the Chamberlain's were committed by their patron in 1594 to begin at two and end before five. Possibly starting times were staggered to help customer choice. The duration of the performances, between two hours and three, seems to have remained standard throughout. We might wonder how cynical was the comment by Dudley Carleton, an assiduous playgoer, when he saw students perform Seneca's *Troades* in Leiden, and wrote to his friend John Chamberlain that 'they began at two of the clock and ended at five', which, he added, 'made the play so much the better, being both short and sweet'.[12] The players could always shorten their maximal playtexts to a more comfortable length, as they did with *Henry V*, which in its quarto form of 1599 and 1600 can run in barely two hours. Two hours' traffic for the stage

---

[11] *1 Henry VI* (1591?), 1.1.1; Marston, *Antonio's Revenge* (1600) Prologue 20, *The Insatiate Countess* (1607–8), 4.5.1; Dekker, *Northward Ho!* (1605), 4.1, *Lanthorne and Candlelight* (1608, *Non-Dramatic Works*, ed. Grosart, III.296). An elegy for Burbage in 1619 orders the stage to be hung with black, but that was a ceremonial reminder of his former days.
[12] *Dudley Carleton to John Chamberlain*, p. 231.

was a routine claim from *Romeo and Juliet* onwards, and less than three was regularly claimed in the 1630s.

It is now a cliché that Elizabethan audiences were hearers before they were spectators, using their ears as much as their eyes. Two of the more potent effects of that disposition were, first, that the audience felt itself to be a crowd, not an assembly of individuals, and second that they were more ready than modern audiences to interact with the players. Both required three-dimensional acting. The assumption that a stage has a front facing the audience and a back from which the actors enter is a modern two-dimensional preconception. All the Elizabethan stages were three-dimensional. That is clearly laid out in the Inigo Jones design for an indoor theatre, probably the Cockpit, the most reliable testimony we have to early theatre design for general audiences. It provides not only two levels of boxes on each side of the stage but also what we consider to be seats 'behind', on the degrees flanking the stage balcony's central music room.

A three-dimensional audience that literally surrounds the players was the Elizabethan norm, a world away from scenic staging. Blocking on a centralized stage was concentric. The official speakers stood in the centre, while the commentators and clowns prowled around the flanks. The audience was closest to the commentators, and the commentators spoke directly to them. In *Richard III* Richard opens the play crouching at the stage edge and speaking in soliloquy to the crowd at his feet. He tells them the truth about his feelings, with intimate frankness. The other characters when they come on speak from centre-stage, and the audience literally backs Richard as they watch him fool them with his acting. His wooing of Lady Anne in the third scene is a bravura display of his arts of deception. That role and that position he sustains until he has the crown. Once he is king, though, he has to occupy the centre of the stage. That is when he loses his proximity and his intimacy with his audience. From then on he is the victim, acted on rather than acting, and he loses the audience's subconscious alliance with him. Iago does the same, as does Vindice in *The Revenger's Tragedy*, using the stage margins to confide in the audience while fooling his centre-stage victims. Hamlet too stands on the margins of the stage, alone and apart from the court when we first meet him in the play's second scene. Comedians, using the marginal *platea* or street area next to the audience rather than the central *locus* or authority position, do the same.[13] Three-dimensional staging admits a radically different dynamic from two-dimensional in the

---

[13] See the handsome discussion by Robert Weimann, *Author's Pen and Actor's Voice: Playing and Writing in Shakespeare's Theatre*, Cambridge University Press, 2000, p. 197.

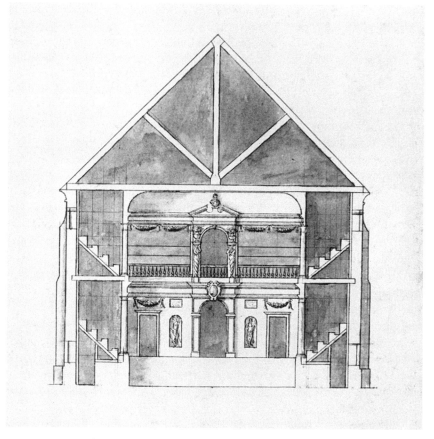

8. A section from plans by Inigo Jones for an indoor playhouse, probably drawn
in c. 1616 for the Cockpit, which was built in 1617, imitating the Blackfriars. This
section shows the stage and *frons scenae*, with a central music room on the stage
balcony, and 'degrees' or benches for seating on either side. The boxes flanking the stage
are shown with raked benches.

intimacies it grants to some of its characters with the audience. There is
still much to be done to recognize the effects of this disposition on the
plays we now read and stage.[14] An Elizabethan audience was a crowd, in
three dimensions. Modern spectators are individuals, thinking and looking
in two.

[14] Good work is being done by Alan Dessen and others. On the configurations of stage blocking, see
Gurr, 'Stage Doors at the Globe', *Theatre Notebook* 53 (1999), 8–18, and subsequent debates in that
journal.

Many other currently incalculable factors remain for study: the effects of interaction between the players and the surrounding and visible crowd as audience, their alertness to the oral rather than visual features, the choreography of three-dimensional staging and its familiar significances, the intertextuality of the story-lines and genres, and the effect of staging signals used to mark tragedy from comedy, not to mention factors that have not yet come to our notice.

THE CHANGING PERSONALITY

Many features of the company's work changed in the course of their forty-eight years. Three examples of change in particular show how the company practices changed: the routine of touring their plays round the country with which all the first sharers' careers started; the custom of performing a jig to conclude the afternoon's entertainment; and the use of music and musicians in the plays. Many other practices would reward study, but these three reflect in best detail the gradual shifts in policy and the pressures the company came under through their remarkable half-century. Other practices, such as maintaining a resident playwright, the familial cross-links and 'brotherhood' that held them together for so long, and the consequences of their being under the monarch's direct patronage for four-fifths of their existence, along with the cautious defences of their position published by Webster, Field, Lowin, and others, are dealt with elsewhere in this book.

First, though, a few of the smaller and less gradual features of their climb in status and self-confidence. These include the colourful symptoms of their rise in eminence. When they were made Grooms of the Chamber, for instance, as the King's Men, the sharers of 1603 became technically and in public the lowest rank of courtiers, gentlemen who were allocated the courtier's scarlet to wear, and who paraded in the king's processions. It was a public elevation that led Beaumont in 1605 to insert into one of his plays a Jonsonian sneer about Shakespeare's humble origins as the son of a glover and his new pretensions.[15] However personal the jibe, it signals the company's rising status which was soon to give them the Blackfriars where Beaumont's play was staged. Whether it was the sharers' courtier status, their consistent success in their profession, or the wealth they generated that made them the subject of such envy is a tangled matter. They did earn envy for what their work brought them. Heminges was said in 1619 to have

---

[15] See Gurr, 'A Jibe at Shakespeare in 1606', *Notes and Queries* 247 (2002), 245–7, and below.

'greate lyveinge wealth and power'.[16] But he was never accused, as other managerial figures like Christopher Beeston were, of exploiting his control of the company's finances for his own profit, so his position cannot have differed from those of Condell, Taylor, and the later leaders.

Most of the other features of the company's work that altered in the course of their career changed much as did those of the other companies, and need no particular account here. The more specific ones include the changes to the repertory dealt with in chapter 4, and new modes in staging, especially the practice that was unique to the King's Men after 1608, shifting their plays between the two venues each year.

The neatest small marker of the changes in their staging practices is perhaps the frequency of performance of each play. This, I think, had a profound yet almost incalculable effect on the staging. The little information we have suggests that in their first incarnation as the Chamberlain's Men their role as one of the two duopoly companies meant that they had to follow the practices so minutely recorded for their opposites by Philip Henslowe. Between 1594 and 1600 the Admiral's Men kept roughly thirty plays in their repertory a year, and performed none of them in London more than a dozen times at most. No play was staged on successive days, and usually the most popular appeared less than once in the six days of each week's performances. With only two playhouses licensed to perform in London and audiences who were frequent visitors, such an intense repertory system must have been seen as essential. The demands that such an intensive practice laid on the players' memories does not bear thinking of. Its basis lay in the practices of travelling, where each play was staged only once at each town. But travelling needed far fewer plays than the Henslowe repertory, so the intensity of the London practice must have told heavily on the companies once they were performing throughout the year at the Rose and the Theatre. When additional playhouses came into use after 1600 the demand for constant novelty must have shrunk a little, and the idea of giving plays short runs on consecutive days must have been introduced through the next decade or so. We are told, for instance, that when a performance of *Henry VIII* burned the Globe down in 1613 it was on the third day of its run. The nine-day wonder of *A Game at Chess* in 1624 was a more special case, but it does suggest that the idea of such runs with a single play had been established by then. To play the same play for several days was much easier on the company than the duopoly practice of a different one each day. This did not affect the speed of preparation for staging very much, since in 1633

---

[16] Chambers, *Elizabethan Stage*, ii.323.

the King's managed to replace their planned performance of Fletcher's *The Tamer Tamed* with *The Scornful Lady* in the course of a single morning.[17] But we know that by the 1630s authors were being paid with the third day's takings, so evidently by then initial runs of a week or more were expected both by the companies and by their audiences. Beyond easing the demand on players' memories, however, there are few clear indications of the effect this continuity of performance might have had on the company's staging practices.

Of all these smaller features of the company's work, the principal one I shall deal with before looking into the three major features of the changes is the set of events that led up to Beaumont's sneer at Shakespeare. It tells us a lot about the lowly status of the sharers initially, and their vulnerability as people who had to succeed through their work rather than their birth. As the new king's servants, a status which in May 1603 made the ten sharers, including Shakespeare, Grooms of the Chamber, it brought them no new income but certainly a sharp rise in their social rank. They could now wear the royal livery, for which they received the only money their new rank brought them. Twelve paraded in their new garb at James's entry into London in April 1604. It was a unique elevation for a group of men who were used only to the rank of common player.

Their scarlet cloaks, doublets, and breeches as Grooms of the Chamber were put on show again in August of that year for the eighteen-day visit of the Spanish Constable of Castile. With a large party of Spanish grandees Castile came to London as the chief delegate to King James's great conference held to make peace and stop the long war between Protestant England and Catholic Spain. The Spaniards were housed at Somerset House, and the King's Men were ordered to attend them throughout their stay. They presented no plays but were paid to wait in attendance on the Spanish daily. They were spare parts, mutes who displayed the king's livery as courtiers before the Spanish guests. Their eighteen days of standing around looking handsome in their distinctive scarlet was a clear mark not only to the Spanish but to all London of their status as royal courtiers (Appendix 2.17).

This elevation did not pass unnoticed. Ben Jonson had already used the company's actors, including Shakespeare himself, to mock the new coat of arms and its motto that Shakespeare had bought for his father in 1597. In *Every Man out of his Humour*, written in 1599 for the Shakespeare company,

---

[17] See N. W. Bawcutt, *The Control and Censorship of Caroline Drama: The Records of Sir Henry Herbert, Master of the Revels 1623–73*, Oxford University Press, 1996, p. 182.

9. The chief members of the Spanish Conference at Somerset House in 1604, at which twelve sharers from the King's Men served as courtiers. Versions of the portrait, by an unknown artist, are at Greenwich and at the National Portrait Gallery. This version is reproduced by permission of the National Portrait Gallery (NPG 665). It shows the Spanish delegates on the left. From the window they are Juan de Velasco, Duke of Frias and Constable of Castile, the delegation's Spanish leader; Juan de Tassis, Count of Villamediana; Alessandro Rovida, a Senator of Milan; Charles de Ligne, Count of Arenburg; Jean Richardet, President of the French Council of State; and Louis Verreycken, Audiencer, from Brussels. The English delegates, sitting on the right are, from the window, Thomas Sackville, first Earl of Dorset; Charles Howard, Lord Admiral and first Earl of Nottingham; Charles Blount, Earl of Devonshire; Henry Howard, Earl of Northampton; and Robert Cecil, Viscount Cranbourne, Chief Secretary and later Lord Treasurer and first Earl of Salisbury.

he made one of the characters boast about the emblem for his own newly acquired coat of arms, a boar's head on a plate and a crest which included a frying pan. His mockers proposed that the motto should be 'Not Without Mustard'. That derisively echoed the emblematic spear on the Shakespeare shield, and aptly underscored the ambiguity of the motto Shakespeare had secured for his father, *Non Sans Droict*, 'Not without right'.

The company was not slow to respond to Jonson's insults. However tolerant the other sharers may have been to the mockery of Shakespeare, the play launched a series of derisive exchanges between Jonson and the company, and an even longer one between the two poets. In 1601 the company staged Dekker's *Satiromastix*, a complex satire aimed at Jonson as part of the so-called 'War of the Theatres'. Shortly afterwards Shakespeare seems likely to have put him on stage as Ajax in *Troilus and Cressida*. It was during this period, when Jonson was writing for the boy companies and first met two of his many protégés, Beaumont and Fletcher, that the second sharp jibe at Shakespeare's ascent was written. Six years after *Every Man Out*, in the first play of Beaumont's that the boys at Blackfriars staged, he produced a sneer about Shakespeare's social ambitions even more contemptuous than Jonson's earlier one. In *The Woman Hater*, printed in 1606, he used John Shakespeare's lowly career as a whittawer and glover to mock his son's social climb as a King's man, Groom of the royal Chamber and thus a new courtier. A character making a speech condemning social climbing at court says 'you shall see many legges [i.e., making a leg, or bowing low] too; amongst the rest you shall behould one payre, the feete of which, were in times past sockelesse, but are now through the change of time (that alters all thinges) very strangely become the legges of a Knight and a Courtier: *another payre you shall see, that were heire apparent legges to a Glover, these legges hope shortly to bee honourable*; when they passe by they will bowe, and the mouth to these legges, will seeme to offer you some Courtship' (italics minc).[18] The allusion to a glover, the trade of Shakespeare's father, together with the pun on 'sockelesse', not wearing the classical comedian's 'soc' or light shoe, is too direct to be accidental or incidental. Such men were once so poor they had no footwear, but now they can make a courtier's 'leg', especially the one who went from being a mere player of comedies to a courtier. The identification, however gratuitous, of the glover's son as a new courtier clearly aggrieved ambitious young gentlemen like Beaumont who, writing for the boy players including those at courtier Burbage's indoor playhouse, were not getting any such rise in status themselves.

Obviously Beaumont's prejudice was prompted by Jonson's chronic gossiping. A regular exchanger of playscripts and poems with Jonson, how else could Beaumont from Leicestershire have known so much about Shakespeare's origins? No doubt his animus was enhanced by the well-known opposition between the 'little eyases' of *Hamlet*, the Blackfriars boy company who were Beaumont's first employers, and the King's at the Globe. The boys were occupying the playhouse that had been originally built for

---

[18] The quotation is taken from the edition by George Walton Williams in *Beaumont and Fletcher, Dramatic Works*, General Editor Fredson Bowers, 10 vols., Cambridge University Press, 1966–96, I.164 (1.3.13–21).

the King's Men. We might choose to see this incident as a mark of the King's Company's lack of ill-will, when first they agreed to buy Jonson's *Volpone* in 1605, and, after they regained the Blackfriars in 1608, took on Beaumont himself with Fletcher to write for them. Their readiness to forgive went with the upward mobility that was now able to take on the Blackfriars audiences.

TRAVELLING

The Chamberlain's Men came into being after working in a long tradition of taking their plays on tour round the country, a tradition in which London was only one of the many stops in a country-wide spread of one-off performances from a limited repertory. They knew that playing to the huge numbers in London was more profitable but also more demanding because of the number of plays they had to stage there compared with the mere three or four that were all they travelled with. The London-based professional companies had to perform twice as many plays in one week as they needed to learn for a whole year of travelling. It has even been suggested that once their footprints were fixed in London the small number of plays they had to take on their travels made touring a holiday. Plague often made it a necessity, but most plague deaths came in the summer, the best time for travelling. Certainly the long-lasting traditions of travel dictated their main practices. Even in London staging was based on mobile resources, the words and the clothing, and the few props that were needed to equip whatever space they could secure to perform in. That practice stayed with them throughout, whether it was used to take plays from their London base to Gray's Inn or Middle Temple Hall or the court at night, or to pile onto their waggons and horses to perform in front of a family of grandees in their country house.

According to the records so far published in the REED volumes and its *Newsletter*, in the first months, the summer period up to Michaelmas 1594, the new company may have ventured to Marlborough, about sixty-five miles west of London.[19] In the following year they were in East Anglia,

---

[19] According to William Harrison's calculations in his *Description*, first published in 1587. I use the edition *The Description of England*, ed. Georges Edelen, Folger, Washington, DC, 1994. Harrison's list of distances in England and Scotland is on pp. 399–405. Peter Davison emphasizes the visits to Marlborough in his edition of the 1597 quarto of *Richard III*, pp. 38–42, and in 'Commerce and Patronage: the Lord Chamberlain's Men's Tour of 1597', in *Shakespeare Performed: Essays in Honor of R. A. Foakes*, ed. Grace Ioppolo, University of Delaware Press, Newark, 2000, pp. 56–71. The Marlborough visits are in the town's records, and Davison does not speculate about whether any nearby hall might have prompted them.

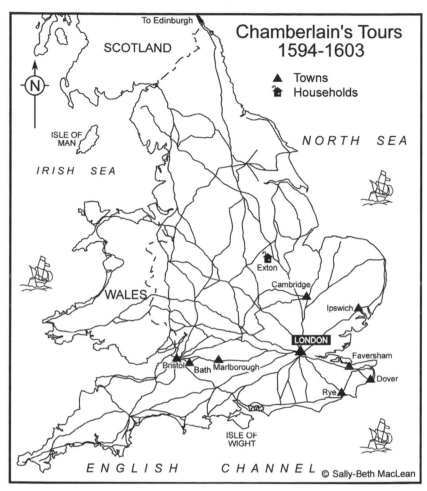

10. A map of the Lord Chamberlain's Men's known touring routes, prepared in 2002 by Sally-Beth MacLean of the Records of Early English Drama project, Toronto.

visiting Cambridge (the town, not an official visit to the university) and Ipswich. In 1597 at the beginning of August they visited Rye and Dover, probably as part of one tour, and in the west Marlborough, Bath, and Bristol in the same summer. None of these trips were very far afield, and the visits to Dover and Bristol most likely led them onto coastal shipping for their return to London. The Bristol visit (in September) may have marked the end of that year's tour, although it is possible that they went from their

11. The Old Hall, Exton, where the Chamberlain's Men played *Titus Andronicus* in 1595.
A photograph of the hall before it was destroyed by fire.

Kentish tour to Dover and thence round by sea to Bristol, taking in Bath
and Marlborough on the land route back to London.[20]

The paucity of visits to towns, and the fact that most of them were undertaken during the summer, suggests that the company may have preferred to
travel when the court was away from London and dignitaries invited them
to play at their country seats. A winter journey happened when Sir John
Harington, later Lord Harington of Exton, summoned them to perform
Titus Andronicus as part of the festivities at his new estate, Exton Hall in
Rutland, on 1 January 1596.

The more than seventy miles up the Great North Road from London to
Rutland (via Waltham, Ware, Royston, Huntingdon, Stilton, and Stamford,
according to Harrison)[21] was a three- or four-day trek in each direction that
they must have felt obliged to do, despite the limited time available between
their three booked performances at court on 26, 27, and 28 December
and 6 January, when they resumed at court after two performances by
the Admiral's. A number of special commissions to give performances
for private entertainment happened in London, such as the two known

---

[20] Alan Somerset, ' "How Chances it They Travel?": Provincial Touring, Playing Places, and the King's
Men', *Shakespeare Survey* 47 (1994), 45–60, provides an excellent overview of the conditions that
travelling companies were used to. He makes the point (pp. 59–60) that travelling with only two or
three plays might have been more restful than staging a different play every day as London required.
[21] Harrison, *Description*, p. 400.

performances at the Inns of Court, *The Comedy of Errors* at Gray's Inn in 1594 and *Twelfth Night* at Middle Temple on Candlemas 1602, and others at private houses such as (probably) *Richard II* for Cecil at Sir Edward Hoby's in the Strand in 1595,[22] and certainly *1 Henry IV* (called *Oldcastle*) at their patron George Carey's house in 1600 for a party that included the Dutch ambassador.[23] They were also booked for *Love's Labours Lost* by the Earl of Southampton at his house in London at Christmas 1604. The possibility that this performance was planned as a special revival of the play for Southampton, who may have known it from much earlier, is mildly ironic, since it became the subject of a tug of war when courtiers were looking for something new to gratify the king. Southampton seems to have lost his private performance at his house in the Strand to the court.[24]

This sort of commissioned performance was additional to the winter commands to play at court. Such commissions could well have been renewed by idle nobles through the long and vacant summer periods they spent, often reluctantly, at their country houses. Far fewer records of visits to country houses survive compared with the payments transcribed by the clerks of the towns, and private estate papers are less readily available to REED editors than town and borough records, so the number of such visits is largely speculation. But the relatively small number of cities and towns visited, and the evident lack of any standard touring route for the company of the kind that the Queen's Men followed each year,[25] strongly implies that there were special reasons for the directions their travels took

---

[22] Whether Sir Edward Hoby's letter inviting Cecil to see 'King Richard' over dinner at his house in the Strand in November 1595 was an invitation to see the Chamberlain's Men's new play or a picture from Hoby's collection of paintings of former kings has been debated. Hoby was the new Constable of Quinborough Castle, and was commissioning portraits of all the former Constables to hang in its hall. Both Richard II and Richard III were former Constables. On the other hand Hoby was the son-in-law of Henry Carey, the Lord Chamberlain, himself an old friend and ally of Cecil's. He may have thought that hiring the Chamberlain's Men to entertain Cecil was nicely tactful.

[23] Chambers, *Elizabethan Stage*, 1.220. Carey was markedly hostile to the Cobhams after he went through a well-known quarrel with them over a failed marriage contract, so he may well have specified the old Cobham-mocking title for his performance. See Paul Whitfield White, 'Shakespeare and the Cobhams', in *Shakespeare and Theatrical Patronage*, pp. 64–89.

[24] In an undated letter in the Christmas season of 1604–5 Sir Walter Cope, secretary to Robert Cecil and employer of Cuthbert Burbage, wrote to Cecil to report on his quest for fresh plays or 'Juglers & Such kinde of Creaturs' to entertain the jaded appetites at court. He could offer only *Love's Labours Lost*, already set to be played the next night at Southampton's house, 'unless yow send a wrytt to Remove the Corpus *Cum Causa* to yor howse in strande. Burbage ys my messenger.' On 15 January Dudley Carleton wrote to John Chamberlain to report that 'The last nights revels were kept at my Lord of Cranborns' (i.e., Cecil's). See *Love's Labours Lost*, ed. H. Woudhuysen, The Arden Shakespeare, 1998, pp. 83–5.

[25] See McMillin and MacLean, *The Queen's Men and their Plays*, chapter 3.

12. Middle Temple Hall, where at Candlemas Night, 2 February 1602, the Chamberlain's played *Twelfth Night* for John Manningham and other Templars. The picture shows Mark Rylance as Olivia in the Shakespeare's Globe memorial production on 2 February 2002.

them in through these years. One impetus to travel was, of course, the all-too-frequent onset of plague in London.

Visits to the universities, a long day's journey away, were a recurrent activity. Cited on the title pages of *Hamlet* and *Volpone*, mockingly acknowledged in the students' *Parnassus* plays at Cambridge, and emphatically asserted by Robert Armin in the prefaces to his pamphlets, the university authorities deplored them. Therefore, as in London, the plays were staged on the verges of the town, in places like Cambridge's Chesterton. Even those visits may have been intermitted up to the time they had the Globe. During their troubles with their London base, from April 1597 until well after they had settled into the Globe in the summer of 1599, they seem not to have gone on tour at all. Apart from the evidence of the *Parnassus* plays of 1599 and after, which is unreliable,[26] there is nothing to say that they resumed touring until 1602–3. Then they went all the way north to

---

[26] Three *Parnassus* plays were staged by students at St John's College Cambridge in 1598–1601. The third of them brought Burbage and Kemp on stage, in not very complimentary terms, having them quote *The Spanish Tragedy* and *Richard III*, and making Kemp refer to Shakespeare as having given Jonson a purge (4.3). That indicates a date in 1601 or later, even though Kemp left the company in 1599. In 5.1, Studioso complains of professional players that 'With mouthing words that better wits

Shrewsbury in Shropshire, and are also on record at Ipswich. Possibly they were drawn to the first location by an invitation from the Pembrokes, where the family had large estates, and stopped at Ipswich en route to one of the great houses of East Anglia. Through 1603–4, during a lengthy closure of the London playhouses for plague, they are recorded at Coventry in the Midlands in late 1603, at Bridgnorth in Shropshire (possibly again heading for the Pembrokes), and in the west at Oxford and Bath. On 31 October Joan Alleyn wrote from London to her travelling husband saying that 'All the Companyes be Come hoame & well for ought we know',[27] though the plague still did not allow the London playhouses to be reopened. All of the excursions that year seem to have been quick ones, since in December the company was at Mortlake, twelve miles upriver from the city, where Augustine Phillips had recently bought a new house. They were probably gathered there out of London because of the enduring plague while they prepared for their court appearances (they opened the festivities with *The Fair Maid of Bristow* on 26 December). Before that opening, on 3 December, they were summoned from Mortlake to the Earl of Pembroke's house at Wilton, to perform before the king.[28] Commissions to play at other great houses in the country may have prompted most of the other recorded visits. The life a touring company led, if it was at all like that derided in Sir Oliver Owlet's Men in *Histriomastix*, cannot have been a major attraction to either of the new duopoly companies. The travelling player's song in that satire about 'we that travel, with pumps full of gravel' (also quoted in *Poetaster*) claims that 'we never can hold together', which was emphatically not true of the Chamberlain's.

After doing heavy duty at court in this and the next season, despite the plague, they were in Devon at Barnstaple in 1604–5. In 1605 they are recorded, improbably, at Fordwich in Kent on 6 October and at Oxford on 9 October. The distance between these locations on either side of London is over 150 miles. The Oxford record may be an error, since they were definitely in the Kentish region at some time in 1605–6, at Faversham and Maidstone. Even coastal shipping round Kent and up the Thames to Oxford would have taken more than two days. In 1605–6 they were recorded at Saffron

have framed, / They purchase lands, and now esquires are named.' That reads like a conflation of Robert Greene's condemnation of Shakespeare in 1592 with the latter's inheritance, when his father died in September 1601, of the title Shakespeare had bought for him.

27 R. A. Foakes and R. T. Rickert, *Henslowe's Diary*, Cambridge University Press, 1961, second edition, 2002, p. 297.

28 Chambers, *Elizabethan Stage*, II.209. They were paid £30 for that visit. See J. Leeds Barroll, *Politics, Plague, and Shakespeare's Theater: The Later Stuart Years*, Cornell University Press, Ithaca, 1991, pp. 112, 114.

13. Wilton House in Hampshire, home of the Pembroke family, where the company performed for their new patron King James in December 1603.

Walden, about thirty miles north of London, and at Marlborough again in 1606.[29] This may have been another lengthy tour with some sea travel round the coast, since they were at Dover on 30 August. On 7 September 1607 they are on record playing at Oxford town, again most likely travelling by boat, and in 1607–8 at Barnstaple and Marlborough again. The return to towns like Barnstaple, Faversham, and Marlborough suggests they came to expect a welcome at such places.

Another dreadful plague epidemic followed, lasting in London for nearly eighteen months. A visit to Coventry is recorded on 29 October 1608, preceded by an East Anglian visit to Dunwich on 10 October. Ipswich received them on 9 May 1609, and they journeyed (perhaps by water) to Hythe on 16 May and New Romney in Kent the next day. They were at Oxford some time in that plague-ruled year, when they played *Othello* to the approval of some university figures,[30] and in the next year at Dover on 6 July 1610 and at Dunwich in East Anglia in October. In 1611–12 they visited Winchester fifty miles to the south-west of London, and in the next year New Romney and the coastal port of Folkestone in Kent. In that

---

[29] Peter Davison, in 'Commerce and Patronage: the Lord Chamberlain's Men's Tour of 1597', pp. 62–3.
[30] The well-known account of the murdered Desdemona evoking tears with her face alone belongs to this visit.

14. Leicester Town Hall, where the Chamberlain's may have performed while on tour.

period they also visited Oxford once again. They went further north in 1614–15, to Coventry and to Nottingham. In 1615 they were in East Anglia at Dunwich and Norwich, and in 1615–16 they appeared at New Romney in Kent. Thereafter the records get more complicated. Partly that was because the regulations and the issue of patents for travel changed, with an effect on the provincial recording processes, and partly because new groups came into existence with licences to use the royal name, but not based in London. The long-held habit of the entire company going on tour may also have changed as time went on, and the sharers who were also housekeepers chose to stay in London to manage the playhouses, sending juniors in their place. The groups travelling under the king's name differed, and the records often leave unclear what group it was they were noting. The company does seem to have also developed at least one spin-off group of their own in the 1620s to tour while the main company was performing in London.

The long closure of the playhouses in London through 1608–10 seems to have led to a number of policy shifts that must have been laid down at about the time the company acquired the Blackfriars. Playing in London was now the central feature of their work, so travelling became an activity

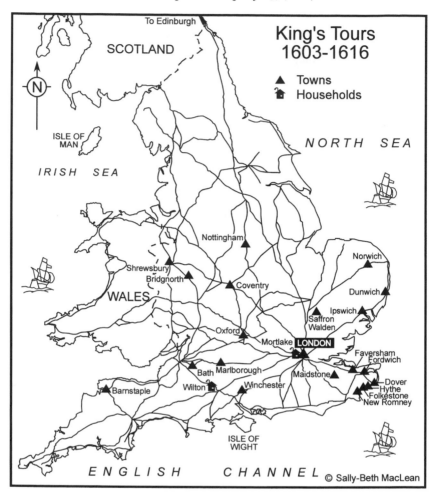

15. A map of the tours made by the King's Men, prepared by Sally-Beth MacLean of the Records of Early English Drama. For the Caroline years the records are noticeably less informative.

the company fell back on chiefly in times of plague. This may explain why in those two winters when plague kept the playhouses mostly shut the company managed to get a payment for the six weeks or so they spent preparing their chosen performances for the court. Heminges received £40 on 4 January 1609, 'by way of his majesties rewarde for their private practise in the time of infeccion that thereby they mighte be inhabled to performe their service before his Majestie in Christmas hollidaies 1609'. On

9 February 1610 he took another £30 for 'beinge restrayned from publique playinge within the citie of London in the tyme of infeccion duringe the space of six weekes in which tyme they practised pryvately for his majesties service'.[31] London was now the absolute priority, while the company was still officially in the service of the king. There are hints that some of the senior sharers such as Heminges and Condell stopped accompanying the company's tours at about this time. Even before that Shakespeare may have been in the habit of leaving them in favour of visits home to Stratford. Cessations of playing were his only chance to go home other than in the forty days of the Lenten closures. By 1610 the company may have begun to think of travelling as simply their shift from one seasonal playhouse to the other. This time marks the final loss of the long tradition that created all the early companies and based their thinking about performance as a travelling show. It may well have spread from the King's Men's realization in 1608 of the Burbage plan of 1594 for playing in London.

This shift in thinking may have been what led to the use of subsidiary groups travelling in the company's name. By 1616 a new system of licensing for the London companies was overdue. Now the only official patrons were the four members of the royal family, and some less-privileged groups were having to fake their licences.[32] The always-itinerant Martin Slater, for instance, was caught presenting a false licence made out to Queen Anne's Men at Norwich in 1616.[33] For his next forgery he used the best name available. In May 1618 the Exeter clerk noted a payment of £2 4s 'paid martyn Slader on [i.e., one of] his majesties players to forbaer to playe'.[34] The same forged licence appeared at Leicester seven years later, when one pound was paid on 15 October 1625 'to one Slator and his Companie being the Kings Playors'. To use the name of the King's Men was an obvious temptation, and matches the REED evidence about groups travelling with forged licences. But it does seem that some of these travellers were genuinely associated with the Blackfriars company. Identifying the London-based travellers is difficult because groups based in York and in Bristol in the 1620s evidently had licences that allowed them to call themselves the King's Men.

Once the licensing system changed in 1616 it was not only forged papers that influenced the recording of visits to towns. While the REED records are wonderfully specific about the company's visits to towns and villages,

---

[31] Chambers, *Elizabethan Stage*, IV.175, 176.
[32] See Gurr, 'The War of 1614–1618: Absolutism, Local Authority and a Crisis of Overproduction', *English Literary Renaissance* 26 (1996), 138–54.
[33] *Ibid.*, p. 149.   [34] See REED *Devon*, ed. John M. Wasson, Toronto, 1986, p. 188.

we have reason to doubt their comprehensiveness in the early seventeenth century as records of all the company's travels. Besides the inadequate records of payments made at great houses and uncertainty about which version of the King's Men might have been calling, there was a marked change in the civic records after 1616. Until Elizabeth appointed a Master of the Revels to control professional playing at the end of the 1570s, it was up to every mayor to view every play offered to the populace he was responsible for before he gave permission for it to be performed in public. It was normal then for the mayor and council to censor the play at a private showing in the guildhall, before the townsfolk could see it. For such special performances the council gave money to the players. The records of such grants provide most of the REED information. After the Master of the Revels took over play-licensing, and the number of companies was reduced by restricting patronage to the higher nobility, the practice of the mayor's private show gradually died out.

It only did so very slowly, in part because councils liked to exercise their authority. But its stopping and the consequent loss of civic records of company visits intensified with the exclusively royal patronage under James and Charles. The system of control in London tightened and the standard authorization became royal patents. As a result, increasingly the civic entries appeared merely as payments to companies to leave the town without playing at all. Companies no longer had access to the guildhalls where the mayor usually saw the play he had to approve, so they used the great coaching inns or inns with large upper rooms converted for playing like the one in Wine Street which the Bristol mayoralty agreed could become an official playhouse. Few records of such activities appeared in the civic records.

In this last period most of the entries in town accounts were for payments made to stop them performing. Such records were made for one group or other of the King's Men at Exeter in May 1618 (Martin Slater's), Leicester in 1620, Canterbury 1621–2, Norwich 15 June 1622, Canterbury 24 April 1623, Bridport, Dorset in 1623, Leicester 22 September 1623, Reading April 1627, Canterbury 9 March 1629, Bristol March–June 1630 and June–September 1631, Worcester 1630–1 'for feare of infeccion', Worcester 1632 'to the king's majesty's players, beinge two companies, to prevent their playinge in this city', Norwich 6 July 1633, Southampton 27 March 1634, King's Lynn 1634 ('his majesties Plaiors of his private chamber in Yorke'), Southampton 1634–5, Bristol June–September 1635, and King's Lynn 1636. These nineteen entries for three or more allegedly 'King's' companies make up nearly

20 per cent of the listings so far obtained by the REED editors for this period of playing.

At other places where the towns still welcomed them and gave them money, the accounts rarely specified which of the three or more groups was travelling under the king's name. Worcester's record in 1632 of 'the king's majesties players, beinge two companies' was typical. Nottingham did distinguish three king's companies in its entries in 1635–6, calling them 'the Kinges Plaieres of Yorke', 'the Kinges playeres of the Court', and 'the Kinges playeres of London'. The York players were acknowledged under that name at other centres, but which London company was 'of the Court' and which of the Globe and Blackfriars it is impossible to tell. A clue to the York-based group appears in the Canterbury records for 25 March 1636, when the mayor complained to Laud, the Archbishop of Canterbury, a dominant figure on the Privy Council, that he had tried to stop a company from playing after eight days of late nights and drunkenness. The names of the leaders of this group were William Perry and Richard Weekes, who are named in other town accounts as leading a King's group based in York. Perry's company was paid by Coventry in 1632 and York in 1633. York named them 'the kings plaiers of the Chamber of yorke Perries Company'. The same group appeared at Nottingham in 1633–4, Norwich and King's Lynn in March 1634, Bristol in 1635, Nottingham again in 1635–6, along with two other King's Men's companies as noted above, and Norwich on 11 May 1636, as well as the Canterbury visit in March 1636, which may have led to the termination of their licence since they had played during the forbidden forty days of Lent. Through this period it is rarely possible to differentiate the entries for the York-based group from those for the London-based company.

Earlier, a company of boys or youths based in Bristol, possibly a choir school, also used the royal name, appearing at Coventry on 9 August 1621 and again at the same date in 1622. This was possibly the group led by a William Daniell[35] ('the cheife of the Kinges Players') who was paid not to play in Canterbury in 1621–2, at Nottingham in 1622–3 ('the Kinges playeres of the Chamber of Bristowe'), Coventry 26 September 1623 ('to the kinges players for bringing xx Bristow youthes in Musick'), Leicester 1624 ('to John Daniell who had a Patent for the Children of Bristoll'), and under the new king at Nottingham in 1626–7 and 1629–30. Again, the

---

[35] William Daniell is nowhere recorded as belonging to the King's in London, but he may have been kin to the John Daniell leading the Bristol youths at Leicester in 1624.

entries for this group may easily be confused with those for the King's from London.

Neither Perry's company based at York nor Daniell's Bristol boys had anything to do with the London-based King's Men. Another group led by Richard Errington is a different case. A hired man in the company, he seems to have been used to lead a branch of the King's as a travelling company between 1622 and 1629. On 22 November 1627 while serving at the door as a gatherer during an evening performance at Ludlow he was assaulted by drunken intruders. The deposition specifies him as 'of the Citty of London, pewterer, aged fiftie yeares or thereaboute'.[36] Errington's group may or may not have been the King's Men who were listed as appearing in Wallingford, Berkshire in 1621–2, Lydd, Hythe, and New Romney in Kent between 19 and 30 April 1622, Leicester on 8 June and 26 August, Norwich on 15 June and Carlisle on 13 September of the same year. His group may be the one identified at Nottingham in 1635–6 as 'of the Court', as distinct from the Blackfriars-based 'London' company.

Errington's is certainly the company identified as 'Mr Irington & other of his Majesties Company of Players' at Norwich in 1622–3. They also did a Kent tour in 1622, repeated in 1623. They were at Canterbury on 24 April 1623 (paid to 'depart the Cittie and not playe'), Hythe on 7 July, Lydd and New Romney on 9 July, and banned at Bridport and Leicester. They were back in Hythe in 1624–5, and possibly at Worcester and Ludlow before that. A sceptical note at Craven in Yorkshire in 1624 records the respectable sum of £3 paid 'to a set of players, going by the name of ye Kings Players, who played 3 times'. A King's company was paid similar amounts at Reading in 1624–5 and at Carlisle on 5 July 1625. Smaller amounts were paid at Bridport and at Kendal in 1625 and November 1626, Gravesend near London, Lydd, Hythe, and Sandwich in Kent, Coventry, Leicester, and Reading in 1626–7, Kendal and Carlisle in August 1627 and Ludlow that November, and at Nottingham and Coventry in 1628 and 1629. A markedly larger £2 was paid by Bristol twice in 1630, and £1 at Doncaster in May 1631. A mere 2s 6d was given to a King's company at Ludlow in 1630–1, and two marks (13s 4d) at Worcester in the same period to stop them playing. The renewed visit 'beinge two companies' in 1632 brought the two groups a total of £1 not to play. Reading gave them £1 in 1631–2, in the following year Ludlow in Shropshire and Fordwich in Kent paid them five shillings, and Dover on 8 April 1633 ten shillings. Norwich gave a King's company £3 to 'forbeare' on 6 July 1633. Dunwich, also in East Anglia, paid them five shillings in 1633–4.

---

[36] See REED *Shropshire*, ed. J. A. B. Somerset, Toronto 1994, pp. 111–12.

On the other hand Coventry on 13 April 1634 paid a generous £2.0s.10d 'to the kinges players who brought a Commission from Sir Henry Harbert'. The Coventry clerks knew that licences from the Master of the Revels had to be authentic. On 27 March 1634 Southampton sent away a company under the same name without playing for five shillings, while on 5 June another port, Dartmouth, gave them £1, and a similar fee on 21 October. Southampton repeated their ban in 1634–5, but Newcastle, also a port, gave them £1 in January 1635. In the same year Thomas Crosfield, a fellow of Queen's College Oxford, noted in his diary that in July a company was playing 'The witches of Lancashire . . . their Tricks, Meetings', at a local inn. This sounds very like the play written for the company the previous year by Heywood and Brome (see Appendix 2.42). Crosfield, who had taken notes about the London companies the previous year, did not identify who the players were.[37] It may have been the Salisbury Court's rival play on the same subject. Given the absence of records of playing in either Oxford or Cambridge, the claims made on title pages such as *Hamlet* and *Volpone* that the company had played there, and Robert Armin's evident familiarity with the universities and their gossip when he dedicated *A Nest of Ninnies* (1608) to the students of Oxford, Cambridge, and the Inns, it is likely that the the main company sustained its tradition of visiting both university cities throughout.

The multiple use of the king's name for travelling companies does not mean that the main company did not also travel, especially in times of plague. What is less evident is whether the senior sharers went on tour. On 17 May 1636 near the beginning of a dreadfully long plague closure the Lord Chamberlain drew up a list, called in the margin a 'Players Passe', authorizing the company to go on tour (Appendix 2.45). It names eight players 'together with Tenne more or thereaboutes of their fellowes in the Blackfryers', their duty to entertain the king on his progress through the country, who while waiting for their summons were to be allowed to play at any towns they pleased. None of the eight players on the list was a sharer. The failure to specify the names of the ten others might have been a means of allowing some of them to choose later whether to go or not, but the named travellers, who must have been expected to guarantee what the company would show, were all minor players.

Nottingham was the farthest north the King's companies went on visits to large towns. Nottingham's three visits from distinct groups of King's players in 1635–6, one of them registered as 'of London', were followed in the next

---

[37] *The Diary of Thomas Crosfield*, Frederick S. Boas, Oxford University Press, London, 1935, p. 79.

years by visits to Lydd and Canterbury in Kent, Gravesend, Windsor in Berkshire twice, Coventry three times, Kendal and Doncaster, all of whom paid a respectable price for the performances. Two out of the three visits to Coventry in 1636 were specified by the local clerks as 'the kinges players of Blackfriers'. On the second of these visits by the Blackfriars company, in August 1636, they were awarded the special distinction of playing in 'the Councel house'. Altogether not more than three of these thirteen visits can be clearly identified as by the King's Men normally playing in London. More there must have been, if only on the assumption that they made a number of country house visits. But most of the tours when several towns in the same region recorded visits might have been by Errington's players.

A few records in household accounts of visits by the King's Men survive, and more will certainly be found in future years. Several of these penetrated well beyond Nottingham. Thomas Walmesley's accounts at Dunkenhalgh in Lancashire, for instance, record three visits at Christmas once every four years, on 18 December 1620, 16 December 1624, and December 1628. Other likely visits to private houses in nearby Cheshire are marked in the accounts for Congleton, a small town close to some of the great houses of the Stanleys, earls of Derby. The Stanleys maintained acting companies under their patronage from 1590 to the 1640s, and a majority of the Chamberlain's Men when formed in 1594 had previously worn the Stanley livery as members of the company patronized by Ferdinando Stanley, Lord Strange.[38] Around Christmas 1621 the Congleton accounts note 'Bestowed uppon the kings majesties players and the Lord of Derbies . . . . xx s'. Again on 13 December 1623, the accounts record 'Bestowed upon the Kings players and the Earle of Derbeys the xiiith daie of december who played at the Swanne'.[39] This link with the Derby family probably stemmed from invitations to play in the Christmas festivities at one of their great houses in Lancashire and Cheshire. Other visits to Congleton are on record for 1615, 25 September 1620 ('Geeven to the Kinges players that were heare on the Election day with consent of the ov'seers . . . . x s'), 27 November 1620, Christmas 1621, in November and on 13 December 1623, and at similar times of year in 1627

---

[38] See Alan C. Coman, 'The Congleton Accounts: Further Evidence of Elizabethan and Jacobean Drama in Cheshire', *Records of Early English Drama Newsletter* 14 (1989), 3–18.

[39] The date more likely records the payment than a single day of two performances at the one inn. On p. 9 Coman notes Murray's conclusion that Richard Errington's separate provincial company was formed from the King's in 1622 (John Tucker Murray, *English Dramatic Companies 1558–1642*, 2 vols., London, 1910, 1.155), and that this and/or the next entry may be for his group. On the other hand, all of the royal family companies performed at Congleton, and the London-based King's had done so before, so he concludes it was more likely to have been the London-based King's Men on these occasions. That is also my view.

and 1630.[40] A summer visit was made in 1634, possibly by a non-London group. William Perry's York-based group visited Nottingham, Norwich, King's Lynn, and other places in 1634, and in 1635–6 Nottingham made its record of the three companies all travelling under the name of the King's Men. The company's focus on playing in London did not noticeably inhibit their travels, even in winter.

JIGS

At the open-air playhouses, at least up to 1612 or so, the normal practice was to end the day's performance with a jig played by the company clown and a few assistants. Always comic, and usually telling a fairly bawdy tale, the jig was enacted in song and dance to the accompaniment of the clown's tabor or side-drum and pipe. Copies of stage jigs that survive were printed as ballads in blackletter, and it is not easy to distinguish between a ballad that was simply written to be sung on any festive occasion and a farcical jig that was composed to be sung as a stage dialogue by different characters. Of those jigs where the ascribed authorship indicates that they were designed for performance on stage, four of Will Kemp's are noted for printing in the Stationers' Register between 1591 and 1595. Sadly, no copies have survived for three of them.[41] The one Kemp jig that survives, and was presumably played by the Chamberlain's Men through the five years that Kemp was in the company, is *Singing Simpkin*, listed in the Register as 'a ballad called Kemps *newe Jigge* betwixt, a souldiour and a Miser and Sym the clown', registered on 21 October 1595.[42] The others in the Register are '*the Thirde and last parte of* Kempes *jigge*', '*A pleasant newe Jigge of the Broome-man*' (Kemp's name is supplied in the margin of the Stationers' Register entry), and 'master Kemps *Newe Jigge of the kitchen stuffe woman*'. The music for a piece called 'Kemp's Jigge' is in Playford's *The Dancing Master* (1651). The Stationers' Register includes two other entries of company jigs, '*Phillips's jig of the slippers*' (1595),[43] and '*Shankes Ordinary*' (1624).[44]

[40] This visit, like others, was listed along with one by the Lady Elizabeth's and the Earl of Derby's, the latter from the family who had for many years run acting companies (see Coman's notes pp. 12–13).

[41] Another, called 'Attowell's Jig', was evidently written and performed for the Admiral's by their sharer George Attewell, once of Strange's. His jig uses the bed-trick that Shakespeare adopted later for *Measure for Measure* and *All's Well that Ends Well*.

[42] The only surviving jig of Kemp's, it is reprinted in C. R. Baskervill, *The Elizabethan Jig*, University of Chicago Press, 1929, pp. 444–9.

[43] Entered in the Stationers' Register, 26 May 1595. No copy is extant.

[44] Not certainly a jig, it was licensed by Herbert on 16 March 1624 as 'written by Shankes himselfe'. Herbert charged the full pound that was the usual fee for licensing a play.

16. Will Kemp jigging his way to Norwich in 1599, dressed as a morris dancer, with his accompanist. From the title page of *Kempes Nine Daies Wonder*, 1600.

The story for '*Singing Simpkin*' was taken from the *Decameron*, VII.6, 'The Gentlewoman of Lyons'.[45] It fairly represents the cuckoldry games found in some other surviving ballad-jigs that may have been used in the theatre. The clown enters wooing the pregnant wife of an old man. When interrupted by a 'roarer', also in pursuit of the wife, he hides in a chest. At the husband's return the roarer tries to hide in the chest but is persuaded by the wife to bluster and pretend to be chasing a thief. Simpkin keeps interjecting asides from his hiding place (for instance that it was the roarer who made the wife pregnant). The wife tells her husband that the thief is hiding in the chest, and the husband persuades the roarer to leave. He then opens the chest to release Simpkin, who, while he is out getting wine, makes up to the wife. On the husband's return the wife says she has been testing the clown, and husband and wife both beat him off the stage. It is a prototypical bedroom farce. Cotgrave's Anglo-French dictionary of 1611 actually defined farce as 'the Jyg at the end of an Enterlude'.

From the descriptions in the Stationers' Register and elsewhere, it seems that jigs were normally written by the company clown. Herbert's 1624 entry for John Shanks's jig specifies that it was 'written by Shankes himself'. The history of stage jigs developed out of medieval fairs and the popular game of presenting stories in song and dance as *Singspiele*. A folk and fairground

---

[45] Baskervill, *Elizabethan Jig*, p. 105. *Singing Simpkin* was first published in Robert Cox's *Actaeon and Diana*, in the 1640s. It was republished in 1656 with other jigs which the title page claimed had been recently acted at the Red Bull, in the period when the short 'drolls' were being acted surreptitiously there. It reappeared in the enlarged edition of Kirkman's *The Wits* in 1673. Short jigs and drolls were still being acted in the country in the eighteenth century.

tradition, it was popular throughout Europe. The morris-dancing tradition and Robin Hood tales were a kindred though more characteristically English activity. The picture of Kemp dancing to Norwich in 1599 shows him in morris costume, unlikely clothing for a stage jig. Ballads, sung either as a narrative or in dialogue, could be romantic and heroic, though usually they were comic and often satirical. Many surviving nursery rhymes reflect the satirical mode. A version of 'The Grand old Duke of York, he had ten thousand men', sung in the eighteenth century about the commander of the British army during the war of American Independence, was reported in 1642 as a Tarlton jig from before 1588, called *Pigges Coranto*: 'The King of France with forty thousand men, / Went up a Hill, and so came downe agen.'[46] Song and dance acts performing ballads in rhyme featured in plays from very early in the sixteenth century, although they seem to have begun to feature as the afternoon's closing event only in the professional companies. They were certainly a feature of Tarlton's performances in the 1580s and then Kemp's.

Inevitably, the popular and bawdy or satirical nature of such acts drew contempt from the more snobbish and learned. Marlowe himself seems to have written the Prologue to *1 Tamburlaine* dismissing the 'jigging veins of rhyming mother-wits / And such conceits as clownage keeps in pay', and as early as 1590 his publisher told the play's readers that

I have purposely omitted and left out some fond and frivolous gestures, digressing and, in my poor opinion, far unmeet for the matter, which I thought might seem more tedious unto the wise than any way else to be regarded, though haply they have been of some vain, conceited fondlings greatly gaped at, what times they were showed upon the stage in their graced deformities.[17]

The author of *The Wars of Cyrus*, published in 1594, said much the same thing. But such dismissals were for the educated reader. The early public stage certainly held jigs in high esteem. English actors who played over the Channel featured jigs with the 'Pickleherring' character, and the Marprelate controversy of 1590 made great use of jigs to voice its satires. Moralistic elements popular in jigs, published as 'Knacks to know knaves', and 'The story of Nobody', were turned into entire plays in the 1590s, just as Antony Munday wrote an urban version of the Robin Hood tales, common at fairs and country festivals like the jigs, for the Admiral's at the Rose.

[46] Baskervill, *Elizabethan Jig*, p. 102.
[47] Quoted from *The Complete Works of Christopher Marlowe*, General ed. Fredson Bowers, 2 vols., Cambridge University Press, 1981, 1.77, 79.

Jigs became the standard way of closing a performance in the 1590s. John Davies's Epigram 17 says that audiences did not leave until 'ended is the play, the daunce, and song'.[48] Jonson in *Every Man out of his Humour* wrote in 1599 a comparison of something following with the inevitability of 'a jigge after a play'.[49] Henslowe appears to have bought two jigs for the Admiral's on 12 December 1597.[50] By 1600, however, when Hamlet lumped jigs with tales of bawdry as evidence of Polonius's gross appetite in playgoing, it was becoming evident that what Kemp supplied was too near the bottom end of the market for the more lordly tastes like Hamlet's own. Hostility to jigs grew, chiefly because of their potential offensiveness, when the fashion for superior forms of entertainment began to impose itself on the players. Even Dekker, not usually a discriminating observer, wrote in 1613 about jigs closing tragedies: 'I have often seene, after the finishing of some worthy Tragedy, or Catastrophe in the open Theaters, that the Sceane after the Epilogue hath beene more blacke (about a nasty bawdy Jigge) then the most horrid Sceane in the play was.'[51] Ben Jonson laid into them heavily in later years. His Induction to *Bartholomew Fair*, written for the new open-air Hope, echoes *Hamlet* by linking jigs with bawdry, condemning 'the concupiscence of jigs and dances'. The authorities took note, too. On 1 October 1612 the Middlesex Court General Session came down on the Fortune players with a ban prompted by the effect of jigs:

An Order for suppressinge of Jigges att the ende of Playes – Whereas Complaynte have beene made at this last Generall Sessions, that by reason of certayne lewde Jigges songes and daunces used and accustomed at the playhouse called the Fortune in Gouldinglane, divers cutt-purses and other lewde and ill disposed persons in great multitudes doe resorte thither at th'end of everye playe, many tymes causing tumultes and outrages wherebye His Majesties peace is often broke and much mischiefe like to ensue thereby, Itt was hereuppon expresselye commaunded and ordered by the Justices of the said benche, That all Actors of every playhouse within this cittye and liberties thereof and in the Countie of Middlesex that they and everie of them utterlye abolishe all Jigges Rymes and Daunces after their playes.[52]

Middlesex controlled the northern suburbs, and the order that every acting company in the city and liberties should also obey the order stretched their control beyond its official limits. Such Orders usually ran into the ground within a year or two in any case. But targeting jigs rather than the whole

---

[48] 'In Cosmum', *The Poems of Sir John Davies*, ed. Robert Krueger, Clarendon Press, 1975, p. 136.
[49] *Works*, III.467.   [50] *Henslowe's Diary*, pp. 74, 85.
[51] *A Strange Horse-Race*, 1613, in *Non-Dramatic Works*, ed. Grosart, III.340.
[52] Quoted in Chambers, *Elizabethan Stage*, IV.340–1.

afternoon's performance was new in 1612, and marks the beginning of a more selective hostility among Middlesex's magistrates than appeared in the angrily sweeping claims of the Lord Mayors.

By then the jig clearly marked the bottom end of the playgoing market. The coincidence of John Shanks abandoning his jig-making when he joined the Shakespeare company in 1613 is notable, and must be ascribed to company policy. William Turner, whose *Dish of Lenten Stuffe* appeared in the next year, wrote

> That's the fat foole of the Curtin,
> And the leane foole of the Bull:
> Since *Shanke* did leave to sing his rimes,
> he is counted but a gull.
> The players of the Banke side,
> The round Globe and the Swan,
> Will teach you idle trickes of love,
> But the Bull will play the man.[53]

In 1613 the fat fool was Will Rowley, playing with the new Prince Charles's Men at the Curtain, while the 'leane fool' was Thomas Greene of the Red Bull. Both were using Middlesex playhouses. Shanks's transfer from Prince Henry's Men at the Fortune to the Globe and Blackfriars evidently required him to give up his practice of closing the day with a jig. Whether that met an already-existing company policy, or whether Middlesex's Order in 1612 helped to set it off, we cannot be sure. Kemp had left the company rather precipitously early in 1599, for reasons that indicate his independence from the rest of the team, most likely because of debate about his main contribution to the plays. It may well be that Feste's simple song ending *Twelfth Night* was the company's new kind of jig, and shows us what it wanted in 1601 to replace the practice that Hamlet deplored. *Twelfth Night* is almost unique among Shakespeare's plays in having such a song as its ending. It may therefore have been written into the script precisely to clarify the new way of doing endings. Such a more musical, less bawdy kind of offering would have suited Robert Armin's range. If so, it seems certain that the Kemp type of jig had gone from the Globe performances possibly as early as 1601.

One piece of evidence adds some force to that view, Lowin's solemn little pamphlet about dancing. He signed it 'I. L. Roscio', the name for Rome's most celebrated actor attached to his initials acknowledging his own status as a player, and called it *Conclusions upon Dances*. It is a plain, sermon-like

---

53 *A Pepysian Garland*, ed. Hyder E. Rollins, Cambridge University Press, 1920, p. 35.

17. Robert Armin, from the title page of his *The Two Maids of More-clacke*, 1609.

pamphlet rather than a book, only twenty pages long, although its contents are given status by a dedicatory letter and an epistle from the printer. All its examples of dances good and bad are from the Bible. But even in the section called 'Of the Unlawfull Dances, which are commonly called prophane', it cites only that of the daughter of Herodias before Herod in Matthew 14. Nowhere is there any mention of jigs. Even in the section 'Of the ordinarie Dances, used everie where, in these dayes', while citing their value for recreation and exercise, he avoids mentioning jigs. The exclusive use of biblical examples and the absence of any mention of modern profane dances resounds through the pamphlet, as if it was a disavowal of the company's former practices.

The extant plays of this period give little clear indication of how the company expected to close its afternoon performances. *A Midsummer Night's Dream, As You Like It,* and others written up to 1599 end with a formal dance, a bergomask, or a wedding round. The surviving comedies staged from 1601 onwards do not. Armin's song ended *Twelfth Night* in 1601, but *Measure for Measure*, *All's Well that Ends Well*, and *The Fair Maid of Bristow* all close simply with a harmonious exit through the central opening, and no explicit indication of any afterpiece. That absence may signal unease, and a shift in thinking about what the right form of closure to the day's performance should be.

What can be said is that up to at least 1600 jigs were the dominant tradition for closing performances in the open-air playhouses. They were performed even after tragedies, a feature of playgoing that Dudley Carleton made use of in a letter to John Chamberlain in 1604. Telling Chamberlain about a rather risible but unfortunate death, he went on to make a joke, introducing it as 'a jig after this tragedy'.[54] That makes it tempting to enquire whether the practice of staging jigs might not explain the rare awkwardness at the end of *Hamlet*, a play in which Hamlet characterizes jigs as fitting the taste only of 'tedious old fools' like Polonius. At the end, in all versions of the play, the dead king, queen, and courtier Laertes are left on stage after Hamlet's body has been carried off. It is tempting to ask whether the three corpses might not have sprung back to life to dance a final jig. Almost all the other tragedies contrive a funeral procession to remove the bodies. *Hamlet*, a play about play acting, is oddly distinctive in leaving so many bodies on stage at the end.[55] The staging difficulty created by the three senior corpses left on stage at the play's conclusion must have been a talking-point among the players. Hamlet condemns the taste for jigs in fools like Polonius. Conceivably the contempt he voices in the play, with all its other games about seeming and acting, set up the right occasion for a jig to make an ironically fitting closure. That in its turn might have led on to the decision to stop performing jigs.[56]

If '*Shankes Ordinary*' was indeed a stage jig written in 1624, which Herbert's fee makes almost certain, it appears that the company's decision to abandon the jig-making tradition in or before the year that Shanks joined the company was reversed in the early 1620s. It may have renewed

[54] In a letter of 21 September 1604, in *Dudley Carleton to John Chamberlain*, p. 65. Carleton also writes, in 1604, of 'all the actors being together on the stage (as use is at the end of a play)' (p. 51). This, an apparent alternative form of closure to the jig, may refer to what later became known as the curtain-call, but might equally be a reference to the full cast that normally assembled for the finale, as in Shakespeare's comedies.

[55] See Gurr, 'Metatheatre and the Fear of Playing', in *Neo-Historicism: Studies in Renaissance Literature, History and Politics*, D. S. Brewer (Cambridge, 2000), pp. 91–110, especially 103–9.

[56] David Wiles, *Shakespeare's Clown*, p. 60, says that 'In *Hamlet*, we see the jig being swallowed up and dissolved within the play.'

the question in the company at the time, because Hamlet's habit of scorning jigs was renewed soon after among the authors writing for the Blackfriars. Massinger in his epistle to *The Roman Actor* printed in 1629 asserted that 'If the gravity and height of the subject distaste such as are onely affected with Jigges, and ribaldrie (as I presume it will,) their condemnation of me, and my Poem, can no way offend me: my reason teaching me such malicious and ignorant detractors deserve rather contempt, then satisfaction.' The Prologue to Fletcher and Massinger's *Fair Maid of the Inn*, staged in 1626 like *The Roman Actor*, said much the same thing. *The Fair Maid*'s Prologue indicates that by the end of James's reign the writers thought the Blackfriars had come to be seen as the home of 'nobler Judgments' than those who applauded jigs. Conceivably Shanks's jig was designed only for the Globe, although Herbert approved it in March while the company was still playing at the Blackfriars. Jigs were popular in the 1630s, since Donald Lupton could still write in 1632 that 'Most commonly when the play is done, you shall have a jig, or dance of all treads.'[57]

There is no direct evidence to tell us why the decision to start buying jigs again was made, but to at least some extent it must have reflected awareness of the way the Blackfriars repertory and its audiences and their tastes were diverging from those of the Globe, so it may be true that Shanks's jig was bought for playing at the Globe, not the Blackfriars. The best evidence for this recognition of divergent tastes in the two playhouses does not really emerge in the company repertoire until the 1630s, by when it was routine to say that jigs marked the different kind of performance available at the amphitheatres compared with the hall theatres. As early as 1624 the Prologue to *The Bondman* could boast that '*Here are* no Gipsie Jigges, *no* drumming stuffe, / Dances, *or other* Trumpery *to delight*, / *Or take, by common way, the common sight.*' Massinger might have written that just for the Cockpit. In the new reign, his epistle that accompanied the printed version of *The Roman Actor* evidently took it for granted that both kinds of playgoer would be at his play, whether it was at the Blackfriars or the Globe, but that in his own ambition the play was designed only for the more refined playgoers.

Attitudes to jigs beyond the Blackfriars changed in the 1620s, but it is still not clear exactly how, why, or where. In 1629 the Praeludium to Goffe's *Careless Shepherdess* could acknowledge the division between townsmen and gentry, making a citizen complain about what the hall playhouse was offering and declare 'I'll go to th'Bull, or Fortune, and there see / A Play for

---

[57] *London and the Countrey Carbonadoed*, 1632, G3v.

two pense, and a Jig to boot.' That assumption of differences marked by pro- and anti-jig tastes was echoed in Davenant's prologue to *The Unfortunate Lovers* (1638), about the citizen playgoers of twenty years before who 'would expect a jig, or target fight'. In Davenant's view it was the northern amphitheatres and their playgoers that were hanging on to the old traditions and their jigs. That view, proclaimed at the Cockpit in *The Bondman* and at Blackfriars soon after in *The Roman Actor*, was affirmed in retrospect (1673) by Henry Chapman, who wrote of the kind of people who did not want anything at 'the *Fortune* play-house, without a Jig of *Andrew Kein's* into the bargain'.[58] At the Globe, never clearly identified with the Fortune and the Red Bull's choices, the Prologue to Shirley's *The Doubtful Heir* did however assert in 1640 that his play was unusual at that venue in having 'No Bawd'ry, nor no Ballads'.

If these socially divisive acknowledgements of divergent tastes were observed by the King's Men, it would have made sense in 1624 to revive Shanks's old practice of doing a jig at the end of performances at the Globe but to sustain the musicians at the Blackfriars. Herbert's vetting of the Shanks script seems to confirm the company's acceptance that they now had to cater for two different sorts of appetite at their two playhouses. In its way, it confirms the tendency of commentators at the time to isolate the Fortune and the Red Bull, an attitude that the Master of the Revels had already conceded in 1616 when he stopped admitting any of the open-air playhouse companies to perform in the court's Christmas revels.[59]

Nonetheless, jigs did survive this period of elevated social contempt. There are hints that short jigs or *Singspiele* were even used to mark interacts at indoor playhouses. Rafe's rhyming song that occupied the final interact of *The Knight of the Burning Pestle* instead of the boys who danced for the previous interact breaks may be an early example by a boy company. The practice of having short breaks between each Act at the indoor playhouses to give time for the candles to be trimmed may have been used for versions of jigs, especially in the 1630s when some of the breaks were made longer. Prynne in *Histriomastix* condemned the 'obscene lascivious Love-songs, most melodiously chanted out upon the Stage betweene each several Action'.[60]

[58] See Gurr, *Playgoing*, 2nd edition, Appendix 2, pp. 259, 255, 261.
[59] Roslyn Lander Knutson questions the division between Globe and Blackfriars status and playfare, using a muddle of evidence, including some dubious claims about the company's travels and ignoring the preponderance of references to the Blackfriars on title pages from the early 1620s. See 'Two Playhouses, Both Alike in Dignity', *Shakespeare Studies* 30 (2002), 111–17.
[60] William Prynne, *Histriomastix, the players scourge*, 1633, p. 262.

MUSIC AND MUSICIANS

Bawdry and ballads marched along in the company of stories from England's history, though no jigs on such subjects have survived. Agincourt and other famous battles feature in ballads, and in some degree the history plays of the 1590s must have been helped to grow as subjects for drama by the popularity of the ballads. On stage, however, the players set aside the jig-maker's pipe and tabor for trumpets and drums. Trumpets, an army's instrument for signalling to cavalry and for calling attention at ceremonies, were used in processions, outdoor events, and especially on stage to herald the arrival of a ruler on occasions like Lear's entry in the opening scene of his play. The players used trumpets for such ceremonials, and commonly for the 'alarum' that called troops into action in a battle. The other war music came from drums, the instrument used for signalling to infantry. It gave the beat for marching soldiers, and was often used to signal an alarm. Most stage directions simply call for an alarm without specifying which instrument, although I suspect that drums were used more commonly. Sometimes both were used at the same time, judging by *Antony and Cleopatra*, where a stage direction calls for '*Alarum, Drummes and Trumpets*' (4.7). One stage direction in the Q2 *Hamlet* 3.2 uniquely calls for '*Trumpets and Kettle Drummes*'. A massed entry of soldiers marching behind their colours would always have a drummer with them.[61] Two stage directions, one of them in *Timon*, specify '*Drum and fife*', a pipe giving a melody to the beat supplied by the drum.

At this time trumpets and drums were not considered to be primarily musical instruments. Trumpets were not used in art music until the first performance of Monteverdi's *Orfeo* (1607) in Italy. For the Shakespeare company they were exclusively for outdoor signalling, either ceremonial fanfares and sennets or military tuckets and 'alarums'. A 'sennet' was a polyphonic trumpet-call, while a 'tucket' could include drumming. Played solo or in unison, the trumpet served no role in orchestral music or in 'consorts' of musicians playing composed music. The sennet or flourish was a signal to announce the arrival of a major dignitary. In battle scenes the approach of a herald or a summons to a 'parley' would have been by trumpet-call, while a battlefield 'alarum' might be either a drum-roll or a trumpet-call. At court the monarch kept a team of trumpeters for ceremonial occasions. The King's trumpeters, who did not belong to the King's

---

[61] See entry under 'drum' in Alan C. Dessen and Leslie Thomson, *A Dictionary of Stage Directions in English Drama 1580–1642*, Cambridge University Press, 1999.

players, are on record[62] hiring themselves around the country showing off their skills, not as musicians but as ceremonial signallers.

In the company's early years music was made on stage by individual actors. The company's trumpeter must have been a specially trained performer, and in several plays was required to appear on stage. The same man probably announced the start of a performance from the platform on the Globe's top. He and possibly others blew to announce the arrival of regal figures such as King Lear, and he probably also played the hunting horn which heralds Lear's second appearance after he has divested himself of his crown. Other music was supplied by the players themselves, who seem to have been trained to play a variety of instruments. We have noted Augustine Phillips's bequest of a bass viol, a cittern, a bandore, and a lute to his trainees. Since all of them were string instruments, he must have been used to plucking a variety of strings on stage. The clown, if playing a Tarlton type of rustic, as Will Kemp often did, might enter playing his traditional and familiar pipe and tabor.[63] He or his accompanist might have used them to supply on-stage music for the jig at the end of the play. If it was a song-and-dance act like 'Singing Simkin' an assistant would have done the playing, as he does in the picture of Kemp's morris-dance to Norwich on the title page of his book (see Figure 16, p. 70). If the clown was doing a solo act, he would intermix his monologue with his own music as he danced.

All of these instruments, whether functional like the trumpets and drums, or used to accompany songs and dances like the clown's pipe and tabor, were played solo. A singer would be accompanied on a lute or viol or other instrument, sometimes played off stage but usually by the singer himself, or by a player alongside him. A singer of lute-songs would usually accompany himself, as Amiens does in *As You Like It* with 'Under the greenwood tree' and 'Blow, blow, thou winter wind'. Songs were often sung by boy players, like Ariel in *The Tempest*, or the boy who sang for Mariana in Middleton's addition to *Measure for Measure*.[64] Robert Armin was clearly a singer used to accompanying himself on stage, since the role of Feste in *Twelfth Night* was written for him.

---

[62] The REED volumes are full of entries of civic payments to the King's trumpeters.

[63] The 'tabor' or 'taber', an English variant of the Eastern 'tambour', is a small side-drum beaten lightly and rapidly. That suggests that its name may be onomatopoeic, pronounced 'tabber' rather than 'tabor', echoing the drum's repetitive 'tabber-tabber' sound. I owe this nice suggestion to Rosemary Linnell. According to the *OED*, in 1587 it was spelled 'tabber'. The clown's pipe and tabor were usually played by the same person.

[64] See Taylor and Jowett, *Shakespeare Reshaped 1606–1623*, Clarendon Press, Oxford, 1993, pp. 123–40.

The great change in the company's musical accompaniment came with the acquisition of the Blackfriars, and its consort of professional musicians. The Blackfriars consort was a feature of the boy company's once-weekly performances from very early on. In Frederic Gerschow's diary of his three-week visit to England with the Duke of Stettin-Pomerania's entourage in September and October 1602 he wrote (in my rough translation from the original German) that

> we went to the boy comedians, whose argument was an open case about a royal English widow. The origin of this boy company is this: the Queen keeps a group of young boys who work hard at the art of singing and learn a wide variety of musical instruments while pursuing their studies. They have special teachers in all the arts, and in particular some outstanding musicians. To help them learn good manners, they are required to act a play once a week, for which the Queen has erected a special theatre and given them many expensive costumes. Those who want to see one of these performances have to pay as much as an English shilling, but there are always plenty of people present, including respectable women, because, we are told, there are useful cases made there, and good doctrine. They do all their plays by artificial light, which makes an impressive effect. For a whole hour before the play begins there is a delightful performance with musical instruments, organs, lutes, bandores, mandolins, violins and flutes, and a boy sings *tremolo* in a double bass so tunefully that we have not heard anything like it in our entire journey, except perhaps for the nuns in Milan.[65]

Like so many foreign visitors, Gerschow was retailing the false hearsay he had been told about the Blackfriars boy company and Elizabeth's entirely fictional support for its playhouse. But we need not doubt the truth of his praise of the consort's musical quality, nor (in spite of the claim about the double bass) the boy's good singing voice.

The evidence from the company's plays after 1608 seems to indicate that the acquisition of the Blackfriars consort led to the reconstruction of the Globe's stage balcony to give it a music room. Some of Fletcher's stage directions assume a curtain across the central section of the balcony behind which the invisible musicians played, and Richard Brathwaite mentioned 'the encurtain'd musique' in 1631.[66] At the outdoor Globe the consort's music must have been markedly less audible than at the indoor Blackfriars, especially when curtained off, yet the company persisted with it at both playhouses. What that says about the choice of plays and the selection of

---

[65] The diary is transcribed (and mistranslated) in *Transactions of the Royal Historical Society* n.s. 6 (1892), 1–35. How the boy could sing *tremolo* in a double bass voice is a mystery that might be explained by a better transcription.

[66] *Whimzies*, p. 51.

which plays best suited which of the two venues calls for more extended analysis than can be made here. The little evidence there is suggests that the company made few concessions to the differences, other than to restrict history plays requiring large-scale battles to the Globe. It may be worth noting that none of Shakespeare's most warlike plays from 1599, *Henry V*, *King Lear*, and *Antony and Cleopatra*, have any of the on-stage fights staged at Shrewsbury in *1 Henry IV*.

The most notable consequence of the company's acquisition of the Blackfriars musicians was that the plays grew act breaks. The boy company plays had all used them, and the King's Men's plays now adopted the practice. Effectively they introduced a pause of a minute or so, while music played from the balcony and gallants got up from their stools on stage to stretch their limbs. From 1609 onwards more and more play-texts in the repertory show act breaks, and make provision for music to be played during the one or two minutes they left the stage clear. The Folio text of *A Midsummer Night's Dream*, for instance, says that the lovers 'sleepe all the Act', meaning the musical interlude between Acts 3 and 4. *The City Madam* has a stage direction, *Whil'st the Act Plays, the Footstep, little Table, and Arras hung up for the Musicians*. *The Fatal Dowry* calls for *a passage over the Stage, while the Act is playing*. All the Blackfriars performances used act breaks, as the 'satyrical puppy called Nim' recorded during his visit.[67] *The Tempest*, with its off-stage mood music, was the only play Shakespeare wrote for the Blackfriars using the newly acquired consort and planned act breaks.[68] The word 'long', inserted at two act breaks (after Acts 1 and 3) in the allowed book of *Believe As You List* in 1631, has been interpreted as meaning that by then some act breaks were turning into substantial intervals.[69] No other evidence exists to confirm this, so far as I know.

A 'consort' comprised five strings: treble and bass viol, cittern, lute, and bandore, with either a recorder or flute as a woodwind. A 'broken' consort used a mixture of strings and wind instruments. Thomas Morley was writing consort music by the 1590s, as did Thomas Ravenscroft, who witnessed Richard Cowley's will in 1618. Consorts lacked the volume of a trumpet or drum or a hunting horn, which were designed for use out of doors. The difference in the decibel levels required by the two types of playhouse demanded different kinds of instrument. Judging from *The Tempest*, the company put the Blackfriars consort to use from the outset, using a cornett

[67] See chapter 1, pp. 38–40.
[68] See Gurr, '*The Tempest*'s Tempest at Blackfriars', *Shakespeare Survey* 41 (1989), 91–102.
[69] Charles J. Sisson, ed., *Believe As You List*, Malone Society Reprints, 1927, p. xxiv.

to replace the outdoor playhouse's brass trumpet, since as a woodwind it was quieter. In the few plays staged at the indoor playhouses that needed trumpet-calls, and in plays that were written for outdoor playhouses but adapted for indoors, woodwinds such as the old cornett almost always replaced the loud brass of the trumpet. Jonson's *Epicene, or The Silent Woman*, written for the boy company in its last days in 1609, and much later adopted by the King's, made a rare intrusion when it blasted the indoor audience by using a brass hunting horn to shock the hyperacusic Morose. Marston's *Sophonisba*, one of the very few plays containing major battle scenes written for the boy company while it occupied the Blackfriars, specifies 'cornetts' for the sennets and flourishes and the battle-signals, where a play written for an outdoor playhouse would have used trumpets.

The Blackfriars consort had already made itself famous as a self-sufficient performing group while the boy companies used the Blackfriars, as Frederic Gerschow testified. After 1608 the King's Men maintained that tradition. In his memoirs, Bulstrode Whitelocke said of his life in the 1630s (dissolute by puritan standards: in the Interregnum Whitelocke was a leading Parliamentarian) that he

> was so conversant with the musicians, and so willing to gain their favour, especially at this time, that I composed an air myself, with the assistance of Mr. Ives, and called it *Whitelock's Coranto*, which being cried up, was first played publicly by the Blackfriars Music, who were then esteemed the best of the common musicians in London. Whenever I came to that house (as I did sometimes in those days), though not often, to see a play, the musicians would presently play *Whitelock's Coranto*, and it was so often called for that they would have played it twice or thrice in an afternoon.[70]

However much Whitelocke was boasting about his skill as a composer of popular melodies, the ambience – an audience happy to come and hear the consort before the play, familiar with its offerings, and ready to call for particular favourites before the play began – was a regular feature of the King's Men's afternoon shows at Blackfriars.

A number of well-known composers supplied music for the Blackfriars consort, and several of them were commissioned to compose melodies for the songs that Fletcher, Middleton, and Massinger wrote into their plays for the company once it had the Blackfriars. The boy companies at Blackfriars and St Paul's had claimed to be choir-school groups, so their singing was always a major feature of their plays. In Beaumont's *Knight of the Burning*

---

[70] Charles Burney, *A General History of Music from the Earliest Ages to the Present Period*, London, 1782–9, II.299.

Pestle, written for the Blackfriars Boys in 1607, the hero's father, an anti-merchant figure called Merrythought, sings almost all his words to popular songs from ballads. He uses more than thirty different tunes, mostly fitting their opening lines into his replies in a kind of *parlando*. The play includes a maylord interact song-and-dance act by the leading boy, probably Nathan Field. Not all the music was from the popular song-tunes of the time, though. Three appear to be 'composer's pieces', written specially for the play, including a love-duet between the hero and heroine and a lament by the heroine over her lover's apparent death. The final chorus may have been specially composed for the play, too. Most distinctively, a composer's song is given to Merrythought to characterize the specially sanguine 'humour' he represents in his role. It opens "Tis mirth that fils the veines with bloud, / More then wine, or sleepe, or food' (2.9.25–38), and goes on to explain the psychological basis for a 'merry' outlook over the mercantile thinking of the others. Sadly, its music has not survived.

Some of the composers who wrote for the King's Men during their occupation of the Blackfriars can be identified. As we know, music took on a particular importance in Shakespeare's last plays, written between c. 1609 and 1613. It appears that in all these plays the company used the king's lutenist, Robert Johnson. He probably wrote music for *The Tempest*, *The Winter's Tale*, *Cardenio*, *Valentinian*, *The Duchess of Malfi*, and *The Devil is an Ass*. First indentured to George Carey, the company's second patron, he was drawn to write for the theatre only after he had become lutenist to King James, the company's third patron, and had written music for the first of the Inigo Jones–Jonson masques of 1605 and after. Most of the other known composers, Alfonso Ferrobosco the younger, who composed the tune for Volpone's song to Celia, John Wilson, who may also have written music for *The Winter's Tale*, and the brothers Henry and William Lawes, all set music that has survived for songs by Shakespeare, Fletcher, and Middleton. Most of these are not likely to be the original settings, though Johnson's music is the most likely to have been written for the plays' first performances, and his settings survive for songs in some of the later plays. In 1640 William Lawes wrote the music for the songs in Shirley's *The Cardinal*, and probably others.[71] On those in Jonson's plays, Mary Chan's book[72] about the concept of music he exercised in his masques and in a

[71] See John P. Cutts, 'William Lawes' Writing for the Theatre and the Court', *The Library*, 5th series 7 (1952), 225–34. Information about John Wilson and Ambrose Beeland is in Andrew Ashbee, David Lasocki, and Peter Holman, *A Biographical Dictionary of English Court Musicians*, Ashgate, London, 1998.

[72] Mary Chan, *Music in the Theatre of Ben Jonson*, Clarendon Press, 1980. See especially chapter 3 on *Volpone* and *The Devil is an Ass*, and chapter 7 on *The Winter's Tale* and *The Tempest*.

few of his plays (most notably the badly received *New Inn* at Blackfriars in 1629) is a complex and sensitive review of the innovations that Jonson used music for. Songs as purified language, songs as satirical intensifiers, and music from the idealizing forms characteristic of masquing demanded close collaboration between author and composer. The King's Men took on a lot of new resources with the Blackfriars consort.

Of the musicians who were actual company members, only a few can be distinguished from the hired men as regular employees. After the individual musician–players like Kemp and Phillips, we can identify among those who belonged to the Blackfriars consort John Adson and Richard Balls in the 1620s and 1630s, both of them City Waits, probably Francis Balls and John Rhodes, plus Ambrose Beeland, a 'fiddler' who later became a royal violinist, and another fiddler, Henry Wilson. William Tawyer must have played the trumpet when leading the mechanicals on stage in a pre-1623 production of *A Midsummer Night's Dream*, since he is named in the Folio text. Some others may be included on the list of the twenty-two 'musicians and other necessary attendantes' set down by Henry Herbert on 27 December 1624.[73] John Wilson was a singer, playing Balthasar in a performance of *Much Ado about Nothing*, since the Folio text identifies him there as 'Jacke Wilson'. He was also possibly the 'cunning Musition' who organized a performance on 27 September 1631, a Sunday, at the Bishop of Lincoln's house, according to a complaint that the bishop was misusing his Sundays.[74] A John Wilson who set the music for the song 'Take O take those lips away' in *Measure for Measure* and *Rollo*, and became Professor of Music at Oxford in 1656, was probably not the same person as the walk-on singer of the 1620s.

Music as an element in playgoing must have excited many people beside Bulstrode Whitelocke. The company's shift to the Blackfriars with its ready-made musical accessory had a profound and durable effect on their products. By the late 1630s William Davenant's long-running desire to create a wholly new kind of scenic and musical drama, an enlargement beyond the limited scope the small Blackfriars could offer, was tugging at their conservatism. Had the close-down not come when it did, they might have started to at least consider introducing operatic theatre.

---

[73] They are identified under their names in Appendix 1.

[74] The complaint claimed that 'one Mr. Wilson a cunning Musition . . . contrived a curious Comoedie, and plotted it so that he must needs have it acted upon the Sunday night, for he was to go the next day toward the Court'. It must have been a kind of masque. See Murray, *English Dramatic Companies*, II.49.

CHAPTER 3

'Will money buy 'em?': company finances

Playing was a business, and it ought to be possible to register an individual company's business activities in modern accountancy terms: turnover, income and expenditure accounts, the sharers' profits, levels of staff pay, and assets. It is not, of course, anything like so simple. The chief assets we know of were the plays, special costumes and properties, the tenant relation with the playhouse-owners, and of course the company's reputation with its customers. To complicate this exercise we have to add the 'housekeeper' or playhouse-owning finances to the company sharers' accounts. In the absence of any papers at all that tell us anything directly about the company's finances, this offer of the facts and figures has to be based largely on guesswork.

COMPANY GOVERNMENT

Playing companies ran the nearest thing to a democratic and non-authoritarian management system in the largely monopolistic Tudor and early Stuart economy. The Privy Council tried to impose monopolistic control by restricting the number of companies licensed to perform and insisting that every company had a patron who was ultimately responsible for their good behaviour. As control tightened, the social level at which patrons were allowed to have companies rose rapidly. In 1572 a statute was passed identifying all 'Fencers Bearewardes Comon Players in Enterludes Mynstrels Juglers Pedlers Tynkers & Petye Chapmen' who were not travelling with a licence from a lord or two magistrates as 'Roges Vacaboundes and Sturdy Beggers', in other words outlaws. In 1598 the right to issue such licences was limited to barons and earls. Under James the only patrons allowed to run a London company were members of the royal family. Essentially an attempt to fix everyone to a specific parish, the 1572 Act tried to ban free travel for non-gentry outside the local parish. It made itinerant merchants, tinkers, and players vulnerable and likely to be arrested

18. An image of Atlas carrying the celestial globe, an engraving by George Glover in
Hondius to *Atlas or A Geographicke description of the regions*, 1636. Some such emblem
showing Hercules carrying the globe is thought to have featured on the Globe's flag and
perhaps over its doors to explain its name. The image ('Hercules and his load too') is
mentioned in *Hamlet*.

in whatever town they visited if they had no licence for their travelling jobs.

In practice from 1572 the few playing companies licensed to tour the whole country had to have a lord or earl as their patron. Under Elizabeth the rank superior to earls, that of duke, died out. The Duke of Norfolk, the last of them, was executed for treason in 1571, and the rank was not revived until King James took over in 1603. So the number of patrons who could license companies to undertake full-time professional travelling was effectively down to not much more than a dozen by the 1570s. Plus, from 1583, the queen herself. Some Privy Councillors who ran companies were barons – notably Henry Carey, Lord Hunsdon, and his son-in-law Charles Howard, Lord of Effingham until he was made Earl of Nottingham in 1598. Those two had special access to the licensing business. All the other patrons of companies from 1594 till 1603 were earls. It was a system of centralized control, with the mightiest in the land confining strictly to themselves and to the monarch the right to license players.

This created the wonderful paradox that the most durable success in an authoritarian society was a thoroughly anti-authoritarian organization. The company system that evolved first with the travelling players in the sixteenth century kept going up to 1642 in the one company as an unlikely success story. The King's Men, and specifically the two Burbage brothers, chose to preserve the old collaborative system against all the profiteering that a more capitalistic and authoritarian system might have offered them. Despite the economic arguments they chose to run their two playhouses with the one company as part of a collective institution. They were able to do so because, in a system dominated by monopoly capitalism, whereas all the other playing companies got their backing from entrepreneurial impresarios, their management system was unique in keeping the sharing co-operative system of the early travellers. In the core of their team they were both tenants and landlords of their own properties. The company financed itself. In the early years of the new century Henslowe gradually came to adopt the more authoritarian practice of impresario–financier, banker and controller of the companies he ran (at least if the 'Complaint' by the Lady Elizabeth's company in 1614 has any truth in it), along with his managerial son-in-law Edward Alleyn. They and others developed a system that favoured the impresario–capitalist over collaborative players, as it has done through the succeeding centuries. Only the King's ran themselves.

There is evidence that, working for impresarios, players in the other companies looked enviously at the King's Men's sharing and playhouse-owning system. The King's Men became a model for their peers in more than their plays and their playhouses. In 1618 the company using the Fortune signed an agreement with their landlord Alleyn that bought them shares in his playhouse, effectively replicating the original Globe system. For the Fortune company, the imitation did not last beyond December 1621, when the playhouse burned down. It was a worse loss for them than the Globe in 1613, because the Fortune burned at midnight, and so took all the company playbooks and costumes with it whereas the Globe's fire during a performance meant that enough bright sparks were on hand to save the company's vital assets. Such a rescue act must have been what saved for posterity the half of Shakespeare's plays that were not yet in print. The Fortune company's playhouse had to be rebuilt with money from financiers, not the players, and throughout its subsequent history, like all the London playhouses other than the Globe and the Blackfriars, it remained in the hands of impresarios, former players though some of them were.

The management system devised in 1599 became a supreme paradox in 1603, when the most uniquely democratic and co-operative organization in the whole of England came under the patronage of the most despotic figure in the country, Britain's most well-argued autocrat. This most privileged, longest-living and most prosperous of all the early Stuart companies ran for forty years as the only one carrying the name of the early Stuart kings. Its consistent financial success in the face of the impresario system that ran its rivals began accidentally at the Globe in 1599, thanks to the generosity (or the desperation, and certainly in retrospect the financial acumen) of five of its sharers. The Globe-born scheme meant that the most anti-authoritarian system of management that ever ran in early modern England came to wear the king's own name as its cover.

Through the course of the sixteenth century the size of playing companies grew from the five players for whom Skelton wrote *Magnificence* in 1519 to the twelve who were licensed as Queen's Men in 1583. In practice the London companies of the 1590s had eight and, later, ten sharers at most. Shares in a company were based on a kind of stock-market valuation. The playing companies were never 'companies' in the sense that modern companies are, restricting their liability to make payouts if they go bankrupt. Professional players were 'servants' to their patron, calling themselves Lord X's 'Servants' or just his 'Men'. Early in the sixteenth century those who 'shared' the group's profits (and losses) would be the entire company of five who played *Magnificence*. When companies first became lodged firmly in London after the 1570s the number of players needed grew rapidly, to a peak of about twenty for a few years from 1588 to 1594, after which it settled back to the fifteen who played *Julius Caesar* at the Globe in 1599 (Appendix 2.12). Of that higher number, not more than ten at most, more often eight, were the 'sharers'. The rest were hired, receiving their wages from the profits made by the consortium of sharers and paid by the year or the week or even the day.

The eight or so sharers were the ones who put up the company's capital, paying for its assets, covering the playhouse rent and other running costs, and making the management decisions. A strong company with eight sharers might be valued at as much as £500. A few figures survive for individual share values, such as the £80 paid to Simon Jewell in the optimistic year 1592 for his share in Pembroke's or the Queen's Men, before the long plague epidemic of 1593–4 drove expectations downwards. In 1596 a share in the Admiral's and probably also the Chamberlain's, when company size and ambitions had shrunk, was valued at £50. A Queen Anne's Men's share in 1612 was £80. On the other hand the value of a King's Men's share in the 1630s when they were supreme was bringing in a profit of £180 a year, so its price by then should have been at least that. Such enormous values – Shakespeare is supposed to have paid only £60 in 1597 for the second-largest house in Stratford – meant that shares might be divided, and aspirant players could buy a half- or a quarter-share in order to get their foot in the door. Horatio in *Hamlet* 3.2 wryly shrinks Hamlet's exultant claim to have earned a fellowship in a cry of players to a half-share. Outlays for the sharers included the rent of their playing-space, amounting at the London playhouses to half the takings from the galleries, and the purchase of the company's capital assets, playbooks, properties, and special costumes. Musical instruments and standard costumes were owned by individual sharers.

A sharer had to buy his way into the company, at a price determined by the market of the time. That money identified his commitment to the enduring good of the company. A sharer routinely took one of the eight major speaking parts and helped with company management. On the principle of egalitarian management usually two sharers had to sign on the company's behalf for any financial transactions. Standard company numbers included, besides the eight or ten sharers, four or more boys and as many as ten hired men, plus in London a 'book-keeper' who looked after the playbooks and a 'tireman' who looked after the special costumes. There were also 'gatherers', the doormen and women who took the money at the various entry-points to the playhouse, and others who did the odd jobs and stage management.

THE CHAMBERLAIN'S/KING'S MEN'S COMPANY ACCOUNTS

Trying to calculate the finances of a company for which so few hard records survive is the sort of strenuous mental exercise rarely rewarded with a fit body and never with a healthy mind. To start with, problematic even for accountants, the flows of income and expenditure are based on subjective rather than objective records, and few exercisers work on the records in the identical way. In the Chamberlain's and King's company case such calculations are also made complex by the nearly fifty years that the few surviving figures have to recount, and the inevitable inflation which ran throughout the period. In fact the basic figure, the cost of admission to the playhouses, does not seem to have varied through the company's lifetime, although other prices and values certainly shifted, especially for capital assets like clothing. As a result, placing the same fixed value on such items in the 1590s and the 1630s falsifies the story more than a little. Equally, giving a modern valuation to the Elizabethan pound does not give an accurate idea of the Elizabethan cost of living. There may be some co-relation between the one Elizabethan penny that throughout the period was the charge for entry to the yard at the Globe and the five modern pounds (eight US dollars) charged for standing room at the new Globe in Southwark. On the other hand, the same penny in the 1590s could buy a pound of bread, while a comparable loaf in England now costs less than one-fifth of that. Given the extremity of the social divisions that were then flaunted between the aristocracy and the artisan, the prices for items of clothing were even more divergent.

Perhaps the greatest anomaly in the evidence about company finances is the fact that the charges for admission remained so constant between the time the first commercial group of playhouses opened in the 1570s and the general closure in 1642. Those seventy or so years saw wide fluctuations in the country's levels of prosperity, and a pattern of price inflation never reflected in the costs of admission to the playhouses. What really changed and moderated the drop in the value of the penny for the company sharers was the shift of customer affluence upmarket from the open-air to the indoor playhouses, with their far higher prices. The existence of the two authorized open-air playhouses of 1594, the Theatre and the Rose, was matched in 1642 by the Fortune and the Red Bull. But by the later date there were three indoor houses as well, plus for half the year the Globe. The Fortune and Red Bull became what James Wright called 'citizen playhouses' in part because their price levels were so much lower than the indoor venues, and so their income was too. After about 1617, when the Master of the Revels stopped calling on the Fortune and Red Bull companies to perform at court, they also lost the payments that brought each King's Men sharer on average at least an additional £10 every year.

The one underlying economic trend through the period that did impact on the playing companies was the country's final lurch from a barter to a monetary economy. That happened in London earlier than in the countryside, but it was so gradual that its effects cannot be allowed for in reckoning the company accounts. In general, Londoners were early cash-entrepreneurs. Even before the building of playhouses first allowed the players direct control over access to their products, they had charged cash instead of taking barter-commodities for admission to their shows. This is unlikely to have applied at the great houses round the country, where a substantial meal and a bed were automatic components of their pay. Still, to maintain the same London prices through a time when inflation was reducing the purchase value of so many commodities seems unnatural. If a beggar's whole family could be admitted for the price of a single place in the yard ('all in for one penny', as John Taylor the water poet wrote),[1] the gatherers must have been prepared to bargain with hesitant playgoers. Custom is a powerful stabilizer of prices, though, and the leap from the simple unit of one penny to two was evidently more than most customers would tolerate.

The most likely explanation for this long-lasting stability in the prices for access is that the pain to the sharers bearing the loss of income from the open-air playhouses when they charged the same minimal one penny for a place in the yard may have been held in check by the need to keep a deliberate contrast with the higher prices charged at the indoor playhouses. If we discount the rebuilding of the Globe in 1614 and of the Fortune in 1622, the last open-air theatre to be built was the Hope in 1614, where playing soon stopped in favour of its use as a baiting-house. The only new playhouses after that were hall theatres with their higher prices, the Cockpit in 1616, built to match the Blackfriars, and the smaller Salisbury Court in 1629. The fact that playing at the Blackfriars after 1608 became much more celebrated than at the Globe has to be seen not just in the light of its more educated audiences, who wrote about it much more, but as a consequence of the fact that the richer clientele became a better source of income, at least by 1619.[2] There are several likely explanations why the King's Men moved

---

[1] John Taylor, *The praise, antiquity, and commodity of beggery, beggers and begging*, London, 1621, C3v.

[2] The rise in the takings at the Blackfriars by 1619 may reflect price increases, or a rise in the popularity of the plays staged there, or, most likely, an increase in the number of the affluent who could afford the price.

upmarket in the second half of their long career, and money is certainly one of them.

A lot of careful study has been devoted to the market economics of playing at this time, but much remains to be done, above all identifying the relative income levels of the different playgoing sections of the community at different times and of individuals in different occupations. Even the relationship between general income levels and playgoing provides a number of surprises. Douglas Bruster noted the apparent anomaly that the 1590s, the period when the Shakespeare company launched their first and greatest period of invention and innovation, was a dreadfully bad time for London's citizens. Throughout the 1590s real income was the lowest for seven centuries. Conditions were dire. An appalling loss of life in the plague epidemic of 1593–4 was followed by seven successive crop failures. The massive expansion of maritime trade, which brought the East India Company of 1600 a return on its investment of 121 per cent for each voyage, soon meant huge amounts of new money flowing in, but that did not trickle down the social chain very readily.[3] For the pastime of playgoing to flourish so strongly under these conditions is a paradox. I think it likely that the contraction of company size after 1594 – the staging of plays with less spectacle and smaller numbers than at the beginning of the 1590s – was more a reflection of the economic conditions and of bad experiences with overly ambitious staging than the different sorts of plays being written.

The value of a penny spent at the Theatre in 1594 was different from the value of a shilling spent at the Blackfriars in 1630, an apparent truism that needs a lot of refining to turn it into useful currency. It was not just that spending power in general was shrinking. At the Theatre and the Globe the basic penny was a form of entry to a social gathering. The community was paying for a product they knew about. The additional pennies were only used to supply some additional comforts, a roof, a seat, and perhaps a cushion, and a place literally superior to the groundlings in the yard. Beggars and fishwives, epitomes of Elizabethan penury, were noted as presences in the yard as much as the hordes of apprentices, whose presence as penny-payers is a chronic anomaly. On the whole, apprentices laboured unpaid throughout their training until they could produce work good enough to be sold in their master's shop, so their presence at playhouses must have been largely dependent on their employers' generosity. At the Blackfriars and the Cockpit the minimum admission price of sixpence separated the

[3] Douglas Bruster, *Drama and the Market in the Age of Shakespeare*, Cambridge University Press, 1992, p. 18.

indoor playgoers from the poor at the outset. The one or two shillings that Inns of Court men like Bulstrode Whitelocke, John Greene, and Edward Heath[4] paid for a seat in the Blackfriars pit through the 1620s and 1630s were used to keep them apart from the *hoi polloi*. A shilling was twelve times the price of a groundling's place, and nearly twice a normal day's wage even for a skilled workman. Jonson reported in 1610 that in the furthest gallery at the Blackfriars it was not an apprentice but 'the shops *Foreman*' who could 'judge for his *sixe-pence*'.[5] Sixpence bought the cheapest seats in the house, the upper gallery, still the cheapest location in modern indoor playhouses.

It has to be said that the totals claimed by contemporary witnesses for particular items of income and expenditure are so unreliable that even the sturdiest sources are of little use. A note in a copy of *A Game at Chess* now in the Dyce Collection in London claims first-hand information from the players that 'they tooke fiveteene hundred Pounde' from the play's run at the Globe.[6] Allowing an average spend of twopence per person, the standard price of a bench in the galleries but twice the yard's penny, such a sum meant almost twenty thousand customers were there on each of its nine days. John Chamberlain claimed not much over three thousand daily, so the figure was at least a sixfold exaggeration. We have good reason to be sorry for the loss of the 'great booke of Accomptes' which was flourished as a stage property in *Believe As You List* in 1631 and might have been the company's real account book.[7]

In assessing the Shakespeare company finances we are faced not only with a range of valuations for the money but with the problem of deeply flawed sets of figures for income and expenditure, plus drastic changes in the conditions that generated income, as well as the radical adjustments that came with the use of two playhouses, and above all shifts in social attitudes to playgoing. The last of these factors meant that the two designated London companies of 1594 began their work with a massive inhibition against making any large investment in their enterprise. Despite the novelty of explicit support from the Privy Council the players must have been seared by their recent memory of the major losses through the years up to 1594, with lengthy plague stoppages and the over-ambitious writing and staging that produced the 'large' plays of 1588–93. The Chamberlain's Men's first years,

---

4 John R. Elliott Jr lists the prices that Whitelocke of the Middle Temple, Greene of Lincoln's Inn, and Heath of the Inner Temple paid, in 'Four Caroline Playgoers', *Medieval and Renaissance Drama in England* 6 (1993), 179–96.
5 Commendatory verses to *The Faithful Shepherdess*.
6 See Sara Jayne Steen, *Ambrosia in an Earthen Vessel*, AMS Press, New York, 1993, p. 51.
7 That is what the book-keeper's note at line 981 calls it. When presented to the Roman Senate at 1116 it is called 'the booke of records', an even more useful relic.

from 1594 to 1603, when they established their reputation as the country's leading company, were also the years their financiers suffered drastic losses with their playhouses.

Sadly, these are the years when the most detailed financial evidence exists in the parallel case of the Admiral's Men and Henslowe's *Diary* with its accounts. The direct association of the two duopoly companies makes the *Diary* by far the most detailed account of the other company's daily income and expenditure, a unique parallel to how the Chamberlain's Men fared in their first years. And yet even Henslowe's entries of income and costs are fragmentary. He served the Admiral's first as landlord and later as banker, not as the company accountant, so his records do not give direct sets of figures for the company's finances. The thirty-one months when he kept a daily record of his rental income, the best guide to the company's takings, ran from May 1594 until January 1597. Through those years, however, his entries are solely those of a playhouse landlord. It was not until 1597 that he began to make entries as company banker and manager, recording the costs of playbooks and clothing and of paying the licence fee to the Master of the Revels. So the best record by Henslowe of company income precedes 1597, while the records of company expenditure only begin after that. Henslowe's entries are hard fact, specifying precise amounts taken in and paid out to run his duopoly company. They provide a firm basis for the tables of likely income and expenditure invented below. But they are seriously incomplete. They make no allowance for the shifts in subjective valuation of the company's work, for instance, the kind of estimate of profitability that generated the value put on a company share. The low valuation of a share in both the two new companies in 1596 (£50) most likely showed the smaller expectations of the two companies that now replaced the single royal company, a pair of newcomers who had not yet established their playing credentials in full.

The fact that the number of company shares increased in the first few years of operation suggests that their value did rise quickly. At the Admiral's the sharers appear to have been ten in 1597, eleven in 1600, and twelve in 1603.[8] The Chamberlain's had eight in 1594 and a similar number in 1603, with the addition of one apparently short-term import from Scotland, Lawrence Fletcher, presumably included as a part-requirement for the new king giving them his patronage. In 1597 one-tenth of the Admiral's enterprise was rated at £50. At its successor the Prince's in 1613 the

---

[8] Carol Chillington Rutter, *Documents of the Rose Playhouse*, Manchester University Press, 1984 (pp. 89, 131, 189), identifies them by their signatures in Henslowe's *Diary*.

value had risen to £70 each for twelve sharers, while a Queen Anne's share at the same time was set at £80, the sum that Simon Jewell recorded for a Queen's Men's share in 1592.[9] Such valuations were subjective, dependent as much on the company's stock of plays in its repertory and its costumes and equipment as on its personnel or the current state of its activities. In practice the valuation seems to correspond roughly with the expected income per sharer for a year or more of regular playing. A rather wild claim in 1625 seems to say that a share in the King's company stock was £500,[10] though when in 1637 during a lengthy closure for plague five men from Henrietta Maria's company, Michael Bowyer, William Robbins, William Allen, Hugh Clark, and Theophilus Bird, joined the King's, their share in the stock was rated at £200 each.[11] It seems that by then the company's stock was a more substantial item for valuation than a share in playing, hardly surprising after more than forty years of acquiring the huge repertory of plays and the stage properties and costumes that went with them, when there were two playhouses to store them in.

The return on shares varied according to the amount of playing that was possible. In a single good year in the later 1590s it could easily cover the capital cost of a share. By the 1630s the scale of income and the cost of a share had both escalated substantially. A share in Prince Charles's (II) Company in the 1630s cost £100.[12] In 1634 the annual income from a King's Men's share was £180, roughly the purchase value of one of their shares if we average out the various figures given through that decade.

Philip Henslowe's daily lists of his rental takings for 1594–7 at the Rose identify his half of the daily income from the galleries. These figures note his take on each performance day from the time the two companies separated in June 1594 for two years and seven months up to January 1597.[13] They provide a basis for the income of the Admiral's through the first years, and thus a broad parallel to what the Chamberlain's might have made, almost up to their loss of the Theatre in April 1597. In those thirty-one months, between 16 June 1594 and 22 January 1597, the Admiral's played on 568 days out of a possible 951 (omitting the non-playing Sundays brings the maxi-

[9] Mary Edmond, 'Pembroke's Men', *Review of English Studies* 25 (1974), 129–36.

[10] That was the 'stock debt' that Thomas Hobbs engaged himself for on 25 May 1625.

[11] Bird gave that figure in a later lawsuit, when he also claimed that a share was really worth only £50 in 1637. See Leslie Hotson, *The Commonwealth and Restoration Stage*, pp. 31–5.

[12] G. E. Bentley, *The Profession of Player in Shakespeare's Time*, p. 29.

[13] On 24 January 1597 Henslowe changed his accounting system, making entries into five columns instead of the previous three. There has been much debate about what the five columns were for (see *Henslowe's Diary*, pp. xxxiii–xxxvii), and it seems best to exclude this section of the accounts from the comparison with the Chamberlain's.

mum possible down to 818).[14] In that period Henslowe's annual rent, half the takings from the galleries, averaged £336. The Theatre was larger than the Rose, so its rent was likely to have been rather higher.[15] That would have left the company the other half, plus the pennies from the yard, which was markedly larger at the Theatre than at the Rose. Any figure for groundling attendance has necessarily to be an estimate, and a rough one, since the weather might have had a bigger impact on enthusiasm for standing in the open air than it had for those who planned to sit under the roofing of the galleries. So a rough guess at the income for that two-and-a-half-year period might raise the annual half-gallery takings at the Theatre to more than £360. That sum doubled, plus the yard's takings, would make a total annual income of well over £900. That was augmented with £140 for the fourteen plays they staged at court in those three seasons (the Admiral's played there only six times), and an unknown amount from private performances and touring. At private venues such as the Middle Temple for *Twelfth Night* in February 1602 the amount paid for a performance would have been less, somewhere between the £2 the Essex conspirators paid to supplement the takings for *Richard II* at the Globe and the £10 which was standard for a court performance. Probably the ten angels, or £5, which the generous Thomas More offered to the visiting company of four men and a boy in Munday's *Sir Thomas More* would be a good sum for such a show. So a gross annual income of perhaps a thousand pounds after the half-gallery rent was deducted seems a reasonable estimate for those first thirty-one months as a preferred company.

These figures match up fairly well with other sets of figures from Henslowe's *Diary*. Neil Carson's scrupulous examination has identified £368.3s as the total amount taken at the galleries between the beginning of August and 13 October 1598, a run of eleven weeks.[16] Re-calculating those figures as an annual income, and adding rather less than half of the gallery amount as the sharers' total from the yard, brings the sharers' annual income to £920 from the galleries, half of it deducted for rent, and £400 from the yard. This would have brought them £1,320 in an unbroken year, of which £460 would normally have gone to pay the playhouse rent. From these calculations we might guess that the Theatre's larger capacity could have

[14] These figures differ slightly from those given by Carol Chillington Rutter, *Documents of the Rose Playhouse*.

[15] Neil Carson, *A Companion to Henslowe's Diary*, Cambridge University Press, 1988, p. 43, finds that the takings at the Fortune, built in 1600 as a match for the Globe, were generally larger than those for the Rose.

[16] *Ibid.*, p. 19.

brought the Chamberlain's annual income to at least £1,500, less £480 rent. As a thumbnail sketch to show the profits that were likely to accrue after the 1599 reorganization to the Chamberlain's sharers who also bought into the Globe playhouse, for each year of full operation Shakespeare would have taken one-eighth of the housekeeper's £480 rent, less maintenance costs, an impressive annual income of more than £50, plus as much as £60 from his proportion of the profits as a sharer. That compares with Thomas Dekker's optimum income from writing for Henslowe of about £20 a year. Unlike Shakespeare, Dekker spent several years in a debtor's prison.

Assuming two hundred performances by the Chamberlain's in a plague-free year, the annual profit per share after all expenses were paid would have easily exceeded its capital value. But that was before deductions for company costs, which were by no means inconsiderable. Company costs included not only paying the hired men but such regular expenses as the charges made by the scribes copying the plays and parts, and the printer's charge for the daily playbills that advertised what was to be shown.[17] A more detailed accounting of the company's income and expenditure adds some flesh to this thumbnail sketch, using some of the other ways to calculate company income at this time. Playhouse rental for Henslowe's Rose came to half the daily takings from the galleries, which between 1594 and 1597 might vary from £3.11s for a revival of *Tamburlaine* on 28 August 1594 to seven shillings at the long-running *Bellendon* on 2 November 1594, giving an average of a little under £1.10s for each day of performance. That amount, the company's income after deduction of the playhouse rent, would have brought in £4 in total per day of playing, rather than the £6 of the Rose figure for 1598 cited above. Such a figure suggests that audiences at the Rose usually occupied rather less than half of the playhouse's total capacity, although Henslowe's figures for the thirty-one months are those for the actual daily takings.[18] Even the Henslowe figures can produce oddly discrepant totals when studied from different angles.

The Rose company was less successful than the Chamberlain's with the number of performances chosen for the court, a weakness which may also have been reflected in the numbers attending its playhouse through the

---

[17] No company ephemera such as playbills survive, though the Henslowe papers include a handwritten one for a bear-baiting. Tiffany Stern has noted entries in the Stationers' Register for the four men licensed to print playbills, who included the play-text printers James Roberts and William Jaggard. See Stern, ' "On each Wall / And Corner Poast": Playbills, Title-pages, and Advertising in Early Modern London', *English Literary Renaissance*, forthcoming.

[18] Roslyn Lander Knutson, *The Repertory of Shakespeare's Company 1594–1613*, The University of Arkansas Press, Fayetteville, 1991, p. 24, calculates that for a 'ne' performance of '*the venesyon comodey*' on 25 August 1594 the Rose had 1,212 in the galleries and a smaller number in the yard.

year. At the Theatre in the same period, assuming slightly better levels of enthusiasm for what their repertory offered, the company's net income would have amounted to perhaps £5 per playing day, or £1,100 for a 220-day year. Such a rate makes the extra £2 that the Essex conspirators paid to have *Richard II* restaged at the Globe on 7 February 1601 a reasonable addition to the income from a play that Augustine Phillips claimed was 'so old and so long out of use'.[19]

There are not many indicators of the level of profit the company made in any period. We might consider as a signifier of the general lack of money the fact that the Burbages failed to pay their licence fees to the Master of the Revels until he took them to court in 1604.[20] So equally could one of Giles Allen's reasons for closing the Theatre when its lease expired on 13 April 1597, that James Burbage owed him over £30 in arrears of rent for the property.[21] Those indicators contrast with the squabble over the difference in income levels registered in the 'Sharers' Papers' of 1635 (Appendix 3). They are signs of the underlying changes of feeling: poverty and risk in the 1590s replaced by secure affluence in the 1630s. Such feelings are subjective, and come more from circumstantial factors such as the precariousness of the company's innovatory and privileged status in the 1590s against established popularity and the protection of the court of the 1630s than from any profit-and-loss account, however ostensibly objective it may be. The feelings were real enough, but they need to be set against the identifiable financial realities.

It seems reasonable to conclude that the average net income from play-house takings in the first years, free as they were from stoppages for plague, was somewhere between £1,000 and £1,760 per annum. Additional sources of income came from court performances and private-house visits, plus whatever else came from touring. Besides these main revenue-spinners there must have been a number of more marginal ways of raising the company income. One of them, where Henslowe's notes give no help, is the sale of food and drink. Henslowe financed the building of the Rose with John Cholmley, a local grocer, by guaranteeing him the income from such sales. Cholmley faded from the scene early on, but nothing in the *Diary* says that Henslowe received any income from selling food and drink. Pedlars of food such as apples, pears, cherries, plums and nuts, water and ale there

---

[19] *Calendar of State Papers Domestic, 1598–1601*, p. 435.
[20] See Mary Edmond, 'Yeomen, Citizens, Gentlemen and Players: the Burbages and their Connections', in *Elizabethan Theater: Essays in Honor of S. Schoenbaum*, ed. R. B. Parker and S. P. Zitner, University of Delaware Press, Newark, 1996, pp. 30–49.
[21] See Charles William Wallace, *The First London Theatre: Materials for a History*, University of Nebraska Studies 13, Lincoln, 1913, especially pp. 248, 278.

certainly were.[22] Possibly they plied their wares independently, but it seems unlikely that the playhouse owner and/or the company would not have demanded a slice of their takings, or at worst the price of admission to the yard. The Globe had a taphouse adjoining the building, with John Heminges as the tapster,[23] though it is not clear whether that was private enterprise for his own profit or whether he shared the takings, either with the other housekeepers or with the sharers. If the latter, then such takings must be counted as an item of the company's income. The absence of such income from Henslowe's figures suggests that it became company income, not a housekeeper profit. Playhouse maintenance costs with licensing and leasehold rents are in Henslowe's accounts, but not any income from a taphouse or pedlars.

The records of performance in Henslowe's *Diary* show how intense the repertory system was. That intensity must have been the same at both playhouses. Through the thirty-one months up to January 1597 the Admiral's 568 performances included 63 different plays. Of those, 44 were new products, introduced at a rate of roughly one every three weeks. The most popular play (*The Wise Men of Westchester*) was staged 30 times, the next (*Faustus*) 24. *The Seven Days of the Week* had 22 stagings, *A Knack to Know an Honest Man* 21, and *The Blind Beggar of Alexandria*, introduced on 12 February 1595, had 19 stagings by 22 January 1597. The older plays *The Jew of Malta* and *Bellendon* had 17 each through the full thirty-one months (*Bellendon* was available at the outset, when there were fewer plays to stage, and most of its performances were in 1594; but it was revived two years later, in July 1596). Marlowe's *1 Tamburlaine* was staged 15 times, as was *Long Meg*. New plays, *Chinon*, *Longshanks*, and *Crack Me This Nut*, all had 14 stagings. At the other extreme, five plays appear to have been staged only once and three only twice, two of them sequels.[24] The average number of times each play appeared in the thirty-one months was fewer than nine. It was a strenuous repertory system, and its financial demands were considerable.

The three weeks that it took to mount a new play meant that resources had to be deployed well in advance of any return on the investment. Returns

[22] Analysis of a section of the remains from the yard at the Rose in 1993 found five cherry stones and a plumstone, in addition to the hazel-nut shells that constituted part of the yard's concrete surfacing.

[23] Gabriel Egan, 'John Heminges's Tap-House at the Globe', *Theatre Notebook* 55 (2001), 72–7.

[24] It is not possible to be sure that Henslowe's variant spellings always refer to the same play. *The Massacre at Paris*, for instance, appears first on 19 June 1594 as 'the Gwies', the name it had on its first appearances in the records in 1593. On 3 July Henslowe noted it as 'the masacer', and it appears thereafter in variant forms of this second title. Other plays varied in name even less recognizably. In general the identifications followed in the *Diary* Index have been accepted in making this tally.

were quite unpredictable, the takings for an old favourite like *Faustus* ranging from £3.12s (Henslowe's figure for 30 September 1594) to five shillings (5 January 1597). Plays marked by Henslowe as 'ne', a note which generally appears to signify a new production, almost always took more than the many repeats, and may reflect higher prices for admission. The weekly takings show consistent features. There were no performances on Sundays, and no particular pattern can be discerned to say which days of the week were more crowded than others. The takings were highest in the week between Christmas and the New Year. In the week of Christmas 1594, for instance, Henslowe took £10 for his half of the gallery takings, although he may have been profiting from the sudden lack of competition, because all that week the Chamberlain's seem to have been absent from London, travelling to and from Sir John Harington's new house in Rutland with *Titus Andronicus*.

What is most difficult and yet most important to calculate are the outgoings in the three principal areas of cost other than the playhouse rent: expenditure on playbooks, costumes, and properties.[25] The Henslowe records from 1597 onwards for these costs do provide us with a distinct idea of what the charges for mounting plays were through this period. Henslowe's own note of the Admiral's Men's total expenditure on playbooks, costumes, and properties between 13 March 1598 and 13 October 1599 amounts to £631.4s.11d over a period of nineteen months,[26] Henslowe's tally rounding it up to £632. This gives an average expenditure for these three items of £7.14s a week.

The fourth major cost was wages for the company's employees.[27] Any calculation of wage costs for the personnel in the company besides the sharers depends on the total number of players required to mount the plays. When he visited the Globe to see *Julius Caesar* on 21 September 1599 Thomas Platter's lack of English meant that he watched rather than

---

[25] The most detailed study yet done of the Shakespeare company's accounts is in chapters 6 and 7 and Appendix 2 of T. W. Baldwin's *The Organisation and Personnel of the Shakespearean Company*. Baldwin, however, begins his calculations well before 1594, ignores outlays on clothing, plays, and other commodities, ignores the outlay on wages for hired men and boys in his estimates of sharer income, and often presents his evidence without clearly distinguishing between player-sharers and housekeepers.

[26] Carson, *Companion*, p. 28.

[27] Some figures are oddly absent in Henslowe. Besides omitting anything about supplies of food and drink, he seems to have made no outlay at all on playbills, the only major form of advertising, which would have meant a daily cost for paper and print of perhaps as much as two shillings. That must have come from the company's own accounts, plus other 'sundry' items not noted by Henslowe. Tiffany Stern has identified a payment for one company's playbills of roughly ten shillings a month (see ' "On each Wall / And Corner Poast": Playbills, Title-pages, and Advertising in Early Modern London').

listened to the players, so his assertion that the number of players on stage
was no more than fifteen (including those dressed as women, for a play
containing thirty-eight named characters, besides carpenters, a cobbler, a
messenger, senators, citizens, servants, and soldiers), is probably a good
indication of the total number of players in the performance, as well as
indicating the intense degree of doubling.[28] This figure, largely confirmed
by the calculations about doubling made by Ringler and others,[29] suggests
that the company expected to use the eight sharers plus at least five hired
men and up to four boys for each play. There are rarely more than eight
significant speaking parts in a Shakespeare play, probably reflecting the
number of sharers. All the other players took wages: cash for the men, and
for the boys bread and board. We do not know how much the sharers who
boarded boys charged the company for their protégés, or indeed whether
they charged the company at all. Henslowe, as his company's manager but
not a sharer, charged the Admiral's three shillings a week for the use of one
of his boys.

Besides the sharers and their boys and the hired men there was an uncer-
tain number of stage hands, some of whom might also do service on stage
as mutes, and a trumpeter. In addition, there were some skilled craftsmen.
Henslowe's Diary notes a book-keeper, a tireman, gatherers, and a few more
occasional craftsmen. They would have received something like London's
standard wages, which themselves are regrettably still matters for dispute.
Plenty of calculations have been made about the working wage in this time,
although apart from the few notes of rates of pay that Henslowe records
they give more context than hard information. William Ingram suggests
that a benchmark wage would have been about £10 a year, or five shillings
a week.[30] Carol Chillington Rutter gives the wage rates from the Statute
of 1588: 'Drapers being hosiers by the yeare with meate and drinke = £4
[i.e, less than 3d a day or one shilling and sixpence a week]. Shoemakers
by the yeare with meate and drinke = £4. Brewers by the yeare with meate
and drinke = £10. Common laborores with meate and drinke by the daye
5d without meate and drinke 9d.'[31] On this basis a wage of five shillings a

[28] A number of pre-1594 plays and 'plots' such as 2 *Seven Deadly Sins* appear to demand twenty-five
or more players. These belong to the 'large play' period, when staging ambitions and personnel
for a while outreached those of the later period. See Gurr, *The Shakespearian Playing Companies*,
pp. 59–60. Such numbers were not used again until the 1620s.

[29] See William A. Ringler, Jr, 'The Number of Actors in Shakespeare's Early Plays', in *The Seventeenth-
Century Stage*, ed. G. E. Bentley, Toronto University Press, 1968, pp. 110–34.

[30] William Ingram, 'The Economics of Playing', in *A Companion to Shakespeare*, ed. David Scott
Kastan, Blackwell, 1999, pp. 313–27, p. 315.

[31] *Documents*, Appendix, pp. 230–1.

week without food and drink for stagehands would have been comparable
to the daily wage of unskilled labourers.

For all the debates about their reality, wage levels are more easily identified
than the actual number of workers the company employed. The Admiral's
sharer Thomas Downton on 25 January 1599 'ded hire [blank for name]
as his covenante servante for 2 yers . . . & he to gef him viijs a wecke as
long as they playe and after they lye stylle one fortnyght then to geve hime
hallfe wages'.[32] That meant an annual income for the hired man of about
£16. After the first year of such service the weekly rate would usually rise.
Henslowe noted on 27 July 1597 'I heayred [hired] Thomas hearne with
ijd pence for to searve me ij yeares in the qualetie of playenge for fyve
shellynges a weacke for one yeare & vjs viijd for the other yeare'. Alleyn
hired William Kendall on 8 December 1597 'for his sayd servis everi week
of his playng in London xs & in ye Cuntrie vs'.[33] A starter wage of five
shillings a week, increasing to one mark, or six shillings and eightpence,
appears to have been the standard rate, £10 a year rising to £12. Henslowe
also has a note that the company owed him for 'my boye Jeames Bristo
wages', the amount not specified. In 1600 it was specified at three shillings
a week.[34] The highest figure of ten shillings a week or £20 in a good year
was probably the hiring rate for established players. How many such wages
were paid is the least clear figure in all these calculations. It must have varied
according to working conditions. My estimate would be for a minimum of
eight hired players at the top rate of ten shillings, and another eight at the
lower rates. That would set the average weekly wage bill at between £6 and
£7. In an average year in the 1590s the total expenditure on wages would
have approached £300.

As the Shakespeare company prospered, especially once the much greater
income from the Blackfriars strengthened its financial position,[35] the numbers it employed grew. In Henry Herbert's protection order for the company's attendants that he issued in December 1624 he wrote down twenty
names, including the book-keeper and musicians.[36] That included none
of the sharers. The acquisition of the Blackfriars in 1608 carried with it
the extra cost of the consort of musicians who were such a potent part
of that playhouse's charisma. We cannot tell exactly when the number of
attendants escalated from the ten we think were necessary at the Theatre

---

[32] *Henslowe's Diary*, p. 45.   [33] *Ibid.*, pp. 138, 268–9.   [34] *Ibid.*, pp. 118, 164.
[35] Under Charles, Henry Herbert's records of his benefit receipts from the Globe and Blackfriars show
him taking twice as much from winter days as from summer. See Irwin Smith, *Shakespeare's Blackfriars
Playhouse*, London, 1966, p. 263.
[36] The Order is quoted in Bentley, *Jacobean and Caroline Stage*, 1.15–16.

and the Globe at the turn of the century into the twenty listed in 1624, but the inclusion of the six or more musicians certainly post-dated the development of the company's capacity at the Blackfriars.

The cost of buying playbooks is one of the many dark sides of the Globe company's large polygon of expenditure. Henslowe ran teams of writers who received an average of £5 for each complete play. Antony Munday received that amount for 'a playe boocke called the firste parte of Robyne Hoode' (*The Downfall of Robert Earl of Huntington*) in full payment.[37] We must assume that the Chamberlain's paid a similar amount, though the surviving plays in their repertory do not give much sign of being produced collaboratively. Shakespeare as the in-house writer seems to have written solo-authored plays for the company during this period, as did Jonson, although Jonson did acknowledge help with *Sejanus*, 'wherein a second Pen had good share', not improbably from the in-house poet.[38] Tourneur (or Middleton) appears to have written *The Revenger's Tragedy* single-handed, as did Barnabe Barnes with *The Devil's Charter*. Few of the other writers of the earliest Chamberlain's company plays can be identified, nor whether they wrote in collaboration. In later years the authors of the plays in the so-called Beaumont and Fletcher canon routinely wrote in collaboration. By then the fee for writing a play had risen, though not by much more than double the early £5. Some of the gentlemanly authors in the 1630s such as John Suckling appear to have scorned payment altogether. In general, and particularly in the Chamberlain's years, Henslowe's standard price of £5 per play is not unreasonable. A significant part of the cost of writing was paper,[39] though again there is nothing to say who undertook it. The writer in *Shakespeare in Love* who so freely discarded the sheets on which he struggled to compose *Ethel the Pirate's Daughter* was not an Elizabethan.

For the cost of clothing, usually reckoned the greatest expense in portable property, certainly greater than the playbooks, we might note a sample of the *Diary*'s entries. Henslowe lent Martin Slater on 28 November 1596 'to by coper lace & frenge for the play of valteger' £3.5s (p. 49); he lent Robert Shaa on 26 November 1597 £4 to buy 8 yards of cloth of gold (p. 72, and p. 85 'for the womones gowne in bran howlte'), £1 to William Birde on

[37] *Henslowe's Diary*, p. 86.

[38] The case for Shakespeare as helper with *Sejanus* is made by Anne Barton, *Ben Jonson Dramatist*, Cambridge University Press, 1984, pp. 93–4.

[39] London's Chamber Accounts specify on 12 September 1585: '24 reams of writing paper bought of sundry persons at divers prices as by the journal appears five pounds eleven shillings and sixpence.' (*Chamber Accounts of the Sixteenth Century*, ed. Betty R. Masters, London Record Society for the Corporation of London, 1984, p. 82). That was 12,000 sheets of paper at about one penny for ten sheets. A play usually filled about thirty sheets.

24 February 1598 'for A wascotte wraght with sylke' (p. 75), and £4.13s.4d on 25 July 1598 'A sewte of satten for the playe of the made manes moris' (p. 94). A contextually revealing entry in 1596 was Henslowe's note of his outlay for his nephew John, son of his brother Edmund. It lists the basic cost of outfitting a young hopeful who was not a gentleman (he needed no sword), but who had to have respectable citizen clothing, two shirts, a hat, a cloak for bad weather, and the cost of altering them to fit him.

> layd owt for edmond henslowe sonne
> John Henslowe as foloweth 1596
> Itm bowght hime a clocke for . . . . xvijs
> Itm pd for mackenge of his aparell . . . . xxijd
> Itm lent hime to bye a hatte . . . . iiijs
> Itm bowght hime ij sheartes . . . . vs vjd
> some 28s 4d[40]

Clothing was the major visual feature in staging any play. Nonetheless, the company stock of stage clothing was limited. Historically accurate costuming was not an important requirement, and Henslowe's records along with the wills of several sharers indicate that players were generally expected to provide their own clothing. Only when the players had to play nobles or regal figures did the buying of expensive cloth come into the accounts. Special dress – Henslowe notes green cloth for the Robin Hood characters in Munday's two plays about the Earl of Huntingdon, and the gowns and hats for monks and cardinals were part of the company stock – was the main cost in the Henslowe inventories along with colourfully rich doublets and cloaks for the noble roles. Dress for the boys to play women was another major expense. The wife's gown for *A Woman Killed with Kindness* cost more than Heywood was paid for the play.

Properties were a less costly item. Unspecified costs along with the clothing noted above were listed for staging *Valteger*. A play like *The Jew of Malta*, with its notoriously complex carpentry and Barabas's cauldron in Act 5, required extra payments whenever it was revived. Henslowe noted 'Lent unto Robart shawe & mr. Jube the 19 of maye 1601 to bye divers thinges for the Jewe of malta the some of . . . £5 / lent mor to the littell tayller the same daye for more thinges for the Jewe of malta the some of . . . xs.' Altogether the properties for the play's revival cost £5.10s (p. 170). Stocks of weapons, swords, pikes, such special items as a wooden hatchet, possibly for on-stage executions, and various scenic properties also appear in the Henslowe inventories. Such items were available both for revivals and for reuse in new

---

[40] *Henslowe's Diary*, p. 77.

plays, as were the company costumes, which were always ready for the tireman to remake in fresh forms.[41]

And there were other costs, not least any copyists needed in addition to the book-keeper, and the printing of playbills. Poor relief paid to the local parish was an important softener of the attitudes of local authorities. The Middlesex authorities adopted various positions at different times, but a letter sent by 'the Inhabitants of Finsbury' to the Privy Council when the building of the Fortune was an issue shows their interest: 'the Erectors of the saied howse, are contented to give a very liberall porcion of money weekelie, towardes ye releef of our Poore, The nomber and necessity whereof, is soe great that the same will redounde to ye contynuall comfort of ye saied Poore'.[42] A similar acknowledgement was made by St Mary Overies in Southwark for payments by the Chamberlain's after 1599. These weekly payments appear to have amounted to roughly 6d per performance, or £5.10s in a good year, though the reference to the 'Erectors' of the Fortune suggests that these payments came from the playhouse owners, not their tenant company. Equally necessary were payments to the Master of the Revels for licensing the playhouse (a landlord expense) and the plays (a company expense). Tilney's legal action in 1604 claiming a lengthy failure to pay him by the Burbages may show them putting off some of the company's costs to a more affluent accounting period, but it does not mean such dues can be discounted.[43] To license a play cost £1, so the forty or so plays that Henslowe paid for in the late 1590s should have been matched by a similar Chamberlain's expenditure. When the demand for new plays shrank in the 1630s the size of payments to the Master of the Revels shrank too. Henslowe's records of his payments to the Master of the Revels suggest they were to license the playhouse, not a company outlay but the landlord's, i.e., housekeeper's. Judging by Tilney's action against the Burbages he was charging them for their playhouse, not the company's plays.

One of the two particularly heavy costs that came to the King's Men with the Blackfriars was illumination. The other cost was even heavier, but it brought some income too. Apart from the extra wage bill to the musicians and the need to apologize to the neighbourhood with poor relief and other sweeteners, the most substantial additional cost of the Blackfriars was its

---

[41] For the 'frippery' (second-hand clothing) element in theatre costumes, see Ann Rosalind Jones and Peter Stallybrass, *Renaissance Clothing and the Materials of Memory*, Cambridge University Press, 2000.

[42] Chambers, *Elizabethan Stage*, IV.328; *Henslowe's Diary*, p. 289.

[43] Mary Edmond, 'On licensing playhouses', *Review of English Studies* 46 (1995), 373–4. Tilney's relations with the Burbages were more businesslike than amiable. Much of his income came from his licensing fees, and in 1604 he sued first Cuthbert and secondarily Richard for arrears going back ten years.

Table 3.1

Rose Annual Income 1594–6		Rose Annual Expenditure 1597–9	
galleries	£672.00	rent (half galleries)	£336.00
yard	£600.00	plays	£150.00
court performances	£20.00	clothing	£150.00
other performances	£20.00	properties	£96.00
incidentals	£15.00	wages	£250.00
travelling	£20.00	licences	£50.00
sale of consumables	£30.00	poor relief	£5.00
		incidentals	£50.00
		sharer profit	£290.00
Total	£1,377.00	Total	£1,377.00

candles. Their price varied according to their quality. According to R. B. Graves,[44] in the 1630s tallow candles cost sixpence a pound and wax cost two shillings. The Salisbury Court hall playhouse, which was smaller than the Blackfriars, was said in 1639 to pay out four shillings a day for half the total illumination, plus another two for torches to light the candles. A daily charge of ten shillings would provide up to forty candles at six in the pound, capable of burning for two hours. Thus lighting the Blackfriars added at least ten shillings a day to the winter running costs.

The other cost came with the Blackfriars but ran for all the year: the music. The musicians were a special category of helper, who could operate for hire independently, but as soon as plays like *The Tempest* that demanded off-stage music entered the repertory, they became a regular addition to the wage bill. As employees, of course, their being hired out could also enhance the company income. They were used at the Globe, since it seems to have been equipped with a musicians' gallery after 1608,[45] but they must also have been frequently available for hire, particularly in the evenings.

In total, then, using Henslowe's figures as the basis for calculating running costs, and adding a wholly hypothetical sum for the profits to the company from sales of food and drink that are so notably absent from Henslowe's accounts, the major components of the Admiral's income and expenditure at the Rose in the first duopoly years might be set out in table 3.1. From this rough attempt to balance the books over two distinct

[44] *Lighting the Shakespearean Stage 1567–1642*, Southern Illinois University Press, Carbondale, 1999, chapter 8, especially pp. 183–7.
[45] See Richard Hosley, 'Was there a Music-Room in Shakespeare's Globe?', *Shakespeare Survey* 13 (1960), 113–23.

periods, one based on Henslowe's figures for his rents and the other based on his expenditure for the company, it appears that the Admiral's company turnover brought the sharers little more than £35 each in a year. That seems minimal, though well ahead of a hired man's takings. Certainly it was not quite enough to warrant valuing a share at £50. But it was still a lot more than Dekker got as a writer for the company.

Comparable tables of income and expenditure for the Chamberlain's and King's Men in the different periods of their operation are much more conjectural. The income from a Chamberlain's share for instance became complicated when shares in the Globe were added to some of the company shares in 1599. At first this had no impact. But by 1635 when there were twelve company sharers the housekeeping shares were in fewer hands, not all belonging to the company sharers because they had passed down by inheritance as property. This process meant that several of the playhouse shares, including the Burbage family half, no longer belonged to the company sharers. That led to management complications, and the issues that were set out in the 'Sharers' Papers', although that dispute was chiefly motivated by the fact that housekeeper shares were much more profitable than company shares. The accounts of the housekeepers are in a number of ways a business distinct from the company accounts, and are dealt with in a separate section below.

So here are some rather hypothetical accounts for the company so far as they can be reconstructed for the whole period of their existence, separated into distinct phases of fairly homogeneous costs between May 1594 and September 1642. Each table tries to present the balance from a sample year with a fairly good run of performances. These are usually calculated as over 220 in the year, with no plague closures. In general the tables ignore the worst effects of the plague, which brought complete closures in London over at least these periods: 22 July–27 October 1596, 19 March 1603–9 April 1604, 5 October–15 December 1605, short periods in 1606 and 1607, July 1608–December 1609, periods in 1610, 1611, 1612, and 1613, 24 May–24 November 1625, 8 July–28 November 1630, 12 May 1636–2 October 1637, 23 July–29 October 1640, and 15 July–9 December 1641.[46] Such closures meant an almost complete loss of company income, and a smaller saving in expenditure on rent and wages. The company's compensation from the king to sustain them through these periods (see Appendix 2.21) has not been included in the annual accounts. The intention is to provide an averaged

---

46 A more detailed account of the plague closures is given in Gurr, *The Shakespearian Playing Companies*, 1996, pp. 87–92. They are less extensive than those calculated by J. Leeds Barroll.

Table 3.2

Average Annual Income 1594–7		Average Annual Expenditure 1594–7	
galleries	£750.00	rent (half galleries)	£375.00
yard	£770.00	plays	£260.00
court performances	£50.00	clothing	£300.00
other performances	£80.00	wages	£300.00
incidentals	£15.00	licences	£50.00
travelling	£30.00	poor relief	£10.00
sale of consumables	£35.00	sharer profit	£435.00
Total	£1,730.00	Total	£1,730.00

Table 3.3

Average Annual Income 1603–8		Average Annual Expenditure 1603–8	
galleries	£800.00	rent	£400.00
yard	£850.00	plays	£250.00
court performances	£50.00	clothing	£250.00
other performances	£120.00	wages	£300.00
incidentals	£40.00	licences	£50.00
travelling	£30.00	poor relief	£10.00
sale of consumables	£35.00	sharer profit	£665.00
Total	£1,925.00	Total	£1,925.00

set of annual income and expenditure figures, taking no direct account of the losses from the plague closures.

In table 3.2, the first period of the Chamberlain's company accounts roughly matches the Rose company's expenditure and income given in table 3.1, with the income inflated to allow for the Theatre's greater auditorium capacity. These are all hypothetical figures based on the analogous totals at the Rose. They indicate a level of annual income for the eight sharers that matches the Admiral's valuation of a share at £50.

The period in table 3.3 offers an average annual turnover for the King's Men during the Globe years, 1603–8. The table of income allows for increased takings as the company's status rose. For five of the sharers who became housekeepers in 1599 the total annual income would have been over £60 for the company share and £80 from the playhouse rents, less the housekeeping costs.

Table 3.4

Average Annual Income 1610–15		Average Annual Expenditure 1610–15	
galleries, stage door (for stools)	£1,100.00	rent	£735.00
		plays	£350.00
yard and pit	£1,200.00	clothing	£300.00
court performances	£180.00	wages, musicians	£450.00
other performances	£50.00	licences	£60.00
sale of consumables	£40.00	poor relief	£5.00
		candles etc.	£130.00
		sharers	£540.00
Total	£2,570.00	Total	£2,570.00

The list in table 3.4 of the average annual income and expenditure (estimated) for the six years 1610–15 begins after the acquisition of the Blackfriars. The income from the two playhouses is grouped together, and the increase reflects the greater takings from the indoor playhouse. It does not reflect the long delay because of plague from 1608 to late 1609 in opening the Blackfriars, nor the extra income that came from the Blackfriars while the Globe was being rebuilt. The figures also ignore the occasional income that might have come from renting the Globe or the Blackfriars for use out of season, since such income would have gone to the housekeepers, not the company sharers. The principal change is the likely increase in rental costs with the two playhouses. While the housekeepers only received their half of the gallery takings from performances, which were halved at each playhouse, probably they took a retainer of some kind to keep the unused one free while the other was occupied. I have guessed that retainer at an additional one-third of the normal rent.

Table 3.5 gives the likely average annual income and expenditure (estimate) for the three years 1616–19. Court records for this period are deficient, and it was the first time that the Blackfriars had competition from the Cockpit. But it was also the time when the Master of the Revels stopped taking any plays from the open-air playhouses for performance at court. Consequently these estimates are even more conjectural than the others.

Table 3.6 gives average annual income and expenditure (estimate) for the six years 1619–25. This ignores the closure of 1619 in mourning for Queen Anne, and the onset of the enormous plague epidemic in 1625, when all the companies were barred from playing in London or, uniquely, anywhere

Table 3.5

Average Annual Income 1616–19		Average Annual Expenditure 1616–19	
galleries and boxes	£1,100.00	rent	£735.00
yard and pit	£1,250.00	plays	£340.00
court performances	£180.00	clothing	£400.00
other performances	£80.00	wages, musicians	£460.00
sale of consumables	£40.00	licences	£50.00
		poor relief	£5.00
		candles etc.	£120.00
		sharers	£540.00
Total	£2,650.00	Total	£2,650.00

Table 3.6

Average Annual Income 1619–25		Average Annual Expenditure 1619–25	
galleries	£1,200.00	rent	£700.00
yard and pit	£1,380.00	plays	£400.00
court performances	£90.00	clothing	£420.00
other performances	£70.00	wages, musicians	£450.00
sale of consumables	£40.00	licences	£60.00
		poor relief	£5.00
		candles etc.	£120.00
		sharers	£625.00
Total	£2,780.00	Total	£2,780.00

else in the whole country, for more than six months. The 1625 closure, and the change of royal patrons, ensured the collapse of all playing companies other than the King's.

Table 3.7 shows average annual income and expenditure (estimate) for the sixteen years 1626–42. While covering nearly three times the period of any other table, these figures are rather more reliable, chiefly because of the detailed evidence from the 'Sharers' Papers'. They make, however, no allowance for royal *ex gratia* payments during the long plague closure in 1636–7. The figure for expenditure on plays is only marginally reduced because although the number of plays bought shrank, the price paid for them must have risen substantially. The figure for the income of the twelve sharers, compared with the statement in the 'Sharers' Papers' that the daily take

Table 3.7

Average Annual Income 1626–42		Average Annual Expenditure 1626–42	
galleries	£1,300.00	rent	£870.00
yard and pit	£1,570.00	plays	£320.00
court performances	£90.00	clothing	£460.00
other performances	£90.00	wages, musicians	£450.00
sale of consumables	£40.00	licences	£60.00
		poor relief	£10.00
		candles etc.	£130.00
		sharers	£790.00
Total	£3,090.00	Total	£3,090.00

per share was approximately three shillings, suggests that the real amount was nearly 40 per cent higher.

The 'Sharers' Papers' argue that costs in 1635, for playscripts, licensing fees, wages for hired men, musicians, stage keepers, book-keeper and gatherers, plus the boys, ran to £3 for each performance day, which would have made a total of about £700 in that year. That is noticeably less than the £830 estimated in table 3.7. Costumes would have been a large additional item, depending on how much of the cost was paid by individuals for themselves or by the company as a collective expense. If anything, these figures underestimate the total left to be divided amongst the sharers. Income from the court grew to £270 in 1633, including £10 for the company's overnight board and lodging for four plays at Hampton Court, and another £10 for rehearsing a play in the afternoon and thus losing a day's takings at Blackfriars (Appendix 2.37).

HOUSEKEEPER FINANCES

It makes sense to follow the designation that Chambers invented,[47] making the holders of shares in the company the 'sharers', and the holders of shares in the playhouses the 'housekeepers'. The first 'housekeepers' were the two Burbage sons, when Cuthbert inherited the Globe and Richard the Blackfriars, although for business purposes they seem to have treated

---

[47] In *The Elizabethan Stage*, 1.357, Chambers states that the playhouse owners 'came to be called' housekeepers. The term first appeared in the 'Sharers' Papers', but was actually his own useful designation to differentiate the sharers who were landlords from those with shares in the company. T. W. Baldwin's study of the housekeepers in *The Organisation and Personnel of the Shakespearean Company* is often confusing when he calls them both 'sharers'.

the two playhouses as a joint possession. In February 1599 they brought in five of the player–sharers, each of whom put up £100 to help pay for the reconstruction of the old Theatre's timbers and fittings on Bankside and to complete the painting and decoration of the new playhouse. The bulk of the Burbages' contribution to the costs was the old framing timbers and all the fittings from the Theatre, while the £500 from the players paid for the builder's work and the new paint. From then on the seven housekeepers doubled the roles of impresario–playhouse-landlord and player–tenant.

The Burbages extended this new sharing-housekeeper principle when the Blackfriars was returned to them in 1608. In what might well be lauded as an unprecedented act of generosity and fellowship the brothers allocated housekeeper shares in the Blackfriars on the same basis as the Globe shares. No money was involved, so it was a free gift, an acknowledgement of the success of the system devised in 1599. In practice it was a gift that made it possible to run both playhouses seasonally. Allocating shares in the Blackfriars to the Globe housekeepers meant that their level of income could be sustained, half the year's rent coming from each playhouse instead of a full year's from only the one. It was not an act of simple-minded generosity. Cuthbert Burbage later said the other housekeepers got their shares in the Blackfriars 'of us for nothing', but the larger agreement, to run the two playhouses in tandem, made the hand-out inevitable.

When the company set out its plan to build the Globe for itself early in 1599 a precise majority of the company's eight sharers put up the money to become housekeepers. Richard Burbage and his brother, and the players Heminges, Shakespeare, Pope, Phillips, and, for a short time, Kemp became the seven housekeeper–sharers. Whether the incoming five were thought to be enough to provide the cash needed for the building, or – the more durable factor – whether adding five more to Richard Burbage as a sharer was thought necessary to create a majority of company sharers, we cannot say. Probably they had both considerations in mind. Bringing in the other sharing players may have been an act of desperation because the Burbages lacked any other source of capital. Yet it certainly served the company's collective interest, and may well have been seen as an ingenious as well as a generous act of mutual self-help. When Kemp divided his holding between the other four non-Burbage housekeepers the six housekeepers still provided a clear majority for company management and decision-making. The new team of housekeepers became the company's capital-holders and financiers.

It was the housekeepers who paid for the playhouse's upkeep and renovations. All founder-sharers in the company since 1594, they must have had in their minds the alternating summer and winter playing-places that Henry Carey wrote the Lord Mayor about in 1594. The six may even have been identified as possible housekeepers because they were the sharers who most warmly supported the idea. They certainly did agree to underwrite the launch of Blackfriars as the second venue in 1608, which finally achieved the plan for seasonal playing-places broached in 1594, and they provided the capital for the Globe's rebuilding in 1614 (Appendix 2.23) which maintained the practice.[48]

On 9 August 1608 Richard Burbage divided the title to the Blackfriars between seven men. Richard and Cuthbert held two shares each, a smaller proportion than they had of the Globe (Appendix 2.20). Phillips and Pope had both died, Pope at the end of 1603 and Phillips in 1605. Their shares in the Globe had gone to Sly and Condell. So to Heminges and Shakespeare, the other survivors from the original housekeepers, the new contract added Sly and Condell as Blackfriars housekeepers. A seventh share went to Thomas Evans, an outside financier, probably kin to or even the same man as the Henry Evans who had leased the Blackfriars in 1600 for the boy company. Sly died while the deal was being completed, so at the final count in 1609 the Blackfriars housekeepers were six, four of them players, with Cuthbert Burbage a fifth, the same number as owned the Globe. There was some subsequent redistribution of the shares, Heminges and Condell taking Sly's portion, and in February 1612 another player, William Ostler, came in as a seventh housekeeper. Later allocations are noted elsewhere. The principle that a majority of the landlords should be company players was always the vital basis for the arrangement.

John Shanks's dispute with the three younger company sharers in 1635 over his acquisition of housekeeper shares, set out in Appendix 3, has a lot to say about the level of profit that could be expected from them. Income from the playhouse rent was markedly higher than the income from a company share. A petition by the Blackfriars residents in 1631 had evoked some remarkable claims about the value of the playhouse. When the question of buying the housekeepers out came up they said it was worth £21,000, whereas the Privy Council's official valuation, which presumably took no

---

[48] T. W. Baldwin has a table listing all the known housekeepers from 1598 (i.e., the initial agreement over the Globe) to 1642, with the succession of their shares, in *Organisation and Personnel*, p. 111. It is slightly speculative, but it does give a general overview of the sequence of property ownership. The various livery allowances made after 1603 once the king became their patron always named twelve men (see *Historic Manuscripts Commission*, Report IV, Part 1, p. 299), but they do not all seem to be sharers.

account of its expected profitability, rated it at £3,000.[49] The Blackfriars residents could not put together even a thirtieth of the lower valuation. By the time of the Shanks dispute the Blackfriars had been running in partnership with the Globe for twenty-seven years. In the course of that time the difference between shares in the two buildings and shares in the playing company had led to a divergence between the players and the property-holders. In his will, Shanks claimed to have purchased one-quarter of the Blackfriars lease and three-eighths of the Globe.[50] As a company sharer he was entitled to do so, and in fact his purchase meant that a player was reclaiming his shares from some non-playing housekeepers. It is probably true to say that Swanston and the other protesters were looking to extend the company sharer as housekeeper principle for their own profit rather than to renew the shaky equilibrium of the company's management system.

Unlike the sharer accounts, some parts of the housekeeper finances are quite well documented. The Globe's housekeepers appear to have maintained consistently the tradition Henslowe followed from before 1594, that the playhouse rent should be half the takings from the galleries. The Cuthbert Burbage counter-petition in the Sharers' Papers confirms that such a share was standard for the Globe when it specified 'halfe the Galleries from the Houskeepers'. An equivalent proportion was taken from the Blackfriars. This housekeeper income included the prices paid by the richest customers, who occupied the boxes at the Blackfriars and entered the Globe by the 'tireing house dore' to get into the lords' rooms.

The actual scale of the profits from the landlord function is speculative, since it depends on estimates of company takings, but it was always regarded as substantial, however fanciful some of the claims in the legal testimonies may be. John Witter, the second husband of Augustine Phillips's widow, claimed in 1619 that the housekeepers' annual rental income from the Globe was about £500 before the fire of 1613, and more after, and that the Blackfriars brought in £140 in 1615 but over £700 by 1619.[51] £500 a year divided among the initial eight housekeepers would have given Shakespeare more than he got from his company share. Once they had the two playhouses, the housekeepers could also take the rent from occasional lettings of the vacant house, as they did from a Dutch tumbler for his use of the

[49] Since the Blackfriars residents could not raise more than £100 towards the price, all the Privy Council bothered to do, in 1633 when the issue had to be settled, was to issue an order about the overcrowding caused by playhouse traffic. See Appendix 2.40.

[50] *Playhouse Wills*, p. 188.

[51] See C. W. Wallace, 'Shakespeare and his London Associates', *University of Nebraska Studies* 10 (1910), 47–76.

Globe in 1630 and 1635.[52] Baldwin claims that the housekeeper income was more than three times that of the company sharers, an estimate based on the sharers' complaint that the housekeepers took home 12 shillings from each performance in 1635 while the sharers took only three. This ignores the much larger number of company men among whom the takings were divided, and the fact that by then most of the housekeepers had multiple shares in both playhouses. It also ignores the housekeeper outgoings. The income per share from the Blackfriars was higher than from the Globe, but the housekeeper totals matched those of the company sharers in their seasonality. In rough terms, income from a single share in the playhouses does not seem to have been very much bigger than that of a sharer in the company from 1610 onwards.

We do know that by the end of 1598 five of the company sharers could afford to put up or were confident enough to borrow £100 each to help build the Globe. From table 3.2 we can assume an annual sharer income of about £50 per year up to then, while the usual cost of living for an ordinary family would probably have been less than £20, so it was quite possible for the five to have amassed at least that amount by 1599. That gives us a clear indication of the level of their current income as well as their confidence in the company enterprise. After the 1599 decision, assuming that a company sharer like John Heminges maintained a similar level of profit from his company share, we can make a rough calculation of how much his likely income from his housekeeper share in the Globe added to his takings. Together the two would have brought him, in all, close to £180 a year. Once the Blackfriars started to bring in a higher level of housekeeper income he probably made more than £200. Up to 1613 Shakespeare was probably making a similar amount.

On the debit side, the housekeepers were responsible for all playhouse maintenance and rents, and the legal costs that went with their ownership of property, a more tangible and therefore litigious matter than a company share. The yearly rent for each of the two plots of the Globe site was £7.15s, an annual debit of £15.10s a year. That compares closely with James Burbage's rent for the Theatre's land, which was £14 a year. The Blackfriars costs were markedly higher, though we have no exact figures. Those were the least of the recurrent housekeeper expenses. Other charges were for maintenance of the sites in the interests of the parish at large. In February 1606, for instance, the Sewer Commission ordered the Globe's

---

[52] Herbert noted (Bentley, *Jacobean and Caroline Stage*, VI.194): 'Reced of Mr Lowins for allowinge of a Dutch vaulter att their house 18 Feb: 1630'. Bawcutt's edition of Herbert (p. 192) also records 'From the Dutchman . . . at ye Globe by Blagrave 16th March 1634.– 2li'.

housekeepers to repair 132 feet of the wharf beside the playhouse, and to remove a set of posts driven into the ditch under the bridge on the other side of the lane from the Globe. A Buildings Return of 1634 (LMA P.92/SAV/1326 f.3 and /1327 f.4), states that the Globe land's rent was worth between £14 and £29 a year, and the adjoining house £4. A lengthy lawsuit between the players and the landowner Matthew Brend that ran in the Court of Requests for several years from 1632 eventually led to an increase in the rent from £15.10s a year to £40.[53] On the other hand, part of the Globe land was rented out, bringing in £6 a year of income. The house was occupied by a tenant, William Millet, gentleman, who paid his rent to the housekeepers. He rather than Heminges may have been the man handling provision of food and drink for the playgoers, though I think that unlikely in view of Heminges's work as tapster and Millet's status as a gentleman.

The housekeepers on occasions also had not inconsiderable legal and administrative costs. John Atkins, the company's longserving scrivener (Heminges's son-in-law), and the lawyers employed for the Brend lawsuit at the Court of Requests in 1632–5, must have generated substantial costs to the housekeepers.[54] Nonetheless, income from the housekeeping shares was the chief reason why John Heminges in particular was acknowledged to be the company's patriarch, and why his family's affluence became such a matter for envy in the 1630s.

The superior income expected from the housekeeping shares influenced Ben Jonson, I believe, when he wrote *The Alchemist* as one of the first plays staged at the Blackfriars in 1610 after the long closure for plague. The play is set in a house 'here at the Friers', occupied by a set of would-be thieves. The rogues Face, Subtle, and Doll are play-actors who for all their plots and deceptions end the play no better off than they were at the start. They fill the play with their tricks and disguises to beguile the gulls of their money when they come to the house in the hope of making their own gains. The gulls represent the gamut of social types in the Blackfriars, a mirror of the theatre audience. The only character who succeeds in acquiring all their pelf at the end is the housekeeper, Lovewit. I have proposed elsewhere that Jonson was renewing his semi-private wit-combats with Shakespeare, evident from the other side in *The Winter's Tale*'s reference to the artist Giulio Romano, and in *The Alchemist*'s matching magus-tale, *The Tempest*. I suspect Jonson applied the winning Lovewit to Shakespeare because he had become a housekeeper of the new Blackfriars. Jonson saw the housekeepers as the

[53] Herbert Berry, *Shakespeare's Playhouses*, AMS Press, New York, 1987, p. 155.
[54] John Atkins is not listed in Appendix 1 as a company employee because he was a Heminges man, and seems to have served as scrivener to the housekeepers, not the players.

affluent idlers who profiteered from the tricks the players entertained their customers with.[55] That was when the Blackfriars venture was still on its first tack as a new voyage for the company, and Jonson could only have been guessing about the relative profitability of the two kinds of share. The fact that the testimonies from 1634–5 in the 'Sharers' Papers' argue that the income for a housekeeper had improved to nearly three times that of a sharer as player suggests that Jonson's gambit was well chosen.[56]

These financial calculations, like those composing the company accounts, are at best approximate, and at worst almost completely speculative. It might be worth noting, moreover, that some individuals such as Heminges, who occupied both kinds of sharer role, stand in a particularly shady area in the company finances. His honesty was always respected, but his control of company finances up to his death in 1630 gave him an unprecedented command of the more marginal sources of income. In the absence of any figures we cannot tell whether his function as tapster, for instance, brought in income profitable for him personally, or as a representative of the company sharers, or as a housekeeper. Henslowe made no entries in his *Diary* about food and drink either as landlord or as company manager and financier. Apart from the 'Sharers' Papers' (see p. 274), there is nothing to say who the concessions held by the sellers of food and drink in the playhouses profited. It would most logically have been a profit to the housekeepers, but that only makes it more strange that Henslowe's *Diary*, mostly a housekeeper's record, makes no mention of any such income. That is why the conjectural accounts tabled above award the pedlar profits to the company.

After the housekeepers acquired shares in the Blackfriars playhouse, the Henslowe-based analysis of their accounts goes haywire. It was a risky venture. The boy companies had performed much less frequently through the week than the adults, and local objections to the newcomers were inevitable, though in the event they were not openly renewed until 1619. The risks to the company and the housekeepers were largely financial, and they bore the weight of what might be considered the management's single most arrogant decision, choosing to leave one playhouse empty while they played at the other, according to the season. The Globe was rented out in winter occasionally for shows like the Dutch acrobat's, but that brought income

[55] See Gurr, 'Who is Lovewit? What is He?' in *Ben Jonson and Theatre*, ed. Richard Allen Cave and Brian Woolland, Routledge, London, 1999, pp. 5–19. For an adroit comparison of *The Tempest* with *The Alchemist*, see Harry Levin, 'Two Magian Comedies: *The Tempest* and *The Alchemist*', *Shakespeare Survey* 22 (1971), 47–58.

[56] Conversely, Cuthbert Burbage claimed that the sharer income had risen in 1635 to £180 a year, more than that of a Blackfriars housekeeper (Appendix 2.43). But he was making a defensive point, and ignoring the duality of housekeeper income.

to the housekeepers as playhouse owners, not the company. Presumably the housekeepers used the empty period at each playhouse for recurrent maintenance. The expenses of repairing and repainting the playhouses were debited to the housekeepers against the rents the company paid them, so they make no appearance in the company's own accounts. But they cannot have been large compared with the incomings. Repainting, especially of the gilded decorations and the posts 'wroughte palasterwise', together with the carved figures (whatever the Globe and Blackfriars had that was equivalent to the Fortune contract's 'carved proporcions called Satiers'),[57] and repairs to the carpentry and plasterwork would have been a constant need. On the other hand, such work was neither major nor very time-consuming. The six months each house stood empty was the time it took to completely build the Fortune and probably the Globe. To keep one playhouse constantly empty was in its way the supreme expression of company, and especially housekeeper, domination, even arrogance. It makes a sharp comment on the company's rise above and beyond what John Cocke in 1614 called the 'brotherhood' of players, that they never let any other company use whichever of their two venues was idle.

The role of the Chamberlain's sharers as team-leaders did of course become more complicated when a majority of the company sharers became housekeepers. It was undoubtedly the housekeeper–sharers who held the reins, and the other company sharers, while eager to climb to the level where they could get the additional profits, must have felt themselves underrated. For most of the first thirty years the new management system with its built-in majorities gave no trouble. But by 1635, with twelve company sharers, the housekeeping shares had shifted into fewer hands through inheritance and purchase, so the division became one of loyalties as well as finance. The playhouses were material assets, not notional valuations like company shares, and they could be passed on either by direct sale or by inheritance. By the 1630s a good proportion of the playhouse shares no longer belonged to the company sharers. That, and the desire of three company sharers to join their two leaders and Shanks in holding shares in the playhouses, was the cause of the 'Sharers' Papers' dispute. Except as a symptom of the profitability of the playhouse-owning end of the enterprise, it had no direct impact on company finances, but what it does confirm is not only an incipient jealousy between the players and their landlords but that to be a housekeeper–landlord was a better source of profit than to be a company sharer. There were fewer housekeepers sharing the profits,

---

[57] See Henslowe's contract for the Fortune, Chambers, *Elizabethan Stage*, ii.437.

and they had much smaller outgoings, even though they had to continue spending on the buildings when plague stopped their source of income. A complaint about the 1642 closure, issued as a pamphlet by the players in 1643, lists the losses not just of the players themselves but of their helpers the door-keepers or gatherers, the boys whose voices were cracking, the clowns, the musicians, tiremen, tobacco-sellers, and poets. But it starts the list of their losses with

first, our Housekeepers, that grew wealthy by our endeavours, complain that they are forced to pay the ground Landlords rents, during this long Vacation, out of their former gettings; instead of ten, twenty, nay thirty shilling shares, which used nightly to adorn and comfort with their harmonious music, their large and well-stuffed pockets, they have shares in nothing with us now but our misfortunes; living merely out of the stock, out of the interest and principal of their former forgotten monies, which daily is exhausted by the maintenance of themselves and their families.[58]

The familiar echoes there of the 'Sharers' Papers' suggest that one of the authors of the complaint was an unemployed King's man, conceivably even a rentless sharer–housekeeper.

[58] THE ACTORS REMONSTRANCE, OR COMPLAINT: FOR The silencing of their profession, and banishment from their severall **Play-houses**, London, 1643.

CHAPTER 4

'Workes are playes': the public repertory

PRIMARY ASSETS

The plays that are the concern of these last three chapters are limited in value because almost all of them exist only in translated forms, for reading, not the scripts the company acted. The written word, the predominant form of record for all early history, is itself a translation not just of the writer's thinking but of the complex processes it tries to record. Playscripts register only a small portion of the whole event involved in staging a play. The words are skeletal, either a pre-script or a residue of the stage action. Words can be delusory. They freeze a moment out of what is invariably a transient and flexible event. Centuries of habituation to the written word have conditioned us to conceive as fixity what is really flux. Words are what Peter Blayney, a student of the printed word who has worked in theatre, has called only the 'raw material' from which the play is staged.[1] Most of the 168 play-texts which give us our only access to the company's repertory stand at a disconcertingly remote distance from the staged events we all too comfortably expect them to record. They are records of what the writers thought the company's audiences would want, rather than the scripts the company actually performed.

The latest editors of the Shakespeare company writer John Webster take care to distinguish the 'poem', as Webster's dedication names the printed text of his *Duchess of Malfi*, from the 'play', the staged text. It is a distinction worth bearing in mind, given the substantial number of the printed plays in the company repertory that were designed to offer a poem rather than a play-script. Not many of Shakespeare's plays may have survived as poems, yet sadly they are not reliable play-scripts either. They do give us the story, but they are not very reliable evidence for how it was staged.

---

[1] 'The author's final draft is essentially only the raw material for performance.' Introduction to *The First Folio of Shakespeare: The Norton Facsimile*, second edition, 1996, p. xxx.

The surviving repertory includes nineteen extant play-manuscripts.[2] At least two of these (*Believe As You List* and *The Swisser*) are in the author's own hand, and a dozen or more are scribal copies made for presentation. Special cases like *A Game at Chess* and *The Royal Slave* survive in several presentation copies, one of the latter made for King Charles, as was the manuscript of *Aglaura*. These and others, *Bonduca*, *The Witch*, *Barnavelt* (a scribal copy made after the Master, George Buc, had censored it), *The Humorous Lieutenant*, *The Tamer Tamed*, *Hengist*, *The Beggar's Bush* (transcribed by the same hand as *Aglaura*), *The Elder Brother*, *The Soddered Citizen*, *The Inconstant Lady*, *The Country Captain*, and *The Court Secret* survive in one or more copies made for reading. Several of them, including *A Game at Chess*, *The Humorous Lieutenant*, *The Witch*, and *Barnavelt*, were copied by the company's regular scribe of the 1620s, Ralph Crane, who transcribed the first Shakespeare plays printed in the 1623 Folio. Others were made by a company book-keeper known as 'Jhon'. In the early 1620s the book-keeper Edward Knight retranscribed two worn Fletcher manuscripts, *Bonduca* and *The Honest Man's Fortune*, the first for presentation and the second to be 'reallowed', copied from what he called Fletcher's 'fowle papers'. The same scribal hand copied *The Court Secret* and *The Country Captain* in the late 1630s or 1640. Some of the manuscripts, notably *Hengist* and *The Court Secret*, have quite substantial variations from their printed versions.

Most of the scribal manuscripts, including several made by the company book-keepers, were made to be read. They were not stage scripts. Almost none of the essential repertory of 'allowed books' have survived, so the deficiencies of the printed texts apply to most of the company's play manuscripts too. The scribal transcripts are mostly versions of the writer's text designed for private study, and therefore remote from the central interest of this book, on the 'poem' rather than the 'play' side of the textual divide. Most of them, notably *Bonduca*, were less carefully copied than the

---

[2] In alphabetical order the plays in manuscript are *Aglaura* (printed 1638), *The Beggar's Bush* (printed in 1647 Folio), *Believe As You List* (1631: not printed), *Bonduca* (printed in 1647 Folio), *The Country Captain* (printed 1649), *The Court Secret* (printed 1653), *The Elder Brother* (printed 1637), *A Game at Chess* (printed 1625), *Hengist, or the Mayor of Quinborough* (1619?: printed 1661), *The Honest Man's Fortune* (printed in 1647 Folio), *The Humorous Lieutenant* (printed in 1647 Folio), *The Inconstant Lady* (1630: not printed), *The Royal Slave* (printed 1639), *The Second Maiden's Tragedy* (1611: not printed), *Sir John Van Olden Barnavelt* (1619: not printed), *The Soddered Citizen* (1630: not printed), *The Swisser* (1631: not printed), *The Witch* (1615?: not printed), and *The Woman's Prize, or The Tamer Tamed* (printed in the 1647 Folio). The locations of these manuscripts are given in Appendix 5. A case might be made for *The Faithful Friends* as another unprinted company manuscript with book-keeper's markings. It is MS. Dyce 10 in the Victoria and Albert Museum. The only reason for thinking it a company play, however, is that a publisher entered it in the Stationers' Register in 1660 as by Beaumont and Fletcher. Its markings include no indications that it was a King's play.

printed versions.[3] Cartwright's *The Royal Slave*, written for staging before royalty at Oxford and only subsequently and reluctantly given to the professionals at Blackfriars at Henrietta Maria's insistence, survives in at least six presentation copies for reading. Middleton's *Game at Chess* also survives in several copies, including two by its author. Shirley's *The Court Secret* may be in the author's hand with modifications by later users.

By far the most notable, because they show what the company was used to doing with its writer's work, are the two surviving 'allowed books' authorized on their last pages by the Master of the Revels: *The Second Maiden's Tragedy* and *Believe As You List*. *The Honest Man's Fortune* is a copy made for the King's from an earlier version and allowed as a fresh transcript. Judging by the players named in it and the manuscript title page it was a Fletcher play originally allowed in 1613 that the King's acquired some years later from its first company, the Lady Elizabeth's. Knight transcribed the old manuscript for Herbert to 'reallow' on 8 February 1625. The manuscript corrects some slips made in the 1647 Folio version, simplifies the language, makes a number of cuts, some of them probably by Herbert as censor, omits one scene from the last act and alters the conclusion.

Besides showing what the censor's concerns were, these three 'allowed books' affirm the truth of Charles Sisson's view that 'a dramatist's copy was . . . anything but sacred to the stage-adapter'.[4] They show the censor's work, but more importantly they show the book-keeper's hand not only adjusting the stage notes, as we would expect, but polishing the text. The manuscript of *Believe As You List* shows Massinger even after fifteen or more years of writing for the company still producing playbooks that needed a lot of changes to ready them for staging. The book-keeper relocated every entry three or four lines before their placing by Massinger, who usually put them where a new entrant first speaks. The book-keeper, Edward Knight, was marking up for the large Globe stage, where it took that number of lines before an entrant could reach centre-stage. He marked act breaks and scenes, noting that two of the interacts should be 'long', perhaps a sign that a more modern concept of interval was creeping into playhouse practice by 1631. He also corrected several textual slips, and added a list of the few properties, chiefly papers and letters, though intriguingly his list omits the 'great booke of Accomptes' which his textual note says should

---

[3] For a careful analysis of the Beaumont and Fletcher manuscripts, see R. C. Bald, *Bibliographical Studies in the Beaumont and Fletcher Folio of 1647*, Supplement to the Bibliographical Society's *Transactions* No. 13, Oxford University Press, 1938, pp. 50–65.

[4] *Believe As You List*, Malone Society Reprints, Oxford University Press, 1927, p. xxvi.

be 'ready' at line 982, and which the Malone Society editor suggests was the company's own account book.[5] *The Second Maiden's Tragedy*, a scribal copy, has additions by the book-keeper, who inserted Robert Gough's and Richard Robinson's names. *Believe As You List* has a total of less than 2,900 lines, and *The Second Maiden's Tragedy* has 2,450, if we include the numerous additions on slips pasted into the copy. These lengths affirm the likelihood that 2,500 was close to maximal for a play-script, and that plays of greater length were still routinely cut for performance. Even in 1635 the Prologue to *Love's Pilgrimage* speaks of 'A good tale, / Told in two hours'. If to this we add the earlier evidence of the quarto *Henry V*, where the company whittled down the 3,400 lines of the author's text to a streamlined 1,700, revising and rewriting to accommodate the many cuts, it is obvious that the company did expect their writers to provide no more than Blayney's 'raw material'. Apart from the three 'allowed books', we have to do some strenuous imagining to identify the finished products from the other 165 cases of raw material.

The 'allowed book' was taken seriously by everyone in the business. It licensed whatever was authorised to be spoken on stage. In the Caroline period Henry Herbert is several times on record as taking a half-fee to license the addition of single scenes or acts to an already approved book. Our tragedy is that so few of these company-authorized texts have survived. A compensation of sorts could be that some of the 'allowed books' may have reached the press after the closure, when they no longer had any value for performance. One play printed in 1657, sadly not a King's Men product, actually reproduced the Master's licence at the end.[6] R. C. Bald's analysis of the plays in the Beaumont and Fletcher Folio of 1647 led him to conclude that as many as twelve have book-keeper's markings such as '*ready*' for properties well before they are needed on stage (one in 4.6 of *The Spanish Curate* specifies '*Pewter ready for noyse*'). Like *Believe As You List*, the twelve texts mark the acts but not scenes. Four, *The Mad Lover*, *The Coxcomb*, *The Chances*, and *Love's Pilgrimage*, name King's Men players. In addition perhaps twenty-two of the plays that did not come into print until after the closure of 1642 had removed the special value of the 'allowed' manuscripts might have been set from them. So it is possible that up to thirty-seven plays might survive in versions with 'allowed book' markings.[7]

[5] Charles J. Sisson, *ibid.*, p. xxv.
[6] The Red Bull's *Walks of Islington and Hogsdon*. See Bentley, *Jacobean and Caroline Stage*, IV.688–90.
[7] Bald analyses the most likely signs of what he calls prompt copies in *Bibliographical Studies in the Beaumont and Fletcher Folio of 1647*, pp. 103–14.

However, since almost all of these late printings were of plays from the 1630s or prepared for revivals in that last period they can hardly be said to be a large segment of the whole repertoire.

What this deficiency really demands, for Shakespeare and all other early modern plays, is a fresh and wide-ranging input by editors of the text, attempting to identify as many features of the original staging as can be found, both for the 'maximal' or allowed-book version and for the 'minimal' texts containing all the likely cuts and changes that would have been made to the allowed book for staging. Some Shakespeare play-texts do seem to be close to the staged versions, plays not poems, most notably the quartos of *Henry V* (1600), *Merry Wives* (1602), *Othello* (1622), and perhaps the 1597 quarto of *Romeo and Juliet*. Future editors need to identify the form of their maximal text and supply all the available information about its likely transition from page to stage. Scholars such as Alan C. Dessen have made a start in identifying the original staging practices, but with the honourable exception of the Cambridge Webster editors the staging has not yet achieved a primary role in translating the texts into editions.

In print or manuscript, early copies of plays for reading were bought chiefly as reminders of performance until well into the eighteenth century. The author's name upheld their poetic value chiefly as familiar contributions to the theatre repertoire. Thomas Walkley's letter, 'The Stationer to the Reader', attached to his 1622 quarto of *Othello*, flaunted the company's primary asset as provider of these raw materials. 'I am the bolder, because the author's name is sufficient to vent his work', wrote Walkley, but that was a late development. The first plays that came into print were identified not by the author but the owners, the company. The first of the Chamberlain's plays to add the author's name to theirs on the title pages were the second quartos of *Richard II* and *Richard III* in 1598, along with the first known quarto of *Love's Labours Lost*. In the next year they put the author's name on *1 Henry IV*, probably to celebrate the inventor of Falstaff. In 1600 *The Merchant of Venice*, *Much Ado About Nothing*, *A Midsummer Night's Dream*, and *2 Henry IV* were all ascribed to 'William Shakes-speare', although the company's version of *Henry V* published in the same year had no author's name. It reappeared on the quarto of *Merry Wives* in 1602, and on all quartos afterwards. Jonson had 'Composed by the author B. J.' on the title page of *Every Man out of his Humour* in 1600, and a year later his full name appeared on *Every Man in his Humour*. Other writers were identified occasionally in the following years, starting with George Wilkins's *Miseries of Enforced Marriage* in 1607, although by then publishers had added *Thomas Lord Cromwell* and *The London Prodigal* to the eight plays already ascribed to Shakespeare.[8] In 1608, when the first quarto of *King Lear* appeared under Shakespeare's name, *The Yorkshire Tragedy* also claimed it. After that, once the company had the Blackfriars and the status and affluence it brought them, no new company plays appeared in print until 1619 apart from Jonson's own publication of his *Catiline* and *The Alchemist* in 1611 and 1612. The year 1619, the company's twenty-sixth, when Richard Burbage died, started the catch-all Beaumont and Fletcher label, on the title page of *A King and No King*. That quarto came out following an order from the Lord Chamberlain to the Stationers' Company 'That no playes that his Majesties players do play shalbe printed without consent of some of them'.[9] This is a useful indicator, because it means that all subsequent printings were made with the company's permission. Indeed, thereafter the company let its plays appear in print regularly, several of Massinger's plays appearing in print within a few months of their first showing on stage.[10] Publication became an additional source of income once a play had passed its first life on stage. During the plague closure in 1637 the Lord Chamberlain issued a further order protecting the company's plays from illicit publication, an order he renewed in 1641.[11]

In 1603 records of performances at court began to supply the titles of the plays the Master of the Revels chose, and occasionally they added the names of their writers. Strictly speaking this was pointless, since the payments were to the company, and the only reason for identifying the product was to distinguish one play from another. But by then the reputation of some writers was evidently as notable as the plays. For the first Christmas season under James the records note several of them. Two of the writers were unknown to the scribes, who copied their names down as they heard them, since 'Shaxberd' was the name put against the first three. Against 'A plaie Caled How to Larne of a woman to wooe' they inscribed 'Hewood', but against a play called 'All Foules' appears the precise 'Georg Chapman', as if that name was familiar to the copyist. Against the fifth entry, called 'Errors', 'Shaxberd' appeared again, as it does against two of the last entries, one inscribed 'the Marthant of Venis', the other 'A play Cauled The Martchant of Venis Againe Commanded By the Kings Majestie'. On the other hand, no writer's name was given to Jonson's *Every Man In* or *Every Man Out*.

[8] Jonathan Hope, *The Authorship of Shakespeare's Plays*, Cambridge University Press, 1994, p. 152, finds *Cromwell* the product of a single author, certainly not Shakespeare. The repertory as a whole must have taken on many (dead) authors.

[9] William A. Jackson, *Records of the Court of the Stationers' Company 1602 to 1640*, The Bibliographical Society, London, 1957, p. 110.

[10] *The Plays and Poems*, ed. Philip Edwards and Colin Gibson, 5 vols., Clarendon Press, 1976, I.xxix.

[11] See Appendix 2 for the orders of 1637 and 1641.

Later court entries cited play titles, possibly because the play was known to the scribe, but almost never the writers.

The popularity of the writers was noted more by booksellers than at court. As the repertory settled, the most popular plays can be identified by what publishers chose to sell. Play quartos were bought to be read from 1594 onwards, as respect for the quality of the company products increased. Histories and tragedies were bought more often than comedies, showing a difference in the book-buyer's priorities from the playgoer's. *Titus Andronicus* went through two reprints before the Folio in 1623, as did *Romeo and Juliet* and the quarto of *Henry V*, while *Richard II* had five, *Richard III* six, *1 Henry IV* six, and *Hamlet* and *Pericles* three each.[12] The most reprinted plays were *Mucedorus*, which went through ten quartos up to 1640 after the first that accredited it to the Globe in 1610, and *The Scornful Lady*. *The Merry Devil of Edmonton* had four and *The Miseries of Enforced Marriage* three. None of the Shakespeare comedies was reprinted as frequently as the history plays. After 1619 roughly half of the Beaumont and Fletcher plays went into quarto before the two Folios of 1647 and 1679. This was also the time when manuscript copies by professional scribes like Ralph Crane and sometimes the author himself began to be made as gifts to interested gentry.

Popularity aside, the identification of 211 play titles and the period of their staging by the company (Appendix 4), and the dates of publication for 160 of the extant texts (if we exclude *Osmond the Great Turk*, published in 1657 as a Queen's play),[13] plus the seven that exist in early manuscripts (Appendix 5), have a rather misleading precision and quantity. Even to have the titles for 211 of the Shakespeare company plays suggests, wrongly, that we know most of the repertory. In fact for the period when the Chamberlain's Men matched the productivity of the Lord Admiral's, between 1594 and 1600, less than twenty Chamberlain's titles survive, whereas the Henslowe records show that through the same period the Admiral's Men staged at least ninety new plays. Almost certainly well over half the repertory in that first six years has been lost without trace. In subsequent years the acqustion of new plays declined quite drastically, but still nearly half the total repertory may never have been noted. A number of the titles of lost plays recorded by Henslowe had only one or two performances, suggesting that the surviving texts were the better products of the system, but the known products still fall well below the true number. That both companies chose to make money by publishing their most popular plays in the years from 1597 to 1601 suggests

---

[12] This listing largely ignores the illegal Jaggard reprints of 1619, although they also testify to the plays' popularity. Two testimonies to the popularity of *Pericles* are quoted in Appendix 2.19 and 2.28.

[13] See note in Appendix 4, plays 1621–4.

that all we have is their best-sellers, so a huge residue of both repertories has certainly disappeared.[14] This long shadow of unknown plays lies behind both duopoly repertories.

Over the next thirty years the shadow did shrink. Plays printed from the repertory grew as the number of new plays bought dwindled, from more than a dozen a year in the 1590s down to as few as four through the 1630s. Some authors, notably Jonson, Barnabe Barnes, and Webster, gave their 'poems' to the press themselves. Perhaps not always rightly, I have accepted as company plays the so-called 'Shakespeare Apocrypha', hyped with the famous name either by the company or their publisher. Booksellers buying the text from the company whose resident writer had already sold so many plays were probably responsible for the mis-ascription.

A similarly scuffed trail marked the arrival of other plays into print. Not until the late 1630s did the company move to secure the Lord Chamberlain's protection of its plays from unauthorized printing (Appendix 2.46, 2.50). Ultimately, Ben Jonson must take the credit for securing nearly half of the surviving repertory. His own Folio of his plays in 1616 certainly prompted Heminges and Condell to think of a Shakespeare Folio (Appendix 2.29). That labour saved eighteen Shakespeare manuscripts from oblivion. Those two great editions in turn prompted Humphrey Moseley to produce a Beaumont and Fletcher Folio in 1647. Between them the three folios brought 52 of the company's 106 pre-1625 plays to the press, most of them for the first time.

A grey fringe also surrounds the known repertory. Some plays for which texts survive may have been in the repertory but were never noted as belonging to the company. This is most likely with earlier plays, either those thought to have been written or partly written by Shakespeare, or others from the time before 1594 when ascriptions of a published text to a particular company were less usual. In her 1999 article 'Shakespeare's Repertory'[15] Roslyn Lander Knutson argues that additional possibilities are *Fair Em*, performed at the Rose by Sussex's along with *Titus Andronicus* in January 1594, *Arden of Faversham*, *Edward II*, possibly *Edward III*, and the lost play *The Tartarian Cripple*. She argues for Marlowe's *Edward II* and the

---

[14] Frederick Gerschow, in the train of the young Duke of Stettin-Pomerania when he visited England between 10 September and 3 October 1602, records two plays the visitors saw. On 13 September they went to a play 'showing how Stuhl-Weissenburg [in Hungary] was gained by the Turks, and then won again by the Christians'. On the 14th they saw 'a tragic play . . . about Samson and the half tribe of Benjamin' (*Transactions of the Royal Historical Society* n.s. 6 (1892), pp. 7, 11). The second of these took place on the afternoon of a day when they were on the river, so the Bankside was the most likely venue. Neither play matches any surviving text in the Chamberlain's repertory at the Globe or Worcester's at the Rose.

[15] *A Companion to Shakespeare*, ed. David Scott Kastan, Basil Blackwell, Oxford, 1999, pp. 349–50.

anonymous *Edward III*, which has been claimed as at least partly Shake-speare's, mostly on the grounds that they belonged to the Pembroke's company of 1593, and that some of Shakespeare's plays moved from Pembroke's to the Lord Chamberlain's. These might have been among the fifty or more plays missing from the repertory in the early years, although since the assembly of Shakespeare's plays for the Chamberlain's seems to have been balanced by a similar assembly of Marlowe's for the Admiral's, they should have been given *Edward II*. The duopoly's dominance over playing might have helped them acquire other old plays to augment their stock in 1594, but the evidence for any being played by the Chamberlain's is inferential.

More useful gains came from the company's dominant status in later years. The King's Men took plays that had previously been staged by now-dead companies, particularly when their title pages featured the names of writers of their other plays. Some originally written for the boy companies like Jonson's *Epicene* and Beaumont and Fletcher's *The Captain* and *The Faithful Shepherdess* seem to have entered the King's repertory in later years through a kind of *droit de seigneur*, although it is rather more likely that several from the Lady Elizabeth's were brought by Nathan Field when he joined the company in 1616. Notes on the plays known to have had a pre-history in other companies are supplied in Appendix 4.

For all the grey fringe and the wide penumbra of which no trace survives, the 168 plays for which we have a text do map the broad landscape of the company's basis for selection of its repertoire over the years. They provide strong hints about the inevitable shifts in taste, and where the King's Men positioned themselves through the years when the number of companies was multiplying and their repertories diverging. The trend in the later years, playing to the company's known strengths and running revivals of Shakespeare and the Beaumont and Fletcher stable, confirms both the kind of audience the company expected and what it thought were the chief demands on its reputation. All of the later plays were marinaded in the earlier repertory, and intertextual links abound in language and in story. The most intriguing aspects of the repertory the company chose to perform appear in the Globe years before they acquired the Blackfriars, when their identity as the King's servants was fully established and they became the most noted entertainers for all levels of society. That period included *Lear*, *Macbeth*, and *Pericles*. Subsequently Shakespeare's early contributions were refined and redefined by Fletcher, and Fletcher and his collaborators built the reputation the Blackfriars lived off till 1642.

In the earliest landscape, stuck with small factual pebbles in a morass of indistinguishable and undistinguished mud, it is easy to lose balance and perspective. Far more pebbles mark the track of the company's relations with the court and the king than its relations with London's ordinary play-goers. This can mislead. The rich soil of the company's daily repertory was always its main path. All plays were tested in the public playhouses first, to an interpretive community sufficiently versed in the rest of the repertoire to guarantee intertextual and metatheatrical exchanges and predictable reactions at every performance. Unlike the court masques, no play was written for any unique occasion. Assumptions that *Troilus and Cressida* was written to be performed only at an Inn of Court, that *Twelfth Night* had its first night in front of John Manningham and his fellow Middle Templars on 2 February 1602, or that *A Midsummer Night's Dream* was written for the celebrations at any one of the eighteen or more weddings scholars have identified as its occasion are nonsense. They ignore the fact that their chief writer provided two plays a year for his company, usually one comedy and one serious play, tragedy or history, and that once it was in their hands it was the company that chose what they did with it. All the plays were tried out first at the company's 'common playhouse'. Even those commissioned to be shown at court were the product of successful staging at the Globe or Blackfriars before the Master of the Revels heard them at the Revels Office in St John's. Every play staged at court was taken from the company's current repertory.

The most potent shaping factor in the repertory was of course the individual aspiration of the writers, and the personal views they put into their raw material. As the company's social position improved, so did the background and education of the writers who supplied the plays. Years before Beaumont and Fletcher were brought in, several writers with university training had started to offer plays. Thirteen of the company's known suppliers, Barnes, Beaumont, Davenant, Denham, Ford, Marmion, Marston, Massinger, Mayne, Middleton, Shirley, Suckling, and Webster, were graduates.[16] By the Caroline period almost all were university men and some were courtiers. But the first writers, like Shakespeare, had their training on the job, working to suit the company's expectations and resources. Tracing the gradual shifts in the tastes of the targeted audiences through the 168 plays that survive, from those tested at the Theatre and around the country to the last Blackfriars plays written and even financed by courtiers like Suckling, is a huge labour that this book does not pretend to undertake. But snapshots of the plays are the best means we have to identify the shifts made to satisfy changing audience demands.

---

[16] See Darryll Grantley, *Wit's Pilgrimage*, Ashgate, 2000, pp. 76–81.

THE SHAKESPEAREAN SEQUENCE

To run a repertory when you are the country's chief performers is likely to make the choice of plays depressingly conservative. Whether in the 1590s when the two companies were given the first-ever licences to perform in London, or in the 1630s when five competed and one had the king himself for their patron, the pressure not to be too radical and adventurous was even greater than the commercial pressure to give regular playgoers the familiar satisfactions. So the Shakespeare company could not possibly be anything but respectful of, on the one hand, popular and, on the other, authoritative expectation. The one major act of defiance, with *A Game at Chess*, and the multitude of unheralded successes like Hamlet and Falstaff, need to be seen framed by that inhibiting and constant need to be careful in what they staged. It was inevitable from the time they started with a few well-known Shakespeares and a rag-tag of older plays from the Queen's Men's repertory that their choices would follow recognizable paths. The extent to which the choice of plays was dictated by popular demand and by fear of innovation must not be underestimated.

Nonetheless, the process of change, whether evolutionary and developmental or radical and revolutionary, was inevitable, and it moved fast. The difference between, say, *The Merchant of Venice* written in 1596 and *Aglaura* written in 1637 is enormous. In 1596 the habit of playing to crowds of thousands in London was still barely twenty years old, and doing so in licensed playhouses was less than two. By 1637 Blackfriars audiences of the great and the affluent knew what they liked, but they still welcomed innovation. By that time radical ideas needed a more subtle and well-disguised dressing-up than mad Hamlet or Prince Henry's fool and jester. Concealed subversion of both dramatic and political traditions can be read throughout the repertory.[17]

As we try to identify what image of the early repertory an Elizabethan playgoer might have, it is regrettable that most of the surviving plays from the first fifteen years are Shakespeare's. Unless we see the company writer dictating everything other suppliers wrote and what the company chose to perform, a deeply suspect assumption, a totalizing idea of the repertory's character through this first period is quite inaccessible. We cannot even be sure which types of play the company chose not to perform. There is nothing, for instance, to say whether they continued to stage plays on

---

[17] The sheer number of the 168 plays helps the impression that the repertory became repetitive and conservative. A more positive idea of its radicality is argued by Simon Shepherd and Peter Womack in *English Drama: A Cultural History*, Blackwell, Oxford, 1996.

biblical topics, like *Hester and Ahasuerus*, which they started with in June 1594. The early mix seems to have been eclectic. Up to 1600 and *Hamlet* the Shakespeare provisions meant a diet largely of history plays – shifting from England to ancient Rome in 1599 – and romantic comedies, together with their most popular play, the romantic tragedy *Romeo and Juliet*. All the latter favoured young love over conservative citizen patriarchy. At least one of the other plays, however, was clearly inclined towards more traditional moral values.

A Warning for Fair Women, staged some years before 1599, is a straightforwardly moralistic citizen tragedy, its story taken from Holinshed, like *Arden of Faversham*. It opens, though, with a peculiar Induction where the genres debate against each other, Melpomene as Tragedy quarrelling with Comedy and History for precedence. Tragedy pessimistically prevails for just the day of the show, handing over to History and Comedy for future plays:

> What now hath fail'd, tomorrow you shall see
> Perform'd by History or Comedy.

As in other Inductions, however, Melpomene is making a major statement about playing, and claims a distinct theatrical identity. *A Warning*'s Induction is an extended argument for a remarkable and noteworthy innovation on the Elizabethan stage as the company conceived it: a new form, domestic tragedy set in London, telling a true tale. The idea was not quite as new as the Induction claims, since *Arden of Faversham*, published in 1592, long preceded it, but it was evidently an innovation for the duopoly company at the Theatre, and the Rose had no comparable play in its repertory.

The Induction actually disclaims the value of all the types of play that we know were running in the company's repertory up to 1599. First Comedy adopts a strong line against Tragedy, deriding its customary form:

> How some damnd tyrant, to obtaine a crowne,
> Stabs, hangs, impoysons, smothers, cutteth throats,
> And then a Chorus too comes howling in,
> And tels us of the worrying of a cat,
> Then of a filthie whining ghost,
> Lapt in some fowle sheete, or a leather pelch,
> Comes skreaming like a pigge half stickt,
> And cries Vindicta, revenge, revenge: (50–7)[18]

---

[18] I follow the through-line numbers assigned by Charles Dale Cannon in his critical edition (Mouton, The Hague, 1975). The text is from the 1599 quarto.

At this Melpomene whips both Comedy and History off the stage, complaining

> T'is you have kept the Theatres so long,
> Painted in play-bils, upon every poast,
> That I am scorned of the multitude,
> My name prophande.   (74–7)

The essence of Melpomene's case is that she is presenting a fresh and better form of tragedy in place of the old revenge drama with its chorus, tyrant and ghost. Instead she will give a truthful account of a real tragedy set in London and presented to Londoners. The story itself, she says, is a well-known piece of recent history.[19] 'My Sceane is London, native and your owne', she declares. For once she is to give her audience the truth. 'I am not faind: many now in this round, / Once to behold me in sad teares were drownd' (95–8). For at least this day the fictions and feigning of the old fashion of tragedy are banished along with History and Comedy.

Tragedy's essential claim is that it is a tale not 'faind' but 'true', unlike the comedies and former revenge tragedies. She reaffirms its truth in the epilogue, returning in order to explain why the play has not concluded with a more theatrical act of revenge.

> Perhaps it may seeme strange unto you al,
> That one hath not revengde anothers death,
> After the observation of such course:
> The reason is, that now of truth I sing,
> And should I adde, or else diminish aught,
> Many of these spectators then could say,
> I have committed error in my play.
>   (2722–8)

Such a boast is an extraordinary assertion to have made on this stage in the years around 1597. It runs counter to almost everything we know of the Chamberlain's company repertory in these first years of duopoly control of London playing. It sets aside Shakespeare's history plays and his comedies and replaces them with a well-known story set in London. As such, apart from the Eastcheap scenes of the 1596–9 *Henry IV* and *Henry V* plays, *A Warning* was unique among the surviving plays of that company as a

---

[19] Like the story of Arden of Faversham's murder by his wife, *A Warning*'s murder is recounted at length in Holinshed.

London story. It was also unequalled by any new play that can be identified in Philip Henslowe's lists for the Admiral's through that time.[20]

Sadly, in its banal narrative and moralistic sentiments, the play that followed the Induction hardly justifies the boast. What is most obviously notable about *A Warning* is the hint that the writer thought the company's repertoire of plays needed reform. Comedies about romantic lovers, history plays full of battles with flag and drums were the popular mode ('once a weeke if we do not appeere, / She shall find few that will attend her here' says Comedy, dismissively), along with the old kind of revenge tragedies like the ur-*Hamlet* and *Titus Andronicus*.

A Warning's discontent with fiddling comedy and drumming history in the Chamberlain's first years up to 1599 not only stands against the other plays surviving from the repertory of that early duopoly period (all Shakespeare's), but argues for an innovation that no company was yet ready to introduce: a play set in London. Jonson's *Every Man in his Humour* in 1598 was located ostensibly in an Italian city, its transfer to London not made until Jonson produced the revised text for his Folio edition of 1616. Chapman's *An Humorous Day's Mirth* launched London-set comedy at the Rose in May 1597. Before that only *Arden of Faversham* (1592) had used an English setting, but a country house in Kent is a long way from the streets of London. *Arden*'s author and company are unknown, and there is little to suggest that it had any link with the Chamberlain's Men, unless one tries to conflate the names of its villains Black Will and Shakebags. Moreover, if *A Warning* was an attempt to introduce a new kind of play to the London stages, as Chapman's play did for citizen comedy, it was far less successful, since no other domestic tragedy of a similar kind has survived. Heywood's enactment of a proverbial phrase from *The Taming of the Shrew* in his moralistic tragedy of 1602, *A Woman Killed with Kindness*, was perhaps the nearest imitation. The closest of the King's repertory, if they did ever stage it, was *A Yorkshire Tragedy*.

In general, avoidance of London locations was a habit the company sustained through most of the repertory. None of Shakespeare's, Fletcher's, or Massinger's plays use a London setting, and even Davenant's prose comedy written for the Globe in 1634, *News from Plymouth*, was deliberately set outside the city. *A Warning*'s London location was diverted in 1598 into the ostensibly Italian setting of *Every Man in his Humour*, the first and

---

[20] Scott McMillin and Sally-Beth MacLean assert that the Queen's Men claimed that their own history plays were distinct from other plays because as history they were telling truths. See *The Queen's Men and their Plays*, Cambridge University Press, 1998, p. 133. Melpomene avoids this point when she dismisses History from the stage.

most popular of the London comedies, initiator of the fashion for satirical 'citizen comedy'.[21] Nonetheless, *A Warning*'s writer did echo some of the Shakespeare plays Melpomene dismisses. Browne the murderer, for instance, asserts his determination by a reference to *Titus Andronicus*, saying that if he does not kill his beloved's husband he will be 'no more worthy to obtain her bed / Than a foul Negro to embrace a Queen'. The play's moral also appears to offer an invitation to the company's writer to pen a second thought about it:

> Then triall now remaines, as shall conclude,
> Measure for measure, and lost bloud for bloud.
>
> (898–9)

Such resonances were natural to an intimate repertory where the same players were in every play and knew that their audiences would recognize the cross-references. It may be wrong to make too much of this play's citizen-minded orthodoxy, but it does argue that the company's repertory values were not exclusively Shakespearean. As an innovation in form, however, it did not compete with Shakespeare.

This chapter is mainly an account of the company's allegiance to their daily flock of playgoers, manifest in the plays and their reception by the London public. From 1594 to 1600 Londoners could go to little beside the plays of the duopoly. The two companies quite deliberately staged their stories in parallel, notably those from English history. Along with that sincerest form of mutual flattery, Henslowe's titles suggest that the Admiral's was the more radical and inventive of the two. They started 'humours' comedy with Chapman's *An Humorous Day's Mirth*, a sleeper in 1597 according to Henslowe. Its record in the *Diary* is unique in showing higher and higher takings in the six days of its first run. Later in the same year the Chamberlain's copied their opposites by taking on Jonson's *Every Man in his Humour* and its successor, though they forsook the fashion after relations with Jonson broke down.[22] That is what led them to add their own staging of *Satiromastix* to that of Paul's Boys in response to the mockeries of their plays Jonson gave them in *Every Man Out*. Staging *Satiromastix* declared the company's opposition to Jonson. It was much more a response to his criticisms of their repertory in *Every Man Out*, which he published in

---

[21] Fear of setting plays in London was evidenced by making the original location of *Every Man In* Florence, and not using London names till the 1616 Folio edition. Brian Gibbons, *Jacobean City Comedy*, Methuen, London, second edition, 1980, sees the fashion for comic satire on London life starting with Jonson but chiefly developed by Marston and Middleton with other companies.

[22] Martin Wiggins succinctly describes the 'humours' plays in *Shakespeare and the Drama of his Time*, Oxford University Press, 2000, pp. 64–71.

1600 as 'Containing more than hath been Publickely Spoken or Acted', than any attempt at an alliance with the new boy companies. The boy companies were an obvious irritant to the ageing duopoly, as a conversation in *Hamlet* noted (despite, or perhaps because of, the fact that Richard Burbage was landlord to one of them). For the Chamberlain's to ally themselves with Paul's in staging Dekker's attack on Jonson must mean that animosity against their critic overrode their hostility to the boys. It proved short-lived, since they took on *Sejanus* barely a year later and *Volpone* two years after that.

They do not seem to have imitated the Admiral's own offering of *Faustus* and plays about devils until some years later, in 1600 or so, and especially 1606, when they took on *The Devil's Charter*. Barnes's play owes some debt to Marlowe's, but at a deliberate distance. The company staged *Macbeth* with its own echoes of *Faustus* in the same year as *The Devil's Charter*, but before that *The Merry Devil of Edmonton* shows them distancing themselves from the *Faustus* mode. References in *The Black Book* and *A Mad World my Masters* of 1603 to *The Merry Devil* indicate that it was very popular, and it remained so for the next forty years. Its echoes of the nocturnal gambols in the forest in *A Midsummer Night's Dream* and *Merry Wives* set it alongside the Admiral's *Englishmen for my Money* and *Two Angry Women of Abingdon*, suggesting a first staging around 1600. Its comic catchphrases such as Blague's 'I serve the good Duke of Norfolk' had started as a fashion with the Shakespeare plays of 1597. Largely a romantic comedy with a Shakespearean allegiance to young love, its Induction sets up the popular trick where a magician plays a joke to outwit the devil. Jonson played from the same suit for the company much later with *The Devil is an Ass*. By that time, 1616, the fashion for *Faustus*-like plays with their fireworks was confined to the open-air playhouses, the Fortune and the Red Bull. When the King's opened at the Blackfriars in 1609 devils and fireworks became an exclusively summertime trick.

The strongest difference between the duopoly repertories was the Admiral's lack of romantic comedy. Love and marriage dominated all the early Shakespeare comedies, with the limited exceptions of *Love's Labours Lost*, the nearest thing to a satirical comedy in Jonson's mode where Jack does not end up with Jill, and *The Taming of the Shrew*, the first comedy about love not before but after marriage. We can too easily underrate the radicality in the 1590s of plays like *Romeo and Juliet* favouring young love over parental authority. The company used its boys thoroughly in its earlier years, especially when parts were written for a tall dark boy playing against a shorter fair one, in *A Midsummer Night's Dream*, *Much Ado*, and

As You Like It. A group of younger boys was available for the fairies in *A Midsummer Night's Dream* and the Falstaff-bewitching act at the end of *Merry Wives*. The Admiral's plays mocked this mode of the Chamberlain's, with for instance a scene in Haughton's *Englishmen for my Money* where a would-be (non-English) lover tries to get up to his beloved's balcony like Romeo but is caught suspended in a buck-basket like Falstaff. In the process Haughton conceded the Chamberlain's anti-patriarchal mode by preferring young love to parental authority, which in his play favoured the foreign lovers at their and the father's cost, but that was a rare feature in the Admiral's repertory.

Towards the end of the duopoly the Admiral's started running plays aimed at rousing the loyalties of a specific segment of their broad range of London audience-types. The first was *The Shoemaker's Holiday* in 1599. As a tribute to the spirit of handicraft apprentice gangs Dekker's ostensible loyalty was to his poorest audience-members from the city. In fact it was chiefly a spirited attack on the ex-Mayor John Spencer and his repressive views, as noted above. The Chamberlain's made no such attacks on their enemy in authority, and none of their surviving plays have anything to match Dekker's proclaimed allegiance to the roughest of the citizen–workers. The only survivor in the company's early repertory that might have appealed to the poor was *Thomas Lord Cromwell*. Staged in the years immediately following *The Shoemaker's Holiday*, it is partly a history play as a personal tragedy but also a rags-to-riches story not far in sentiment from Simon Eyre's story in Dekker's play. Taken from Foxe's 'Book of Martyrs' like several Admiral's plays of the time, *Cromwell* is the nearest the company came to the Admiral's worker allegiance, which strengthened in the next decade and took the two companies off on divergent tracks. The Globe never adopted the artisan-loyal trend that the Admiral's shared with Worcester's in their years at the Red Bull. Worcester's mounted Heywood's *Four Prentices of London*, a tale of four brothers, all apprentices-errant yet sons of a nobleman, who journey through the Levant fighting the heathen in a fanciful narrative that Beaumont burlesqued at Blackfriars in *The Knight of the Burning Pestle*. Beaumont's boy company play, deriding *The Four Prentices* and its allies, asserted the boys' radical divergence from the audience-targets at the open-air playhouses towards the lovers of satire at the indoor venues, a divergence which confronted the King's when they finally acquired the Blackfriars for themselves.

So long as the duopoly ran at their two open-air playhouses, appealing to city and artisan values was their chief response to the wide spread of audience types. The advent of the boy companies with their higher prices and less frequent performances showed the alternative value of appealing to more 'select' audiences. With this division went divergent repertories. The boys at Blackfriars from 1600 set their aim at gentry and lawyers, feeding them cynical and sexual satire, while the amphitheatres other than the Globe appealed to positive city values. With the one exception of *Satiromastix*, written for the Paul's boy company as part of the *Poetomachia* or 'War of the Theatres' but co-staged at the Globe, the company's repertory between 1600 and 1609 seems to have avoided either extreme. Up to the acquisition of the Blackfriars it played a number of lukewarmly citizen plays, domestic tragedies in the *Warning* mode like *A Yorkshire Tragedy*, and one which evoked the Shakespeare romantic principle to the point of involuntary parody, *The Miseries of Enforced Marriage*. Its author appears to have been that odd writer George Wilkins, associated at the same time with Shakespeare's biggest innovation, following the last of what Bradley called the 'central tragedies', *King Lear* and *Macbeth*, his introduction of *Pericles* and the new tragicomic mode in 1606. There is no evidence for the popularity of individual plays in the repertory before *Pericles* other than *Romeo and Juliet*, *1 Henry IV*, and *Hamlet*, though it is worth noting that three of the four plays Simon Forman went to at the Globe in 1611 (*Macbeth*, *Cymbeline*, *The Winter's Tale*, and an otherwise unknown *Richard II*) were Shakespeare's.

However innovative the company was in its control of its finances and its playhouses, the cautious conservatism of its repertory points up Shakespeare's late tragicomedies, soon to be copied and developed by Fletcher, as its most radical innovation. Through the 1590s the Chamberlain's simply added to the historics and romantic comedies already in their stock. Playscripts came to them in fairly complete form, so they had to swallow large lumps of their dramatic intake whole, with little time for digestion and rewriting or much discriminatory selection. Saying yes or no as a team to buying a play, after the whole company had spent an evening reading through the playbook at a tavern among food and drink,[23] led to a vote that might be influenced by quite small local discomforts and inspirations. It needed only one or two strong advocates to encourage the adoption of a play that ventured into new territory, but through the first years, when the speed of processing new plays onto the stage was most intensive, innovations were rare. Apart from copying the Admiral's with Jonson's *Every*

---

[23] *Henslowe's Diary*, p. 88, has a vivid entry for five shillings on 13 March 1598 'lent at that tyme unto the company for to spend at the Readynge of that boocke at the sonne in newfyshstreate'. The 'boocke' was inscribed as 'the famos wares of henry the fyrste & the prynce of walles'. A further note on the same page tots up a second five shillings spent at the Sun Inn 'for good cheare'.

Man in his Humour in 1598, which legend has Shakespeare backing against the general vote, the company's main innovation came in 1597 when they started launching their best plays into print, though that was chiefly a help in managing the financial strains of losing their Theatre. In 1599 their resident writer, after completing his series of plays from English history, first turned back to the politics of Roman history that he had launched with *Titus Andronicus* in 1592, and then abandoned history altogether to rewrite *Hamlet*.[24] That could have been his own decision, made easy because he was a company sharer and now a housekeeper as well. The most positive shifts of direction for the repertory are only evident in some signals put out after the company became the King's Men.

A few technical innovations did come. The company or their writers gradually modified traditional elements such as the old social distinction of making serious characters speak in verse while servants, working men, and comics spoke in prose, notably in plays like *Much Ado* and *Hamlet*, and increased the ostensible realism of staging by the use of devices like mid-speech entries, as in the opening of the fourth scene in *Richard II* when Richard enters saying to his followers 'we did observe' as an answer to what one of them said to him before they entered, without specifying what it was he had seen. Formal verse speech shed the Marlovian mighty line, parodied by Ancient Pistol, perhaps because Burbage preferred characterizations like Hamlet to Alleyn's strutting and bellowing. But old habits such as closing scenes and adding moral emphasis with a rhymed couplet persisted in the non-Shakespeare plays. Couplets provided endings in *A Warning for Fair Women*, *Thomas Lord Cromwell*, and others down to Wilkins's backward-leaning *Miseries of Enforced Marriage* of 1606, and even *The Revenger's Tragedy*, long after Shakespeare moved on. One of the 'safe' plays chosen for the first Christmas season at court for their new patron King James, *The Fair Maid of Bristow*, ends eleven of its fifteen scenes with a rhyme.[25]

---

[24] Shakespeare's version was not itself an innovation, since Thomas Lodge saw the company perform an earlier *Hamlet* at the Theatre in 1596. Both plays were rooted in contemporary politics, *Titus* in its opening scene putting heredity, election by merit, and democratic selection as alternative bases for government, while *Julius Caesar* set monarchic tyranny against what the Brutus of *Coriolanus* calls the 'liberties and charters that you bear / I'th'body of the weal' (2.3.166–7), and *Hamlet* played games with incest and the Scottish succession (see Bruce Thomas Boehrer, *Monarchy and Incest in Renaissance England*, University of Pennsylvania Press, Philadelphia, 1992, and Lilian Winstanley, *Hamlet and the Scottish Succession*, Edinburgh, 1920, plus 'Hamlet and the Essex Conspiracy. Part I', *Aberystwyth Studies* 6 (1924), 47–66, and 'Hamlet and the Essex Conspiracy. Part II', *Aberystwyth Studies* 7 (1925), 37–50. See also Roland Mushat Frye, *The Renaissance Hamlet: Issues and Responses in 1600*, Princeton University Press, 1984.

[25] Wiggins, *Shakespeare and the Drama of his Time*, pp. 91–2, writes helpfully about the shifts in this fashion, as does Russ McDonald, *Shakespeare and the Arts of Language*, Oxford University Press, 2001.

The Fair Maid of Bristow seems a good example of the repertory at the end of the company's run as the Chamberlain's. The Fair Maid's story was as innocuous as it well could be, reflecting many of the King's Men's new concerns, especially a shift away from the young-love and anti-patriarchal priority of Shakespeare's early comedies. It avoids dealing with London's citizenry by transferring the action to Bristol. Its love story concerns not young lovers but a wife's loyalty to her transgressing husband. A story about proclaimed murder but with a happy ending, the complex game of non-standard justice that closes it is enacted by a king, Richard I, arriving at the port just in time to perform an act of royal justice. By contrast, Wilkins's renewal of the young love priority in the loud claim made on the playbills for *The Miseries of Enforced Marriage* seems reactionary in comparison with Shakespeare's own immensely popular new venture, possibly with Wilkins, into the torn-apart families of *Pericles*.

A more striking example of the current and therefore transient concerns of the early period is *A Larum for London*. So long as the threat of invasion by the Spanish Armada could still cause national panics, as it did up to 1599, to dramatize what the Spanish did to the great city port of Antwerp made a forthright attack on citizen complacency. Making a play from Gascoigne's old pamphlet, the 1576 *Spoil of Antwerp*, at such a time was to give a noisy echo to civic fears about the defence of London. The Chamberlain's staged it as blatant propaganda aiming to warn government and city fathers. In its manifestation of the common concern at a time of crisis it ranks with *A Game at Chess*, though without the same danger of royal ire.[26]

Innovation in either practical or political matters seems never to have been an urgent priority. The most conspicuous developments in this first period were technical, Shakespeare-inspired, and soon copied by the Admiral's. One idea in particular, broached occasionally in pre-1594 plays, was the device augmenting the fashion for individual comic characters by the use of identifying catchphrases. Comic or clown catchphrases were not in themselves new, but Shakespeare relaunched the idea in his great successes of 1596 and 1597, the *Henry IV* plays. Starting after Bottom and the mechanicals of *A Midsummer Night's Dream*, whose idioms are prosaic and 'boorish' but not individualized, it set sail with Falstaff and his Eastcheap crew, especially in the extensions of the Eastcheap company scenes in

---

[26] Roslyn Lander Knutson, 'Filling Fare: the appetite for Current Issues and Traditional Forms in the Repertory of the Chamberlain's Men', *Medieval and Renaissance Drama in England* 15 (2003), 57–76, provides a context for two plays of 1599, the lost *Cloth Breeches and Velvet Hose*, and *A Larum for London*. See also Gurr, 'The Condition of Theatre in England in 1599', in *The Cambridge History of English Theatre*, Cambridge University Press, 2004, 1.264–81.

2 Henry IV in 1597 which introduced Pistol's iambic strutting and bellowing and Nym's comic allusions to Jonson with his 'And there's the humor of it', and in the next history play Llewellyn's distinctive Welsh idioms. Falstaff's own chief verbal characteristic, his constant use of the key of 'If . . .' about which there is more to be said below, was part of that game. I suspect the individual idioms of the urban Eastcheap characters may have been created to block the familiar clown-speak of country folk. As a new fashion the London-speak Eastcheap idioms did not outlive this early phase of the company's repertoire, though they renewed their popularity whenever the plays were revived. Compositor B of the First Folio showed his enthusiasm for Llewellyn in 1619 when he set the third quarto of *Henry V*, since he chose to make his own enhancements to Llewellyn's comic encounter with Pistol in the final Act.[27] The other half of the duopoly picked the idea up in 1599 with Simon Eyre in *The Shoemaker's Holiday* and the clown's proverbs in the Admiral's own play about a pair of wives of a Berkshire town on the Thames, its name neatly competitive with *The Merry Wives of Windsor*, *Two Angry Women of Abingdon*.

In later years the changes were more substantial, although they still suggest a knowing and defensively conservative policy. They mark the repertory out by the breadth of its appeal and its refusal to exploit sensationalism. No plays explicitly appealed to London's groundlings like *The Shoemaker's Holiday*. So far as we know, the sole exception to this policy was *Satiromastix*. Otherwise the company avoided overt social satire or anything that signalled allegiance to any one social grouping. Once they repossessed the Blackfriars for themselves they certainly never took on the anti-citizen satire of their predecessors at Blackfriars, the boy company. Jonson tried it in *The Alchemist*'s satire, which was aimed at every social level in the Blackfriars precinct and even at the company's own housekeepers, but that was unique, and part of the package they bought with the return to Jonson. Later innovations were mainly devoted to the merging of genres, especially in Fletcher's versions of the tragicomedy launched with *Pericles* in 1607.

Jonson was a positive influence on the repertory in several ways, not just the plays he wrote for them intermittently. He made them dip their toes into the satirical and moralistic element of city comedy, first with his Humours plays and later with *The Alchemist*. Loudly and consistently he gave them his views on the company's repertory. His opinion of their older plays was advertised in his overt contempt for battle scenes, with 'four

---

[27] See *The First Quarto of Henry V*, Cambridge University Press, 2000, p. 113.

or five most vile and ragged foils / Right ill disposed in brawl ridiculous',
mocked in the 1616 Prologue to *Every Man In*, and in the scorn he expressed
in *Bartholomew Fair*'s Induction in 1614 about tastes that have not moved
since *Titus* and *Jeronimo*. His voiced dislike of the last Shakespeare plays
may be linked to his jealousy over their influence on Fletcher's work for
the company. Fletcher's plays took a route far from Jonson's own, which
from 1612 onwards dealt exclusively with immediate London matters. He
always demanded more change and innovation than the company liked,
a pressure it reacted against by staging *Satiromastix*, though it marked a
fracas that may have stopped Shakespeare from writing any more romantic
comedies.

The most positive change may well have been the abandonment of
Kemp's old-fashioned jokes with the groundlings, noted in *Hamlet*, in
favour of the less audience-confiding form of playing that was affirmed
in the Fletcherian modes prevailing from 1614 onwards. Richard Brome's
Antipodes in 1638, a comedy that mocked gentlemanly fashions of the 1630s
with some force, has a play-loving lord contrast the old days of Tarlton
and Kemp on the 'elder stages', and their 'interloquutions with the au-
dients', against the modern stage, 'purged from barbarism, / And brought
to the perfection it now shines with' (*Antipodes*, 2.2). One wonders how
deeply Jonson's ex-servant had his tongue in his cheek when he made
the lord assert how perfect staging had become by the 1630s, given that
jigs and other clownage still prevailed at the Fortune and Red Bull (*The
Antipodes* was written for Queen Henrietta Maria's Men, playing at the
Salisbury Court). But by then the social divisions in audience tastes were
clear-cut.

Jonson's relations with the company were so intense and fluctuating that
it is almost impossible to paint them in a non-moving picture. While selling
them his six great early plays over twelve years, he was from the outset the
company's most pungent critic. He used his plays to voice social criticism
as a radical alternative to the company's romantic comedy tradition. The
best evidence for their uneasy relation with his work and his principles was
their staging of *Satiromastix*. Jonson, Marston, and Dekker's quarrel that
gave the name 'Poetomachia' to their 'War of the Theatres' was fought from
the Blackfriars on one side, where Jonson was the resident poet and whose
boys played *Poetaster*, and on the other the boys of Paul's and the Globe
players, both of whom staged *Satiromastix* in or a little before October 1601,
the year that Shakespeare's last romantic comedy, *Twelfth Night*, was first
staged.

In James P. Bednarz's reading of the text,[28] Jonson certainly knew of the plan for the double production of Dekker's attack on him at the two playhouses before it came out, from his double references to the 'world' and the company that '*bespawls*' the time. The real puzzle is why the boy company and the Chamberlain's Men should have so openly ganged up together against Jonson. The Paul's motive is obvious. They started life in 1599 with Marston as their writer, and would logically take his side against the chief writer of the other 'private' playhouse, its open rival. That is Cyrus Hoy's view. He reckons that Dekker had 'a joint commission' from the Chamberlain's and Paul's for the attack in *Satiromastix*, simply because Paul's were backing Marston.[29] We cannot ignore the fact that its staging came not long after the Chamberlain's acknowledged itself jealous of the new boy companies' success in *Hamlet* (Q1, 1603, which has some relation to the version first staged in 1600, refers to the 'Tragedians of the Citty' being driven out of town by 'private playes, / And . . . the humour of children', an early reaction to the boy companies as competition for the adult groups).[30] It seems most likely that the company's alliance with Paul's started with Jonson's ridicule of the Chamberlain's repertory in *Every Man Out of his Humour*. The play's publication in extended form in 1600 might have prompted the company to share a public reprisal early the following year. This assumes a heavy animosity against Jonson which proved remarkably transient, however, since not long afterwards they bought his first major tragedy, *Sejanus*. What led them to take up Dekker's play is intriguing, and perhaps ultimately inexplicable. To share the performance of any play was almost unprecedented, unless it was simply a commercially motivated way of cashing in on the current noisy scandal. What it argues most positively is the company's rejection of Jonson as a loyal company writer.

Some hint of the thinking is evidenced by the nature of the attacks. Dekker charged Jonson with misuse of 'application', allusions to real people, in his characterization of 'the humorous poet' by asking how could 400 out

---

[28] James P. Bednarz, *Shakespeare and the Poets' War*, Columbia University Press, New York, 2001, p. 246.

[29] Cyrus Hoy, *Introductions, Notes and Commentaries to Texts in 'The Dramatic Works of Thomas Dekker*, ed. Fredson Bowers, 4 vols., Cambridge University Press, 1980, 1.180.

[30] Roslyn Lander Knutson, *Playing Companies and Commerce in Shakespeare's Time*, chapter 5, claims that the 'little eyases' reference in the Folio text (1623) was an insertion made in 1606–8, after the Blackfriars boys had stirred up trouble for themselves. The version of the reference quoted here from Q1 must have been made much earlier, and certainly close to the time of the 'Poetomachia'. This early reference might of course be read as not an attack on but a puff for the new boy companies, which makes sense not only because of the company's link with Paul's shown by the staging of *Satiromastix* at the Globe but because Hamlet was being played by the man the Blackfriars boys were renting their playhouse from.

of the 500 at the Blackfriars 'point with their finger in one instant / at one and the same man' if the application was not blatantly obvious?[31] Conceivably that was an attack to disguise Dekker's own applications, since the balding Adam Prickshaft in *Satiromastix* may be a thinly concealed depiction of the Chamberlain's chief writer. Roslyn Lander Knutson claims, I think rightly, that the basic reason for attacking Jonson was to set up a defence at Paul's and the Globe of the traditional repertory of plays which both companies were running and which Jonson scorned. She cites Dekker's constant references to well-known old plays, from *Gorboduc* to *Tamburlaine*, and allusions to recent productions such as Paul's *The Wisdom of Dr Dodypoll* and the Globe's *Hamlet*, the Falstaff of the *Henry IV* plays, and Justice Shallow from *2 Henry IV* and *Merry Wives*.[32]

Standing up for the old repertory on such grounds, however, was a departure from the Chamberlain's Men's usual middle-of-the-road path. Normally they did not partake in obvious games of 'application', and their own repertory did not venture into anything directly relevant to current affairs, bar the marginal *A Larum for London*, until they took on the dangerous *Sejanus* in 1603 and the sycophantic *Gowrie* in 1604.[33] That is what in the first place makes the company's decision in 1599 to stage the acerbic *Every Man Out* so striking. It may be that *Every Man In* with its fresh version of the comedy of humours and its satirical portraits of citizen Londoners had been a colourful enough success to warrant them taking on Jonson's second play, and most likely the script they staged lacked much of the acid that is in the subsequent printed text. Jonson's play survives as his poem, not the allowed book, so what we have may not be the dish that was originally served at the Globe. In print it mocked four of the company's most successful plays, all by its resident writer, *Romeo and Juliet*, *1 Henry IV*, and the two successes of 1599, *Henry V* and *Julius Caesar*, and had its in-joke about the same writer's gentrification. But at least some of this must have been in the original staged text. The inferences are not really very clear. To present such jokes against themselves shows a tolerance quite unlike the partisan hostility that in the next year led the company to stage *Satiromastix*.

---

[31] Bednarz, *Shakespeare and the Poets' War*, p. 216.
[32] Roslyn Lander Knutson, *Playing Companies and Commerce in Shakespeare's Time*, pp. 137–40.
[33] It might be argued that both *King Lear* and *Richard II* were exceptions to that rule. *King Lear* in 1605 certainly was, and advertised the fact in its opening lines, as noted in chapter 5. But the political edge in *Richard II* when composed in 1595 was more oblique. Its 'application' by the Essex followers in February 1601 made use of a play written six years before in a very different situation. The reference to Essex in *Henry V* is a more obvious case, but that was upbeat, with none of the satirical point of the issues laid out in *Poetaster* and *Satiromastix*.

It may be that the Chamberlain's Men realized only gradually that Jonson was attacking their whole repertoire of plays, and that some kind of counter was needed. That would explain *Satiromastix*'s flood of allusions to the standard repertory. Shakespeare delivered his own counter to Jonson about the nature of comedy with *As You Like It* in 1599 and *Twelfth Night* in 1601, and it has been claimed that in 1602 he made a less defensive, more personal counter-attack with the 'application' of the character of Ajax to Jonson.[34] Such a reading supports the idea that he voted for the staging of *Satiromastix*. Tolerance of *Every Man Out* in 1599 and the purchase of *Sejanus* in 1602, straddling as they do the attacks in *Satiromastix* and *Troilus*, leave room for a lot of speculation about shifting policies and the mobile relations between Jonson and Shakespeare.[35] The company used *Satiromastix* to defend the romantic comedy so richly lodged in their stock of popular Shakespeares. After that they must have felt that their current repertoire needed no further innovation or alteration, so they withdrew from the 'salt' of Jonsonian satire, though they were happy to take on his first tragical history. Tolerance and love as ruling themes put the plays of the hawkish Blackfriars eyasses at an extreme which the Shakespeare company felt they should never indulge in. The fact that they took on *Volpone* little more than two years after they had taken up Jonson again in 1603, perhaps thanks largely to the unknown 'happy *Genius*' who Jonson thanked for his help with the stage version, and that they chose to forget the initial troubles that *Sejanus* got into at its first staging, shows how tolerant, or possibly how generous, they and their choosers of plays were.[36] Between *Sejanus* in 1602 or so and *Volpone* in 1605 they did opt to restage both *Every Man In* and *Every Man Out* in 1604, since both plays were chosen for the court that Christmas.

What was the concept of a play that determined the early repertory choices? An answer is not far to seek, at least in Shakespeare. In 1977 Maura Slattery Kahn published an elegant article about Touchstone's 'improvisation in the key of If'.[37] It identified the thinking about fantasy and the

[34] This is the theme of Bednarz's book. The whole of chapter 2 argues for Jonson being personified as Ajax in *Troilus and Cressida* in 1602 (*Shakespeare and the Poets' War*, pp. 32–52).

[35] Jonson's acknowledgement that the stage version of *Sejanus* contained contributions by 'a second Pen', written by 'so happy a *Genius*', who would most likely have been the producing company's resident writer, adds some credibility to the idea that Shakespeare was instrumental in helping Jonson back in 1602–3. He was not, however, likely to have been the company's chooser of playbooks. For all his alleged generosity to Jonson, it is not right to assume that the company used Shakespeare to appraise the playscripts offered them, in view of Henslowe's indications about the Admiral's practices and their evening meetings at taverns for a read-through before they agreed to buy a play.

[36] The hostility to *Sejanus* at its first performances is well attested.

[37] Maura Slattery Kahn, 'Much Virtue in "If"', *Shakespeare Quarterly* 28 (1977), 40–50.

conditional basis of many of the stories told in the early repertory. Similar thinking can be found in the lawyers' tradition of moot games, where improbably extreme cases were put up for debate. It was a tradition made explicit in Touchstone's treble clef and Falstaff's conditionals. A later version of the moot game appeared in Fletcher's invented plots, where extreme situations put questions of honourable morality and conduct to the test. The moot game as an intellectual exercise was traced and analysed thoroughly and neatly by Joel Altman in *The Tudor Play of Mind*.[38] It sees drama and the persuasive arts at the heart of the Tudor educational system. Rooted in the teaching of rhetorical debate, it recognizes that the skills of lawyers and preachers began with the assumption that the aim of education was the art of persuasion. Theology and law alike, the chief occupations of university graduates, made the composition of persuasive arguments the highest priority. The lawyer's moot game of 'put case that . . .' used extravagant or extreme situations to test such skills. Extreme situations being the essence of a good dramatic plot, the plays, whether comic or tragic, provided a model for such debates. Altman traced the game from the early Tudor interludes through to Lyly and Marlowe, concluding with a superb analysis of the plotting of *The Comedy of Errors* as an epitome of the game. The dramatic basis for a comic, often a tragicomic, and sometimes a tragic situation was almost always a similarly extravagant hypothesis. Fletcher based most of his tragedies and tragicomedies on such games, exercises in the key of 'if'.

Falstaff constantly uses extreme conditionals. Starting with a searching paradox in his first scene (*1 Henry IV*, 1.2), 'now am I, if a man should speak truly, little better than one of the wicked', he uses versions of the 'if . . . then' structure four times in that scene and four times more in the next (2.2). In the confrontation over his cowardice at Gadshill and the play-scene that follows he uses versions of it twenty-three times in a dialogue of 350 lines, and five more in 3.3. At Shrewsbury (5.3) he uses it thirteen more times. That notoriously tricky play *All's Well that Ends Well* concludes similarly with Bertram being conditional. All will indeed be well, '*If* it end so meet'. Like *Measure for Measure*, which challenges and complicates the theological assumption inherent in its own title, *All's Well* calls a familiar truism into question.

Shakespeare's extension of that concept envisaged plays, at least his earlier comedies, as special kinds of dream. That wonderfully liberating concept is

---

[38] Joel B. Altman, *The Tudor Play of Mind: Rhetorical Inquiry and the Development of Elizabethan Drama*, University of California Press, Berkeley, 1978. His concept of the interrelations between drama and the law is developed strikingly by Luke Wilson, *Theaters of Intention*, Stanford University Press, 2000.

what Hippolyta implies in *A Midsummer Night's Dream* when she responds in puzzlement to Theseus's eloquent speech about lunatics, lovers, and poets and their excess of imagination. She says that the real mystery of the story the four lovers have told about their night in the forest is that they all had the identical dream. Their improbable experiences cannot be dismissed as easily as Theseus thinks.

> But all the story of the night told over,
> And all their minds transfigured so together,
> More witnesseth than fancy's images,
> And grows to something of great constancy;
> But howsoever, strange and admirable.

What the four went through was transfigured *so together*. They were like a theatre audience, sharing an experience that was fantastically strange, meaning abnormal, a matter for alienation and admiration, that grows into constancy. Such an experience was Shakespeare's idea of how audiences find a play in a theatre. It is a fantasy that works on the collective mind like a shared dream, of great constancy because remembered and replayed. It is memorable and faithful to itself, and yet like all dreams it is unreal. It warrants Hamlet's dismissal of the Player emoting only 'in a fiction, a *dream* of passion'. The unreality of theatre is shared by the whole audience, and accepted willingly for its emotive power. As Stephen Greenblatt says in *Shakespearean Negotiations*, 'the theatre elicits from us complicity rather than belief'.[39] Stage realism, the game of cinematic illusionism that rules modern audiences, is alien to theatre as a community event. How Shakespeare's concept of a play staged as a dream was subsequently transformed by the rewriting of *Hamlet*, where all the parts demand role-play and disguise, is too large an issue for this story. *Hamlet* was a pivot on which many people's thinking was levered, not least the adoption of metatheatre as a means of confronting reality.

History, whether as stories from the chronicles or some other form of tragedy, was a rather different matter from the moot games and the dreams of comedy. A history play narrates ostensible and sometimes well-known facts. One of the more notable features of Shakespeare's English history plays is their earthliness and ostensible reality. Between the procession of vengeful ghosts in *Richard III* and the 'spirit' of Caesar appearing to Brutus

---

[39] Stephen Greenblatt, *Shakespearean Negotiations: The Circulation of Social Energy in Renaissance England*, University of California Press, Berkeley, 1988, p. 119. Other comments on the early modern attitude to stage illusionism are in Gurr, 'Metatheatre and the Fear of Playing', in *Neo-Historicism*, ed. Robin Headlam Wells, Glenn Burgess, and Rowland Wymer, D. S. Brewer, Cambridge, 2000, pp. 91–110.

and Cassius nothing in any of the plays shows faith in divine intervention. Richard II claims angelic backing, but never gets it. The Archbishop in *Henry V* asserts orthodox Anglican Protestant doctrine in saying that the age of miracles has passed while announcing his plan to bribe Henry to protect the church. The pungent scepticism of Samuel Harsnett, author of two attacks on credulous magic devoured by Shakespeare,[40] and of Harsnett's pragmatic mentor Archbishop Bancroft, display the same healthily hard-headed reluctance to believe myths and folklore that Reginald Scot flaunted in his *Discovery of Witchcraft* in 1584, and that the Holinshed authors used more cautiously in their *Chronicles*. Earthly realism, even *realpolitik*, became a feature of the history play with its inherent claim that unlike comedy it represented true stories from the past.[41] In this concept it stood as an opposite to the fantasies of comedy. Subsequently *Hamlet*, aided in complex ways by the evolution of Shakespeare's history plays, helped to push the repertory towards a more complex view of what drama can do.

From the perspective of the intricate games played with realism in the tragedies Shakespeare wrote between 1600 and 1606, the tragicomic mode fostered by the success of *Pericles* and developed by Fletcher was a retreat to moot games and fantasy. In its new form, however, the Fletcherian mode served to redirect the fantastic games of the comedies into the more obviously serious and substantial subjects touched on so delicately in *Cymbeline* and *The Tempest*. Nor did these new games ignore politics. Fletcher made tyranny an explicit feature of his tragedies and tragicomedies, a point to be considered more extensively in the next chapter, on company attitudes to their royal patrons. The merger in tragicomedy of the serious 'truths' of history with the extreme and fantastic situations of comedy renewed the orthodox moral frame of the drama. But it did so in complex ways.

An enormous amount of attention has been given to the Shakespeare history plays, both as an innovation from 1590 and as a revelation of Shakespeare's political attitudes. On the whole it has told us more about the political perspective of the analysts than about the man's own thinking. Many post-*Hamlet* plays in the repertory, whether histories, tragedies, or tragicomedies, invoked God's will in their final judgements, as Antonio does when he says 'Just is the law above' at the end of *The Revenger's Tragedy*. Even in that tragic farce, though, sending the triumphant revenger Vindice and his brother to execution is done on the practical ground that 'You that

---

[40] See F. W. Brownlow, *Shakespeare, Harsnett, and the Devils of Denham*, University of Delaware Press, Newark, 1993, particularly pp. 93–131.

[41] McMillin and MacLean in their history of the Queen's Men make a good point about history as perceived reality. See especially pp. 133–38.

would murder him would murder me.' The same earthly view is expressed in Lear's contemptuous reaction when Albany says 'All friends shall taste / The wages of their virtue, and all foes / The cup of their deservings.' This earthliness became a durable innovation. By 1605 several of the company's writers were expressing doubts about the simplicity of the moralistic and providential closures of plays like *A Warning for Fair Women*. They prepared the way for the extreme test-cases of tyrants in love that Fletcher developed.

LATER INNOVATIONS

To a degree the advent of the Blackfriars as a venue for the company was matched by the rise of the Fletcherian repertory, which slowly took the dominant place in the repertory from Shakespeare's plays. The relationship was, however, much more intricate than a simple cause-and-effect process. The transition from the company's assumption of the primacy of audiences at the Globe to those at the Blackfriars was so gradual that few indicators can be noted as clear markers of the shift. The Globe remained eminent for years beyond 1610. Foreign dignitaries visited it, and in 1611 an attendant in Prince Otto of Hesse-Kassel's train noted that of all London's playhouses 'the most important is the Globe'.[42] Even in the 1620s the Globe was for a while named on title pages as often as the Blackfriars. Rebuilding the Globe in 1614 and maintaining the summer and winter repertory through to the end shows the persistence of the company tradition first conceived in 1594 to play for all the range of London society. Even the choice of the Globe to stage *A Game at Chess* and *The Late Lancashire Witches* was a matter of making hay while the authoritarian suns were shining outside London rather than of appealing to a down-market audience. James Shirley's prologue to *The Doubtful Heir*, proclaiming that it had not been written for a Globe audience, is sometimes cited as the clearest mark of the repertory's recognition of the gulf between Globe and Blackfriars tastes. In fact it is careful to make no such suggestion. The play had been written originally for Shirley's Dublin audiences, and was revised for the King's on his return in 1640. His apology for the absence of the bawdry and swordfights normally expected by a Bankside audience does not say that the play was designed only for the Blackfriars.

The influence of the Blackfriars on the repertory is most evident in the plethora of Jacobean and Caroline plays devoted to questions of love and honour. That was the actual title of a play by Davenant in 1634, designed to

[42] Chambers, *Elizabethan Stage*, II.369.

sieve the grit out of Fletcher's innovations in his tragicomedies and tragedies since 1609. Fletcher's most common theme was the gentry's concept of honour in extreme situations where love, oppressed by royal or brotherly tyranny, put it to the test. That theme was the essence of his first plays written for the King's, *Philaster*, *The Maid's Tragedy*, and *A King and No King*. *The Maid's Tragedy* offers a king who marries his mistress off to a young man to cover his sexual involvement, trusting the new husband to conceal the situation once he learns the truth. He is agonized like Hamlet, but will not take revenge on his king. The mistress's brother, however, a soldier, chooses revenge. The play splits Hamlet's dilemma over revenge into its alternatives. This kind of story based on courtly lechery led to a mass of reinventions of the old stories as writers struggled to compose variations on familiar themes. The nearly forty Shakespeares and the fifty 'Beaumont and Fletcher' plays that were roosting in the repertory by 1625 cast a long shadow over the Caroline writers.

New plays in the Fletcherian moot-game mode flowed in more and more slowly. Repeating old favourites in the 1620s and 1630s was a simple effect of the sheer quantity of plays the company now owned. The time, risk, and expense of mounting new plays discounted their novelty value against the old faithfuls. It is hardly surprising that once it had been established with Shakespeare's and then Fletcher's plays the company's Blackfriars repertory should offer a familiar menu. Even at court in the years from 1616 to 1642 the company presented more than twice as many revivals as new plays, seventy-one against thirty. Some new plays were offered at court more than once on their first showings, *The Maid in the Mill* appearing three times in the 1623–4 season. Through the Caroline period a 70:30 ratio of revivals over new plays at court was the norm, which suggests that there must have been a much higher ratio of old plays at the Blackfriars and Globe.

One of the company's most durable innovations was its practice of sustaining a resident writer. Bentley, in his study of the business of writing plays, identifies only two writers who can be counted as being held on professional contracts, Heywood and Shakespeare.[43] A lawsuit about the failure of one writer to obey the terms of his contract for the regular provision of plays does survive from the 1630s, but no actual contracts. It seems likely that Christopher Beeston made a contract with Heywood and the Chamberlain's had one with Shakespeare as players and writers for their companies. Fletcher, after some years collaborating with Shakespeare and others, and writing for the residual boy companies, seems to have developed

---

[43] G. E. Bentley, *The Profession of Dramatist in Shakespeare's Time*, Princeton University Press, 1971.

19. John Fletcher, an engraving by John Marshall from the Folio of 1647.

a resident status as chief of the collaborators for the King's by 1616, working perhaps on the same terms that Henslowe's writers did in the 1590s.

Shakespeare's contract, however hypothetical, of course came to guarantee the long shadow in the repertory. Other players, notably Ben Jonson, wrote plays that they sold to the company, but the Chamberlain's seem to have been the first to have paid a writer to work with and sell his plays to the company exclusively. Since the first occupant of the residency was Shakespeare, a player and sharer as well as an author, his membership in the company can easily be misrepresented. From the company's perspective his inclusion was a gift from the main sponsors of the duopoly because of his existing plays. He had acted alongside several of the other sharers, notably Richard Burbage, so he could hardly have been considered an intruding outsider. Yet if the myths about the small roles he took in his own plays have any validity, he was valued more for his writing than his playing. The allocation of all his earlier plays to the Chamberlain's is strikingly like the delivery of Marlowe's plays from various companies to the other half of the duopoly. Such an allocation guaranteed the chief resource for each company. Marlowe was dead in 1594, but Shakespeare was an active participant in the growth of the newly licensed duopoly, and his continuing presence guaranteed its great rise.

Judging from the dates that can be ascribed to his plays, Shakespeare each year wrote one comedy and one serious play, history or tragedy. Such work was almost certainly a requirement of his contract. A version of the same divide can be identified in the later writers, too. Like his successors in residence, Fletcher, Massinger, and Shirley, Shakespeare sold all rights in his plays to the sharers, and did nothing to get them into print in the way that non-residents like Jonson and Webster did. It was the company that owned them, and that allowed them to get into print. Most of the Beaumont and Fletcher plays that were issued as quartos while Fletcher was in the company seem to have been printed from scribal transcripts originally made for presentation to private enthusiasts.[44] Of the four writers in residence only Shirley, freed by the stoppage of playing, took his plays directly to the press, and that was not until eleven years after the 1642 closure.

The company evidently saw a resident writer as an asset, because they renewed the concept in the reorganizations of 1608–9, 1625, and 1640.

---

[44] One such was Sir Henry Neville, to whom the publisher of the first quarto of *A King and No King* in 1619 presented the book, thanking him for 'that which formerly hath beene received from you'. Possibly some of the other Beaumont and Fletcher plays that came into print in 1619–23 were released by the company when income was short because of Burbage's death and the closure of playing during the mourning for Queen Anna.

Not that Shakespeare's replacement was made quickly. He left playing and moved back to Stratford in 1609 or so, and a lengthy period of non-resident writing in collaboration followed before John Fletcher succeeded him, some time after Shakespeare sold his shares in the company. Fletcher wrote in collaboration much more than his predecessor is thought to have done, starting by sharing with Shakespeare the composition of at least three plays, *Two Noble Kinsmen*, *Cardenio*, and *Henry VIII*. Fletcher had already collaborated with Beaumont for the Blackfriars boys. Collaborative writing does not seem to have figured largely in the Chamberlain's repertory, unlike the Admiral's. Henslowe employed teams of up to five writers who shared the composition of speeches and dialogue, one of them laying out the general plot and allocating writing slots to the others according to their particular skills. Fletcher worked with fewer fellow-writers, and more interactively. Judging by the difficulty analysts have had differentiating one writer from another in his early collaborations with Beaumont, Fletcher seems to have worked side by side with his various co-writers and to have made tighter revisions of the completed scripts. His collaborative writing for the King's was holistic. After working with Beaumont and Shakespeare he linked up with several other writers, including Massinger, Field, and possibly Middleton, who wrote six plays for the company and collaborated in the writing or at least the revision of several others, including *Measure for Measure* and *Macbeth*. The so-called Beaumont and Fletcher corpus of more than fifty plays shows Fletcher keeping tight control of his collaborative teams.

For some years while Fletcher was first writing for the company he continued to write plays for the ex-boy company, the Lady Elizabeth's. He may not have actually become the company's resident until Field left the Lady Elizabeth's for the King's bringing with him Fletcher's other plays.[45] It was Fletcher who established the value of a resident writer who could co-ordinate his various collaborators. When he died in 1625 Massinger succeeded him, keeping the job till his death in 1640. He was buried alongside Fletcher in St Saviours, now Southwark Cathedral, near Shakespeare's youngest brother, an evident mark of the company's continuing commitment to the Globe. The majority of innovatory intrusions by writers using other styles came during Massinger's tenure. When he died in 1640 the company fetched Shirley back from Dublin to do the job for the last years. As a company practice the resident writer was unique, probably the most lasting

---

[45] Authorship of collaborative texts was mystifying to everyone. *Rollo* was noted in the Stationers' Register in 1639 as by '*J.B.*' The title page of the 1639 London quarto made it '*B.J.F.*' The second quarto, printed in Oxford in 1640, made the author 'John Fletcher *Gent.*' Moseley listed it as 'by Francis Beamont, and John Fletcher' in 1660 and in the Stationers' Register the same year.

effect of Shakespeare's presence in the founding membership, even though none of his successors played or shared in the company as he did. The overlaps meant that in all Shakespeare worked for twenty years, Fletcher for sixteen, Massinger on and off for nearly twenty-five, and Shirley for two and a half up to the closure. Overlaps and long-lasting tenures ensured they were all thoroughly familiar with the existing repertoire and could maintain its anti-radical continuity.

It was not all conservatism, however. Fletcher became a quite basic influence on the repertory after 1610, and a more potent influence than Shakespeare after 1625. Critics like Philip Finkelpearl and Gordon McMullan have done valuable work on his political attitudes, and his focus on women in his plays and his audiences is now getting closer attention. His views about male–female love were laid out before he started writing for the King's, in the unhappily received *The Faithful Shepherdess* for the Blackfriars boys. He seems to have been the first writer to show much awareness of the female component in Blackfriars audiences, and took care to cater for it. *The Tamer Tamed* ignored Bianca's eyelash-fluttering, offering instead a solo woman who runs the wives' revolt and ends in triumphal independence of men. In *Philaster* and *The Maid's Tragedy* he portrayed sexual extremes that ruled the plot, happily with Megra, Arethusa, and Bellario in *Philaster*, and tragically in the contrast between Aspatia and Evadne in *The Maid's Tragedy*. *Bonduca* and later tragedies extended the range, while other comedies besides *The Tamer Tamed* kept up the celebration of female control. His tragicomedies played with the danger of taking love and honour seriously.

Fletcher was an innovator, but not a dangerous one. It is in the nature of any settled company where audience expectations are well enough known to dictate a familiar repertory that new plays are never very radical. Their audiences wanted them to be reliable in production standards and in the range and type, and nobody could withstand the nobility who took over the Blackfriars. That situation Fletcher, Massinger, and Shirley went along with. Their plays ran down a narrow channel of inventiveness on familiar and intertextual themes. The few plays that could really be called innovatory in the repertory after 1610 came from the non-resident writers of the 1630s, of whom the most notable were the courtier poets, chiefly William Davenant, who took control of the Blackfriars repertory for a while in the 1630s. Even he felt bound to renew the prime Fletcherian subject of honour in love.

As both royal and public favour raised plays in status, the question of the best poetic style for plays became a respectable subject for poets to debate. A new order of gentlemanly poets seeking to make their names at court, notably Davenant and Thomas Carew, started writing for the Blackfriars

20. William Davenant, from the engraving by John Greenhill on the Frontispiece of the 1673 edition of his *Works*.

audiences, and their assumption of superiority over the professional writers soon drew blood. Several professionals, Massinger, Shirley, Heywood, and John Ford, then had their say about what they thought good plays should be, and how their verse should sound. The contest began with Carew making a fuss about the failure of Davenant's *Just Italian* at Blackfriars in 1629. In a prefatory verse written for its publication in 1630 Carew lamented how Beeston's players at the indoor Cockpit and outdoor Red Bull were emptying the benches at the Blackfriars with their cock and bull stories. Taste should move forward. Davenant's style was fresh and full of bright metaphors, and in Carew's mind the Blackfriars repertory needed that novelty. The argument grew wider as a friend of Carew attacked the resident Massinger's 'flat / dull dialogues frought with insipit chatt', in contrast with Carew's own 'sweete Muse, which sings / ditties fit only for the eares of Kings'.[46] Ford, who had spent years paring down his own style down till it was free of the extravagances of Davenant's metaphors, left the King's for Beeston around this time, as did Shirley.[47]

Davenant ruled the King's roost for years, writing and stimulating his courtier friends to write most of the company's new plays from 1631 to 1637. In 1634 he became the court's sole writer of masques and therefore the company's chief access to courtly tastes. Massinger was still the resident writer, loyally writing Fletcherian plays, even explicitly rewriting his *Lovers' Progress* with *Cleander* in 1634, but it was Davenant who drew the Blackfriars repertory closest to the court's interests, till his ambition to stage a more operatic kind of theatre took him away during the long plague closure in 1638.

Cause of another intrusion by outside writers, and another mark of the company's intermittent entanglement in political issues through the 1620s and 1630s, was a likely intervention by the Lord Chamberlain. He seems to have prompted the company to pay Heywood and Brome to write *The Late Lancashire Witches* for staging while a rehearing of the Pendle witches case in London was imminent (Appendix 2.42). Like the manoeuvres that led to the staging of *A Game at Chess* ten years before, it seems to have started with a Pembroke, this time William Herbert's younger brother Philip, his successor as Lord Chamberlain, who at the time was engaged in sorting out the company's affairs over the Sharers' Papers. His chief enemy on the Privy Council, Archbishop Laud, found the judgement at the original trial in Lancashire unsatisfactory, and brought the accused to London with the various testimonies for a fresh trial. Someone on the Council with access to the papers gave a biased selection to Heywood and Brome to make into a play, the selection omitting the chief accusers' retractions. That was probably Pembroke, because in August 1634 his agent the Master of the Revels blocked another play on the subject by a different company until the King's Men's version had its run. The same machinery of control that

[46] The 'untun'd kennell' debate is discussed in *The Shakespearean Stage 1574–1642*, Cambridge University Press, third edition, 1992, pp. 218–20, and on pp. 85–9 of the book on Ford cited below.
[47] The potent taciturnity of his verse in *The Broken Heart* also appears in the other FIDE HONOR plays, published in 1633–4, 1638, and 1639 under the anagram of his name, IOHN FORD. Michael Neill's collection of essays, *John Ford, Critical Re-Visions*, Cambridge University Press, 1988, includes several that deal with his style and the intrusion of the new writers who made him leave the King's.

licensed and brought Middleton's anti-Spanish play to the stage in 1624 seems to have worked in 1634 to influence people against Laud's scepticism, though that was evidently shared by the players, on the evidence of a visitor who happened to witness a performance of the play, and wrote about it to entertain his master in Somerset.[48]

While it may oversimplify the history, the most direct way of tracking the shifts in the company repertory is to follow the resident writers and the way they built on their predecessors. The bias of Shakespeare's plays has been sketched already. A look at similar features from Fletcher and Massinger and from Shirley's brief tenure should mark the line of the company's path and some of the flowers that grew alongside it.

To modern readers and playgoers the fifty-two plays of the Beaumont and Fletcher canon and the plays of Massinger and Shirley lack the human intimacy found in the Shakespeare plays. That loss was not unintended. It followed the distinctive concept of playmaking that Fletcher developed in all three of the genres he used. The idea of drama apparent in Fletcher's essential form, tragicomedy, interlocks as an innovatory genre with several of Shakespeare's last plays, but its essence was his own. By the 1620s plot-driven dramas of love, danger, and the peril of death featured in almost all the new plays, whether the outcome was comic love or tragic death. Tragicomedy left the audience guessing which would be the outcome. The danger that might lead either to a tragic or a comic ending was inherent in many of the new plays written between 1610 and 1642. It became almost a defining characteristic of the company repertory. The plays listed in Appendix 5 show how specific and durable this concept of a play's genre became.

Rather too much has been made of the variants on the generic term 'tragical history' on the title pages of the Shakespeare quartos, and the uncertainty evident in the misgrouping of plays such as *Cymbeline* in the First Folio. The three genres on stage in the Induction to *A Warning for Fair Women* reflect the binary nature of the serious and comic division that was standard under Elizabeth. Tragicomedy entered as a distinct genre with Fletcher, and gradually crystallized. By the time Shirley became the company's resident playwright, the spread of genres he supplied seems decidedly prescriptive. In the two-and-a-half years after his return from Dublin to replace Massinger he wrote two comedies, two tragicomedies, and one tragedy. In fact until the Caroline period genre was not often clearly identified. Of the 160 plays listed in the Appendix, the title pages of only

---

[48] The story is told clearly and the letter quoted in full by Herbert Berry, 'The Globe Bewitched and *El Hombre Fiel*', in *Shakespeare's Playhouses*, AMS Press, New York, 1987, pp. 121–48.

twenty-four say they are comedies, twelve are called tragicomedies, four-teen are tragedies, one (*Hamlet* Q1) is a tragical history, and four (including *The Merchant of Venice* and *Troilus and Cressida*) are said to be histories. *A Warning*'s distinct genres were certainly not recognized on the early play title pages. Almost all the confident genre specifications come from the 1630s. The first use of 'tragicomedy' on a title page was in 1630, although the 1604 entry in the Stationers' Register for *The Malcontent* had called it one. Of the fifty-two plays in the collected Fletcher edition of 1679 one (*Four Plays in One*) is a curious morality and probably not a King's play, ten were designated tragedies, twenty-four comedies, and ten were named and another seven were in effect tragicomedies. That roughly matches the ratio of Massinger's and Shirley's plays, and is not far out of step with the proportion in Shakespeare. In the earlier part of the period *Richard II* and *Richard III* were both called tragedies while *Hamlet* was a tragical history. The *de facto* Shakespeare pattern of writing one comedy and one serious play, tragedy or history, annually broke down after 1602, after which the tragicomedies like *Pericles* and *Cymbeline* destroyed any parity. Fletcher's di-vision of twenty-four comedies to twenty-seven tragedies or tragicomedies became the new pattern. Their chief value was that because they could go either way Fletcherian tragicomedies kept newcomers guessing. In contrac-tual terms, though, they evidently belonged in the 'serious' half of Fletcher's supply to the company.[49]

 The Fletcher repertory reflects the stability the company had acquired by 1610. Where its earlier writers had dramatized stories already in print, from Holinshed's *Chronicles*, Painter's tales, or an old pamphlet by Gascoigne (*A Larum for London*), Fletcher created his own stories. While the older plays took stories largely ready-made, generating the source-hunting industry which is still a major feature of most modern editions, Fletcher and his peers and successors largely invented their own plots. The proof of that can be seen in modern editions where the hunt for Fletcher's sources can only offer a despairing trawl through a multitude of vague parallels, mostly of extreme situations. Fletcher took elements from many stories and plays – his own are infused with elements from Shakespeare[50] – and wove new plots out of components familiar in the whole playstock of the time. The essence

---

[49] See Philip Edwards, 'The Danger not the Death: the Art of John Fletcher', in *Jacobean Theatre*, Stratford-upon-Avon Studies 1, 1960, ed. John Russell Brown and Bernard Harris, Edward Arnold, London 1960, pp. 159–78.

[50] An elegant demonstration how Beaumont and Fletcher incorporated Shakespearean strands and motifs in their early plays can be found in H. Neville Davies, 'Beaumont and Fletcher's Hamlet', in *Shakespeare, Man of the Theater*, ed. Kenneth Muir, Jay L. Halio, and D. J. Palmer, University of Delaware Press, Newark, 1983, pp. 173–81.

of the company's post-Shakespeare repertory was original plots contrived to test honour and morality in extreme situations.

The reason for this change to plot-driven stories can be partly ascribed to a new kind of confidence in this second generation of writers, their security matching the company's own. Fletcher invented his plots because his concern was to make up complex moral and political situations that the play resolved in suitably testing ways. Love and lechery test a man's honour. That meant losing Shakespearean individualism. Most of the characters in Fletcher's plays are types who might have features of Hamlet, Othello, or Macbeth, but spend more time chasing the plot than revealing the inner man. Many of the plot-devices were familiar from Sidney's *Arcadia*. The man disguising himself as a woman appears in *The Honest Man's Fortune*, *Monsieur Thomas*, *The Humorous Lieutenant*, *Love's Cure*, and *The Night Walker*. Daughters disguised as pages not recognized by their own fathers, starting with Rosalind in *As You Like It*, were used by Fletcher from *Philaster* (where a father is shown up when he accuses his daughter, disguised as a page, of male sex with the play's heroine), to the comforting revelation to a defeated king in *The Humorous Lieutenant* that the heroine, beloved of the prince his conqueror, is his own daughter. Fletcher developed heroic women as an active plot-device to test honour in men. His plays anticipated the prioritizing of women's roles in the plays that came to prevail in the 1630s. His constant and honourable heroes are all women. It is the men in his plays who suffer torments of moral choice.[51] His values were complex, and at the outset markedly individual. *Philaster* depended on Sidney and Spenser, whose *Faerie Queene* Bk IV gave him the idea of a woman being accused of sex with a man who was a woman in disguise, from Ate's accusation of Amoret and Britomart. *The Faithful Shepherdess*, which the company revived for Henrietta Maria in 1633, creates a remarkable typology of love-types in its three pairs of different kinds of love.

In many respects it is Fletcher rather than Shakespeare who stands at the heart of the company repertory for its last thirty years, dependent on themes from Shakespeare though he was. Fletcher learned his art in collaboration, first with Beaumont, then with Nathan Field, and finally with his successor Massinger. His plays with Beaumont were sold to the Blackfriars boys, then he wrote for their successor the Lady Elizabeth's, whose leader Field, later a collaborator with Fletcher and a King's player, was

---

[51] On what he calls 'Romance Exhausted', see Richard Hillman, *Intertextuality and Romance in Renaissance Drama: The Staging of Nostalgia*, Macmillan, Basingstoke, 1992, pp. 155–71.

their most celebrated name.[52] Fletcher did write regularly for the King's from 1609 onwards, but his learning-base was wider than theirs. Some of his plays for the Lady Elizabeth's such as *The Knight of Malta* come closer to being the broad prose comedy he wrote for the boy company than the plays he designed for the King's at Blackfriars from 1609. His kind of play, from *Philaster* onwards (it opens with a greeting for the King's customers), was designed specifically for the company and its women-dominated Blackfriars audiences.

Fletcher's innovatory plotting was not an instant success. In the first period after the company started using its two playhouses, the comments by playgoers do not show much approval of the repertory's shifts. The gossip-conscious John Chamberlain, for instance, wrote in 1615 that 'our Poets braines and invention are growne very drie insomuch that of five newe playes there is not one pleases, and therfore they are driven to forbish over theyre old, which stand them in best stead, and bring them most profit'.[53] We cannot be sure how widely true that was, nor how far it reflected the stability of the open-air repertory and its old plays in contrast with the Blackfriars and its novelties. Chamberlain may have been obliquely echoing Jonson's view expressed in *Bartholomew Fair* where he mocked those who 'will swear *Jeronimo* or *Andronicus* are the best plays yet', on the grounds that such sound judgements had stood unchanged for the last twenty-five or thirty years. That illustrates Jonson's sense of the changes in playwriting over the last decades, though it also acknowledges the strength of audience preference for the now-familiar traditions. Clearly, both writers were recognizing a divergence in audience fashions. As playgoing became more respectable the increase in the number of companies took away the duopoly's need for constant novelty, so old favourites could be repeated more easily. Jonson's and Chamberlain's comments appeared when the King's Men were settling into their most lasting practices, giving preference to the Fletcherian fashion that drew them inescapably into courtly pockets. The broad implication, that the open-air playhouses, including the Globe, held on to the older plays while the indoor playhouses, including the Cockpit from 1617, went upmarket with the new, is still a matter for debate.

In fact the company's move upmarket with the Blackfriars was surprisingly gradual. The higher pricing at the indoor venue must have set an

---

[52] They seem to have been taken into the King's repertory when Field joined them in 1616.
[53] *The Letters of John Chamberlain*, 1.567.

immediate distinction between the two playhouses which the company's repertory took a surprisingly long time to reflect. Its elevated social status in the 1630s was not clearly evidenced in its first decade. Title pages of company plays began to advertise performance at the Blackfriars ahead of the Globe only in the 1620s, when the company resumed the publication of its plays. Even then naming the indoor playhouse first seems largely a hangover from the boy company days when indoor performances snobbishly and wrongly claimed to be 'private' whereas the amphitheatres were 'public'. That formal distinction lost its point once the boy companies came under the authority of the Master of the Revels in 1606 or thereabouts, but the snobbery persisted so the adjectives became fuzzier. Ford's *Lover's Melancholy* was advertised in 1629 as 'acted at the private house in the Blacke Friers, and publikely at the Globe', yet in the same year Carlell's *Deserving Favourite* appeared as acted 'publikely at the Black-Friers'. Performances at Blackfriars were proclaimed on title pages much more than at the Globe through the late 1620s and 1630s, their claim to be 'private' flaunting their social pretensions, as the title pages printed in Appendix 5 show.

The most intricate twist in the long trail of the company's public repertory and its innovations is what went on under the royal shadow. Like any courtier, the company's privilege of proximity to the royal presence meant fawning, but it also allowed the occasional explicit statement of concern. Some of these twists are discussed in the next chapter, including Fletcher's use of the role of women and love at court as a metaphor for concern about political authority and its misuse. In general Massinger continued Fletcher's programme, giving priority to the gentlemanly questions of love and honour, though he got into much more trouble than Fletcher with his political comments. It was Massinger who picked up the royalist term of abuse 'the many-headed multitude' applied to democrats and parliamentarians, but he put it into the mouth of Domitian Caesar, a tyrant who is justifiably murdered (*The Roman Actor*, 3.2.34).[54] While *The City Madam* dismissed the social pretensions of the wives of London's citizen magnates in emphatically conservative terms, *Believe As You List* and other plays were caught even in the loose net of the Caroline censor. Charles himself read play manuscripts such as Davenant's *The Wits*, ruling that its oaths were acceptable when Herbert had ordered them changed, but he was much

---

[54] A thorough survey of the term is given by Christopher Hill, 'The Many-Headed Monster', in *From the Renaissance to the Counter-Reformation, Essays in Honor of Garrett Mattingly*, ed. C. H. Carter, New York, 1966, republished in Hill, *Change and Continuity in Seventeenth-Century England*, Weidenfeld and Nicolson, London, 1974, pp. 181–204.

harsher in censoring political references from several of Massinger's plays. Charles noted a speech about forced taxation in *The King and the Subject* as 'insolent, and to be changed'.[55]

Massinger died in March 1640, and in April James Shirley returned from Ireland to take on the resident's functions. It is not known for certain whether he sailed over by invitation or heard of Massinger's death and took the chance. I think it most likely that he was invited, since the timing is too neat to be a coincidence. In his London years of the early 1630s he had been associated with Massinger in his conflict with the courtier poets. Moreover, the chief opponent in that struggle, Davenant, had now taken over the Cockpit, to which Shirley had given twelve years of his writing until leaving for Ireland in the plague of 1636–8. He was the most obvious professional writer to fill Massinger's vacated role, and he did represent the old opposition to Davenant. To the King's he brought one play he had already staged in Dublin, *Rosania*, which in June joined the repertory at the Globe as *The Doubtful Heir*, a tragicomedy with a prologue proclaiming that it had definitely not been written for the Globe's audiences (Appendix 2.49).[56] Subsequently he appears to have been paid to write two plays a year, of which he completed five down to the closure in September 1642, which prevented his last play from being staged. In 1653 he published all five of his King's plays plus *The Doubtful Heir* in a collection called *Six New Playes*. They were actually registered for printing in 1646, when the times were still unfavourable for plays, but not published for another seven. In the 1653 publication the five written for the Blackfriars were *The Imposture*, a tragicomedy licensed by Herbert on 10 November 1640; *The Politic Father, or, The Brothers*, a comedy licensed on 26 May 1641; *The Cardinal*, a tragedy licensed 25 November 1641; *The Sisters*, another comedy licensed 26 April 1642; and another tragicomedy, *The Court Secret*, which there was no time to perform.

ALONG THE WAY

The quick and short-lived flowering of *A Game at Chess* in 1624 and *The Late Lancashire Witches* ten years later have been noted already. Most of the other flowers that bloomed on the way were more incidental gains, though two in particular exploited the company's pre-eminence rather shamelessly.

---

[55] Bawcutt, *The Control and Censorship of Caroline Drama*, pp. 203–4.
[56] See Gurr, *Playgoing in Shakespeare's London*, pp. 193–5. The original composition for a Dublin audience that prompted the prologue's disclaimer is noted above.

In the late 1620s and 1630s, for instance, the King's appear to have used their privilege as the premier company to take up players and even plays from other companies. Evidence for the first of these acts of privilege appears in a peculiar order of 6 May 1633 by the Lord Chamberlain. It said that several 'principall Actors' of the company had died or were sick, so they could not produce their necessary entertainments for the king without enlisting some new recruits. Consequently they were authorized to choose whoever they wanted from 'any of the lycensed Companyes within & about the Citty of London' (Appendix 2.39). In fact none of the sharers had died since Heminges in 1630. The text of the Order makes it look suspiciously as if the king had complained that one or more of the company's sharers had been absent from a play at court in the recently completed season, and had mentioned it to Philip Herbert, who took the action he thought necessary. No new sharers appeared in the lists at this time, and it may be that the company simply wanted to improve the quality of its hired men. It was, none the less, a unique sign of the company's pre-eminence and the leverage that the king's patronage could now give them.

The second privilege is implied by their acquisition in the 1620s of several plays written originally for boy companies, specifically Jonson's *Epicene* and some early Beaumont and Fletcher plays, *The Coxcomb* (played at court by the Queen's Revels in 1612, and by the King's in 1622), *Cupid's Revenge* (at court by the Queen's Revels in 1612 and 1613, by the King's in December 1624), *The Faithful Shepherdess* (a flop at the Blackfriars in 1608, at court triumphantly with the King's in 1634), *The Scornful Lady*, and possibly *Alphonsus Emperor of Germany* (at court in 1630 and at the Blackfriars in 1636 to honour the queen's guest). We cannot be sure how the company acquired these plays. Some, including *The Faithful Shepherdess* and *Cupid's Revenge*, were in print, but others were not. All the companies that originally staged them were gone, so they may have been acquired by a process of purchase or by more dubious inheritance from the heirs of the original companies. The Beaumont and Fletchers probably came with Field when he was recruited from the Lady Elizabeth's in 1616. Later interventions by the Lord Chamberlain in 1637 and in August 1641 over the printing of play-texts and the rights to specific plays by the King's and by Beeston may have been responses to this privilege. His 1641 letter lists 61 King's plays (Appendix 2.50), including *The Coxcomb*. Since the list was issued while the plague had closed all the playhouses, it must reflect the company's wish to get extra income from publishing. It certainly upholds the view that they thought all these plays were their rightful property. The longer the repertory ran, the more the company revived older favourites and the more they cashed in on their Beaumont and Fletcher resource by selling older plays to the press.

The plays best representing what was expected to attract a Blackfriars audience in the 1630s include Arthur Wilson's *The Swisser*. When the company staged his play in 1631 Wilson was thirty-six, having served as secretary to the Earl of Essex for fifteen years. He was evidently familiar with many of the Blackfriars plays, since *The Swisser* is full of echoes from the repertory's plays such as *Hamlet*. The title role was seen both by author and company as appropriate for Lowin, who played the part, since it refers to a 'great beard' that was his false identity, 'and bulke' (3.2.111), apparent in his depiction as Falstaff in *The Wits* (figure 4, p. 28). The play's verse, full of speeches voicing extreme emotions in extreme situations, is sturdy, but the plot is maggot-ridden with contorted versions of familiar plot devices. Its model was *The Malcontent*, its finale full of similar tragicomic twists. The Swisser is a disguised malcontent, commenting like a licensed Fool on the misdoings of courtiers and soldiers, until he and his friend have to confront the fact that their king has raped the friend's beloved. She turns out to be the Swisser's daughter, who, like Bellario in *Philaster*, disguised herself as a boy to follow her beloved. Should they take revenge? The tragicomic ending, more contrived than its other model, *The Maid's Tragedy*, allows both would-be revengers to forgive, a reversal set up through loving interventions by the king's sister and the raped daughter. The unrelated subplot sets up a pair of lovers with fathers who are Montague-and-Capulet enemies. Opposed to their love, one father tells his son that he must not marry the other's daughter because he is her half-brother. The lovers, having already secretly married and assuming their union is incestuous, drink poison. Being a tragicomedy, the poison turns out to be a sleeping-potion like Imogen's, so that the father can admit to them he lied and they can live happily ever after. It is not easy to avoid feeling how easily such tragicomic plot-contortions can turn into farce.

Two writers among the occasionals, one Jacobean and one Caroline, exemplify the non-resident writers' services to the repertory. Thomas Middleton was a contributor from as early as 1607 up to his apotheosis in 1624. Unless we count *The Revenger's Tragedy* as his, written in 1607 when he was seeking fresh employment after his early patrons the boy companies faded, his first five plays for the King's belong to the latter half of the second decade while the Blackfriars was asserting its supremacy. A sixth might have been *The Second Maiden's Tragedy* of 1611, although the manuscript does not name its author. *A Game at Chess* was a later commission. Of the central five, *The Widow* (1615?) and *The Witch* (1615–18, surviving in a Ralph Crane manuscript) both caught the Fletcherian comic mood of the time. So did *More Dissemblers Besides Women* (1615?) and *Anything for a Quiet Life* (1618–21), although *More Dissemblers* is a blacker comedy than any by Fletcher. It uses the role-playing conceit to expose male trickery. *The Widow* was an intricately plotted and fast-moving comedy, with sympathy for women's victimization typical of Fletcher. *The Witch*, containing a song also used in *Macbeth*, may have failed or been blocked on stage because of its affinities with the trial of Frances Howard.[57] The fifth was Middleton's most popular play for the King's, his tragedy of ancient Britain, *Hengist, or The Mayor of Quinborough* (1616–18?), set in the early British period like Fletcher's *Bonduca*. Its comic subplot about the new mayor and a company of con-man players proved durably popular, featuring in drolls during the closure and full revivals in the Restoration.

The second major occasional writer was Davenant in the 1630s. Much more aggressive and ambitious than Middleton, allied with the courtier poets who later gave the company plays like *Aglaura*, he began with *The Cruel Brother*, a Fletcherian tragedy in 1627, and then the tragicomic and yet anti-Fletcherian *Just Italian* (1629). An extension of the old subject of love after marriage first broached in *The Taming of the Shrew*, *The Just Italian* sets its eponymous hero at odds with his new rich wife, who is determined to be a shrew and to keep her riches from her new husband. The husband tries to correct her, and to

> Shew
> Her crime to spring, not from poison'd malice
> But, from the feminine mistakes of wit:
> For, modern courts now preach, wit doth reside
> In ladies' subtle riots, and their pride.

He brings his sister to his new wife, who has never met her, pretending that in reprisal for her shrewishness he is going to make the newcomer his concubine. To counter that challenge the wife brings in a Florentine who she says will be her paramour. These gambits go into reverse when the sister and the Florentine fall in love with each other and the Florentine then spurns the wife, who consequently repents her 'stern pride'. Davenant explicitly does not let the play become a 'black tragedy', ending it with a

---

[57] See Anne Lancashire, '*The Witch*: Stage Flop or Political Mistake?', in '*Accompaninge the Players': Essays Celebrating Thomas Middleton, 1580–1980*, ed. Kenneth Friedenreich, AMS Press, New York, 1983, pp. 161–81.

dance of three pairs of lovers, including husband and wife. Carew's defence of it against the Cock and Bull crew was chiefly spurred by the play's inventive images. One simile says that 'life is like the span / Forc'd from a gouty hand, which, as it gains / Extent and active length, the more it pains'. It also has some deeply erotic phrasing. Lovers are to be 'wrapt in curlings intricate', enjoying sex in 'slippery closures' while suspended in an arcadian hammock, 'the Indian net', ''tween two shady poplars'.

After *The Just Italian* flopped, Davenant wrote nothing for four years. He returned to the King's and Blackfriars with *The Wits*, a raunchy comedy, which in 1633 Charles was persuaded to read in order to pass judgement on its language when it was condemned by the Master of the Revels. The king upheld it against Herbert (Appendix 2.41). Davenant then launched two other ambitious plays, the first's title exemplifying the Blackfriars concerns, *Love and Honour* (1634), the second aimed at climbing into the queen's favour, *The Platonic Lovers* (1635). This openly pandered to Henrietta Maria's *précieuse* taste for love purified from sex, though on the evidence of his other sex-driven plays for the Blackfriars the new concept must have been distasteful to the tongue in his cheek. Setting two pairs of lovers in contrast, one aiming at pure love, the other at sexual consummation, it introduced the sort of extreme case, a youth who has never seen a woman, that Davenant was to use much later for his operatic version of *The Tempest*, where Miranda's ignorance of men is matched by Hippolito, her unknown and previously well-hidden brother. The epilogue made the poet dismiss the audience's men on the grounds that sex was all they were after, appealing to the ladies: '*For you (hee knowes) will thinke that Doctrine good, / Which entertains the Mind, and not the Blood.*'[58]

In this period Davenant wrote one play specifically for the Globe, *News from Plymouth*. A blunt citizen comedy set not in London but at one of Britain's main seaports, its heroes are sea-captains detained in harbour by contrary winds, who set their caps at a rich widow as rivals for two landlubber knights named Sir Solemn Trifle and Sir Furious Inland. One of the captains, Topsail, closes Act 1 with a couplet that shows the play's intended level: 'Small hands, full breasts, soft lips and sparkling eyes! / If I can board her, she'll prove lawful prize.' Davenant's expectation of the Globe's audiences shows in the drunken captains, who sing a serenade that begins

> O thou that sleep'st like pig in straw,
> Thou lady dear, arise!

---

[58] See *The Platonic Lovers*, ed. Wendell W. Broom Jr, Garland, New York, 1987, p. 241.

The plot is over getting money as much as sex, and it avoids any of the questions of honour that the tragicomedies and tragedies harped on. It is easy to see how calculatedly patronizing this was. Davenant left the company during the plague closure of 1636–8 while he worked up his idea of musical drama with a grand plan for a huge new playhouse in the Strand. In 1638–9 he wrote another tragedy and two comedies for the King's, but was then called on to replace the disgraced William Beeston as impresario at the Cockpit, where he had little time to develop anything new.

The cautiously innovatory repertory at the Blackfriars was an understandable necessity, constrained as the company was by its high-society audiences and the very length of its tenure. When the Blackfriars became high society's chief resort, as it was in the eyes of the money-hunting Nim, no company made up of commoners could easily ignore what its dignitaries wanted. The Lord Chamberlain himself kept a key to his special box alongside the stage and got into a quarrel with the king's uncle over his exclusive right to it, as happened when a new play opened in January 1636 (Appendix 2.44). With such patronage, the company was unlikely to be too radical in its choice of new plays. But its politics were never blindly loyal to their patron, and many issues on which the court's cliques took variable attitudes were on occasions canvassed in the repertory. The company's writhings under the political whips of the various patrons are the subject of the next chapter.

CHAPTER 5

Royal loyalties

PRACTICAL SUPPORT

The claim that professional playing by the duopoly in London was needed for them to practise their skills if the queen was to have proper entertainment every Christmas became the Privy Council's stock defence of playing in the later part of her reign. A Minute of 19 February 1598 copies a letter addressed to the Master of the Revels and the Justices of Middlesex and Surrey. They, one having authority over all playing, the others authority in the suburbs where the duopoly's playhouses stood, were instructed to suppress a third company trying to intrude on the duopoly. The reason was that 'licence hath bin graunted unto two companies of stage players retayned unto us, the Lord Admiral and Lord Chamberlain, to use and practise stage playes, whereby they might be the better enhabled and prepared to shew such plaies before her Majestie as they shalbe required at tymes meete and accustomed, to which ende they have bin cheefelie licensed and tollerated as aforesaid'.[1] No similar authorization existed for any other company. In this narrow view, shows to the public were merely rehearsals for the real aim, to entertain the queen. The patrons of the duopoly on the Council were renewing the practice originally set up when the queen had agreed to become patron of a new company back in 1583. From then until 1642 the monarch's name was explicitly invoked to protect playing.

There was perhaps some truth in the claim that Elizabeth enjoyed plays. A letter from the Council to the Middlesex Justices, signed by the duopoly patrons and Cecil on 8 April 1600, shortly before the Fortune opened in the suburb they controlled, declared that Elizabeth herself wanted Alleyn to return to the stage. It stated that 'Whereas her Majestie (haveinge been well pleased heeretofere at tymes of recreacion with the services of Edward Allen and his Companie, Servantes to me the Earle of Nottingham, wheareof,

---

[1] *Acts of the Privy Council of England*, ed. J. R. Dasent, 32 vols., HMSO, London, 1890–1907, XXVIII.327.

of late he hath made discontynuance) hath sondrye tymes signified her pleasuer, that he should revive the same agayne'.[2] Therefore the magistrates must allow Alleyn to complete the Fortune. That was Charles Howard's personal argument: why the queen's desire to see Alleyn on stage again should justify completion of his playhouse was not spelt out. The familiar argument that playing companies supplied the queen with an essential pleasure at Christmas and needed playhouses to practise in was left implicit. Howard was using Alleyn's name to implement his intention to continue the duopoly at its two new playhouses, the Globe and the Fortune. He could not have applied such strong leverage if there was not some truth in the claim that Elizabeth wanted to see Alleyn playing again. The letter makes more personal the Council's claim that entertaining the queen justified the two playing companies and their playhouses.

King James's charter giving his patronage to London's leading company (Appendix 2.16) took a different line.[3] The new king's patent of 19 May 1603 stated that the company was needed 'aswell for the recreation of our lovinge Subjectes, as for our Solace and pleasure when wee shall thincke good to see them, during our pleasure'. Royalty itself now asserted directly that the pleasures of playgoing were not just the monarch's but the people's. That did not stop James from raising the level of royal generosity in the first season of Christmas entertainments at court. The initial performance, when the King's Men were summoned to perform at Wilton, brought them £30 instead of the £10 which was standard at Elizabeth's court. The persistence of plague that took them out of London and required the court entertainments to be held at Hampton Court brought the company another £80 that Christmas for six plays.[4] The addition to those payments of an extra £30 to compensate them for the long closure during the plague epidemic was a further innovation, an explicit gesture of royal support for the company the king had given his name to. It implies that the first Stuart saw court performances as a standard feature of courtly life, and perhaps as a public manifestation of his new country's best talents. That may explain the appearance of Lawrence Fletcher's name in the company's new patent. Fletcher was an English player from Edinburgh, who could only have been added on the king's instructions. He does not seem to have taken a major part in company affairs, though in 1605 Augustine Phillips left him a bequest

[2] Chambers, *Elizabethan Stage*, IV.328.

[3] I owe this observation to Melissa Aaron. The formula recurs in the Lord Chamberlain's 'Players Passe' of 1636 (see Appendix 2.45).

[4] 'Dramatic Records in the Declared Accounts of the Treasurer of the Chamber 1558–1642', *Malone Society Collections* 6 (1962), 38–9.

in his will. James clearly had his own ideas about his new servants, since he chose to use them in their royal liveries as decoration at Somerset House when the Spanish delegation lodged there during the peace negotiations of August 1604. They were not sent there for their professional skills.

The royal takeover of playing in 1603 lasted till 1642. From 1603 onwards all patrons of the companies licensed to play in London were members of the royal family. King James, after taking on the Chamberlain's for himself, gave the second duopoly company to his elder son Henry and the more recently established third, Worcester's, to his wife Anne. She also took one of the two boy companies, the Blackfriars group, until her controller Samuel Daniel made the mistake of giving them his own *Philotas*, with its unhappy connection to the Essex coup, after which she had to dissociate herself from them. From then on the Blackfriars boys, like the Paul's company, ran without any patron. By 1608, when both had been closed, a new company calling itself the King's Revels had a brief run,[5] its name suggesting the sort of access to royal approval that was used in later years by groups formed outside London.[6] By 1608, though, James's two younger children were considered old enough to become patrons of companies, and new ones were formed in their names, at least one of them absorbing some of the ex-Blackfriars boys.

Such patronage, at least in the first years under James, did not have just a one-way flow of loyalty. James took care at least in the early years to attend every performance by his company at court, as did the other royal patrons. In the 1603–4 season the nine-year-old Prince Henry attended seven court plays, including all five by his own company. James went to twenty, including all eight by his servants. Royal patronage ruled the company till the end. It was an apt irony that one of the last two plays Henry Herbert licensed for the King's in 1642 should be called *The Fatal Friendship*. Royal favour was most explicit in the financial rewards, but they were far from being the only benefit the players received. Royal patronage was an explicit protection that raised the royal companies to a status and durability they never had under Elizabeth. Court politics in her reign were hazardous and much more variable.

However determined were the Privy Councillors who set up the duopoly, they had their own political agendas, and the effects of their multiple interests were not consistently supportive of their companies. There is for instance the mystery of what happened at court over Christmas 1596. Henry

---

[5] For an extended and imaginative history of this peculiar group, see Mary Bly, *Queer Virgins and Virgin Queans on the Early Modern Stage*, Oxford University Press, 2000.

[6] Some of these are noted in chapter 2, on the names of the travelling groups who used the king's name.

Carey was dead, his son had taken the company on as Hunsdon's Men, and yet had signed the petition against the company using the Blackfriars. William Brooke, Lord Cobham, the new Lord Chamberlain, had recently insisted that the name of his ancestor Oldcastle be removed from the company's latest hit so they had to rename him Falstaff. Brooke, whose name was misused with a trick of reversed Falstaffianization in *Merry Wives* in 1597, was hardly likely as Lord Chamberlain to be as close an ally to the company as the first Lord Hunsdon. Yet that Christmas, uniquely in the whole period of the duopoly, Hunsdon's Men were called on to deliver all six plays at court while the Admiral's gave none. In the first duopoly season, 1594–5, the two companies had each staged three plays at court. In 1595–6 the Chamberlain's played five while the Admiral's played four. Afterwards, in 1597–8, Hunsdon's, now again the Chamberlain's, played four to the Admiral's three, and for the two seasons following the two companies each played three. Whatever was going on at court that Christmas to cause the great anomaly after they lost their old patron and their access to the Blackfriars? There is no ready explanation for Brooke's peculiar act of generosity. A letter about his brief tenure of the Chamberlain's office shows him hot-tempered, waving his white rod of office to keep the audience in their places, but that show of temper happened some time after the decision was made to give the company its one-year monopoly of plays at court.[7] Conceivably the gift of exclusive access to George Carey's company that Christmas was Brooke's way of appeasing his rival for the Chamberlain's office, though that seems unlikely given the continuing animosity between the Brookes and the Careys. Carey as Lord Chamberlain was hostile enough to Brooke's heir to entertain the Flemish Ambassador at his house in the Blackfriars in March 1600 with the original 'Oldcastle' version of *1 Henry IV*.[8] Under a martinet like Elizabeth courtiers constantly played their own status games, and the companies suffered from them. Life did become more straightforward and rewarding when patronized by the Stuarts.

After 1603 with royal patrons the duopoly licensing system changed. The royal patents issued to the companies that year were a more potent kind of licence than the ones formerly issued by Tilney as Master of the Revels, and more durable. That innovation called for redress some years later. When in 1615 the Privy Council summoned representatives of the 'foure companyes' to see them, they met, besides Heminges and Burbage from the King's, two

---

[7] Paul Whitfield White analyses Brooke's short career as Lord Chamberlain in 'Shakespeare, the Cobhams, and the Dynamics of Theatrical Patronage', *Shakespeare and Theatrical Patronage in Early Modern England*, pp. 64–89.

[8] See Chambers, *Elizabethan Stage*, 1.220.

each from the Prince's, the Queen's, and Prince Charles's, which because of the shortage of London playhouses had recently merged with the Lady Elizabeth's. The royal patents had been copied and misused by companies touring round the country, so the Council wanted to cull the forgeries. The introduction first of a Master of the Revels in 1578 as censor and then in 1603 of royal patrons abolished the old system where companies had to perform their plays in the local guildhall to the mayors and bailiffs before the town could see them. Now equipped with their royal patents they could perform at whatever inn would take them. But most local authorities still insisted on seeing their licence and the Master's signature on their 'allowed books' that authorized performance, and on occasion bribed them to leave without performing in spite of their patents. In this vetting process several local councils caught companies travelling with forged patents, and that was bad for the royal image. In time the king's protection of playing overrode all local authority, and was acknowledged, often reluctantly, throughout the country. The King's Men in particular benefited, securing royal subsidies during plague closures (£100 in the 1630 closure), and royal support when the Blackfriars residents renewed their complaint in 1619 and 1631. Such possessiveness had its effect on Parliament's thinking in September 1642.

That the King's company took seriously the new role of service to a royal master cannot be doubted. Ideas about how to gratify the company's new patron were met initially when the resident writer included complimentary references to James's books, which had been hurriedly republished in London in 1603, in *Measure for Measure*, the play staged at court on the seasons' chief night, 26 December 1604. For the first Christmas season in 1603 they brought out eight of their already successful plays, including *The Fair Maid of Bristow* and *A Midsummer Night's Dream*. For the second Christmas, however, they tried to get closer to the royal sentiment. Besides *Measure for Measure*, that was evidenced by their choice of the Gowrie story as one of the first plays that they thought to offer for the second season of royal junketing. By 1604 the story of the killing of the two Gowrie brothers in 1601 at their house in Fife was well known, published in several pamphlets. Indeed King James himself, being the only survivor of his encounter with the brothers, was the sole source for the story. Its immediate tellings, readily available in England, all gave full credit to James. So it must have seemed a natural choice for his new servants to stage a play that celebrated his survival from the attempt to assassinate him. The timing, in December, is what suggests the company intended it to be played at court. But staging such a story about England's new king could not avoid presenting one of its chief participants, the king himself, on stage, and that broke one of the few rules that the Master of the Revels always insisted on, that no living person could be shown. James himself took no part in the consequent fuss, and might indeed have thought the publicity about his great escape helpful. But the Privy Councillors who were said to be offended did their work and had it suppressed. As John Chamberlain reported,

the tragedie of Gowrie with all the action and actors hath ben twise represented by the Kings players, with exceeding concourse of all sortes of people, but whether the matter or manner be not well handled, or that yt be thought unfit that princes should be plaide on the stage in theyre life time, I heare that some great counsaillors are much displeased with yt: and so is thought shalbe forbidden.[9]

That gave the company a first lesson in the function of royal servants. It must have rankled, because Fletcher invoked it as late as 1619.[10] No text of the play survives, so its suppression was comprehensive. It is possible that James never knew of his servants' aborted attempt to reproduce his story on stage, although he did have a high regard for it, because he had already set down 'Gowrie Day' to be celebrated in England every year on its anniversary, 5 August. Sermons on it were preached annually at Paul's Cross. According to Thomas Crosfield at Oxford the annual celebration only stopped some time after James died.[11]

What the consequences of this lesson were for the staging of other plays in the repertory is unknown, though if *Henry V*'s quarto text of 1600 is any evidence they had already rejected the idea of staging a version containing Captain Jamy with his Scottish accent. *Henry V* was staged at court soon after the Gowrie fiasco in the same Christmas season, on 7 January 1605. Not for another two Christmases did their refreshed presumption allow them to open the court season with another explicitly pro-James play. That was a rewrite of the old *King Leir* supporting, on the face of it, the royal case for uniting the kingdoms, set in a dystopian view of a kingdom divided between a Duke of Cornwall and a Duke of Albany. Its direct political applicability when the play was put on for the court on 26 December 1606 says a lot about the company's sensitivity to the handling of royal affairs after the Gowrie fiasco. Some high-level backstage planning involving the Master of the Revels and his own masters was needed before *King Lear* was

[9] Written 18 December 1604, *Letters*, I.199.

[10] 'Examine all men / branded with such fowle syns as you now dye for, / and you shall find their first stepp still, Religion: / Gowrie in Scotland, 'twas his main pretention: / Was not he honest too?' *Sir John Van Olden Barnavelt, The Dramatic Works in the Beaumont and Fletcher Canon*, Gen. Ed. Fredson Bowers, VIII, 1992, p. 588 (5.3.134–8, TLN 2938–42).

[11] *The Diary of Thomas Crosfield*, ed. Frederick S. Boas, Oxford University Press, London, 1935, pp. 5, 6.

chosen for that symbolic evening, since Prince Charles was the Scottish Duke of Albany and his older brother Prince Henry had recently been made Prince of Wales and Duke of Cornwall.

No comment on James's own reaction to the startling first lines of *King Lear* is known. There is in fact only one case of a notable royal reaction to the staging of any play at court. It came in the 1619–20 season, when, as the Venetian Ambassador reported, a play by Prince Charles's company 'moved the king in an extraordinary manner, both inwardly and outwardly'.[12] The play, the Ambassador told his Doge, involved a king with two sons. He 'has one of them put to death, simply upon suspicion that he wished to deprive him of his crown, and the other son actually did deprive him of it afterwards'. That account should make us wonder how James could have had no visible reaction in 1606 to the names Cornwall and Albany in the opening lines of *King Lear*, and yet have been so moved in 1619, unless he knew beforehand in 1606 that *King Leir* had been rewritten in his own interest. As Shakespeare's play represented not the utopian union but a dystopian division of the kingdom, James could conclude that Lear was an opposite to himself. Giving it pride of place as the Christmas season's first play means that the Master of the Revels expected such a royal reading.

The years that followed the staging of *King Lear* at court on Christmas night of the 1606–7 festivities saw royal support maintained and, under Charles, made into almost as explicit a reflection of royal thinking and self-presentation as the court masques in which selected King's players took the speaking roles. Leaving aside the question of the Folio text of *King Lear* being a rewrite made to suit the politics of 1611,[13] *Cymbeline* followed *Lear* in that year as a celebration of the mythic union of Great Britain. We do not know, however, if this follow-up of Shakespeare's was acted at court at any time before 1634. The company's allusions to royalist politics under James were distinctly edgy. Their culmination with the staging of *A Game at Chess* shows, indeed flaunted, their freedom from sycophancy. Mounting *The Roman Actor* under the new king Charles showed a similar edginess. But it was under Charles that royal protection enveloped and finally swallowed them completely.

Charles soon showed his interest in protecting the establishment the company had developed at Blackfriars. He gave them his patronage quite quickly, during the dreadful plague epidemic when James died (Appendix 2.34). On 29 December 1633 he chose to sit in on a Privy Council meeting

---

[12] *Calendar of State Papers Venetian 1619–21*, p. 111.
[13] See the New Cambridge Shakespeare edition by Jay L. Halio, Cambridge University Press, 1992.

when the problem of the traffic jams caused by coaches parked near the playhouse was up for discussion. A month previously, in response to complaints from the Lord Mayor and the Aldermen of the precinct, the Council had issued an order to restrict parking in the playhouse's immediate vicinity (Appendix 2.40). Pressure from dignitaries inconvenienced by the order meant that they were now under pressure to soften it, and Charles sat there to ensure it was done. The new order was painfully self-justifying:

Upon Informacion this day given to the Board of the discomoditie that divers persons of great quallity especially Ladies and Gentlewomen, did receive in goeing to the Playhouse of Blackfriers, by reason that noe Coaches may stand within the Blackfriers Gate or retourne thither dureing the Play, and of the prejudice the Players his Majesties Servants doe receive therby. But especially that the Streetes are soe much the more incumberred with the said Coaches. The Board takeing into Consideracion the former order of the 20th of November last concerning this busines, did thinke fitt to explaine the said order, in such manner that as many Coaches as may stand within the Blackfriers Gate, may enter and stay ther, or retourne thither at the end of the Play, but that the said former order of the 20th of November be duly observed in all other parts.[14]

George Garrard, reporting from London to Lord Strafford in Dublin, wrote on 9 January that the order 'is disorder'd again'.[15] Barely tactful to the complainants, under pressure to backtrack on its own original order, the decision shows it was 'persons of great quallity' and the players who now had the power in the Blackfriars neighbourhood, and that the king was backing them.

ROYAL SUPPORT

Identifying political allegiances is never straightforward when the form of government is monarchy. Few people in England even after 1642 raised serious questions about whether a monarchy was preferable to, for instance, a republic. Semi-republics there were, in Venice and more intimately in England's and Britain's closest Protestant ally, the Dutch Republic. Just as Antwerp had been the great republican port rivalling London until Spain sacked it in 1574, so Venice was the semi-mythical republic governing the Mediterranean.[16] Those two eminent and self-governing sea powers upheld

[14] *Malone Society Collections* I.4–5, 1911, 388–9.
[15] Thomas Wentworth, *The Earl of Strafforde's Letters and Dispatches*, ed. William Knowler, 2 vols., London, 1739, I.175.
[16] In 1600 John Chamberlain called Venice 'a commonwealth so generally esteemed for justice and wisdome'. *Letters*, II.89–90.

the great anomaly inherent in the common assumption that monarchy was the best form of government, based on a reading of Aristotle. The truly potent anomaly was that ancient Rome rose to its greatness as a republic. In that frame of thinking *Julius Caesar* and its sequel can be read as the sharpest political plays ever written for the company's repertoire. The first play set Brutus's reservations about the common loss of liberty if a tyrant took the crown against the callous profiteering of the monarchists Antony and Octavius, before the sequel, *Antony and Cleopatra*, traced the effects of the struggle for power between individual tyrants. The unsuccessful Brutus is the only noble Roman of all the politicians shown in the two plays. *Coriolanus*, with its newly headless Rome, took the issue of the republic and a tyrant's personality still further. Monarchy under Tudor and Stuart rulers was a given, so the political concerns of the plays in the company's repertory found their chief focus in the honour or dishonour of the ruler. That focus lit up Shakespeare's history plays, most sharply *Richard II* in 1595 and 1601.

For all the priority of performing to the public two or three hundred times a year at the Globe and Blackfriars, a potent aspect of the company's concern from 1603 onwards was their staging of plays that might gratify their royal patron. This makes the pre-1603 plays all the more crucial as revelations of the company's political outlook. The degree to which the Shakespeare plays uphold royalism and its policies has been the dominant form of their interrogation in recent years. To many critics it has seemed simple-minded to find in them the blind loyalism to Tudor orthodoxy that is now ascribed to the readings of E. M. W. Tillyard and his predecessors (manifested especially in studies of Shakespeare's English history plays, and predominant up to Stephen Greenblatt in 1982). More recent studies of the plays abound with claims for ironic misrepresentations and subversive undermining of the castles of Tudor orthodoxy.[17] The questioning of authority in its different aspects pervades the Shakespeare plays. One, the company's consistent undermining of parental authority, has been looked at above. The plays written about monarchy, especially those which deliberately acknowledged the royal patrons who supported the company for forty of its forty-eight years, are the subject here.

[17] See for instance Tim Spiekerman, *Shakespeare's Political Realism. The English History Plays*, State University of New York Press, Albany, 2001, and Erica Sheen, ' "The Agent for his Master": Political Service and Professional Liberty in *Cymbeline*', in *The Politics of Tragicomedy*, ed. Gordon McMullan and Jonathan Hope, Routledge, London, 1992, pp. 55–76. Sheen poses the classic question of whether a servant should carry out his master's unjust order, though she does not test it on Pisanio's actions after Posthumus orders him to kill Imogen.

The range the company used in its popular repertory to acknowledge the royal patrons is wide, from the Gowrie story in James's second year to *A Game at Chess* twenty years later, a year before James died, and from Davenant's homage to Henrietta Maria in *The Platonic Lovers* to what Martin Butler calls the 'opposition' range of political views within the court.[18] This chapter's concern is to find political markers in the mass of materials that underlay the few public acts of allegiance to the patron. Plays venturing to offer political support for the king's policy, above all *King Lear*, stood (and in that instance still stand) in the popular repertory long after their political occasion vanished. Their 'local reading' needs to be retrieved in any history of the company that hatched them. How deep the company's loyalty to its royal patrons was, and how strongly that loyalty impacted on the basic social allegiances that the mass of plays in the repertory reflect, is the most testing characteristic of all the company's long life.

In politics I tend to count allegiances as starting from emotion rather than reason, largely instinctive and often subconscious. As a team working in a duopoly of London's playing companies, their loyalties had to be specific and explicit, in both general policy and detailed design. Loyalty may well therefore not reflect any basic allegiance with much precision. Obviously the company's underlying allegiances gradually shifted as they and their playhouses became an accepted social feature of London society. They clung to their popular audiences at the Globe until well after 1614, when they rebuilt the Globe, while overt loyalty to their royal patron after 1625 dragged their policy and repertory more and more towards the court's interests. Social allegiance, even to the grandees going to the Blackfriars in the 1630s, kept them on the middle ground of populist feeling, while recognition of their royal patrons and courtly followers gradually summoned them into political camps that had little to do with that basic allegiance. Then again, their overt loyalty to their audiences had to change once they let the Blackfriars usurp the Globe as their main venue. Chapter 4 dealt with their allegiance to their common audiences and their upward social shift, while this chapter deals with their loyalty to their patrons. Yet since critical interests mostly aim to test Renaissance writers' and companies' political commitments by identifying forms of subversion in the drama, it is necessary here to consider the company's varying loyalty to the royal interest that killed them along with their fellows in 1642.

---

[18] Martin Butler, *Theatre and Crisis 1632–1642*, Cambridge University Press, 1984, p. 2.

The story and the many questions about *A Game at Chess*, by far the most famous of the company's displays of political non-allegiance to their royal patron, have been amply recounted. How much that nine-day wonder was a product of the company's secret collusion with the authorities who ostensibly served the king, in particular Henry Herbert as licenser and the Earl of Pembroke as Lord Chamberlain and protector of Herbert and the players, has been debated at length. It is a question central to views about the company's loyalties in 1624, since the play was so blatantly a populist argument against James's policy over Spain, probably inspired and certainly protected by a substantial faction of courtiers. While useful as litmus paper to test the acidity of the company's political attitude in 1624, policies and political attitudes do shift all the time, and questionable loyalty to James in 1624 says nothing about the company's policy in 1594 or 1604 or 1634. *Gowrie* in 1604 misplayed the role that *King Lear* filled much better at court in 1606. Explicit loyalty to the patron was an annual requirement at court, but loyalty to the multitudes who went to the plays throughout the year, including the court's factions, was a much more basic determinant of choice in the repertory, as Middleton's play shows. Individual allegiances and loyalties differed from writer to writer and even within the same writer. Fletcher's and Massinger's company loyalties have to be set against the subversive commentaries in many of their plays.

In collaboration with its writers and other more shadowy figures the company did cultivate a recognizable political stance that was its own. Its defiance in staging *A Game at Chess* was encouraged by the staging five years earlier of *Barnavelt* as a current political issue. On the other hand putting on *The Late Lancashire Witches* ten years after *A Game at Chess* was the result of subservience to the Lord Chamberlain. There is little doubt that the players enjoyed collusion with sponsors and playgoers when they staged such comments on governmental policy. As John Holles, the only commentator who actually saw *A Game at Chess* in performance, noted, 'surely thes gamsters must have a good retrayte, else dared thei not to charge thus Princes actions, & ministers, nay their intents: a foule injury to Spayn, no great honor to England, rebus sic stantibus. every particular will beare a large paraphrase'.[19] Such paraphrasing must also have been in mind when the company staged *The Roman Actor* in 1626 to comment on how a tyrannical patron could murder his company of players.

---

[19] For a full transcript of Holles's report, see Appendix 2.30. For this and other reports, see *A Game at Chess*, ed. T. H. Howard-Hill, Revels Plays, Manchester University Press, 1993, pp. 198–200.

THE CASE OF *RICHARD II*

The most serious tension, when the company's political attitudes were most sensitized, came in the nine years before they were made royal servants. It was a fraught time, with a repressive monarch and no obvious heir to her throne. The best evidence for this tension comes from *Richard II*, written in the company's first year and revived for the Essex coup in 1601. However much tact it was written with in 1595, by 1601 it was a highly flammable issue for everyone. Parallels between the queen and her predecessor were common talk in the 1580s and 1590s. The company's first patron Henry Carey, her own cousin, once asserted his bluff simplicity at court by claiming 'I was never one of Richard II's men.' He meant that he was no flatterer, no Bushy, Bagot, or Greene.[20] E. M. Albright called Richard II Elizabeth's 'political nickname'. Other commentators did precisely what Carey disavowed. When the Essex coup failed after his followers had commissioned a performance of *Richard II* on the day before the coup, Elizabeth herself complained about its frequent performances and its applicability to her.

In its composition even more than its afterlife *Richard II* declared the company's political mind. Besides the obvious parallels, insulation from the people by flatterers, the sale of benevolences and unjust taxes, in 1595 Elizabeth's reign had two elements that made her identification with Richard explosive. Shakespeare took care to depict both of them in the sequence of plays that he began to write in 1595. One was the question of royal hands red with the blood of their kindred. Richard's killing of his uncle Woodstock, the Duke of Gloucester, was uncomfortably close to Elizabeth's execution of her cousin Mary Queen of Scots. The other was the nagging question of succession after a ruler who left no clear heir, a subject Elizabeth forbade anyone to speak of. Richard's own lack of an heir brought on the Wars of the Roses between the usurping Lancastrian Henrys and the dubiously patrilinear Yorkist Richards and Edwards, which oft the stage had shown. The latter traced their line through the Mortimer who was a claimant in *1 Henry IV* and (much more quietly in Shakespeare's presentation) the treacherous Cambridge of *Henry V*. After Elizabeth put a Parliamentarian in the Tower for writing about her likely successor, as she did to Peter Wentworth the year before Shakespeare wrote *Richard II*, it was to say the least disingenuous to write a play that showed how the door first opened to disgorge the horrors of civil war in a state with no heir apparent.

[20] Cited by Evelyn M. Albright, 'Shakespeare's *Richard II* and the Essex Conspiracy', *PMLA* 42 (1927), 686–720, p. 691.

When he composed it in 1595, its writer renewed the political analysis of the *Henry VI* plays to show monarchy's problem with the two recognized kinds of tyrant. One kind might be a legitimate ruler by inheritance yet rule wrongly. The other might rule rightly but lack the endorsement of linear descent. In either case, what should the oppressed subject do?[21] According to Barbara Hodgdon, by 1598 the Earl of Essex had become comparable to *Richard II*'s Bullingbrook in more ways than Shakespeare can have expected in 1595. As she puts it, Bullingbrook's

situation closely corresponds to what Essex saw as his grievances against the Crown: exile from court, if not from England; loss of revenue, royal favor, and title; disgraced honor. And indeed, the questions Essex poses in his 18 October letter to the Lord Keeper, Sir Thomas Egerton – a letter brought against him later as evidence of seditious interest – sound remarkably like Bolingbroke: 'When the vilest of all indignities are done unto me, doth religion enforce me to sue? Doth God require it? Is it impiety not to do it? What, cannot princes err? Cannot subjects receive wrong? Is an earthly power or authority infinite? Pardon me, pardon me, my good Lord, I can never subscribe to these principles.'[22]

By 1598 everyone recognized the parallels between Essex and Shakespeare's usurper. The play seemed to invite it almost openly. Everard Guilpin compared Essex to Bullingbrook quite explicitly and with great hostility in *Skialetheia*, Satire 1. Moreover, Lily Campbell tells us that the reference in 2.1 to the royal practice of extortion by benevolences was registered in the intensely scrutinized evidence cited at Essex's trial in 1601 as a clear instance of Elizabethan practices being applied to the case against Essex as examples of Richard's abuses, so that 'the times of Elizabeth rather than those of Richard II were in question'.[23]

That was true, although with different nuances, in 1595 as much as in 1601, and it may have registered with the powers that be even more than with the groundlings. On 7 December 1595, just a few months before Robert

---

[21] Throughout the century the monarchomachs of Europe, including James's tutor George Buchanan, whose doctrine James later repudiated, debated this question. Tyrants might misrule *in exercitio*, which Pope ironically called the 'Right Divine of Kings to Govern Wrong', or *absque titulo*, when however lawfully they ruled they lacked a title to authorize their claim. Who had authority to depose tyrants was an issue over which religions diverged. James said only God could do it. The Catholics said the Pope could, while Calvin upheld the 'lesser magistrates'.

[22] Barbara Hodgdon, *The End Crowns All. Closure and Contradiction in Shakespeare's History*, Princeton University Press, 1991, p. 124. Lilian Winstanley registered the mirroring of events and theatre when she wrote that 'Essex . . . went into Ireland with the reputation of a Henry V and came out of it with the reputation of a Hamlet' ('Hamlet and the Essex Conspiracy. Part I', *Aberystwyth Studies* 6 (1924), 47–66, p. 62).

[23] Lily B. Campbell, *Shakespeare's 'Histories' Mirrors of Elizabethan Policy*, Huntington Library, San Marino, 1947, p. 201.

Cecil succeeded his father as Elizabeth's chief minister, Sir Edward Hoby invited him to dinner. The incentive was 'as late as it shall please you, a gate for your supper shall be open, and K. Richard present himself to your view'.[24] Hoby, as Constable of Quinborough Castle in Kent, had in 1593 commissioned a series of pictures of former Constables to hang in the castle's hall, starting with Edward III and John of Gaunt and ending with himself. His commissioned pictures would have included Richard II and Richard III, and he may have planned to show off one of them to Cecil. But 1595 was also when Shakespeare's *Richard II* was first staged at the Theatre, and Hoby was Henry Carey's son-in-law. Showing the new offering by Carey's servants may have been designed by Hoby as both a gesture of loyalty to his father-in-law and a revelation to the Privy Councillor of this latest comment on Elizabeth's nickname.

The subsequent plays of Shakespeare's second series from English history show a similar sensitivity to the political issues. In Act 4 of *Richard II* Bullingbrook summons Parliament to endorse his succession to Richard, claiming the rule of law over royal tyranny. *3 Henry VI* had shown the weakness of Parliament, when the power of the sword made it endorse both of the rival claimants to the crown without regard to their right. Might's role as defender of the law was upheld in the later plays. At the end of *2 Henry IV* the new king tells the Lord Chief Justice to 'still bear the balance and the sword' of justice, affirming that the law should be free of the king's will. Such a gesture renewed the point famously made by Trajan on his accession as Roman Emperor. Handing the sword of justice to the Prefect of Rome, he declared '*Pro me si mereor in me*', use it for or against me as I deserve. The monarchomach George Buchanan had this motto engraved on the medal struck to celebrate the birth of James VI in Scotland. When the grown James became king of England his new medal repudiated Buchanan's motto, declaring that the king gives his authority to the law. Whether the king ruled the law or the law the king was an issue that in 1608 had Lord Chief Justice Coke on his knees begging forgiveness after he told James that the law protects the king, an incident echoed and questioned in *Philaster* and other Fletcher plays.

JACOBEAN POLITICS

From *Richard II* to *King Lear* was a long step for the company's resident writer. However readily we may believe Augustine Phillips's protestation of

---

[24] *Salisbury MSS*, v.487. See also chapter 1, note 22, p. 57.

innocence over the play that set out the two kinds of tyrant in 1595 and was commissioned for restaging by the Earl of Essex's followers in February 1601 (Appendix 2.14, 2.15), the Chorus in *Henry V* which hailed Essex's expected return triumphant from Ireland in 1599, and more curiously the addition of a Scottish Jamy to the English-supporting captains at Harfleur, were striking signals of concern with Elizabeth's political problems in 1599. We cannot be sure of Shakespeare's own political attitude to the union of Britain, but in 1599 he clearly expected that James VI of Scotland would succeed Elizabeth, and well before that happened he recognized its political consequences for the islands and kingdoms of Britain, not least the expectation that the two kingdoms would be united. These questions cross the boundary between the company under the Lord Chamberlain as patron and under King James. While the most explicit acknowledgement of the king as the company's patron is in the rewriting of the old Queen's Company's *King Leir* in 1605, Shakespeare's own understanding of the political future in 1599 is evident from the Folio text of *Henry V*.

In *Lear* the King's Men overtly took the royal side on the issue of the divided kingdoms. This apparently royalist alignment favouring a united Britain fits with incongruous intimacy into what I think is the single most inexplicable feature of *Henry V*, first staged six years earlier, nearly four years before James came to the English throne. If written in 1599, the scene of the four variably accented 'brothers', the national captains from England, Wales, Ireland, and Scotland, was remarkably prophetic. The one scene in which the four captains meet and quarrel flouts all the evidence from its main source in Holinshed and blandly ignores its own advertising, in the second scene of its first Act, of the threat from the 'old alliance', Scotland with France, which Shakespeare took from Holinshed and highlighted as a feature of English planning for the invasion of France.

A Scottish Jamy did accompany the historical Henry V to France and fought alongside him, a story also recorded in Holinshed. He was in fact King James I, ancestor of Scottish James VI who was to become James I of England. That might have justified the insertion of an unhistorical Captain Jamy in the play, but to do so in 1599 was either extraordinarily prophetic both of the Scottish James's eventual accession to Elizabeth's throne and his subsequent wish to unite the divided kingdoms, or a crass joke designed merely to exploit the comic potential of regional accents. A Welsh presence alongside English Gower made good sense in 1599, for all the weight of rebel Glendower in the preceding plays and Henry's own long experience as a prince in real history of siege warfare in Wales. Roger Williams and other Welsh captains made names for themselves fighting for England against

Spain in the Low Countries throughout the militant decade of the 1590s. Conceivably too the employment of loyalist Irish contingents in Essex's 1598–9 campaign against O'Neill and the Irish rebellion, however much it worried the Privy Council, might have justified the presence of Macmorris in France. But there was less than no historical justification in 1599 for adding an alien Scottish captain called James to the English, Welsh, and Irish in France. The 'main intendment' of the Scots that Henry provides against in 1.2 was to attack the English, not the French.

As we noted in chapter 2, Scottish accents were not a laughing matter at James's court in 1605 when *Henry V* was staged there. So to add a comic Scot to the comic Welshman and Irishman would have been dangerous at court in 1605 and conceivably even in 1606 for *Macbeth*. It is most likely that if Jamy ever appeared on the Globe's stage he would have been excised from the text for the court performance in 1605, possibly along with the talk of protecting England against the Scottish weasels and their main intendment. The strongest evidence that the company cut the scene with the three 'British' captains even for the first performances in 1599 is its absence from the 1600 quarto along with all the Choruses.

The deletion of Jamy from the quarto text of 1600, however, stands against its retention of the reference to the threat from Scotland and of another to the Scottish king. This second reference made a striking change from the Folio version. When Henry warns his court of the danger of an incursion from the north, the quarto 'Bishop' replies that England in the past

> . . . hath herself not only well defended
> But taken and impounded as a stray
> The King of Scots
> Whom like a caitiff she did lead to France.

This compounds the Shakespeare version, omitting the reference to Edward III, who had the Scottish King David in his train. Henry had the Scottish King James I in his train as a long-term prisoner, and did take him to France, where at the siege of Melun he tried to order the Scottish defenders to defect to him.[25] This omission in the quarto conflates the two historical actions. Evidently the company's revisers of the Shakespeare manuscript had a rougher grasp than he did of the political issues.

King Lear was the most explicitly loyal of all the plays Shakespeare wrote for the company's royal patron in the Jacobean period, even more than the acknowledgement of James's royal lineage in *Macbeth*. It was designed to

---

[25] They refused, denying James's authority over them, so Henry had them all executed for treason when he finally conquered the town. The story is in Holinshed.

uphold, at least on the face of it, James's policy of uniting his kingdoms by its demonstration of the effects of a divided kingdom. The declension of authority in the play, where royal Lear hands power to ducal Cornwall and Albany and in the end Albany offers to abdicate in favour of the surviving pair of earls, is remarkably consistent. It maintains a steadily downward progression in the ranks that pretend to authority in the British kingdom. The declension from king to earl was recognizable on stage in the difference between the king's crown, the ducal coronets, and the ornamented velvet bonnets of the two earls, all on show in the opening scene of the play.[26] Elizabeth had killed off the last of her English dukes thirty-four years before. In 1605 James's two sons were a novelty as dukes of English Cornwall and Scottish Albany. Charles added the title of Duke of York on 6 January 1605 to his earlier Scottish title of Albany, but his older title remained in use. By replacing the old *Leir's* two western Kings of Cambria and Cornwall with one westerner and a Scot, the opening scene of *King Lear* replicated the royal priority and the royal headgear of the English court under James with the actual names of its two younger-generation dukes.

The direct applicability of the names of the two dukes in *Lear's* first lines to the young dukes of James's court was potentially sensational. Yet we know it caused no uproar, and the Master of the Revels chose the play for the Christmas night performance.[27] The debate about the differences between the two texts of 1605 and 1611 (the Folio text) has passed over this overt application of a story about ancient Britain with its retitled dukes and the way it flaunted the company's allegiance to its royal patron. *King Lear* and *Cymbeline* were Shakespeare's contributions to the idea of a united kingdom that was their patron's dream.[28] In 1605 when Shakespeare first rewrote

[26] For some context to this argument, see Gurr, 'Headgear as Paralinguistic Signifiers in *King Lear*', *Shakespeare Survey* 55 (2002), 43–51. See also Charles Spinosa, ' "The Name and All th'Addition": *King Lear's* Opening Scene and the Common Law Use', *Shakespeare Studies* 23 (1995), 146–86. It should be noted that one of the subtler of the many managerial shifts that take place through the course of *Lear's* five acts works better in the Folio version than it does in the quarto. If it is Edgar who speaks the last words in the play, as he does in the Folio text, rather than the quarto's Albany, then the declension from duke to earl leaves hope for a single successor as ruler. If Albany speaks the conclusion, Lear's great mistake is forgotten.

[27] Gary Taylor in his essay on possible censorship in *King Lear* in *The Division of the Kingdoms* (Oxford University Press, 1983, p. 104) notes the mockery of James's enthusiasm for hunting but not the names of the two dukes, except to say that Albany would have signified Scotland. Leah Marcus (*Puzzling Shakespeare: Local Reading and its Discontents*, University of California Press, Berkeley, 1988), gives attention to the naming of the dukes as a feature of the St Stephen's Night court performance, and takes up the link with the current issue of the divided kingdoms, but she does not draw the obvious conclusion about the absence of censorship.

[28] Allusions to royalty go deep into the post-1603 plays. Brian Gibbons, *Shakespeare and Multiplicity*, Cambridge University Press, 1993, pp. 23–9, makes the point that *Cymbeline* is in some ways an oblique commentary on its author's previous writing, including *Lear*, and that King Cymbeline is given (unhistorically) two sons and a daughter, like James.

the old *King Leir* James was trying to persuade the English Parliament to unite his two kingdoms of England and Scotland. As it happens, neither kingdom wanted to join the other, an attitude not entirely unknown today, and for similar reasons. So James had a fight on his hands. The proposal to unite the two kingdoms was the major political issue of 1605, and it caused the first open conflict between the new Scottish king and the old English Parliament. The opening of *King Lear* proclaimed the company's involvement with the most contentious political issue of the day and its evident support for James's current policy with blatant and self-confident bravado.

James did have three assets that Elizabeth lacked, of course, his children. In Shakespeare's play they took a strikingly direct role in the addition of Scotland to the older play's western British equation. Changing Cambria or Wales to Albany made Scotland explicitly a part of Lear's united kingdom. The renaming suggested that Cornwall ruled the west, including Wales, while Albany had Scotland, leaving the third, intended to be Cordelia's (and Lear's) most opulent slice of Lear's map, as England, where James now resided. Lear's opening announces that his policy is exactly the opposite of James's. He will disunite his kingdom, not leaving it to just one of his sons-in-law, nor even giving half each to them, as the earls wondered in the play's first lines, but splitting it into a wholly unexpected three parts. That was radically in excess of the status quo in 1605. Wales had been united with England since Edward I's time. Even Ireland had become a putative colony by the time *Henry V* added Macmorris to Gower and Llewellyn. It is easy to see without hindsight James's vision of a united kingdom comprising all the parts of Britain as the obvious bound for the empire of London's ruler, as it evidently was to Shakespeare back in 1599. From that perspective, the debate in 1605 over disuniting the ancient kingdom was a version of the Fall.

The readiness with which the company could broach the subject of 'the division of the kingdoms' at court in 1606 is an almost unique case of their daring use of 'application' in connivance with the court dignitaries who controlled plays. Only *A Game at Chess* shows the same intimacy with figures in power, and that did not reach anywhere near the top as *King Lear* may have done. The two cases are part of the long story of censorship and its much-used opposite, the two-step art of 'application' that according to Jonson had grown into a trade by 1607. The two steps of the art were propter hoc and post hoc, before and after the event of composition. The first is the more notorious, since it features the author's pre-text freedom to choose any topic, and hence was subject to the formal censorship processes applied to theatre texts. Shakespeare might allude harmlessly to Marlowe in *As You Like It*, or Middleton might write *A Game At Chess* more dangerously to fit the Spanish question. These were authorial applications, calculatingly set out in the text, with consequences that were gauged by the evident political impact. They were matters for which controlling machinery existed in the person of the Master of the Revels and his 'allowing' of the playbooks. But for the Essex followers to fit *Richard II* to the Essex rebellion was a matter of post-hoc audience response. Even innocent texts can be reapplied to a new event, as modern productions of Shakespeare regularly struggle to do. In some cases both post- and propter-hoc applications might come into issue. *Philotas*, which Daniel claimed he had written most of before the Essex rebellion, was a case where the author's protestations of innocence in 1604 did not in the event prevail against the outrage of the implicated earl and other ex-Essex loyalists who Daniel called on to support his claim that he was innocent and that they were making a purely post-hoc application. On balance, except for the special case of *A Game at Chess*, the post-hoc applications which people so easily made served the playwrights much worse than their own identifiable propter-hoc applications. Given James's readiness to make his own applications about sons usurping their fathers, the boldness of *King Lear's* evidently propter-hoc application to the union of the kingdoms is all the more remarkable.

There is no direct evidence that the company sustained such a bold attitude to such dangerous ventures with other plays. One positive statement does exist, however, made not long after the company had undergone their troubles with *A Game at Chess*. In *The Roman Actor*, written in 1625 during the lengthy cessation of playing in the worst plague epidemic ever, begun even before the new king had given the company his name, Massinger wrote a speech for the leading player in Rome to defend acting to the Senate.

> If any in this reverend assemblie,
> Nay e'ne your selfe my Lord, that are the image
> Of absent *Caesar*, feele something in your bosome
> That puts you in remembrance of things past,
> Or things intended tis not in us to helpe it.
>
> (1.3.136–40)

It is the hearers and beholders who are responsible for making what applications they choose. The force of any play, he has already argued, is for the good.

There was some point in that argument. When he was so upset by the otherwise unknown Prince Charles's company play in 1619, James was doing no more than many of his people did in the work of application, especially at court. The surviving evidence about post-hoc applications that survives is all at the gentry and courtier level, like Philip Herbert's notes in his edition of Chapman's *Bussy*,[29] comparing the French court of the play to Charles's court in the 1630s, when he was Lord Chamberlain, or Fulke Greville's destruction of his own plays, including his *Antony and Cleopatra*, out of fear that they would be misapplied to contemporary situations. This did not mean that the writers could not provide an ample supply of their own propter-hoc applications. But the most evident ones are innocuous, patriotic, and easily recognized, aimed at the public not the court. Dekker's *Whore of Babylon* at the Fortune mythologized the victory of Elizabeth's England over the Armada, setting a female Pope as demonic Anti-Christ against Elizabeth as a female Fairy Queen. The printed text made its application overt by identifying the chief historical figures in the Dramatis Personae and in the margins. The prologue claimed that they were presenting

> Matter above the vulgar Argument
> Yet drawne so lively, that the weakest eye,
> (Through those thin vailes we hang betweene your sight,
> And this our peice) may reach the mistery.[30]

For eyes weaker than the weakest the quarto's Dramatis Personae identified the major allegorical figures such as '*Titania the Faerie Queen: under whom is figured our late Queene Elizabeth*', and the margins identified '*Paridel*' as Dr Parry, '*Campeius*' as Edmund Campion, and '*Lupus*', also called '*Rupus*' in the 1607 text, as Dr Lopez. Dekker's play offered an easy application because it was innocuously patriotic. The propter-hoc application Shakespeare offered in *King Lear* was far more risky, and yet it appears to have given no offence.

After the court performance on St Stephen's Night 1606 there is no record of *King Lear* ever reappearing before royalty. An amateur company staged the 1608 quarto text under the auspices of the Catholic Sir Richard Cholmeley at Gowthwaite Hall in Yorkshire in 1610, but otherwise it is not recorded anywhere before Nahum Tate's altered version appeared after the Restoration. If it was revised in 1611, there must have been further

---

[29] A. H. Tricomi, 'Philip, Earl of Pembroke, and the Analogical Way of Reading Political Tragedy', *Journal of English and Germanic Philology* 85 (1986), 332–45. The earl read the play in print, though his attention may have been drawn to it by revivals at the Blackfriars in 1634 and 1638.

[30] The quotation is taken from the Folger Shakespeare Library copy of the 1607 quarto.

performances at the Globe or the Blackfriars before 1642, but none is on record. The more overt propter-hoc applications aged quickly.

THE POLITICS OF BEAUMONT AND FLETCHER

The joke about Beaumont and Fletcher being arrested when they were overheard in a tavern plotting to kill the king has more force than its recorder, Thomas Fuller, had in mind when he wrote about the collaboration.[31] We do not know which play they were discussing, but it could have been *The Maid's Tragedy* or almost any that Fletcher wrote subsequently. Hardly any of the stories dramatized by Fletcher and his various collaborators upholds royalism in the way that Coleridge and other early critics assumed.[32] Most of their plots use the dystopian aspect of monarchy in what Sandra Clark has called 'tyrant plays'.[33] Fletcher, as the controlling influence over his collaborators, revelled in devising plots which questioned how rulers conducted their courts and kingdoms, and how subjects should respond to tyranny.[34] Even *Philaster*, the first play he and Beaumont wrote for the King's Men, starts with a tyrant ruling over two kingdoms like patron James, but unjustly. The hero, rightful heir to the second kingdom, secures his throne and by implication eventually the tyrant's as well by marrying his good daughter. The marriage at the end put him in a position to become lawful ruler over two kingdoms, like James in 1609. As noted in chapter 4, *The Maid's Tragedy* sets up in its two leading characters Hamlet's choices as a subject wronged by his king, either to suffer in Christian patience or to take arms and kill the tyrant and suffer the consequences. One character takes the suffering option, the other commits the murder that Hamlet accepts once he damns himself by killing Polonius. Fletcher was always alert to the moral complexities of what a subject should do when his honour is put to the test. The intensity of his subtle and democratic politics show him to have been a thoroughly political animal.[35] To write *Barnavelt* within three

---

[31] *The Worthies of England*, 1662, sig. oooiv.

[32] Coleridge's view is considered at more length in chapter 6.

[33] *The Plays of Beaumont and Fletcher: Sexual Themes and Dramatic Representation*, Harvester, London, 1994, p. 101.

[34] Kathleen McLuskie has a set of summaries of several King's Men plays in her overview of the period 1613–42, including four from the 'Beaumont and Fletcher' canon, *The Custom of the Country*, *The Elder Brother*, *The Fatal Dowry*, and *Love's Pilgrimage* (*The Revels History of Drama in English Vol. IV: 1613–1660*, pp. 175–85). Philip J. Finkelpearl, *Court and Country Politics in the Plays of Beaumont and Fletcher*, Princeton University Press, 1990, and Gordon McMullan, *The Politics of Unease in the Plays of John Fletcher*, University of Massachusetts Press, Amherst, 1994, both offer insightful accounts of the politics in these plays.

[35] We should, however, bear in mind Walter Cohen's cautionary note: 'the method of symptomatic reading, whatever its intellectual rigour, may be a form of wishful thinking, a procedure designed

months of the events it relates was a daring and certainly a radical choice of political subject (Appendix 2.28).[36] Fletcher's work consistently set up virtuous women as tests for male society, and used good and bad love to test monarchy. Love was the ostensible subject of his plays and male honour their politics. Fletcher set an agenda that the company maintained till 1642.

Political choices are rarely simple. It is chronically likely that an individual's fundamental loyalty will find itself forced to make choices between grossly over-simplified options. Political loyalties have to be simple and collective, crowd politics, while personal choice is always individual. Many supporters of the Parliamentary cause hated the decision to decapitate Charles. The kinds of personal choice that had to be made between crown and Parliament in the commonwealth, so delicately laid out in Marvell's 'Horatian Ode', had to be simple, but were always painfully complex to the individual. The history of the commonwealth period and the immense body of record it generated about personal doubts over Cromwell's role as Protector reflect in surprisingly exact ways the concerns already expressed in plays of the 1630s about royal morality and conduct. Charles's own sexual morality was never in question, but he was seen as a tyrant, and there is ample evidence for resistance to tyranny in the flood of plays like Davenant's *The Unfortunate Lovers*, which show rulers misusing their power in the interests of love. From *Philaster* and *The Maid's Tragedy* onwards love at court became a metaphor for the impact of royal misrule on the subject. As Martin Butler puts it of the 1630s, 'The decade's drama is replete with absolute kings tyrannizing over their realms, subjects trapped between their loyalty to the crown and their need to speak out, contrasts between government built on trust and enslavement built on fear, evil counsellors undergoing anatomization, bad kings reduced to penitence, courtiers and countrymen attempting different compromises and agreements.'[37] This was the repertory's stock commodity. Indeed, *The Unfortunate Lovers* develops soldier Melantius's moral dilemma from the earlier play with some precision. Other plays used the more *Hamlet*-influenced dilemma of his opposite Amintor. *The Swisser* incorporated both. Political readings of the plays have to accept the intricacy of

to discover a radicalism unavailable to seventeenth-century audiences and most modern readers alike . . . . political commitment predetermines critical position.' ('Prerevolutionary Drama', in *The Politics of Tragicomedy: Shakespeare and After*, ed. Gordon McMullan and Jonathan Hope, Routledge, London, 1992, pp. 122–50, 143).

[36] On *Barnavelt*, a play about a political confrontation in the Low Countries that took place barely three months before the play was staged and therefore dealt with a living ruler, see Ivo Kamps, *Historiography and Ideology in Stuart Drama*, Cambridge University Press, 1996, chapter 5, pp. 140–67.

[37] Martin Butler, *Theatre and Crisis*, p. 23.

situations and the inevitable fact that they have to be resolved, like modern voting, through an oversimplifying choice. The Fletcherian tradition of basing plays on plots using the moot game and Shakespearean 'what if . . .' concept took a fresh lease of life with the love dilemmas of the King's Men's plays in the 1630s.

None of these deliberately generalized concerns should be allowed to overlie the occasions when the company did choose to reflect current events in their plays. *Barnavelt* was one under James, *A Game at Chess* the second. Each was an independent attempt to energize public concern by staging current events. Each was carefully planned, and *A Game at Chess* at least was almost certainly created with the censor's connivance. It was staged at the Globe in August while James and the court were away at Newmarket. One man who was still in London, John Holles, Lord Haughton, sent the Earl of Somerset a synopsis that shows close engagement with the play and its applicability, which he called its 'paraphrase'. It was so easily applicable that the crowds who flocked there made getting a place difficult. Holles's whole letter is quoted fully in Appendix 2.30.

I was saluted with a report of a facetious comedy, allreddy thryce acted with extraordinary applause: a representation of all our spannishe traffike, where Gundomar his litter, his open chayre for the ease of that fistulated part, Spalato &ca. appeared uppon the stage . . . the descant was built upon the popular opinion, that the Jesuits mark is to bring all the christian world under Rome for the spirituality, & under Spayn for the temporalty: heeruppon, as a precept, or legacy left those disciples from their first founder Ignatius Loyola, this their father serves for the prologue, who admiring no speedier operation of his drugg, is inraged, & desperate, till cumforted by one of his disciples, the plott is revealed him, prosperously advanced by their designe uppon England: with this he vanisheth, leaving his benediction over the work. The whole play is a chess board, England the whyt hows, Spayn the black: one of the white pawns, wth an under black dubblett, signifying a Spanish hart, betrays his party to their advantage, advanceth Gundomars propositions, works under hand the Princes cumming into Spayn: which pawn so discovered, the whyt King revyles him, objects his raising him in wealth, in honor, from meane condition, next classis to a labouring man: this by the character is supposed Bristow: yet it is hard, players should judge him in jest, before the State in ernest . . . at last the Prince making a full discovery of all their knaveries, Olivares, Gundomar, Spalato, Iesuite, spannish bishop, & a spannish evenuke ar by the Prince putt into the bagg, & so the play ends . . . surely thes gamsters must have a good retrayte, else dared thei not to charge thus Princes actions, & ministers, nay their intents: a foule injury to Spayn, no great honor to England.[38]

---

[38] Quoted with some smoothing from *A Game at Chess*, ed. T. H. Howard-Hill, Revels Plays, pp. 198–9.

Whatever good retreat the players had, very likely a secret pact with the Lord Chamberlain but most immediately Henry Herbert's licence as Master of the Revels, they were hotly pursued at first, specifically over the licence that they flourished to protest their innocence (Appendix 2.31). It soon cooled off, the players suffering no more than a short closure. Their letter of apology and submission to Herbert that December (Appendix 2.32), may have been part of an oblique process of appeasement for his troubles over the issue.

There was another side to the repertory's fascination with politics: the view of some in authority that interest in fictions conveniently took attention away from political realities. That dismissive idea was behind Sir Thomas Roe's letter to Elizabeth of Bohemia, Charles's sister, during a long closure for the plague in 1630. On 29 October he wrote 'Your Majesty will give me leave to tell you another general calamity; we have had no plays this six months, and that makes our statesmen see the good use of them, by the want: for if our heads had been filled with the loves of Pyramus and Thisbe, or the various fortunes of Don Quixote, we should never have cared who had made peace or war, but on the stage. But now every fool is enquiring what the French do in Italy, and what they treat in Germany.'[39] Staging the prickly side of the repertory explains why *Barnavelt* got the company into trouble with the censor in 1619, and *A Game at Chess* in 1624. But Roe's dismissive attitude to plays, while it may help to explain the laxity of Stuart censorship compared with later centuries, does acknowledge the concerns of courtiers and senior government figures who attended the Blackfriars in the 1630s.

CAROLINE INTERVENTIONS

It was under Charles and Henrietta Maria that the company became most clearly identified as royal servants.[40] Besides bringing players to court more often than ever, Henrietta Maria's personal visits to the King's Men at Blackfriars in the 1630s haloed the playhouse as the first public playing-place that royalty ever graced. Her four private visits were a remarkable exhibition of how high the Blackfriars had raised the company's social

---

[39] *S. P. Dom. Chas I*, 174. Doc. 102. The Duke of Buckingham's visit to the Globe in 1628 to see *Henry VIII*, and his departure after watching the execution of his predecessor in Act 2 (Appendix 2.35), marks another use of playgoing for politics.

[40] Sophie Tomlinson, in 'She that Plays the King: Henrietta Maria and the Threat of the Actress in Caroline Culture', in *The Politics of Tragicomedy*, ed. Gordon McMullan and Jonathan Hope, pp. 189–207, uses this kind of evidence to argue for the dominance of the women at indoor playhouses.

credit. No wonder that the prologue written for the presentation of *The Faithful Shepherdess* for the court at Somerset House on 6 January 1634 does not just praise Charles as 'this Islands God; the worlds best King', but acknowledges that the whole occasion was thanks to Henrietta Maria. 'Bless then that Queen; that doth his eyes invite / And ears, t'obey her Scepter, half this night.' The letter-writer John Pory reported two occasions when Charles showed his favour to his company. In one, dated 3 November 1632, Pory reported that the king, meeting the Lord Privy Seal, 'did highly congratulate and extoll unto him the rare and excellent partes of his sonne Mr Walter Montague, appearing in that Pastorall which hee hath penned for her Majesty her Ladies, and maydes to act upon his Majesties birthday'. Pory footnoted that 'Mr Taylour the Player hath also the making of a knight given him for teaching them how to act the Pastorall.' He concluded that Davenant, the King's Men's writer and author of all the court's future masques, was also in line for a knighthood thanks to his latest poem. Neither accolade was actually given, but the rumour shows the level of benefit and social elevation the king's favouring of theatre was expected to bring the company. In the event, Taylor became Yeoman of the Revels and Lowin the King's Porter in 1639, both posts profitable reminders of their patron's power.

Pory's second note was about a show laid on for the king and queen earlier in the same year by Philip Herbert, dedicatee of the Shakespeare First Folio and now Lord Chamberlain in succession to his brother and co-dedicatee William. In a letter dated 5 May 1632 Pory reported that 'On Thursday night my lord Chamberlaine bestowed a feast and a playe upon the king and Queen at his lodging in the Cockpitt, which cost his lordship £1500. This expense was noble both in respect of those that were feasted, and of him that made the feast.'[41] I think Philip Herbert must have chosen to use the King's Men for his entertainment, since they were the most eminent company, and he rewarded them accordingly. To use the king's own servants at the Chamberlain's banquet played a nice game with the concept of Charles's supreme command as a monarch. In the Civil War, Herbert supported the Parliamentarians.

Charles was a reader as well as a beholder of plays, especially the repertoire of the King's Men. He owned at least nine Beaumont and Fletcher play-quartos, which survive in the Bodleian Library (Malone 217), and wrote annotations in them all. They were *Philaster* (Q4, 1639), *The Maid's Tragedy*

---

[41] William S. Powell, *John Pory / 1572–1636. The Life and Letters of a Man of Many Parts, Microfiche Supplement: Letters and Other Minor Writings*, The University of North Carolina Press, Chapel Hill, 1977, Microfiche pp. 321, 257.

21. King Charles I, the Shakespeare company's fourth patron, by Mytens, painted in 1631 (NPG 1246).

(Q4, 1638), *A King and No King* (Q4, 1639), *The Scornful Lady* (Q4, 1635), *The Elder Brother* (Q1, 1637), *Rollo* (Q2, 1640), *Cupid's Revenge* (Q2, 1630), *The Knight of the Burning Pestle* (Q2, 1635), and *The Two Noble Kinsmen* (Q1, 1634). He also annotated his copy of the second Shakespeare Folio (1632). His notes on *The Maid's Tragedy* show him making a serious attempt to polish some of its more awkward features.[42] When the Master of the Revels Henry Herbert objected to the oaths in Davenant's *The Wits* in 1634 (Appendix 2.41), Davenant got Endymion Porter to take it to Charles to read, and Herbert had to accept the king's judgement as his authority, while registering his own doubts (Appendix 2.41). Charles did much more for the Blackfriars company than read its plays. We have already noted that he made sure the Privy Council modified its order over parking coaches in 1633, and he gave them subventions in plague closures. Through the Lord Chamberlain's mediation Charles privileged them more than any other company.

The company's now-chronic apprehensions about being the King's servants were put on show rather bravely in *The Roman Actor*. Massinger wrote the play during the longest of all the closures for plague, at a time when the company's life was in serious danger. The plague epidemic of 1625–6 was so drastic that for once the Privy Council had to extend the usual ban on London playing to cover the whole of England,[43] and nobody could tell how long the stoppage would last. Charles had his own company, Prince Charles's Men, so until he relicensed the King's as his on 26 June 1625 there was no guarantee that the old king's company would receive the new king's patronage and name. In the event they kept their old title and took another subvention to help them through the closure. They were actually the only company to survive this closure. Till playing restarted Massinger spent the time trying to show what could happen to a company if its new patron was a dangerous tyrant. Its leader, solicited by the new empress, is murdered on stage 'to the life' by Diocletian himself, playing the revenging husband. The play's players, unemployed and desperate until the emperor befriends them, reflect the King's Men's position through Charles's first months as king. For Massinger to write his tragedy as an ominous prophecy that was meant to be staged at the first festivities of the new court seems quite likely, though in the event to either the Master of the Revels or the company it must have

---

[42] The Beaumont and Fletcher collection and especially Charles's notes on *The Maid's Tragedy* were examined by Percy Simpson, *Bodleian Quarterly Record* 8 (1935–7), 257–62.

[43] From before 7 July 1625: 'the Lord Chamberlain . . . hath given Order to the Master of the Revels, not to suffer any Players to play in any Part of *England*, during the time of this Infection'. Bawcutt, *The Control and Censorship of Caroline Drama*, p. 162. The closure lasted almost to the end of the year.

seemed too daring. It is our tragedy that the records of court performances in this period do not give the titles of the King's Men's twenty-two plays they provided for Christmas 1625 or 1626. The 1629 quarto of *The Roman Actor*, however, carefully does not say that it was performed at court. It boasts of being played 'with good Allowance' at the Blackfriars, but unlike its peers such as Carlell's *The Deserving Favorite*, also printed in 1629, and Suckling's *Aglaura* (Appendix 2.48), it is silent about any court showing. Presumably the company, while painfully sympathetic to the image it presents of the victim role that a playing company could suffer under a tyrant, thought it less than tactful to show its own patron such a story.[44] During his seventeen years in power Charles seems to have invoked his dictatorial powers quite frequently but always on the company's behalf, especially through 1633, when he not only ensured that the Privy Council did nothing about the latest complaint over Blackfriars but ordered the Lord Chamberlain to give them that peculiar warrant of authority to take up players from the other London companies.

Davenant's dominance of the mid-Caroline repertory shows how carefully the company obeyed the dictates of royal taste in the 1630s. The dates when his *Love and Honour*, *The Platonic Lovers*, and *The Fair Favourite* were licensed, 20 November 1634, 16 November 1635, and 17 November 1638, identify them as the plays he expected to have staged at court for those Christmas seasons. In the previous winter, 1633–4, the company's plays for the court had a mixed reception. Henry Herbert noted that the first two, *Taming of the Shrew* and its sequel *The Tamer Tamed*, were 'Likt', and Fletcher's 'Very well likt'. His *Loyal Subject* was 'very well likt by the king' (not the queen); *Cymbeline* was 'Well likte by the kinge'; *The Guardian* was 'well likte'. *The Tale of a Tub* by the queen's company was 'not likte'. *The Winter's Tale* was 'likt', and neither the king nor the queen gave any opinion on the last plays, *The Wits* and *The Night Walker*. The season's main hit was on Twelfth Night, after *Cymbeline*. It was 'Fletchers pastorall called The Faithfull Shepheardesse, in the clothes the Queene had given Taylor the year before of her owne pastorall'. Henrietta Maria's preferences were gaining control. After Davenant learned of the king's only partial liking for *The Wits* ('the kinge commended the language, but dislikt the plott and characters'),[45] he made sure that for the next season *Love and Honour* was

---

44 Its famous defence of playing has been much debated, including the question of whether it deliberately makes a less than convincing case for the power of plays, since none of its three plays within the play succeed in doing what they are designed to achieve. See in particular Martin Butler, 'Romans in Britain: *The Roman Actor* and the Early Stuart Classical Play', in *Philip Massinger: A Critical Reassessment*, ed. D. Howard, Cambridge University Press, 1985, pp. 131–70.

45 Bawcutt, *Control and Censorship of Caroline Drama*, pp. 185–7.

22. Queen Henrietta Maria, by an unknown artist (NPG 1247). The background, which may be meant to depict Inigo Jones's Queen's House at Greenwich, is by Henrick van Steenwyck.

written to the queen's taste, following it a year later with his most fawning play, *The Platonic Lovers*.

Charles showed care for his servants during the 1625 plague closure and again in the long shut-down of 1636–8, when the Privy Council issued an order securing a special release for the company from the plague restrictions (Appendix 2.47). Towards the end of that first empty time he gave them a grant of 100 marks to help them through. A mark is two-thirds of a pound, so that was more than twice as generous as the £30 his father had given them for the long closure in his first year, 1603. The company was a royal possession, and seen with the hindsight of 1642 Massinger's play at the outset of the reign was ominously prophetic.[46] The company flew high, but it did so in the claws of the monarchy. When at the Restoration William Killigrew, the brother of one of the two new duopoly impresarios, wrote a new prologue for the staging of *Epicene* on 19 November 1660, he summed up the general feeling of the new playgoers who associated the restored plays with the restored royalty:

> This truth we can to our advantage say,
> They that would have no KING, would have no *Play*:
> The *Laurel* and the *Crown* together went,
> Had the same *Foes*, and the same *Banishment*.[47]

By then royal support for playgoing had been a given for most of the century. Royalty and plays went down together. In 1649 the Solicitor General's indictment of Charles expressed the wish that he had studied the Bible rather than Jonson and Shakespeare.[48]

LATER POLITICAL CONSEQUENCES OF ROYALISM

Shakespeare's plays remained a distinctly political potato for many years after his death, as Nahum Tate's handling of *Richard II* under a lawless monarch attests. The nineteenth century marketed it for its show of the glories of militant heroism and monarchism, more prosaically it was used to teach English history to schoolchildren, and most recently it has been baked, roasted, and chipped by interpreters as diverse as Tillyard and Greenblatt.

---

[46] *The Roman Actor* is analysed closely in different aspects by Martin Butler (see note 44, p. 194, above), and by Jonas Barish, 'Three Caroline "Defenses" of the Stage', in *Comedy from Shakespeare to Sheridan*, ed. A. R. Braunmuller and J. C. Bulman, University of Delaware Press, Newark, 1986, pp. 194–214.

[47] Quoted in Leslie Hotson, *The Commonwealth and Restoration Stage*, pp. 208–9.

[48] See Jeffrey Knapp, *Shakespeare's Tribe: Church, Nation, and Theater in Renaissance England*, University of Chicago Press, 2002, p. 6.

Readings of the politics in the plays have mirrored the conflicts of the last three centuries. The same forms of cookery are now being applied to more and more other plays in the repertoire. Massinger, whose social conservatism is transparent in *A New Way to Pay Old Debts* and *The City Madam*, has been proclaimed a radical dissident against the monarchy of Charles I. He wrote about court politics in his Blackfriars plays, raising some of the philosophical questions about right rule that have been found in Shakespeare. His importance probably lies more in the reciprocal effect, the way his voicing of the political issues of tyranny was listened to by and shaped the thinking of his Blackfriars clients. Most of the participants in playing, like Davenant with his extravagant exploits during the war fighting and gun-running for the monarchy, and the players who followed the king to his exile at Oxford, voted with their feet for the royalist option, but many others, like Philip Herbert and other Blackfriars playgoers such as the Speaker of the Commons Bulstrode Whitelocke, and the player Eliart Swanston, made the opposite choice.

One question closely related to the company's allegiance to royalty but better concealed was their likely religious affinities. Catholics were always more inclined to favour playing than the puritan wing of the Church of England. The impresario Sebastian Westcott who ran the first Paul's Boys, Christopher Beeston, player and later impresario at the Red Bull and the Cockpit from 1604 to 1639, and Richard Gunnell, player and impresario at the Fortune and Salisbury Court playhouses, were all avowed Catholics. None of the Chamberlain's or King's Men were known to be recusants, although Davenant is said to have become a Catholic during the Civil War, and was certainly one in the Restoration.[49] In the 1630s his association with the King's as writer marched in time with his masque-writing for the court, though his allegiance to the company faded fast when he saw the chance to become an independent impresario with his Dorset House plans and his takeover of the Cockpit in the last few years of playing. Still, neither his nor any other of the King's Men's plays of the 1630s make any reference to religious issues. The only exception, a complex and prophetic aside, came earlier. That was *Barnavelt*, where the eponymous victim's followers were Remonstrants or Arminians, the sect that Archbishop Laud and Charles came to uphold eventually. James, who read deeply into the religious tracts of the time, disliked the religious position of Hugo Grotius, the chief exponent of Arminian views. He favoured the Contraremonstrants

---

[49] Massinger had Catholic relatives, including an uncle imprisoned for recusancy, but so did the Dean of St Paul's. See Donald S. Lawless, 'The Parents of Philip Massinger', *Notes and Queries* 213 (1968), 256–8.

in the Netherlands rather than Grotius and Barnavelt, so the play should have had some appeal for him.[50] The speed with which Fletcher and the others set about composing the play after Barnavelt's execution in May 1619 suggests there might have been a stimulus from somewhere on high rather like the later promptings that produced *A Game at Chess* and *The Late Lancashire Witches*. Barnavelt's fate was a matter of some debate in England, as John Chamberlain testified, although more over the justice of his execution than his religious position.[51] As written, the play did not really invite its audiences to take up strong attitudes on the matter. Anti-Spanish emotions aside, religion was truly too sensitive and perhaps too personal a question for overt public comment. In later years the popular view found Charles's Arminianism dangerously close to Rome, and his queen was openly Catholic. In such a tense and sensitive situation, with religion and politics entangled like snakes, special sects flourished among the commoners but the affiliations of courtiers other than the queen were mostly kept well hidden. The absence of any explicit sign of religious allegiance in the plays written in this reign simply reflects the acknowledged need to keep quiet about religious differences.

For the company to revive *The Faithful Shepherdess* and to commission *The Platonic Lovers* shows how close was its affiliation to Henrietta Maria. How genuine that was and how far the Blackfriars bias spilled into the Globe plays of the 1630s there is no clear evidence. There is nothing to say that either play was staged at the Globe. Some of the writers in the 1630s do seem to have thought that the Globe repertory should differ from what they were writing for the Blackfriars, but it is not entirely obvious that the company did much to affirm the differences. Their politically inspired plays of 1624 and 1634 were both staged at the Globe in August, but that says as much about the absence of authority from London in that season as about their appeal to the populace. The Fletcher concern to set out questions of honour for the gentry, re-emphasized by Massinger, Shirley, and Davenant, shows one side of the company's coinage with its new repertory. The reverse, though, still kept *The Merry Devil of Edmonton* and Falstaff current even at court through the 1630s. Thomas Roe's wish that Pyramus and Cervantes would keep people's minds off political questions

[50]   Grotius visited England in 1613 in the hope of making it the place for a meeting between the Reformation churches and moderate Catholics, while James was pursuing his own policy of reconciliation. James admired Grotius, but rejected his and Barnavelt's political opposition to the Prince of Orange. See W. B. Patterson, *King James VI and I and the Reunion of Christendom*, Cambridge University Press, 1997, pp. 142–5.

[51]   See *Letters*, II.223, 236, 239.

ignored both the repertory's general concern about political morality and the assimilative effect on its audience's subconscious absorption of political values. Roe thought politics was gossip about current issues, not a formative influence on attitudes to tyranny. Yet we cannot read the hundreds of Jacobean and Caroline plays aimed at the most powerful figures in the period without identifying some of the grounds for the people's dismissal of monarchy in the 1640s.

CHAPTER 6

The afterlife

THE CONSEQUENCES OF ROYALISM

Since the plays, printed or written, are the only durable product of the company's life, its afterlife with only one exception is an intricate weave of reputations, of the plays and their authors. The exception is the Globe. By the time Edmond Malone at the end of the eighteenth century started leafing through and transcribing passages from the mass of Alleyn's papers left in the care of Dulwich College, Shakespeare was almost the only surviving object of general interest in the company's long history. It was then that, in the absence of much information about the Theatre or the Blackfriars, the Globe's distinctive design, so different from the operatic theatres of the eighteenth and nineteenth centuries, gave a fresh impetus to knowledge of the company's relics besides its plays. Tacit or subconscious contempt for the stage at first made antiquarian study of the original context entirely dependent on the status of the texts. Only as scholars slowly rescued the plays from the priority that put solitary reading above the idea that Shakespeare wrote scripts for staging in special playhouses was the contextual frame enlarged to its present shape. Malone's work appeared in a decade when as many as eighteen different editions of Shakespeare were on the market. After Malone the Globe, for all the last-chance fortuitousness of its building and its secondary role to the Blackfriars, built before it and superseding it as the company's chief venue, slowly took on its current sacred status as Shakespeare's workplace. He wrote *Hamlet*, *Othello*, and *Lear* for it, so, viewed as the setting for his greatest creations, it is valued as the vital nurse of all his drama. 'Shakespeare's Globe' has become the romantic's vision of the ideal setting for the plays. The workplace could as easily have been the Theatre, which gave the Globe its skeletal shape, or the Blackfriars, the Globe's predecessor and successor. Even as an idealized setting the Globe is more potent as a vision than as the location for what the company did to the play-texts when staging them. So this concluding chapter about the company's afterlife follows two main threads, the reputation of the plays and their revivals when their authors' standing shifted, and that subsequent growth of interest in the context which began as an antiquarian study of the playhouses and staging.

The struggle to keep any acting company going is a matter for recurrent negotiation between managers and audience. The loss of a playhouse is one factor, but when the company owns its own plays another factor starts operating: the need for caution in the repertory on which its reputation is based. The later story of the Shakespeare company is remarkable above all for the fame of that long and conservative repertory. Its survival after the company's demise in 1642 is thanks to its almost continuous run in print and on the stage, entwined and inelegantly put on show in the contorted and unhappy opposition that still exists between those two kinds of venue.

THE IMMEDIATE AFTERLIFE

As we have seen, the royal family, especially Henrietta Maria and her court, took a personal hand in the King's Men's affairs in the last fifteen years. Her influence can be found in the company's choice of repertory; her courtiers wrote plays to match her interest in 'platonic love' and gave them to the company. She graced the Blackfriars playhouse with her presence. When the division between king and Parliament became an open power struggle, the King's Men had no choice over which side they would support. Their whole profession was dependent on royal protection. When it disappeared, the players' livelihoods went too. The company's afterlife has always lain in the shadow of that long allegiance.

At Christmas 1640–1 the King's Men were the only company to perform at court, offering perhaps as many as sixteen plays. In the following Christmas festivities they performed the only play staged at court, *The Scornful Lady*, on Twelfth Night 1642. It was a bad time for celebrations, now the division had opened up between king and Parliament, with the Army Plot incriminating Suckling and Davenant, and Parliament's execution of the king's strong man Strafford. *The Scornful Lady* was performed for the twelve-year-old Prince Charles, both of his parents staying away. Four weeks later, on 4 February 1642, after the king's abortive attempt to arrest the 'Five Members' and his departure for the north to gather his army, the House of Commons debated playgoing, and several puritanical speakers produced 'a great complaint against the Play-houses, and a motion made for the suppressing of them'.[1] This followed a debate in the House on 26 January, when a motion to close all playhouses was blocked by two unusual allies, the puritanical poet Edmund Waller and the Parliamentary leader John Pym, one of the 'Five Members'. But on 2 September the puritans had their way when Parliament laid down its official ban on playing, on the grounds that 'publike Sports doe not well agree with publike Calamities, nor publike Stage-playes with the seasons of Humiliation'. The humiliation was the king's, and what he gave his patronage to was finished.

The fact that it was Parliament which ordered the closure, whereas all previous ordinances over playing had been issued by the Privy Council, shows how complete the transfer of power in London was. The last long plague closure happened between July and December 1641, when the Privy Council issued its usual order to stop playing. There were not enough plague deaths on the lists from London's 126 parishes to close it in 1642, although the fear was always there. By September Parliament knew that the plague would not erupt as it had the previous year. They did not know how long the 'publike Calamities' would last, but the debate in February had already shown how strong the hostility of many Parliamentarians was to playing, however much (or little) others saw plays as a nursling of the court. So Parliament did what under the earlier regime had been done by the king's council, and laid a ban on playing.

Martin Butler has argued that the closure was not originally intended to last anywhere near as long as the eighteen years that it eventually did.[2] That may be true, but in political terms the major point is that by ordering the ban, the first time Parliament ever did anything about playing, it was pre-empting a function formerly in the hands of the Privy Council. It was Parliament that gave the order, and Parliament renewed it in 1647 and 1649. Dutifully and ironically, it was also Parliament that in 1646 had to authorize payment of the arrears owed for pre-1642 court performances to the remnant King's Men. The fact that it required the restoration of Charles II in 1660 to bring playgoing back into London's sportive resources may be an over-simple mark of how plays were seen as a feature of royalism. It was more the social liberalism of the second Charles than his official approval of playgoing as an establishment practice that brought Davenant and a remnant of the long-defunct King's Men back to work in London. The return was, explicitly, meant to be part of the general 'restoration' of

---

[1] For a thorough and still reasonably reliable account of this period, see Leslie Hotson, *The Commonwealth and Restoration Stage*, chapter 1.

[2] 'Two Playgoers, and the Closing of the London Theatres, 1642', *Theatre Research International* 9 (1984), 93–9. See also Gurr, *The Shakespearian Playing Companies*, pp. 157–8.

the old order. England was always divided over playgoing. The best that can be said is that between 1640 and 1660 its authorization depended on who was in power, and that when the king left London so did authorized playing.

During the Interregnum, the sharers in the King's Men with one exception showed a continuing loyalty to their former patron. In 1642–3 a number of them made their way to the royal headquarters at Oxford, and several took arms on the king's side. One sharer, the clown William Robbins, was said to have been killed at the siege of Basing House in 1645, fighting for the defending royalists. There may even have been a tradition of loyalty to the monarch among company families, since Henrietta Maria, hurrying south to join her husband at Oxford in 1643, slept one night on the way at New Place in Stratford as the guest of Susannah Hall, Shakespeare's elder daughter. The chief exception to this continuing loyalty to the company's patron was Eliart Swanston. A supporter of Parliament against the king, he left the company and became a London tradesman for the last nine years of his life. The main group, though, tried to keep together, and when the fighting was over they re-formed in London and tried to run plays when the Parliamentary soldiery was not looking. The renewal of group activity was stimulated and perhaps fortuitously subsidized by Parliament's payment in 1646, and by the Beaumont and Fletcher Folio in 1647, to which most of the ex-sharers gave their names.

Despite these attempts to renew their skills and their income the divisions of the war split most of the King's Men apart, probably more for personal and financial reasons than their wartime allegiances. In 1655 Theophilus Bird claimed in a lawsuit that Thomas Pollard and Michael Bowyer had with some others sold off the company's apparel and playbooks, and that they owed him a share. Along with Bird, William Allen, Hugh Clark, Robbins, and Stephen Hammerton, Bowyer had in January 1641 been named as a Groom of the Chamber, which signified that he was a company sharer. Who else among the sharers set up the sale of company assets is not known for sure, but it evidently did not include Bird. As one of the youngest sharers he was almost the only one left by 1660 to carry the company's practices on into the Restoration.

When the Folio edition of thirty-four Beaumont and Fletcher plays not previously in print appeared in 1647, the signatories who put their names to the book included ten of the sharers of 1642, Taylor and Lowin, Richard Robinson, Robert Benfield, Thomas Pollard, Hammerton, Clark, Allen, Bird, and, surprising only if one forgets the teamwork by which the company ran, Eliart Swanston. Bowyer had died in 1645. The order of the names in the dedication was Lowin, Robinson, Swanston, Clark, Hammerton, Taylor, Benfield, Pollard, Allen, and lastly Bird. This defiant publication of so many plays at a time when Parliament was renewing its Act against plays and players was accompanied by a substantial collection of poems praising the collaborators. It was only the third Folio of playwriting authors to appear, following Jonson's of 1616 and 1640 and Shakespeare's of 1623 and 1632. Between them the three Folios contained seventy-nine of the King's Men's plays. When the second Beaumont and Fletcher Folio appeared in 1679 it added another eighteen. Altogether, the three/four collections of plays in their Folios contained well over half the 160 plays printed from the King's repertory.[3] They survived more happily than the players.

After the war ended with Parliament's victory in 1645, several ex-King's Men in London tried to create a new playing group. Several of the ten who signed the Beaumont and Fletcher Folio in 1647, including Taylor, Pollard, and Lowin, were arrested by the army when they tried to play *Rollo* at the Cockpit on 5 February 1648. They had played *Wit Without Money* at the Red Bull two days before, and it is possible that the army had warning of their second show. Six days later a Parliamentary ordinance renewed the old Elizabethan statute, declaring that all 'Players shall be taken as Rogues', and the Lord Mayor was authorized to pull all the remaining playhouses down.

As before, that proved easy to order but difficult to carry out. The Globe had disappeared in 1644 after the company's lease of the land expired, and tenements now stood on the site, but other playhouses were held freehold, and no Lord Mayor dared to confront householders over their properties before the catastrophic emergency of the Great Fire of 1666, when whole rows of houses were pulled down to make firebreaks. The Cockpit survived, though damaged by the soldiery, and was even reopened briefly for playing in 1661 after the Restoration. Of the others, two of the three older open-air playhouses, the Fortune and Bear Garden (originally the Hope), gradually followed the Globe. Soldiers dismantled the Fortune in 1649, but its owners, now Dulwich College, refused to lease it for any purpose except as a playhouse, and its ruins were not pulled down entirely until 1662. In February 1656 seven bears belonging to the Bear Garden were shot by the military, and the building was destroyed and replaced with tenements, like the nearby Globe. Only the Red Bull stayed in intermittent use. The Blackfriars playhouse remained unused until soldiers smashed all the interior in 1649. It was never used as a playhouse again, and in

---

[3] For a full listing, see Appendix 5.

August 1655 the interior ruins were dismantled and tenements rebuilt in the hall, returning it to what it had been when James Burbage purchased it sixty years before. The entire Blackfriars complex disappeared in the great conflagration of 1666, and a new Apothecaries' Hall occupied the site, the first major reconstruction after the fire.

Hostility to plays never dies. An Act of 11 February 1647 renewed the arguments against playing, enhancing the statutes about players as vagabonds, calling them 'incorrigible Rogues', ordered all the playhouses to be demolished, and specified that anyone caught at a play should pay a fine of five shillings to the poor of the local parish. That law haunted several subsequent attempts to stage plays at the surviving playhouses. When Taylor, Lowin, and others were caught playing *Rollo* again at the Cockpit, for instance, according to James Wright,

They ventured to Act some Plays with as much caution and privacy as cou'd be, at the *Cockpit*. They continu'd undisturbed for three or four Days; but at last as they were presenting the Tragedy of the *Bloudy Brother*, (in which *Lowin* Acted Aubrey, *Tayler* Rollo, *Pollard* the Cook, *Burt* Latorch, and I think *Hart* Otto) a Party of Foot Souldiers beset the House, surprized 'em about the middle of the Play, and carried 'em away in their habits, not admitting them to Shift, to *Hatton-House* then a Prison, where having detain'd them sometime, they Plunder'd them of their Cloths and let 'em loose again. Afterwards in *Oliver's* time, they used to Act privately, three or four Miles, or more, out of Town, now here, now there, sometimes in Noblemens Houses, in particular *Holland-House* at *Kensington*, where the Nobility and Gentry who met (but in no great Numbers) used to make a Sum for them.[4]

The same legislation explains the military's attack on a performance at the Red Bull in May 1655. One of the newsletters flourishing in this period, the *Weekly Intelligencer*, printed a lurid report of the event, when the audience was penalized along with the players. The soldiers collected the prescribed five-shilling fine from everyone present, on the stage or in the audience, and were prepared to take clothing in place of cash.

This Day proved Tragical to the *Players* at the *Red Bull*, their Acting being against an Act of Parlament, the Soldiers secured the persons of some of them who were upon the Stage, and in the Tyrin-house, they seized also upon their cloaths in which they acted, a great part whereof was very rich, it never fared worse with the spectators then at this present, for those who had monies payed their five shillings apeece, those who had none to satisfie their forfeits, did leave their Cloaks behind them, the Tragedy of the Actors, and the Spectators, was the Comedy of the soldiers. There was abundance of the Female Sex, who not able to pay 5s. did leave some gage or other behind them.

---

[4] Quoted in Bentley, *Jacobean and Caroline Stage*, II.695.

The newsletter added tactfully that some of the items of clothing, the 'gages' forfeited by the women, were later returned to them.

Intermittent attempts to stage plays continued through the 1650s during Cromwell's Protectorate, although by then few of the sharers were still involved. Richard Robinson, Lowin, Benfield, Bird, Clark, Hammerton, and Pollard signed a bond to pay a debt to Bowyer's heirs in January 1648, two months before he died. Allen had already died, and most of the others were dead by 1655. A few survivors, including Richard Baxter, were in the group who played at the Red Bull in 1655 and had to fight the raiding soldiers to save their properties. Bird and a Richard Baxter, who may or may not have been the former King's Men's Baxter, were almost the only survivors from 1642 to sign up for the new King's Men in 1661.

By then Davenant had returned to the scene. The scale of his ambitions as an impresario had become evident through the 1630s, when he tried to commandeer the King's Men's repertory. His ambitions show in his aborted plan during the 1636–8 plague closure to build an enormous theatre in the Strand staging plays with music and dancing. By 1657, after a colourful career fighting for the king and queen, a term of exile with young Charles in Paris, and then capture by Parliament on a ship taking him to Virginia, he could at last set about renewing his ambition for operatic theatre. Before that, back in England in 1650 after a period of detention in the Tower by a surprisingly tolerant Parliament, he ran into trouble for debt. That is hardly surprising after his wartime investments in royalist gun-running and the fact that he had worked for the losing side. He solved the problem in 1654 by returning to France to marry a rich widow, his third wife. Financially secure at last, he finally realized his ambition to stage operatic plays in 1658. He used the word 'opera' for his entertainments to shelter them from the hostility that 'play' or 'theatre' might still attract, and operatic they certainly were. Starting with a show consisting of a medley of songs and spoken 'declamations' at his house, which a ballad of the time said was 'Made a la mode *de France*',[5] he ran a variety of public shows, all at locations reminiscent of the pre-1642 theatres, and all full of song and dance. He used the old Apothecaries' Hall at Blackfriars adjacent to the former Blackfriars playhouse, St John's in Clerkenwell near the Red Bull, and Gibbons's Tennis Court near the Cockpit in Drury Lane. For his major opera in 1659, *The Siege of Rhodes*, he appears to have used the Cockpit

---

[5] The best account of the renewal of staging at this time is in Mary Edmond's *Rare Sir William Davenant*, Manchester University Press, 1987, chapters 8 and 9. The ballad is quoted on p. 123.

itself.[6] There is no doubt that in using these places Davenant was looking to remind prospective playgoers of, if not to actually restore, the old habits. He was well prepared when the Restoration of Charles II in 1660 opened the royalist floodgates.

A royal restoration it was. Pepys reported in his diary that the king's two brothers, the Dukes of York and Gloucester, had been to see a performance of *Epicene* at the old Red Bull by Michael Mohun and a new company within a week of Charles's arrival in London at the end of May.[7] In these months the players and impresarios did their best to restore as many of the old practices as they could. Restoring playgoing soon led to a duopoly of companies markedly like the old pair of 1594. After a period of what Mary Edmond has called 'feverish manoeuvring',[8] when three different groups were trying to establish themselves, Thomas Killigrew was licensed to start a new King's Men under Mohun. They were sworn in as household servants to Charles II as his company on 6 October 1660, while Davenant set up a second company called the Duke of York's. It restored the two approved companies with royal patrons, the king and his brother. The nostalgia of the mind-set became evident when Killigrew and Davenant skirmished over which company had the right to perform Shakespeare's plays, already seen as the best prizes from the earlier period. In the end Killigrew's King's Men got most of the old repertory, but Davenant kept eleven of the most popular, *The Tempest, Measure for Measure, Much Ado, Romeo and Juliet, Twelfth Night, Hamlet, King Lear, Macbeth, Henry VIII, The Duchess of Malfi*, and *The Sophy*.[9]

Nostalgia was the chief sentiment in the first years, and the reopening of the theatres was staged as an exercise in memory of the good old 1630s. Even Henry Herbert returned to his former office as Master of the Revels, though he never succeeded against Killigrew and Davenant in restoring his old authority or profits. Ostensibly the former status quo returned, King's Men and all. In practice, it introduced to London for the first time the radically anti-Shakespearean staging that the exiled court had learned

[6] See John Orrell, *The Theatres of Inigo Jones and John Webb*, Cambridge University Press, 1985, pp. 63–77.

[7] *The Diary of Samuel Pepys*, transcribed and edited by Robert Latham and William Matthews, 1.171.

[8] *Rare Sir William Davenant*, p. 141.

[9] A full list of the plays allocated to Killigrew and Davenant is given in Irwin Smith, *Shakespeare's Blackfriars Playhouse*, London, 1966, pp. 502–4. See also *The London Stage 1660–1800*, ed. William Van Lennep and others, 5 parts (11 vols.), Southern Illinois University Press, Carbondale, 1960–8. Part 1, 1660–1700, pp. 151–2, reprints a list of c. 12 January 1668, of 111 King's plays now 'allowed' to the new King's company. No similar list exists for Davenant's Duke of York's company. Pepys saw *Macbeth, Twelfth Night, Henry VIII*, and *The Wits* at the Duke of York's in 1668, none of which are in the King's list. Davenant adapted *The Tempest* for York's.

to admire in Paris. Both companies used only indoor playhouses.[10] Their impresarios introduced for the first time in public view women actors and scenic staging with 'scenes' painted on grooved flats, and footlights to separate stage from audience. Most innovatively, Davenant pulled ahead of the opposition with his use of music and dance, which now became valued features even of the old plays.

Both new managers also tried to follow the old King's practice of setting up sharers not only in their company's playing assets but in their new playhouses. Unlike the original King's system this was introduced as a means of spreading the costs rather than of keeping control in the players' hands. Both of the Restoration companies were run by their impresarios, as Davenant did in 1641 when he briefly ran the Cockpit company, and as Christopher Beeston had always done. Neither Killigrew nor Davenant ever worked as players themselves like Taylor and Lowin.

The membership of both Restoration companies appears to have included a few remnants of the King's Men who remembered the attractive arrangement of holding shares in the company and the playhouse. Those we know of were in the new King's. Davenant's team was made up mostly of young actors, none of whom can be identified in the former company, although it was claimed later that their eventual star, Thomas Betterton, had learned his trade from those who knew the old King's. Pepys worshipped Betterton's acting from the time he saw his Hamlet in 1661, when he was playing for Davenant's company. Nostalgic commentators insisted that the tradition of Shakespearean acting had been handed down directly, and that the Restoration actors learned how to play Hamlet and other figures in accordance with the style of Taylor and Lowin. For all Davenant's familiarity with the company's work in the 1630s, and his work with Betterton and his young leads, much of that sentiment must have been wishful thinking. John Downes, for instance, enthused over a performance of *Henry VIII* in 1663 by the Davenant company that 'the part of the King was so right and justly done by Mr *Betterton*, he being Instructed in it by Sir *William*, who had it from Old Mr *Lowen*, that had his Instructions from Mr *Shakespear* himself'.[11] That is quite a long line of hand-me-downs.

Killigrew's King's Company had most of the older actors. Its experienced leader Michael Mohun had worked for the Beestons at the Cockpit, Charles Hart had been a boy player with the King's, and Nicholas Burt

---

[10] The old Red Bull was used for a time, as it had been during the Interregnum.
[11] Downes, *Roscius Anglicanus*, 1708, p. 24.

had been trained by Shanks with the King's before joining Mohun at the Cockpit in 1638. In the Interregnum he was one of the players caught acting along with Lowin, Taylor, and Pollard. Another in Killigrew's troupe, Richard Baxter, was a name from the old King's lists. The early Baxter was first noted playing for Queen Anne's Men in 1605, and was in his sixties by the Restoration. He played for the King's Men from 1625. In 1663 he deposed that 'hee hath beene an Actor in Stage playes for above 50 yeares'.[12] The only other well-known and certainly senior survivor and former sharer was Theophilus Bird, who had spent two years in the old King's just before the closure. He joined the Killigrew King's in January 1662. A son-in-law of Christopher Beeston, his own eldest daughter was Mohun's wife. Bird acted with the new King's until his death less than two years later.

Published histories of London's theatre after 1660 are prolific compared with the earlier period. Langbaine produced his *Account of the English Dramatick Poets* in 1691, Wright brought out *Historia Histrionica* eight years later, and in 1708 John Downes, book-keeper to the Restoration King's Men for forty or so years, published his detailed retrospect *Roscius Anglicanus*.[13] Practical memories as well as nostalgia set the basis for the new order of royally patronized companies in London, but it is not easy to tell from these accounts how far the old King's Men's tradition of playing was restored. Early historians like Downes were keen to assert how much was transferred, but that was at a time when Shakespeare was already beginning to emerge as the great model to be imitated. Dryden's famous *Essay of Dramatic Poesy*, written in 1668 when he was himself creating the classic drama of the early Restoration period, upheld Jonson as a more serious model than Shakespeare, but that was for writing, not for staging. In practice there was little feeling of any need to copy the original staging of either of the King's Men's two greatest sets of plays. In 1663 Downes asserted the value of direct inheritance from the old company's pre-1642 practices, but that was before the physical structures of two-dimensional staging in the French style and their mental consequences for plays using Davenant's music and dance had really established themselves. It did not take long for the new theatres, the new actors (not playing now, but acting), and the new audiences to set off on their own roads to glory.

---

[12] Judith Milhous and Robert D. Hume, 'New Light on English Acting Companies', *Review of English Studies* 42 (1991), 487–509.
[13] See *Roscius Anglicanus*, ed. Judith Milhous and Robert D. Hume, Society for Theatre Research, London, 1987.

Dryden did an establishment job in his elegant 'Essay of Dramatick Poesy' when he chose to make an 'examen' of *Epicene* (*The Silent Woman*) rather than a Shakespeare comedy as the exemplar of what he found best in the earlier theatre. Restoration drama was settling into its selective choices. Jonsonian citizen comedy and well-plotted plays on the Fletcher model were the fashion now. Even though neither of the new duopoly companies succeeded in capturing the rights to perform all the Shakespeare plays, they staged them differently, and Davenant's operatic adaptations proved far more popular than traditional staging or unmodified versions of the plays. The real struggles were over the other plays. *Rollo* and other Fletchers were being revived more than the Shakespeares, most of which the producers used to test the water, allowing many of them to drown. Pepys in the ten years of his *Diary* records seeing 360 plays, of which 71 were by Beaumont and Fletcher, 48 by Shakespeare, and 26 by Jonson. The absolute supremacy of the Shakespeares does not appear until the early eighteenth century. All the King's plays gradually acquired the status in the Restoration repertories of 'classics', and many of them were restaged, but of the three writers the Beaumont and Fletcher canon was the one that that ran through most vigorously into the eighteenth century, only slowly dropping off as new fashions emerged.

The old repertory was soon being rewritten, both in Davenant's operatic versions and as developments of the tradition started during the closure, making short farces or 'drolls' out of the comic scenes. A version of *The Taming of the Shrew* called *Sauney the Scot* held the stage from 1667 to 1886. Such adaptations were done to a wide range of the old King's repertory. A droll from 2.1 of *The Beggar's Bush* called 'The Lame Commonwealth' was staged in the closure and printed in *The Wits* in 1661. Later versions of the play included *The Royal Merchant or the Beggar's Bush*, staged at the Theatre Royal and printed in 1706 unchanged from the 1647 Folio text. In 1768 it was made an opera and in 1815 an altered stage-play, cutting a lot for censorship reasons and adding a beggar scene.[14] *Rollo*, the play most notoriously restaged during the closure, was revived as a King's Company play on 6 December 1660, 28 March 1661, and 17 September 1668, when Pepys saw it, and it appeared to royalty on 9 November 1674 and 19 April 1675, 1685, and 1687. It was revived again in 1705 and 1708.

---

[14] John H. Dorenkamp, ed., *John Fletcher and Philip Massinger, 'The Beggars Bush'*, Mouton, The Hague, 1967.

When plays first returned to London in 1660, it was some time before new work appeared on stage, as one might expect. A check on the winter seasons, October to December, for each decade from 1660 to 1710 shows that the King's Men's staples, Beaumont and Fletcher, Shakespeare, and Jonson (in that order of frequency), moved gradually from being simply the old familiar favourites to become the recurrent classics of the two companies' repertories. In the last three months of 1660 the old King's plays made up seventeen of the twenty-five plays that playgoers like Pepys recorded themselves as seeing. They were *The Tamer Tamed*, *Philaster*, *The Beggar's Bush* (twice), *Wit Without Money* (three times), *Rollo*, *A King and No King*, *The Humorous Lieutenant*, *The Chances*, and *The Elder Brother* from the Fletcher and Beaumont canon, Shakespeare's *Othello* (twice), *1 Henry IV* (twice), *Merry Wives of Windsor* (twice), Jonson's *Epicene* (three times), and *The Alchemist*, together with *The Scornful Lady*, *The Widow*, and *The Unfortunate Lovers*. These ratios are not very different from the old company's last years up to 1642.

Ten years later, from October to December 1670, only eight of the old plays were still in performance, including *Macbeth* and the Davenant–Dryden musical version of *The Tempest*. New theatre resources invited the conversion of the more likely classics into operatic forms. Davenant and Dryden's rewrite of *The Tempest* with more parts for women was given operatic wings in 1670 and 1674, and a parodic *Mock-Tempest* appeared a year later. By this time women taking the female roles together with music, song, and dance had grown to become the most popular offerings on stage, and the practice of rewriting the old favourites as musicals was well under way. In the three-month season from October to December in 1680 the only old King's play was *Richard II*, and that, being still a politically sensitive subject, ran in Nahum Tate's disguise as *The Sicilian Tyrant* for two nights before the authorities woke up to his evasion of their censorship. During the Exclusion crisis the Lord Chamberlain also banned Crowne's adaptation of *2 Henry VI*. Ten years after that only *The Prophetess* (*The Maid's Honour*) was on stage from the earlier repertory besides some Shakespeare. This was the beginning of the downturn of the Beaumont and Fletchers. The United Company that ran from 1682 to 1694 was dominated by Betterton, heir of Davenant in his own thinking, whose love for his Shakespeare roles brought them to the forefront among what were now considered the English classics.

The last season of the century, October to December 1700, saw the old plays openly staged as classics, revived in new versions of their original forms as well as in thoroughgoing rewrites. Of nineteen plays recorded in the autumn season in 1700, seven were King's plays: Fletcher's *The*

Pilgrim, *The Prophetess*, *The Island Princess*, and *Rule a Wife and Have a Wife*, plus a revival which may have been Shakespeare's *Henry VIII*, and Jonson's *Epicene* and *Volpone*. Ten years after that, nine out of the forty-three plays performed in London were Fletcher's *The Maid's Tragedy*, *The Pilgrim*, and *The Chances*, Shakespeare's *1 Henry IV*, *Hamlet*, *King Lear*, and *Macbeth*, and Jonson's *Epicene* and *Volpone*. The 4:3:2 ratio of 1710 marks the beginning of the Shakespeare canonization in theatre. The year before that, Tonson had canonized him in print by publishing Rowe's great new edition of Shakespeare, who by now stood out high above his peers.

Shakespeare-worship grew throughout the century, though with readers more than playgoers as the number of collected editions of plays for the reader accelerated. By the end of the eighteenth century, between 1793 and 1800, eighteen editions of Shakespeare were on offer. Pope, Theobald, Hanmer, Warburton, Johnson, Capell, Rann, Steevens with his Johnson Variorum, and in 1790 Malone commanded an audience of readers around the country quite distinct from London's playgoers. Up to 1709 plays were likely to be printed because of their success on stage. After the Rowe edition the stage began to use what the press had made popular. For theatre enthusiasts there were the Bell and other single-play editions printed from the prompt copies of the two groups licensed after *The Beggar's Opera* crisis of 1737, the Princess and Theatre Royal companies. Editors and other readers were interested only in Shakespeare's words, which they reckoned were precious stones to be rescued from the dross of the players and their interpolations. Pope blamed the players even more than the early printers for sections of dialogue that he thought fell below Shakespearean quality. He announced in his edition of *The Tempest*, for instance, that Sebastian's and Antonio's comments in 2.1 while Gonzalo is attempting to comfort Alonzo were players' interpolations. Theobald derided Pope's view, but not in defence of the players.

A footnote in Malone's variorum edition of 1790 confirms the depth of the eighteenth-century gulf between canonizing readers and paying playgoers. On Prospero's famous 'Our revels now are ended' speech in *The Tempest* he noted as a speculation of his own not to be found in any previous edition the thought that the line 'Leave not a rack behind' should perhaps be corrected to 'Leave not a *wreck* behind.' No previous editor had raised that as a possible correction, but it was far from a new idea in the theatre, and had in fact been mischievously published by Pope in marble. In 1742 for Peter Scheemakers's inscription on the Westminster Abbey marble statue that he helped to raise funds for, Pope altered the text a little to make it more suitable for a funeral elegy, and one of his more gratuitous changes turned 'rack' into 'wreck'. Visitors noted the emendation, and as a result every prompt-book edition of the play published from 1745 onwards gave the theatre's version of the word as 'wreck'. Like Johnson, who for all his close links to Garrick, the greatest of the mid-century actor–managers, was not a theatregoer, Malone sat so far away from the theatre (and presumably from Westminster Abbey) that he believed the emendation was his own invention.

For playgoers, the rush of editions meant that attention spread to many of the older plays that had remained classics. In 1734–5 a price war between Tonson and Alexander Walker meant that the market for books was flooded with cheap one-play Shakespeare editions. Shortly after that the Shakespeare Ladies Club started to encourage a return to the original texts. Print made the plays easily accessible, and the stage followed the trend. They stimulated the stage's first retreat from the operatic Davenant tradition, opening the way for Garrick to offer a fresh approach to something more like the original Shakespeare. He had sound commercial reasons for that too. On stage the Licensing Act of 1737 ensured that the classics became standard offerings at London's two official theatres. On the one hand they were free from any of the usual constraints over getting a licence to perform, and on the other they saved the producers the cost of an author's benefit night. As a consequence in the decades after 1737 over 50 per cent of the plays staged dated from before 1700, 20 per cent of them by Shakespeare.[15] When Garrick launched his career in 1740 his progress was marked by his Shakespeare roles. Other remnants of the old King's repertory came back with him, and new editions and collections, of Jonson, Massinger, and others, made revivals easy. While scholarly editors gave most of their time to Shakespeare, in 1744 the extraordinary Robert Dodsley produced his wide-ranging *Select Collection of Old Plays*, using the Bell Quartos from London's two licensed theatres to augment the Shakespeares and the second (1679) Folio of all the Beaumont and Fletcher plays. His volumes captured all and more of the old King's Men plays that had a place on stage in the eighteenth century, including Middleton's *The Widow* and *Hengist, or the Mayor of Quinborough*. His editions and imitations by Chetwood and others spurred the publication of selections of dramatic verse throughout the century, including a coffee-table *Beauties of the English Drama* in 1777, and Lamb's *Specimens of English Dramatic Poets* in 1808.

[15] Julie Stone has three remarkable chapters on the printing of plays between the 1590s and 1760, in Julie Stone Peters, *Theatre of the Book, 1480–1880: Print, Text, and Performance in Europe*, Clarendon Press, 2000.

It was in the eighteenth century that England sanctified Shakespeare. Even in the 1630s his plays had been used to generate an idea of English country life that came to be known, with characteristically anachronistic spelling, as 'Merrie England'. Milton, of all people, helped to inscribe the poet of the forest of Arden and the middle English countryside in common thinking. His celebration in *L'Allegro* (1645) of 'sweetest Shakespear fancies child' who could 'Warble his native Wood-notes wilde' helped transform the plays, from *As You Like It* to Falstaff's Windsor, into a nostalgic vision of an idyllic past. The tourist route to Stratford started its beaten path in those years, though it took a century before Shakespeare was fully relocated away from London. In 1767 Garrick tried to capture the right to Shakespeare as the theatrical spirit of England by launching a belated anniversary festival at Stratford. In contrast with the 126 or so others that survived from the repertory, Shakespeare's plays came to epitomize what people saw as England's age of Elizabethan innocence. According to this myth an Englishman's nature came from whatever was 'native' to Shakespeare. Such purity had no political attachments, although the general assumption was that Shakespeare's 'nature' naturally made him a monarchist. His Eastcheap was sanitized, his advocacy of young love against parental authority became safe in its familiarity.

The nineteenth century brought the longstanding division between readers and viewers of plays into the open, prompting the Romantics' famous opinion (lasting till Bradley in 1904 and beyond) that *King Lear* could not work on the stage. That was a self-fulfilling prophecy. Coleridge, Lamb, and Hazlitt were theatregoers, but they had little chance of attending anything that we might think of now as a faithful rendition of Shakespeare. Kemble's version of *The Tempest*, the only one seen on the London stage between 1789 and 1837, copied the Davenant plot, opening not with the storm scene but with Prospero saying to his daughter 'Miranda, where's your sister?' Lamb and the other Romantic critics had access only to Kemble's rewrite of Davenant's revision with its augmented parts for women. Not till Macready in the 1830s started a policy of staging versions of the original texts in the now-standard collected editions did the Restoration's rewrites fade from the London repertory. By then very few of the Beaumont and Fletcher plays and almost as few of Jonson's still had classic status matching the popularity that kept Shakespeare on stage. Romantic readers like Coleridge could go through the plays afresh thanks to Dodsley's collections, and Hazlitt in particular radicalized thinking about their politics. The early nineteenth century saw new editions of much of the King's repertory, some of it bowdlerized along with Shakespeare. Byron's publisher Murray in

1830 issued selections from Massinger's plays 'adapted for family reading'. Mostly, as readers, alone or in family groups, everyone dwelt on the eloquent speeches rather than theatricality.

When in the second half of the century Shakespeare was taken up into the new education system, the same kind of enthusiasm led to students memorizing and reciting famous speeches. The New Education Code for England of 1882–3 actually required students to learn their English history directly from the plays, sceptred isle, once more unto the breach, and all. *Richard II* and *Henry V* became the most-sold copies of all the plays of the King's Men's repertory. In the 1890s a rather more radical body of thinking about the plays, unmodified by editorial intrusions of scene locations and decorative stage directions, prompted William Poel's attempts to renew the original kind of staging. Such moves were in part a reaction to the schoolroom takeover, though they also reflected hostility to scholarly and editorial modernizing. By then what had started with Malone and the Dulwich archives as an antiquarian curiosity about the life and times of Shakespeare had developed into a more positive urge to restage the works in their original forms. In the 1830s Tieck considered using the Dulwich contract with its dimensions for the Fortune as the basis for Leipzig's new opera house. Poel's marking-out of the Fortune contract's specifications in a curtained room to make a square stage in the 1890s gradually led to a series of attempts worldwide to reconstruct the Globe, from a half-size theatre at the Earl's Court Exhibition of 1912 (an openly fanciful design by Lutyens) to the new Globe in Southwark in 1997. The chief impetus behind the first moves towards a National Theatre in 1910 was the idea of building a version of the Globe. So far only one attempt to reconstruct the Blackfriars has been completed, at Staunton, Virginia. The Rose, the only playhouse from the time for which the entire foundations survive and have been analysed by archaeologists, is the one most capable of being reproduced, though not quite in the form it was given for *Shakespeare in Love*.

From Poel's time on the orthodoxy of fascination with the words on the page began to crumble, replaced with a new priority, not just of modernized reconceptualizations on stage with filmic scenery (film rapidly overtook the theatre's comparatively hopeless attempts at stage realism), but as endeavours to retrieve what was slowly recognized as Shakespeare's original idea of publication, the plays staged as he expected them to be. The slow march of this kind of evolution, and the enduring tenure of hagiographic worship of the words on their own, is evident in the multitude of ludicrous doublings-up in theatre and film, using precise scenic backdrops without any attempt to cut the text's references to locations and scenic features that were there precisely to tell the early audiences what the original stages did not show. The redundancy of words like Horatio's telling us so beautifully that the morn is coming in russet mantle clad when a filmed sun is visibly rising in the background has made no small contribution to the grossly unhistorical assumption that even on film the plays have to run for at least three hours if we are not to feel cheated of the poetry.

In the monarch's Jubilee year, 2002, the Royal Shakespeare Company at Stratford staged five and a possible sixth of the 168 extant plays from the full Chamberlain's/King's Men's repertory. They were the familiar staples *Much Ado About Nothing* and *Antony and Cleopatra* at the main theatre, together with (at the smaller and far more congenial Swan) *The Malcontent*, *The Island Princess*, and *The Roman Actor*. The sixth was the conjecturally Shakespearean *Edward III*, also at the Swan. A company with royal patronage (and government financing) still upholds the Shakespeare company canon, although its home at Stratford rather than London does reflect the eighteenth-century hagiographic and touristic element in its makeup. Royal support for Shakespeare has been a durable commodity. Shakespeare's words are not only the jewel in the crown of the British national teaching curriculum but are embedded in the whole English-speaking world and flourish in many other cultures. That drags the texts a very long way away from their context in the Shakespeare company's work. Post-hoc applications of Shakespeare are unavoidable, and sometimes they can enhance modern cultures richly. But they would be even richer if we could get a better knowledge of the propter-hoc Shakespeares.

The players

This is an alphabetical list of the players known to have worked for the Chamberlain's/King's Men. The evidence is chiefly taken from Chambers, *Elizabethan Stage*, II.299–349; Bentley, *Jacobean and Caroline Stage*, II.344–622; Nungezer, *A Dictionary*; Eccles, *Notes and Queries* 23; and occasional other sources noted in footnotes, at Appendix 2.33, and in the Bibliography. It owes a particular debt to David Kathman's 'Biographical Index of Elizabethan Drama before 1660', accessible on <shakespeareauthorship.com/bd/>.

John Adson

Hired man and musician, c. 1634; played the cornett for the Duc de Lorraine in 1604, when aged nineteen; a city wait in 1614, probably one of the Blackfriars consort; in *The Late Lancashire Witches* in 1634 a stage direction specifies '*Enter an invisible spirit. J. Adson with a brace of greyhounds*'; lived in the parish of St Giles Cripplegate; wrote *Courtly Masquing Ayres for Violins, Consorts, and Cornets* (1621); played in Shirley's masque *The Triumph of Peace*, 1634; m. Feb. 1614, one child (1615).

William Allen

Hired man 1640–2; a Queen Henrietta's player in the 1630s; as player made a Groom of the Chamber in Lord Chamberlain's list of six new King's Men's employees 22 Jan. 1641; in the dedicatory list of the Beaumont and Fletcher Folio (1647).

John Allington
Hired man 1636–7; his name is added in the margin to the Lord Chamberlain's list of eleven King's Men's employees, 12 Jan. 1637.[1]

Robert Armin
(See figure 17, p. 74). Sharer 1599–1610; known as a jester and ballad- or jig-writer in the 1580s; b. King's Lynn; apprenticed to a goldsmith in Lombard Street, 1581, free in 1591; Richard Tarlton is said to have first met him as a wit at his tavern in Gracechurch Street, and declared him his heir (*Tarlton's Jests*, 1611); like Tarlton, used to extemporize in verse on themes thrown to him by audiences, sometimes in song; travelled with Chandos's Men and probably also solo, doing ventriloquist acts with his 'bauble' or jester's stick; joined Chamberlain's either early in 1599 at the Curtain, or later when Kemp left the company; the dedication to his *Quips upon Questions* (29 Dec. 1599) identified him as playing at the Curtain with Chamberlain's or possibly with Oxford's Men;[2] its republication in 1606 said he was of the Globe; a small man, he played Touchstone (an apt name for a goldsmith) in *As You Like It*, marking the company's shift from the country clown of Kemp to the court jester or fool; he was probably Carlo Buffone in *Every Man Out*, Feste in *Twelfth Night*, Lear's Fool,[3] and Abel Drugger in *The Alchemist* (who asks 'did you never see me play the fool?', 4.7); took over Dogberry in *Much Ado*; he may have played Frog in *The Fair Maid of Bristow*, Matthew Flowerdale in *The London Prodigal*, and the clown in *The Miseries of Enforced Marriage*;[4] named in the cast-lists for *The Alchemist* and the Shakespeare First Folio; wrote plays for boy companies (*Two Maids of Moreclack*, *Amends for Ladies*) and pamphlets (*Fool upon Fool*, *Quips upon Questions*, *A Nest of Ninnies*); lived in the parish of St Botolph's Aldgate; four children 1603–6; acquired a coat of arms like Phillips and Shakespeare; appears to have left playing in 1611, since he is not in the cast-list for *Catiline*; the prologue to *Henry VIII* (1613) may be an apology for his failure to enact the role of Henry's jester Will Somers; d. Nov. 1615.

[1] The Lord Chamberlain's note is reproduced in *Malone Society Collections* II.3, 1907, p. 380.
[2] The dedication says he is on his way to Hackney to wait on his lord. Oxford had a house there. The Chamberlain's was using the Curtain, but may have left it free for other users over the Christmas season. They played before the queen at Richmond Palace on 26 December.
[3] Some readers such as John Southworth, *Fools and Jesters at the English Court*, p. 134, reckon Lear's Fool must have been played by a younger person than Armin, and may have been the boy doubling as Cordelia. Southworth reckons Armin would have played Edgar.
[4] David Wiles, *Shakespeare's Clown*, chapter 10, identifies the obvious series of Armin's roles.

Edward Ashborne

Hired man c. 1624; his name is added in the margin to a list of the company's 'Musicians and other necessary attendantes', 27 Dec. 1624; he may be the 'Ashton' named in the revival of *Love's Pilgrimage*, 1635.

John Bacon

Hired man 1635–7; named in revival of *Love's Pilgrimage*, 1635; in the Lord Chamberlain's list of eleven King's Men's employees, 12 Jan. 1637.

Francis Balls

Hired man, c. 1631; noted as attendant in Massinger's *Believe as You List* in May 1631; possibly also a musician.[5]

Richard Balls

Musician 1608–22; cited as a Blackfriars musician and City Wait by John Adson, his brother-in-law; d. 1622.[6]

Richard Baxter

In King's 1625–42; b. 1593; boy, hired man, and sharer in Queen Anne's Men 1605–24; named in the cast-lists for *The Mad Lover* and *The Lover's Melancholy*; Titus in *Believe As You List*; in Lord Chamberlain's list of eight names plus ten not named on 17 May 1636 to attend the king on his summer progress, and of eleven King's Men's employees 12 Jan. 1637; the list specifies him as the chief reason for producing the list: 'Wheras the Bearer heerof Richard Bagstare hath beene & is imployed by his Majesties servantes the Players of the Blackfryers & is of spcciall use unto them both on the Stage & otherwise for his Majesties Disport & service, for which cause it is his Majesties pleasure that hee bee freed from all unnecessary trouble or molestation by Arrest or otherwise wherby Hee may bee withdrawne from the Company & they disabled to performe their service'. Still acting in 1648, and joined the new King's Men under Killigrew at the Restoration.

Ambrose Beeland, or Byland

Member of the Drapers Guild, freed in 1619; hired man and musician (fiddler), c. 1624–40; listed with 'Musicians and other necessary attendantes' exempted from arrest for military service by Herbert, 27 Dec. 1624; arrested by Heminges with Henry Wilson, another fiddler, 14 Dec. 1628; played in

---

[5] See C. J. Sisson, ed., *Believe as You List*, Malone Society Reprints, p. xxxiii.
[6] Mark Eccles, 'Elizabethan Actors: A–D', *Notes and Queries* 236 (1991), 39.

Shirley's masque *The Triumph of Peace*, 1634; royal musician 1640; as royal violinist exempted from subsidy payments 17 April 1641; surrendered his post in March 1672.

Christopher Beeston

Boy player or hired man 1598–9; b. c. 1580; apprenticed to Augustine Phillips in the Chamberlain's, who left him 30 shillings in 1605; named his son Augustine in 1604, while living in St Leonard's Shoreditch; joined Worcester's 1600; named in the cast-list for *Every Man in his Humour* (1598) but not *Every Man out of his Humour* (1599); later a Queen Anne's player at the Red Bull, and later still manager of various companies as owner of the Cockpit playhouse, chief rival to the Blackfriars, and the Red Bull; m. 1602 to Jane Sands, a recusant; five children (1611–16); d. 1638.

Robert Benfield

Hired man and sharer 1615–42; Lady Elizabeth's 1613–14; probably replaced William Ostler when he died at the end of 1614; his presence in the livery list of 1622 indicates that he was a sharer by then; became a housekeeper in the Blackfriars and Globe in 1635;[7] took over Ostler's part of Antonio in *The Duchess of Malfi*, Lovewit in *The Alchemist*, Junius Rusticus in *The Roman Actor*, King Ladislaus in *The Picture*, the King in *The Deserving Favourite*, Marcellus in *Believe as You List*, Degard in the 1632 revival of *The Wild Goose Chase*, and the doctor in *The Soddered Citizen*; in cast-lists for *The Knight of Malta*, *The Double Marriage*, *The False One*, *The Mad Lover*, *The Humorous Lieutenant*, *The Island Princess*, *The Custom of the Country*, *The Prophetess*, *The Spanish Curate*, *The Maid in the Mill*, *The Pilgrim*, *The Little French Lawyer*, *The Lover's Progress*, *A Wife for a Month*, *The Spanish Viceroy*, *The Lover's Melancholy*, *The Soddered Citizen*, and *The Swisser*; signed the Dedication of the Beaumont and Fletcher Folio (1647); lived in the parish of St Gregory by St Paul's, three children (two 1609–10; remarried 1615); d. July 1649.

George Birch

Boy player under Heminges, hired man 1618–25; probably played Mistress Would-Be in *Volpone* and Doll Common in *The Alchemist* after 1616; played Morier in *Barnavelt*; in cast-lists for Beaumont and Fletcher's *The Island*

---

[7] The legal documents relating to Shanks's action in 1635 (Appendix 3) assert that Benfield was not a housekeeper. In July of that year he joined Swanston and Pollard in a petition to take up a share in the Globe, which secured them a division of Shanks's share in the Blackfriars among them.

Princess, The Laws of Candy, The False One, The Double Marriage (1618–21), *The Prophetess, The Lover's Progress,* and *The Pilgrim* (1621–4), *A Wife for a Month* and *The Spanish Viceroy* (1624); received black cloth for King James's funeral procession; lived in the parish of St Saviours Southwark; married Richard Cowley's daughter Jan. 1619; one child (1623); d. 1625?

Theophilus Bird

Sharer in King's Men c. 1640–2; Queen Henrietta's to 1637; b. 1608; Christopher Beeston's son-in-law; named in ticket of privilege for King's 19 Jan. 1641; one of the six men named as Grooms of the royal Chamber, 22 Jan. 1641, with Michael Bowyer, William Robbins, William Allen, Hugh Clark, and Stephen Hammerton; joined new King's at Restoration; d. 1663.

Richard Bowers

Hired man 1636–42; in list of privileged players 12 Jan. 1636; d. 1646.

Michael Bowyer

Sharer 1637–42; player in Queen Henrietta's and friend of Richard Perkins; as player made a Groom of the Chamber in Lord Chamberlain's list of six King's Men's employees 22 Jan. 1641; in 1655 Theophilus Bird claimed that Bowyer along with Pollard and others took the King's Men's apparel, hangings, and playbooks to sell when the playhouses were closed in 1642; lived in the parish of St Botolph's Aldgate, two sons (1621–2); d. 1645.

George Bryan

Sharer May 1594–7; in Denmark with Kemp and Pope 1586–7; Strange's 1590–4; payee for Chamberlain's at court 21 Dec. 1596; not in *Every Man in his Humour* cast-list of 1598; in cast-list for Shakespeare First Folio; lived in the parish of St Andrew in the Wardrobe; m. 1592, one son (1600); recorded as a Groom of the Chamber 1603, 1613; d. 1612.

Alexander Bullard

Hired man c. 1624; his name is added in the margin to a list of the company's 'Musicians and other necessary attendantes', in Herbert's list of King's Men exempted from arrest, 27 Dec. 1624.

Cuthbert Burbage

Company landlord and manager, May 1594–1636; servant to Sir Walter Cope who was usher to Lord Burghley, 1591; b. 1566; he inherited the Theatre's lease from his father James in February 1597, then with his brother took a half-share of the Globe; in 1608 he and his brother took shares in the Blackfriars, and issued others to the housekeepers who already had shares in the Globe; at his death he owned nearly a quarter of the Globe and one-eighth of the Blackfriars; as a family associate and part-owner of the playhouses he worked for the company, though never as a sharer; his 1635 testimony, signed by himself and Richard's widow and son, is a remarkable history of the playhouse enterprises run by the Burbages (see Appendix 3); Nicholas Tooley, former boy under Richard Burbage, lodged and died in 1623 at Cuthbert's house in the parish of St Leonard's Shoreditch; two children; d. Sept. 1636.

Richard Burbage
Sharer May 1594–March 1619; b. 1569,[8] younger brother of Cuthbert, son of James Burbage who built the Theatre and the Blackfriars playhouses; after his death Cuthbert claimed that Richard had been an actor for thirty-five years, which would mean he started in 1584; first noted in a lawsuit over the Theatre, Nov. 1590, where in a quarrel with the claimants he was said to have used a broomstick against Nicholas Bishop, and 'scornfully & disdainfullye playing with [Bishop's] nose, sayd, that yf he delt in the matter, he wold beate him also, and did chalendge the field of him at that time'; in Strange's 1591, named as a player in *The Dead Man's Fortune* and as Gorboduc and Terens in the plot of *2 Seven Deadly Sins*; probably then Pembroke's and Sussex's 1591–4, with Shakespeare, Sly, and others after Alleyn quarrelled with James Burbage and took the Strange's group from the Theatre to the Rose in May 1591; the most celebrated actor of his time,[9] he very likely played all of Shakespeare's leading parts, including almost certainly Richard III, Hamlet, Othello, and Lear; known to have played Malevole in *The Malcontent*, Volpone, Subtle in *The Alchemist*, and Ferdinand in *The Duchess of Malfi*; famous for his realism – John Chamberlain (*Letters*, II.77), wrote in 1617 that the wife of Sir Edward Coke had 'declaimed bitterly' against her husband, 'and so caried herself that divers said Burbage could not have acted better'; his father bequeathed him the Blackfriars in 1597, while Cuthbert inherited the Theatre; he put up half the cost of the Globe with Cuthbert in 1599 (most likely with the value of the Theatre's timbers);

---

[8] His date of birth is identified by Bernard Capp, 'The Burbages at Law (Again)', *Notes and Queries* 245 (2000), 433–5.

[9] His praises are sung by many writers; for his style, see Gurr, 'Who Strutted and Bellowed?' At his death, Middleton, omitting as others did any mention of Queen Anne's death ten days before, wrote 'Astronomers and star-gazers this year / Write of but four eclipses; five appear, / Death interposing Burbage; and their staying / Hath made a visible eclipse of playing.' (*Works*, ed. Bullen, VII.413). See also Appendix 2.25.

23. Richard Burbage, from the portrait in the Dulwich Gallery (DPG 395).

in 1608 he allotted shares in the Blackfriars to Cuthbert and the other Globe housekeepers; lived in the parish of St Leonard's Shoreditch; had eight children between 1607 and 1619, of whom only William survived; his widow married Richard Robinson of the company; in May 1610 the city commissioned him to deliver a speech to Prince Henry at a water pageant on the Thames; in March 1613 he painted an *impresa* for the Earl of Rutland, to Shakespeare's design; William Cartwright's notes on his collections of paintings now in the Dulwich Gallery ascribes one of a woman to him, though the famous portrait of him is unlikely to have been a self-portrait; a legatee in Shakespeare's will in 1616; evidently a generous man, on the evidence of his sharing the Blackfriars in 1608, and that when he died his assets were markedly smaller than Shakespeare's: John Chamberlain wrote to Dudley Carleton saying 'Burbage, the great actor, dead, worth £300 in land';[10] d. 13 March 1619.

---

[10] *The Letters of John Chamberlain*, ii.222–3.

Nicholas Burt
Possibly a King's boy player under John Shanks up to 1635; in Beeston's Boys 1638–42; in 1648 was playing Latorch in *Rollo* at the Cockpit with Lowin, Taylor, and Pollard when it was raided.

William Carver
Hired man c. 1624; his name is added in the margin to a list of the company's 'Musicians and other necessary attendantes', 27 Dec. 1624.

William Chambers
Hired man c. 1624; listed with 'Musicians and other necessary attendantes', 27 Dec. 1624; d. Nov. 1629.

Hugh Clark
Hired man and sharer 1640–2; played in Queen Henrietta's 1629–38, taking female lead in *The Wedding* and other plays; as King's sharer made a Groom of the Chamber in Lord Chamberlain's list of six King's Men's employees 22 Jan. 1641; signed dedication to Beaumont and Fletcher Folio (1647); d. Oct. 1653.

Robert Clarke
Hired man c. 1624; listed with 'Musicians and other necessary attendantes', 27 Dec. 1624; lived in the parish of St Anne's Blackfriars; one son.

Henry Clay
Hired man c. 1624; listed with 'Musicians and other necessary attendantes', 27 Dec. 1624; lived in the parish of St Giles Cripplegate; two children, 1620–6.

Walter Clun
Boy player, c. 1640; Wright (*Historia Histrionica*, p. 3) wrote 'Hart and Clun, were bred up Boys at the *Blackfriers*; and Acted Womens Parts.'

Edward Collins
Hired man 1636–7; in Lord Chamberlain's list of eleven King's Men's employees 12 Jan. 1637.

Jeffery Collins
Hired man c. 1624; listed with 'Musicians and other necessary attendantes', 27 Dec. 1624.

Henry Condell
Sharer and housekeeper, 1598(?)–1627; possibly the 'Harry' named in 2 *Seven Deadly Sins* in Strange's along with Burbage and others; in cast-lists for *Every Man in his Humour* and *Every Man out of his Humour*, 1598–9; portrayed as himself on stage in the Induction to *The Malcontent* 1604; and in cast-lists to 1619 (Richard Robinson had taken over his role as the Cardinal in *The Duchess of Malfi* by 1623); acted Mosca in *Volpone* and Surly in *The Alchemist*; in cast-lists of *The Mad Lover*, *The Queen of Corinth*, *The Knight of Malta*, *The Loyal Subject*, *The Humorous Lieutenant*, and in the Shakespeare First Folio; became a housekeeper of the Globe by 1608, when acquired a share in the Blackfriars; had one-sixth of the Globe and one-eighth of the Blackfriars, half of his Globe shares going to Taylor and Lowin, probably in c. 1625; edited the Shakespeare First Folio in 1622–3 with John Heminges; lived in the parish of St Mary's Aldermanbury, near Heminges; m. Elizabeth Smart in 1596, who brought him property in the Strand, Helmet Court; nine children (1599–1614); a legatee in Phillips's will in 1605, Cook's in 1614, Shakespeare's in 1616, Tooley's, and Underwood's; in 1619 he was described as 'of great lyveinge, wealth, and power'; made his will at his country house at Fulham, five miles from the city; d. Dec. 1627.

Alexander Cook
Boy player under Heminges, hired man, later a sharer; in the cast-lists for *Sejanus*, *Volpone*, *The Alchemist*, *Catiline*, *The Captain*, and the Shakespeare First Folio; lived in the parish of St Saviours Southwark; m. before 1603, four children 1605–14; a legatee in Phillips's will, 1605; own will made requests of Heminges and Condell; d. Feb. 1614.

Richard Cowley
Hired man; his name was pronounced as spelt, 'Coolye'; in Strange's in 2 *Seven Deadly Sins*; probably joined Chamberlain's in 1594; payee at court 1601; played Verges in *Much Ado*; lived in the parish of St Leonard's Shoreditch; four children, wife dying Sept. 1616; daughter Elizabeth married George Birch shortly before Cowley died; legatee in Phillips's will; own will witnessed by Cuthbert Burbage, John Heminges, John Shanks, and Thomas Ravenscroft; d. March 1619.

Ralph Crane
Scribe for the King's Men between 1618 and 1624. Manuscripts of *Sir John Van Olden Barnavelt* and *A Game at Chess* are in his hand; the printers of

the First Folio of Shakespeare's plays in 1622–3 used his transcripts of the first five plays in the Folio.

Samuel Crosse

Listed as a player in Shakespeare's First Folio (1623), but not otherwise known; a 'Samuel Crosse' was born Sept. 1568 at St Lawrence Pountney; Heywood praised Crosse in *An Apology for Actors*, saying he acted before Heywood's time.

Rowland Dowle

Hired man 1631–7; in Lord Chamberlain's list of eleven King's Men's employees 12 Jan. 1637; probably the 'Rowland' of *Believe As You List* (1631); in *Love's Pilgrimage* (1635), *The Coxcomb* (1636), *The Chances* (1638).

John Duke

Hired man, c. 1598; in *2 Seven Deadly Sins* with Strange's 1590; named in cast-list for *Every Man in his Humour* (1598), but not in *Every Man out of his Humour* (1599); left for Worcester's and Queen Anne's 1602; lived in the parish of St Leonard's Shoreditch; m. 1596, nine children (1596–1611); d. 1613.

William Eccleston

Hired man 1609–11, 1613–25; b. 1590; played Kastril in *The Alchemist* and in cast-list for *Catiline*; in Lady Elizabeth's 1611–13; in cast-lists for *Bonduca*, *The Mad Lover*, *The Loyal Subject*, *The Humorous Lieutenant*, *The Laws of Candy*, *The Island Princess*, *The Sea Voyage*, *The Spanish Curate*, and other plays to about 1624; Tooley's will (1623) released him from his debt to Tooley.

Richard Errington

Hired man; possibly in a travelling company of King's Men, 1622–9; on 22 Nov. 1627 he was assaulted by drunken intruders during a performance at Ludlow at 10 pm, while serving as a gatherer; the deposition of the case specifies him as 'of the Citty of London, pewterer, aged fiftie yeares or thereaboute'.[11]

---

[11] See REED *Shropshire*, pp. 111–12.

24. Nathan Field, from the portrait in the Dulwich Gallery (DPG 385).

Nathan Field

A probable sharer 1615–19, playwright, and housekeeper of the Globe; boy player with Blackfriars boy company 1600–8, King's Revels 1609–11, and Lady Elizabeth's 1611–15; co-authored *The Fatal Dowry* and other plays with Massinger for the King's, and wrote a defence of the stage; in cast-list for *The Mad Lover*, *The Queen of Corinth*, *The Knight of Malta*, *The Loyal Subject*, and the Shakespeare First Folio; son of John Field the Blackfriars preacher, who attacked playgoing; his brother became Bishop of Llandaff; wrote a letter of protest in 1616 to a preacher at St Mary Overies in Southwark objecting to his using the pulpit to complain about playing – 'Though, like other trades, that of actors hath many corruptions, it is not condemned in Scripture, and, being patronized by the King, it is disloyal to preach against it';[12] left the King's Men in 1619 after a scandal over fathering a child on the Countess of Argyll; d. 1620.[13]

Lawrence Fletcher

A player in Scotland, 1595–1601; named as a King's man in the royal patent of May 1603, but not listed as a company actor in the Shakespeare First Folio, so probably added in 1603 by the king's order; lived in the parish of St Saviours Southwark; d. Sept. 1608.

William Gascoyne

Hired man c. 1624; his name is added in the margin to a list of the company's 'Musicians and other necessary attendantes', 27 Dec. 1624 (Appendix 2.33); named in *Believe As You List* (1630); two children 1640–1.

Samuel Gilbourne

Phillips named him as his 'late apprentice' in 1605; in the Shakespeare First Folio list of players, 1623; his signature occurs by his name in a Folger copy of the Folio.

Alexander Gough

Hired man 1636–7; b. Aug. 1614; son of Robert Gough; in cast-lists for woman's parts in *The Roman Actor*, *The Picture*, *The Soddered Citizen*, *The Swisser*, *The Wild Goose Chase* (1632); wrote dedicatory epistles for three plays; named in Lord Chamberlain's list, 17 May 1636, of eighteen King's Men to attend the king on his summer progress.

Robert Gough

Hired man; probably named (as 'R.Go') in *2 Seven Deadly Sins* for Strange's (1590), playing a woman; later in Admiral's; played Memphonius in *The Second Maiden's Tragedy* (1611), and attendant in *Barnavelt*; listed as a player in the Shakespeare First Folio; brother-in-law to Phillips; legatee in Pope's will (1603), and witness to Phillips's (1605); lived in the parish of St Saviours Southwark; m. 1603, four children, one of whom, Alexander, became a boy player; became messenger to the Chamber 1621; d. 1625.

---

[12] *Calendar of State Papers, Domestic, 1611–1618*, p. 419.
[13] A reasonably thorough account of what is known of Field's career is given by Roberta Florence Brinkley, *Nathan Field, the Actor–Playwright*, Yale University Press, New Haven, 1928.

Curtis Greville
Hired man in King's 1626–33; joined King's Revels company by 1634; in cast-lists for *The Swisser, The Two Noble Kinsmen* (1625), *The Roman Actor, The Lover's Melancholy, The Soddered Citizen*, where he played Mountain, a goldsmith, and *Believe As You List*; m. 1616, one child (1622).

Stephen Hammerton
Boy player and hired man 1632–42; in Nov. 1632 Beeston petitioned the Lord Chamberlain to recover 'a boy named Stephen Hamerton' from the Blackfriars; played Oriana, heroine in *The Wild Goose Chase* (1632); played in *The Doubtful Heir, The Goblins, The Parson's Wedding*; Wright (*Historia Histrionica*) said he played Amintor, the young lover in *The Maid's Tragedy*; as player made a Groom of the Chamber in Lord Chamberlain's list of six King's Men's employees 22 Jan. 1641; signed dedication to the Beaumont and Fletcher Folio (1647).

Charles Hart
Boy player, c. 1640; Wright (*Historia Histrionica*, p. 3) said that he was apprenticed to Robinson, played the Duchess in *The Cardinal*, and that 'Hart and Clun, were bred up Boys at the *Blackfriers*; and Acted Womens Parts'; after the Restoration, in *Euterpe Restored* (1672), Richard Flecknoe wrote 'Beauty to the eye, and musick to the ear, / Such even the nicest criticks must allow / Burbage was once and such Charles Hart is now.'

William Hart
Hired man 1636–7; in King's Revels 1634–5; named in Lord Chamberlain's list, 17 May 1636, of eighteen King's Men to attend the king on his summer progress; in Lord Chamberlain's list of eleven King's Men's employees 12 Jan. 1637; three children; d. 1650.

Richard Hawley
Hired man 1636–40; travelling player 1630; named in Lord Chamberlain's list dated 17 May 1636 of eighteen King's Men to attend the king on his summer progress; in Lord Chamberlain's list of eleven King's Men's employees 12 Jan. 1637; m. 1630, six children, 1632–8; d. 1640.

John Heminges

Sharer May 1594–1630; b. Droitwich, 25 Nov. 1566;[14] Queen's 1588–94; made a freeman of the London Grocers Company in 1587; most frequently named as company payee at court 1596–1630; named as acting in plays up to *Catiline* (1611); played Corbaccio in *Volpone*; in 1599 he got his neighbours to witness a deed changing the half-interest of himself, Kemp, Phillips, Pope, and Shakespeare in the ground-lease of the Globe into a tenancy in common, which allowed each of them subsequently to dispose of their share; a housekeeper of the Globe (one-sixth, up to one-quarter by 1630) and Blackfriars (one-sixth, up to one-quarter by 1630); was tapster at the Globe's tavern, and built a house in the Globe's grounds;[15] one of London's ten measurers of sea-coals;[16] represented all London playing companies to the Master of the Revels in 1618; edited the Shakespeare First Folio with Condell in 1622–3; apprenticed several boys to the Grocers who played for the King's, including Alexander Cook, George Birch, John Wilson, Richard Sharpe, Thomas Holcomb, Robert Pallant, and William Trigg; lived in the parish of St Mary's Aldermanbury, near Condell, where he was a churchwarden; m. William Knell's widow, Rebecca, March 1588; fifteen children 1590–1611; daughter Thomasine (b. 1595) m. William Ostler, and after his death in 1614 brought a court action against her father over his Globe and Blackfriars shares; legatee of Phillips, Shakespeare, Underwood, Condell; his coat of arms was confirmed in 1629, and states that his father was of Droitwich, Worcestershire; his will calls him 'citizen and grocer' of London; d. Oct.1630.

Thomas Hobbs

Hired man 1626–37; in York's 1610; Prince Charles's 1614–25; Calistus (along with Richard Baxter) in *Believe As You List*; named in list for an allowance of cloaks, 6 May 1629; named in Lord Chamberlain's list, 17 May 1636, of eighteen to attend the king on his summer progress; lived in Shoreditch; m. 1615, two children.

Thomas Holcomb

Boy player apprenticed to Heminges, hired man 1618–25; named by Shanks in his 1635 petition as one of the boys he had acquired for the company; Provost's wife in *Barnavelt*; in cast-lists for *The Queen of Corinth*, *The*

[14] J. M. Nosworthy, 'A Note on John Heminge', *The Library* 3 (1948), 287–8.
[15] See Gabriel Egan, 'John Heminges's Tap-House at the Globe', *Theatre Notebook* 55 (2001), 72–7.
[16] See Mark Eccles, 'Elizabethan Actors II: E–J', *Notes and Queries* 236 (1991), 458.

Knight of Malta, The Custom of the Country, Women Pleased, The Little French Lawyer, The Prophetess; one son; d. 1625.

John Holland
Hired man in Pembroke's 1593, Chamberlain's 1594.

John Honyman
Boy player, named by Shanks in his 1635 petition as one of the boys he had acquired for the company; b. 1613; played Domitilla in *The Roman Actor*, Sophia in *The Picture*, Clarinda in *The Deserving Favourite*, Sly in *The Soddered Citizen*, and First Merchant in *Believe As You List*; in cast-lists of *The Lover's Melancholy* and *The Wild Goose Chase* (1632); made Groom of the Chamber 15 April 1633; Benfield and William Burbage witnessed his will; d. April 1636.

Edward Horton
Boy player and singer 1629–30; played Mariana in *The Deserving Favourite*; named as a boy in a stage direction in *The Mad Lover*.

Humfrey Jeffes
Possibly a hired man 1594–7; probably the 'humfrey' in *3 Henry VI* with Pembroke's, 1591–3; joined Pembroke's at Swan 1597, then Admiral's; b. 1576; d. 1618.

Will Kemp
(See figure 16, p. 70) Sharer 1594–9;[17] with Leicester's 1585–6 in the Low Countries and June 1586 in Denmark with Bryan and Pope as comedian and musician; later with Strange's and Alleyn, 1591–4; his 'merrimentes' were linked with Alleyn's name on the title page of *A Knack to Know a Knave* (1594); payee at court for Chamberlain's with Burbage and Shakespeare, 1595; left the Chamberlain's in 1599, after paying £100 along with Shakespeare and three other sharers to buy a share in the Globe, perhaps because Armin had joined the company, or more possibly to win a bet that he could dance all the way from London to Norwich, a nine-day marathon as a solo entertainer which he enacted in February 1600 during Lent, and described in *Kemps nine daies wonder* (1600), followed by another dance over the Alps; in the pamphlet about his dance to Norwich he wrote that

---

[17] Chapter 3 of David Wiles, *Shakespeare's Clown. Actor and Text in the Elizabethan Playhouse*, pp. 24–42, is entitled 'Kemp: a Biography.' He regards Kemp as a Bottom-like character (p. 37).

'I have daunst my selfe out of the world'; joined Worcester's on his return in 1601, when Henslowe lent him five shillings for some buckram 'gyente hosse' for *Oldcastle*, probably to play Sir John of Wrotham, a parodic version of Falstaff;[18] played Peter in *Romeo and Juliet*, Dogberry in *Much Ado*, and Cob in *Every Man in his Humour*; probably played Falstaff; linked for fame with Burbage by Cambridge students in *2 Return from Parnassus*; a mimic and dancer, he had a sturdy but agile physique and a squint, and may have used a rustic accent for some of his clown roles;[19] famous for his jigs, of which five are recorded in the Stationers' Register, although only *Singing Simpkin* survives, and probably *Rowland*, of which four texts survive, printed 1599–1603;[20] lived in the parish of St Saviour's Southwark; d. Nov.1603.

Anthony Knight

Hired man c. 1624; listed with 'Musicians and other necessary attendantes', 27 Dec. 1624, in same list as Edward Knight.

Edward Knight

Hired man, and company book-keeper, c. 1624; listed with 'Musicians and other necessary attendantes', 27 Dec. 1624; his hand is identifiable in the manuscript of *Believe As You List*;[21] paid the Master of the Revels a £2 fee to license Jonson's *Magnetic Lady* on 12 Oct. 1632; on 21 Oct. 1633 Herbert wrote him over his corrections to Fletcher's *The Tamer Tamed*: 'Mr Knight, In many things you have saved mee labour; yet wher your judgment or penn fayld you, I have made boulde to use mine. Purge their parts, as I have the booke. And I hope every hearer and player will thinke that I have done God good servise, and the quality no wronge; who hath no greater enemies than oaths, prophaness, and publique ribaldry, which for the future I doe absolutely forbid to bee presented unto mee in any playbooke, as you will answer for it at your perill.'[22]

---

[18] The likelihood that he played Falstaff is examined by Wiles, *Shakespeare's Clown*, chapter 9. Wiles suggests that he played Wrotham, pp. 134–5.

[19] Wiles, *Shakespeare's Clown*, cites Samuel Rowlands in 1599 condemning Pope and Singer for speaking 'so boorish'. He analyses Kemp as a 'country fellow' clown, against Armin as fool, concluding like others that parts were added to older plays for him, such as Launce in *Two Gentlemen* and Peter in *Romeo and Juliet*. As original parts Wiles claims he took Bottom, Dogberry, Cob in *Every Man Out*, and, above all, Falstaff.

[20] See Baskervill, *The Elizabethan Jig*, pp. 112, 219–20, and Wiles, *Shakespeare's Clown*, pp. 43–60.

[21] *The Plays and Poems of Philip Massinger*, ed. Philip Edwards and Colin Gibson, 5 vols., Clarendon Press, Oxford, 1976, III.299.

[22] Bawcutt, *Control and Censorship*, p. 183.

John Lowin

Hired man and sharer, 1603–42, and housekeeper of the Globe and Black-friars; from 1626 onwards was usual co-signatory with Joseph Taylor for all court payments; in Worcester's 1602–3; b. 1576 at St Giles Cripplegate, son of a carpenter, the date affirmed by the inscription on his portrait in Ashmolean Museum; apprenticed to a goldsmith in 1593 (as freeman of the Goldsmiths appeared in show designed with Munday at Lord Mayor's pageant 1611, when Sir James Pemberton of the Goldsmiths was Mayor); left the trade for Worcester's, for whom took payments from Henslowe, and toured with them during plague closure in 1603; then joined the King's; one of the eight named as playing in *Sejanus*, and in *The Malcontent* Induction played himself; did not start as a sharer since not in the King's Procession list of March 1604, probably buying Augustine Phillips's share when he died in 1605;[23] wrote a solemn little pamphlet about dancing in 1606, published in 1607, called *Conclusions upon Dances*, all its examples of dances good and bad taken from the Bible; played Bosola in *Duchess of Malfi*, Domitianus Caesar in *The Roman Actor*, Eubolus 'an old Counsaylor' in *The Picture*, Iacomo in *The Deserving Favourite*, 'Undermyne – A wealthy Cittizen' in *The Soddered Citizen*, Flaminius in *Believe As You List*, the title role in *The Swisser*, where he is described as having a 'great Beard and Bulke', Belleur in revival of *The Wild Goose Chase* (1632); delivered prologue to *The Platonic Lovers* (1635), claiming thirty years of service; said to have played Henry in *Henry VIII*; in the cast-lists for *Sejanus, The Mad Lover, The Queen of Corinth, The Knight of Malta, The Loyal Subject, The Humorous Lieutenant, The Laws of Candy, The Custom of the Country, Women Pleased, The Island Princess, The Little French Lawyer, The False One, The Pilgrim, The Double Marriage, The Prophetess, The Sea Voyage, The Spanish Curate, The Maid in the Mill, The Lover's Progress, The Spanish Viceroy, The Lover's Melancholy*; according to Wright, *Historia Histrionica*, p. 4, he acted '*Falstaffe, Morose, Vulpone*, and *Mammon* in the *Alchymist*; *Melancius* in the *Maid's* Tragedy' (see figure 4, p. 28); named with Taylor and Swanston as payee of £220 on 27 April 1634 for 20 Christmas plays at court, £240 on 12 March 1637 for 22 plays, £150 on 15 March 1638 for 14 plays, and £300 for 24 plays on 12 March 1639; named with Taylor and Swanston as payee by Lord Chamberlain of £230 for 21 plays, and £160 for Christmas plays in March 1641; owned one-eighth of Globe and Blackfriars as housekeeper from 1627–42; lived in the parish of St Saviours Southwark, near Paris Garden; m. 1607 at

---

[23] Joseph Quincey Adams, 'The Housekeepers of the Globe', *Modern Philology* 17 (1919), 1, reckoned that Lowin and Taylor only became sharers in 1627, after Condell's death, but Adams confuses shares in the company with shares in the playhouses, which was what Lowin acquired in 1627.

25. John Lowin, from a portrait in the Ashmolean Museum. His age is marked as sixty-three, which indicates that the portrait was painted in 1639–40.

St Botolph's Bishopsgate to Joan Hall, and in February 1620 to Katheren Woodden (they dined with Edward Alleyn on 13 August 1620); at least one son (1639); legatee in Underwood's will (1624); oversaw Elizabeth Condell's will in 1635; made King's Porter in 1639 when Taylor became Yeoman of the Revels; first signatory to the Beaumont and Fletcher Folio (1647); after closure ran the Three Pigeons tavern at Brentford; he was acting Aubrey in *Rollo* at the Cockpit when it was raided in 1648; d. 1653.

William Mago
Hired man 1624–31; in Prince Charles's c. 1621; b. 1579; listed with 'Musicians and other necessary attendantes', 27 Dec. 1624; played walk-on parts

in *Believe As You List*; of Irish descent; his father John built the stage and galleries of the Boar's Head in 1599; William was bound over in 1600 along with Pope in a dispute with the lessee Thomas Woodliffe; d. 1632.

William Ostler

Sharer 1609–14; boy player in Blackfriars boy company from 1600, playing in *Poetaster* (1601); housekeeper of Blackfriars 1611 and Globe 1612; played in *The Alchemist, Catiline, The Captain*, Antonio in *The Duchess of Malfi, Valentinian, Bonduca*; John Davies of Hereford wrote a poem in his praise (*The Scourge of Folly*, [1611], Epigram 205): 'OSTLER thou tookst a knock thou wouldst have giv'n, / Neere sent thee to thy latest home; but O! / Where was thine action when thy crown was riv'n / Sole king of actors; then wast idle? No: / Thou hadst it for thou wouldst bee doing; thus / Good actors' deeds are oft most dangerous: / But if thou plaist thy dying part as well / As thy stage-parts thou hast no part in hell'; m. Thomasine Heminges in 1611, one son; d. Dec. 1614.

Robert Pallant

Boy player apprenticed to Heminges 1620, hired man in King's 1620–5; b. 1605, christened at St Saviours Southwark; probably son of another Robert Pallant, who played in *2 Seven Deadly Sins*, in Worcester's and Queen Anne's; appears to have played Cariola in *The Duchess of Malfi*, c. 1619;[24] listed with 'Musicians and other necessary attendantes', 27 Dec. 1624.

William Patrick

Hired man 1624–37; played a Senator in *The Roman Actor* and minor parts in *Believe As You List*; listed with 'Musicians and other necessary attendantes', 27 Dec. 1624; named in Lord Chamberlain's list, 17 May 1636, of eighteen King's Men to attend the king on his summer progress; in Lord Chamberlain's list of eleven King's Men's employees 12 Jan. 1637; lived on Bankside; one daughter (1622) christened at St Saviours Southwark.

William Penn

Hired man 1626–37; boy player in Whitefriars boy company, playing in *Epicene* (1609); Prince Charles's 1616–25; played Julio Baptista in *The Picture*, and small parts in *Believe As You List, The Swisser*, and *The Wild Goose Chase* (1632); in cast-list for *The Lover's Melancholy*; cloak allowance

---

[24] For a comment on the odd ascription of multiple parts to Pallant in the *Duchess of Malfi* quarto of 1624, see Bentley, *Jacobean and Caroline Stage*, 11.519.

26. Richard Perkins, a painting by the School of Gerard Soest, from the portrait in the Dulwich Gallery (DPG 423).

as King's man 1629; named in Lord Chamberlain's list, 17 May 1636, of eighteen King's Men to attend the king on his summer progress; lived in the parish of St Leonard's Shoreditch; m. 1617, two children at St Leonard's (1617–19), two at St Giles Cripplegate (1636).

Richard Perkins
Sharer (?) 1623–6; in Worcester's/Queen Anne's 1602–19, Red Bull company 1619–23; in Queen Henrietta's 1626 on; given King's livery of scarlet in 1623, and black for James's funeral 1625; lived in Clerkenwell; wife died March 1621, remarried Nov. 1621; d. 1650.

Henry Pettingham

Hired man 1636–7; in Lord Chamberlain's list of eleven King's Men's employees 12 Jan. 1637.

Augustine Phillips

Sharer 1594–1605; in *2 Seven Deadly Sins* with Strange's 1590–4; 'Phillips his gygg of the slyppers' entered in Stationers' Register in 1595; housekeeper of the Globe from 1599; in cast-lists for *Every Man in his Humour*, *Every Man out of his Humour*, *Sejanus*, and Shakespeare First Folio; spoke for the company about the performance of *Richard II* on 7 Feb. 1601 at the trial of Essex; lived in the parish of St Saviours Southwark; had a coat of arms; acquired a house in Mortlake 1604; five children, one of whom married Robert Gough; legatees Heminges, Burbage, Sly, Shakespeare, Condell, Beeston, Lawrence Fletcher, Armin, Cowley, Cook, and Tooley, and bequeathed costumes and musical instruments to his boys Gilbourne and Sands; d. May 1605.

Thomas Pollard

Hired man, sharer 1613–42; probably came to the company with Shanks; cited in John Shanks's petition (Appendix 3) as formerly his boy, probably when Shanks was at the Fortune;[25] a comedian, he played small parts in *The Duchess of Malfi*, *Barnavelt*, *The Roman Actor* (Aelius and Stephanus), and *The Picture*; Pinac in *The Wild Goose Chase*, Brainsick and other parts in *The Soddered Citizen*, the title role in *The Humorous Lieutenant*, Berecinthius in *Believe As You List*, and Timentes in *The Swisser*; appears in the cast-lists for *The Queen of Corinth*, *The Laws of Candy*, *The Island Princess*, *The Spanish Curate*, *The Maid in the Mill*, *The Lover's Progress*, *The Spanish Viceroy*, *The Lover's Melancholy*, *The Cardinal*; possibly m. 1629, 1635; playing the Cook in *Rollo* at the Cockpit in 1648 when it was raided; Wright (*Historia Histrionica*, p. 10) reported that he 'Lived Single, and had a Competent Estate; Retired to some Relations he had in the Country, and there ended his Life'; in his Chancery suit of 1655, Bird claimed that he died worth £500.

Thomas Pope

Sharer 1594–1603; played in Denmark 1585–6; in Strange's 1590–4; payee at court with Heminges 1597–9; housekeeper of the Globe from 1599; in cast-lists for *Every Man in his Humour*, *Every Man out of his Humour*, and

---

[25] That is Bentley's conjecture, *Jacobean and Caroline Stage*, II.532.

the Shakespeare First Folio; called 'Pope the clown' by Samuel Rowlands (1601); involved with Curtain playhouse, and with the Boar's Head, 1600; a gentleman, lived in the parish of St Saviours Southwark; Robert Gough was a legatee; John Holland named in his will as his tenant; d. 1603.

John Rhodes

Hired man and either wardrobe keeper or musician c. 1624; member of the Drapers Guild from 1625; listed with 'Musicians and other necessary attendantes', 27 Dec. 1624; the musician d. Feb. 1636.

John Rice

Boy player and hired man 1607–10, 1614–25; boy under Heminges, 'a very proper Child, well spoken', in 1607, when he gave a speech before the king at the Merchant Taylors Hall; in a City pageant as a nymph with Burbage to honour the Prince of Wales in 1610; joined Lady Elizabeth's 1610; rejoined King's Men c. 1614, and in livery list 7 April 1621; played Marquess of Pescara in *The Duchess of Malfi*; in *Barnavelt*, and *The Spanish Viceroy*; listed in Shakespeare First Folio; lived in the parish of St Saviours Southwark; joined St Saviours as clerk c. 1625; oversaw Heminges's will in 1630.

George Rickner

Hired man 1623–5; named in 1624 revision of *The Honest Man's Fortune*; name deleted from Herbert's list of exemptions from military service 17 Dec. 1624; associated in 1636 with George Bosgrove at the Fortune.

William Robbins

Hired man 1640–2; in Queen Anne's/Red Bull company 1617–25; in Queen Henrietta's 1625–37; as player made a Groom of the Chamber in Lord Chamberlain's list of six King's Men's employees 22 Jan. 1641; known as 'Robinson the Fool'; d. 1645; Wright, *Historia Histrionica*, pp. 7–8, reported that he 'was Killed at the Taking of a Place (I think *Basing House*) by *Harrison*, he that was after Hang'd at *Charing-cross*, who refused him Quarter, and Shot him in the Head when he had laid down his Arms; abusing Scripture at the same time, in saying *Cursed is he that doth the Work of the Lord negligently*'.

Richard Robinson

Boy player, later sharer, 1611–42; played in *Catiline* (1611), a lady in *Second Maiden's Tragedy*, *Bonduca*, *The Devil is an Ass* where he may have played Merecraft, the young hero, who wishes there was a '*Dick Robinson*' available when he has to disguise himself as a Spanish lady; a captain and an ambassador in *Barnavelt*, took over Condell's role of Cardinal in *The Duchess of Malfi*; Aesopus in *The Roman Actor*, Count Orsino and the hermit in *The Deserving Favourite*, Lentulus in *Believe As You List*, and Lacastre in *The Wild Goose Chase* (1632); in cast-lists for *The Double Marriage, A Wife for a Month, The Spanish Viceroy*, and the Shakespeare First Folio; witnessed Richard Burbage's will in 1619; lived in Shoreditch; m. Winifred Burbage, widow of Richard; signed Dedication to Beaumont and Fletcher Folio (1647); d. March 1648.

Will Rowley
Played in King's 1623–6, after ten years of service in Prince Charles's; lived in Clerkenwell; played a fat clown, including probably the Fat Bishop in *A Game at Chess* (the fat clown roles of Bustopha in *The Maid in the Mill*, Tony in *A Wife for a Month*, the Cook in *Rollo*, Cacafogo in *Rule a Wife and Have a Wife*, and the Clown in *The Fair Maid of the Inn* were created during his time in the company); in cast-lists for *The Maid in the Mill* and *The Spanish Viceroy*; d. Feb. 1626.

James Sands
Boy player, apprenticed to Augustine Phillips; legatee in his will (1605) and Sly's (1608); lived in Southwark.

William Saunders
Musician c. 1624; listed with 'Musicians, and other necessary attendantes', 27 Dec. 1624; city wait 1634.

Edward Shackerly
Hired man c. 1624; exempted by Herbert from military service in list of 'Musicians and other necessary attendantes' in a separate warrant, 27 Dec. 1624.

Will Shakespeare
Sharer 1594–1614; b. 1564; housekeeper of Globe from 1599 and Blackfriars from 1608; played in *Every Man in his Humour, Every Man out of his Humour*; seems to have specialized in what John Davies of Hereford called kingly parts ('Some say good Will (which I, in sport, do sing) / Had'st thou not plaid some Kingly parts in sport, / Thou hadst bin a companion for a King; / And, beene a King among the meaner sort.'); retired from playing

c. 1609; probably sold his housekeeper shares when asked to pay his portion of the rebuilding costs for the Globe after the July 1613 fire; d. 1616.

John Shanks

Sharer 1613–36; a member of the Weavers Guild; Pembroke's either 1591–3 or 1597–1600, Queen's either 1593–4 or 1600–3 (he claimed in his petition about housekeeper shares in the Blackfriars and Globe to Phillip, 4th Earl of Pembroke, in 1635 that long before he had served the earl's father, the second earl, and Queen Elizabeth; such service could have made him a Queen's man with Heminges and a Pembroke's man with Richard Burbage, Sly, and others: see Appendix 3);[26] sharer in Prince's/Palsgrave's 1610–13; mostly played a clown famous for his jigs ('Bass for a ballad, John Shanke for a Jigg', according to William Heminges's *Elegy on Randolph's Finger*, c. 1632, although he was mocked in 1613 for having given them up in order to join the King's Men: 'Since *Shanke* did leave to sing his rimes, / he is counted but a gull');[27] he returned to composing and presumably playing jigs in the 1630s; as a comedian played Sir Roger in *The Scornful Lady* according to Wright (*Historia Histrionica*, p. 4); in cast-lists for *The Prophetess* (1622), the Shakespeare First Folio (1623), *The Spanish Viceroy* (1624), *The Lover's Melancholy* (1628), Hilario in *The Picture* (1628), *The Wild Goose Chase* (1632); as Hodge, a country fellow, in *The Soddered Citizen*, played by the King's in 1630, he punned on his own name, speaking the part in a west-of-England (mummerset) accent; as freeman of the Weavers apprenticed several boy players, including Pollard and Honyman; involved in dispute over housekeeper shares, 1635 (see Appendix 3); m. Feb. 1610; a son was buried in 1610 and a daughter christened in Feb. 1612 in St Giles Cripplegate, and six others are registered (1615–29); a citizen of London and a weaver, his will cites his property as including leases of one-quarter of the Blackfriars playhouse and three-eighths of the Globe; d. Jan. 1636.

Richard Sharpe

Boy player apprenticed to Heminges 1616, sharer 1624–32, playing the Duchess in *The Duchess of Malfi*, and later male romantic leads, such as Parthenius in *The Roman Actor*, Ferdinand in *The Picture*, Lysander in *The Deserving Favourite*, and Sir Witworth and Prologue and Epilogue in *The Soddered Citizen*; in cast-lists for *The Mad Lover*, *The Knight of Malta*,

---

[26] Chambers, *Elizabethan Stage*, II.339, thinks he must have been in the Pembroke's that started at the Swan in 1597, and after that with the travelling Queen's Men.

[27] See Gurr, *Playgoing*, Appendix 2, no. 99.

The Loyal Subject, The Laws of Candy, The Humorous Lieutenant, The Custom of the Country, Women Pleased, The Island Princess, The Little French Lawyer, The False One, The Double Marriage, The Prophetess, The Lover's Progress, The Spanish Viceroy, and *The Lover's Melancholy;* exempted by Herbert from military service 27 Dec. 1624 in warrant added to main list; in livery lists 24 June 1625 and 6 May 1629; had a 'base-born' son in 1631 christened at St Giles Cripplegate; d. Jan. 1632.

John Sincler

Hired man 1594–c. 1606; in *2 Seven Deadly Sins* with Burbage and others in Strange's 1590, moving from Strange's in 1591 to Pembroke's before joining the new Chamberlain's in 1594; named in Pembroke's *3 Henry VI* and *The Taming of the Shrew;* named in the quarto of *2 Henry IV* as the beadle whom Doll calls 'you thin man in a censer'; evidently a distinctly small and skinny player, had several parts specially written for him in the post-1594 plays: Nym, the beadle, and Slender in *2 Henry IV, Henry V,* and *Merry Wives,* Aguecheek in *Twelfth Night,* possibly Thersites in *Troilus and Cressida,* and probably Robert Faulconbridge, the Bastard's brother, in *King John,* where at 1.1.140–3 he is described in similar terms; in Jonson's plays a markedly small player took the part of Shift in *Every Man out of his Humour;* probably Nano the dwarf in *Volpone,* who has a larger speaking part than the hermaphrodite and eunuch; he was in *The Malcontent,* and may also have been Asinius Bubo in Dekker's *Satiromastix,* and the 'very little man' in *The London Prodigal* in 1605.

Will Sly

Sharer 1594?–1608; named in *2 Seven Deadly Sins* plot with Richard Burbage and others of Strange's, c. 1591, probably then with Burbage in Pembroke's and possibly Sussex's; housekeeper at Globe 1605, and of Blackfriars 1608; on 11 Oct. 1594 Henslowe sold him 'A Jewell of gowld seat with A white Safer' for 8 shillings, which he paid for by instalments up to 17 January 1595; in his inventory of clothing drawn up on 13 March 1598 Henslowe listed 'Perowes sewt, which William Sley were', presumably a memory from the days when the plot of *2 Seven Deadly Sins* was drawn up, where his name appears along with Burbage and others who were later in the Chamberlain's (unless 'Perowes' is the Berowne of *Love's Labours Lost,* which may have been a Strange's play: the allusion is unknown); named in the Induction to the Globe production of *The Malcontent,* where he enters pretending to be a gentleman wanting to sit on the stage on a stool, and demands to see 'Harry Condall, Dick Burbage, and Will Sly'; Sincler then meets him dressed as a fellow-gallant, and three players, Burbage, Condell, and Lowin, join them to discuss the play and make other jokes before Sly introduces the performance; the same Induction has him playing with his hat and using Osric's lines from *Hamlet*; in Q1 *Hamlet* (1603) Osric is described as '*a Bragart Gentleman*', whereas in Q2 he is a '*Courtier*', and 'young *Ostricke*': probably this signals a change of actor for the part between Q1 and Q2; listed in Shakespeare First Folio; lived in Southwark; had a 'base-born' son in 1606; d. Aug. 1608; legatees included Cuthbert Burbage, James Sands. The portrait labelled 'William Sly' in the Dulwich Picture Gallery is not of him.

Antony Smith
Hired man 1626–31; in Prince Charles's 1616–25; minor parts included Philargus, 'a rich Miser', in *The Roman Actor* and others in *The Deserving Favourite*, *The Soddered Citizen*, and *The Swisser*; in cast-list for *The Lover's Melancholy*.

William Styles
Hired man 1636–7; his name is added to the Lord Chamberlain's list of eleven King's Men's employees 12 Jan. 1637; lived in the parish of St Ann's Blackfriars; m. 1634, five children (1635–43).

Eliart Swanston
Sharer 1624–42, housekeeper 1635–42; in Lady Elizabeth's 1622; a burly player, Shanks reckoned him the most 'violent' of the three petitioners in 1635 who urged their right to shares as housekeepers; often a signatory for payments to the company along with Taylor and Lowin; played Caesar's spy Aretine in *The Roman Actor*, Ricardo, one of '2 wild courtiers', in *The Picture*, Count Utrante in *The Deserving Favourite*, Chrysalus in *Believe As You List*, Melantius in revivals of *The Maid's Tragedy*, possibly Philaster,[28] Alcidonus in *The Swisser*, and Lugier in the 1632 revival of *The Wild Goose Chase*; Wright (*Historia Histrionica*) said he used to play Richard III and Othello; he appears in cast-lists for *The Spanish Viceroy* and *The Lover's Melancholy*; third to sign the Beaumont and Fletcher Folio (1647) after Taylor and Lowin; named as payee with Lowin and Taylor of £120 for plays

---

[28] David George, 'Early Cast Lists for Two Beaumont and Fletcher Plays', *Theatre Notebook* 28 (1974), 9–11, suggests that a manuscript note 'Ey' in a copy of the 1635 quarto of *Philaster* may indicate that he played the title role in the 1636 performance at court.

at court 22 Feb. 1632, of £270 for 23 plays and one rehearsal at court on 16 March 1633, £220 for 22 plays on 27 April 1634, £240 on 6 July 1637 (Swanston endorsing it for £200), £150 on 15 March 1638 ('John Lowen, Joseph Taylor & Eillart Swanston or any of them for themselves & the rest of the Company'), £240 signed for by Swanston alone on 5 June 1638, £300 on 12 March 1639 for 24 plays, £230 on 4 April 1640 for 21 plays, and £160 on 20 March 1641; lived in the parish of St Mary's Aldermanbury; m. 1619 at St Gregory by St Paul's, ten children (1620–39); when the playhouses were closed in 1642 he left playing, supporting the Parliamentary side in the Civil War yet adding his name to the 1647 Folio; d. 1651.

William Tawyer

Hired man (musician?) 1620(?)–5; the Folio *Midsummer Night's Dream* names him as leading on the mechanicals with a trumpet at 5.1.125; his name is added in the margin to a list of men exempted by Herbert from arrest for military service 27 Dec. 1624; servant of Heminges; d. 1625.

Joseph Taylor

Sharer and housekeeper in King's 1619–42; probably joined as replacement for Richard Burbage (performed in *Inner Temple Masque* with Prince Charles's in February 1619, but was in King's by May); in York's 1610, Lady Elizabeth's 1611–15, Prince Charles's 1615–19; b. 1586; replaced Burbage as Ferdinand in *The Duchess of Malfi*; according to Wright (*Historia Histrionica*, p. 4) he played Hamlet, Iago, Mosca in *Volpone*, Face in *The Alchemist*, and Truewit in *Epicene*; according to Edmund Gayton (*Pleasant Notes on Don Quixot*, 1654, p. 25) played Amintor in revivals of *The Maid's Tragedy* and Arbaces in *A King and No King*; played Paris in *The Roman Actor*, Mathias in *The Picture*, the Duke in *The Deserving Favourite*, Antiochus in *Believe As You List*, Arioldus in *The Swisser*, Mirabell in the *Wild Goose Chase* revival (1632); in cast-lists for *The Humorous Lieutenant*, *The Laws of Candy*, *The Custom of the Country*, *The Island Princess*, *Women Pleased*, *The False One*, *The Pilgrim*, *The Little French Lawyer*, *The Double Marriage*, *The Prophetess*, *The Sea Voyage*, *The Spanish Curate*, the Shakespeare First Folio, *The Maid in the Mill*, *The Lover's Progress*, *A Wife for a Month*, *The Spanish Viceroy*, *The Lover's Melancholy*; housekeeper of Globe and Blackfriars from 1630; regular payee for court performances with Lowin; made Yeoman of the Revels in 1639; signed the Dedication to the Beaumont and Fletcher Folio (1647); lived in the parish of St Saviours Southwark; m. 1610, seven children 1612–23; was playing the title role in *Rollo* at the Cockpit when it was raided in 1648; d. Nov. 1652.

John Thompson

Boy player and hired man 1619–34; named by Shanks in his counter-petition of 1635 as a former boy, now deceased, who he acquired for the company at a cost of £40; played the Cardinal's mistress in *The Duchess of Malfi*, Domitia in *The Roman Actor*, the Queen in *The Picture*, Cleonarda in *The Deserving Favourite*, Undermine's daughter Miniona in *The Soddered Citizen*, and Panopia in *The Swisser*; in cast-lists for *The Pilgrim*, *The Maid in the Mill*, *The Lover's Progress*, *The Lover's Melancholy*; lived in the parish of St Giles Cripplegate; one daughter (1632); d. Dec.1634.

Nicholas Tooley, or Wilkinson

Boy player and hired man 1600(?)–1623; as a boy belonged to Richard Burbage, whose will he witnessed in 1619, from before 1605; from 1610 played Ananias in *The Alchemist*, Corvino in *Volpone*, Forobosco and a madman in *The Duchess of Malfi*, and other adult parts in *The Queen of Corinth*, *The Loyal Subject*, *The Custom of the Country*, *The Laws of Candy*, *Women Pleased*, *The False One*, *The Pilgrim*, *The Little French Lawyer*, *The Double Marriage*, *The Prophetess*, *The Sea Voyage*, and *The Spanish Curate*; named in the Shakespeare First Folio; legatees Cuthbert Burbage, family of Richard Burbage, Condell, Joseph Taylor, John Underwood, William Eccleston; d. June 1623; buried from Cuthbert Burbage's house in Shoreditch.

William Trigg

Boy player apprenticed to Heminges, hired man 1625–37; Beeston's Boys 1637–42; named in Lord Chamberlain's list, 17 May 1636, of eighteen King's Men to attend the king on his summer progress; played Julia Titus in *The Roman Actor*, Corsica, 'Sophias woman', in *The Picture*, Modestina in *The Soddered Citizen*, Selina in *The Swisser*, Rosalura in the *Wild Goose Chase* revival in 1632; in cast-list for *The Lover's Melancholy*; m. 1641.

Thomas Tuckfield

Hired man c. 1624; listed with 'Musicians and other necessary attendantes', 27 Dec. 1624; in revival of *The Two Noble Kinsmen* (1624).

Nicholas Underhill
Boy player, musician apprenticed to Ambrose Beeland of the Drapers in 1620, and hired man c. 1619–32; listed with 'Musicians and other necessary attendantes', 27 Dec. 1624; very likely the 'Nick' noted in *Barnavelt* as Barnavelt's wife, and in minor parts in *Believe As You List*;[29] played Shackle in *The Soddered Citizen*; at Cockpit when played violin in Shirley's masque *The Triumph of Peace*, 1634.

John Underwood
King's sharer 1608–24; boy player at Blackfriars 1600–8, playing in *Cynthia's Revels* (1600) and *Poetaster* (1601); became housekeeper of Globe and Blackfriars, possibly buying from Thomas Pope; played Delio in *The Duchess of Malfi*; in cast-lists for *The Alchemist, The Queen of Corinth, The Knight of Malta, The Loyal Subject, The Custom of the Country, The Laws of Candy, The Humorous Lieutenant, Women Pleased, The Island Princess, The Little French Lawyer, The False One, The Pilgrim, The Double Marriage, The Sea Voyage, The Maid in the Mill, The Lover's Progress, A Wife for a Month*, and the Shakespeare First Folio; lived in the parish of St Bartholomew's; five children; legatees Heminges and Lowin; d. 1624.

George Vernon
Boy player apprenticed to Lowin, hired man 1617–30; listed with 'Musicians and other necessary attendantes' 27 Dec. 1624; in livery lists 5 May 1625 and 6 May 1629; minor roles in *The Roman Actor* and *The Lover's Melancholy*; lived in parish of St Saviours Southwark; three children (1626–30).

Thomas Vincent
Book-keeper c. 1624; John Taylor the water-poet wrote an anecdote about him and John Singer, specifying his function (1638) 'that was a Book-keeper or prompter at the Globe playhouse'.

Henry Wilson
Hired man c. 1624; listed with 'Musicians and other necessary attendantes', 27 Dec. 1624; arrested with Ambrose Beeland, another fiddler, on a complaint by Heminges, 14 Dec. 1628; named as a lute player in *Believe As You List*.

---

[29] See Bentley, *Jacobean and Caroline Stage*, II.516–17 and 609.

John Wilson

Musician, apprenticed to Heminges in 1611, freed of the Grocers in 1622; b. 1595; named in Folio *Much Ado* (1623) as Balthazar, singer of 'Sigh no more ladies'; wrote songs for King's from 1614; a city wait from 1622, lutenist in King's Music 1635; professor of music at Oxford 1656; possibly the 'Mr Wilson a cunning Musition' who organized a performance of *A Midsummer Night's Dream* at the Bishop of Lincoln's house on a Sunday, 27 Sept. 1631, which gave offence to puritans.

Documents about the company

The following passages, most of them referred to in the text, are presented here either transcribed or checked from the original documents, with their printed sources acknowledged in a parenthesis at the end. They are placed in roughly chronological order.

1. A recollection of 1594–1599 by Cuthbert Burbage in 1635
– The father of us Cutbert & Richard Burbage was the first builder of Playhowses & was himselfe in his younger yeeres a Player. The Theater hee built with many Hundred poundes taken up at interest. [For a fuller quotation and the context, see Appendix 3, Sharers' Papers.]

2. Title pages of 'Titus Andronicus', first quarto of 1594, and
second quarto of 1600
[1594] THE MOST LA-mentable Romaine Tragedie of Titus Andronicus: As it was Plaide by the Right Honourable the Earle of *Darbie*, Earle of *Pembrooke*, and Earle of *Sussex* their Servants. / [1600] As it hath sundry times beene playde by the Right Honourable the Earle of Pembrooke, the Earle of Darbie, the Earle of Sussex, and the Lorde Chamberlaine theyr Servants. (Quoted from the original titlepages)

3. A letter from Henry Carey, Lord Chamberlain, to the Lord Mayor,
8 October 1594
where my nowe companie of Players have byn accustomed for the better exercise of their qualitie, & for the service of her Majestie if need soe requier to plaie this winter time within the Citye at the Cross kayes in Gracious street, These are to requier & praye your Lordship the time beinge such as thankes be to god there is nowe no danger of the sicknes) to permitt & suffer them so to doe; The which I praie you the rather to doe for that they have undertaken to me that where heretofore they began not their Plaies till towardes fower a clock, they will now begin at two, & have don

betwene fower and five and will nott use anie Drumes or trumpettes att all
for the callinge of peopell together, and shalbe contributories to the poore
of the parishe where they plaie according to their habilities. (*Malone Society
Collections* 1.1, 1907, p. 74)

4. A letter from the Lord Mayor and Aldermen to the Privy Council, 13 September 1595

Wee begin to have experience again within these fiew daies since it pleased
her highnes to revoke her Comission graunted forthe to the Provost
Marshall, for fear of home they retired themselfes for the time into other
partes out of his precinct but ar now retorned to their old haunt & frequent
the Plaies (as their manner is) that ar daily shewed at the Theator & Bankside: Whearof will follow the same inconveniences whearof wee ar humble
suters to your good Lordships & the rest to direct your lettres to the Justices
of peac of Surrey & Middlesex for the present stay & finall suppressing of
the said Plaies aswell at the Theator & Bankside as in all other places about
the Cytie. (*Malone Society Collections* 1.1, 1907, pp. 77–8)

5. November 1596 Petition to the Privy Council by 31 Blackfriars residents

To the right honorable the Lords and others of her Majesties most honorable
Privy Council, – Humbly shewing and beseeching your honors, the inhabitants of the precinct of Blackfryers, London, that whereas one Burbage
hath lately bought certaine roomes in the same precinct neere adjoyning
unto the dwelling houses of the right honorable the Lord Chamberlaine
and the Lord of Hunsdon, which romes the said Burbage is now altering
and meaneth very shortly to convert and turne the same into a comon
playhouse, which will grow to be a very great annoyance and trouble, not
only to all the noblemen and gentlemen thereabout inhabiting, but allso a
generall inconvenience to all the inhabitants of the same precinct, both by
reason of the great resort and gathering togeather of all manner of vagrant
and lewde persons that, under cullor of resorting to the playes, will come
thither and worke all manner of mischeefe, and allso to the great pestring
and filling up of the same precinct, yf it should please God to send any
visitation of sickness as heretofore hath been, for that the same precinct
is allready growne very populous; and besides, that the same playhouse is
so neere the Church that the noyse of the drummes and trumpetts will
greatly disturbe and hinder both the ministers and parishioners in tyme of
devine service and sermons; – In tender consideracion wherof, as allso for

that there hath not at any tyme heretofore been used any comon playhouse within the same precinct, but that now all players being banished by the Lord Mayor from playing within the Cittie by reason of the great inconveniences and ill rule that followeth them, they now thincke to plant them selves in liberties; – That therefore it would please your honors to take order that the same roomes may be converted to some other use, and that no playhouse may be used or kept there; and your suppliants as most bounden shall and will dayly pray for your Lordships in all honor and happines long to live. Elizabeth Russell, dowager; G. Hunsdon; Henry Bowes; Thomas Browne; John Crooke; William Meredith; Stephen Egerton; Richard Lee; – Smith; William Paddy; William de Lavine; Francis Hinson; John Edwards; Andrew Lyons; Thomas Nayle; Owen Lochard; John Robbinson; Thomas Homes; Richard Feild; William Watts; Henry Boice; Edward Ley; John Clarke; William Bispham; Robert Baheire; Ezechiell Major; Harman Buckholt; John le Mere; John Dollin; Ascanio de Renialmire; John Wharton. (*Calendar of State Papers, Domestic, Eliz.* Cclx.116)

6. 13 April 1597 Deposition on the lease of the Theatre site, and its expiry, in the Court of Requests, Burbage v. Allen, ex parte Burbage (15 May 1600)
[William Smythe] saythe he hathe seene An Indenture of Lease whereby it appeared that the defendt and Sara his wyffe did about the thirteenthe daye of Aprill in the eighteenthe yeare of her majesties raigne that nowe is demise unto him the said James Burbadge Certayne garden groundes lyinge and beinge in Hollywell in the parishe of St Leonardes in Shoreditche in the Countye of Middlesex for the terme of one and twentye yeares yealdinge and payinge therefore yearlye duringe the said terme Foureteene poundes per Annum with provisoe in the same lease that the defendt within or at thend and terme of the first ten yeares in the said Lease he the said defendt should make him the said James Burbadge or his Assignes A newe lease for one and twentye yeares then to Commence at thend of the said firste tenn yeare . . . he knowethe the Complainant did about twoe yeares nowe laste paste or there aboutes and diverse tymes synce then, require the said defendt to make him A new Lease of the premisss accordinge to the Agreement mencioned in the First lease, but the Defendt denied to make him any suche lease, alledginge that the premisss weare not bettered by James Burbadge according to his Covenant, and that there weare Arerages of Rent behind and unpayde. (Court of Requests, Req.2/184/45, quoted by Charles William Wallace, *The First London Theatre*, pp. 237–8)

7. A letter from the Privy Council to the Master of the Revels and the Justices of Middlesex and Surrey, 19 February 1598

licence hath bin graunted unto two companies of stage players retayned unto us, the Lord Admiral and Lord Chamberlain, to use and practise stage playes, whereby they might be the better enhabled and prepared to shew such plaies before her Majestie as they shalbe required at tymes meete and accustomed, to which ende they have bin cheefelie licensed and tollerated as aforesaid, and whereas there is also a third company who of late (as wee are informed) have by waie of intrusion used likewise to play, having neither prepared any plaie for her Majestie nor are bound to you, the Masters of the Revelles, for perfourming such orders as have bin prescribed and are enjoyned to be observed by the other two companies before mencioned. Wee have therefore thought good to require you uppon receipt heereof to take order that the aforesaid third company may be suppressed and none suffered heereafter to plaie but those two formerlie named belonging to us, the Lord Admyrall and Lord Chamberlaine. (*Acts of the Privy Council of England*, ed. J. R. Dasent, 32 vols., HMSO, London, 1890–1907, XXVIII.327)

8. A note in Jonson's 1616 Folio, 'Every Man in his Humour'

This Comoedie was first Acted, in the yeere 1598. By the then L. Chamberlayne his Servants. The principall Comoedians were.

Will. Shakespeare.	Ric. Burbadge.
Aug. Philips.	Joh. Hemings.
Hen. Condel.	Tho. Pope.
Will. Slye.	Chr. Beeston.
Will. Kempe.	Joh. Duke.

With the allowance of the Master of REVELLS. (Jonson, *Works*, III.403)

9. Francis Meres, 'Palladis Tamia', 1598

As *Plautus* and *Seneca* are accounted the best for Comedy and Tragedy among the Latines: so *Shakespeare* among the English is the most excellent in both kinds for the stage; for Comedy, witnes his *Gentlemen of Verona*, his *Errors*, his *Love Labors Lost*, his *Love Labours Wonne*, his *Midsummers Night Dreame*, & his *Merchant of Venice*; for Tragedy his *Richard the 2*, *Richard the 3*, *Henry the 4*, *King John*, *Titus Andronicus* and his *Romeo* and *Juliet*. (Sig. OO2)

10. Giles Allen's complaint in Star Chamber, 23 November 1601
The said Cuthbert Burbage having intelligence of your Subjectes purpose
herein, and unlawfullye combyninge and confederating himselfe with the
sayd Richard Burbage and one Peeter Streat, William Smyth and divers
other persons to the number of twelve to your Subject unknowne did
aboute the eight and twentyth daye of December . . . ryotouslye assemble
themselves togeather and then and there armed themselves with divers and
manye unlawfull and offensive weapons, as namelye, swordes daggers billes
axes and such like And so armed did then repayre unto the sayd Theater And
then and there armed as aforesayd in verye ryotous outragious and forcyble
manner and contrarye to the lawes of your highnes Realme attempted to
pull downe the sayd Theatre. . . . And having done so did then also in
most forcible and ryotous manner take and carrye awaye from thence all
the wood and timber therof unto the Banckside . . . and there erected a
newe playe howse with the sayd Timber and wood. (Public Record Office
Req. STAC5/A.32. Wallace, *First London Theatre*, pp. 278–9)[1]

11. Testimony by Cuthbert Burbage, 1632, on lease of Globe site in 1599
his Indenture of lease tripartite bearing date the One and twentith day of
January in the One and Fortith yeere of the raigne of our late soveraigne
Lady Queene Elizabeth made betweene him the said Nicholas Brend on
the firste parte the said Cuthbert Burbadge and Richard Burbadge of the
second parte And William Shakespeare Augustine Phillips Thomas Pope the
said John Hemings and William Kempe of London gentlemen on the third
parte for divers greate and valuable Consideracions him thereunto especially
movcing in the said recited Indenture specified did demise graunt and to
ferme lett unto the said Cuthbert Burbadge Richard Burbadge William
Shakespeare Augustine Phillips Thomas Pope John Hemings and William
Kempe All those before cited parcells of ground or garden plotts with
thappurtenances in the said recited Indenture specified for the terms of
one and thirtie yeeres from the Feast of the Birth of our lord God then
last past . . . the said Cuthbert Burbadge and other the said lessees did
then enter into and upon the aforesaid recited demised premises by force
and virtue of theire said lease and demise . . . and did at theire owne
proper Costs and chardges expend disburse and lay out in the erecting
newe building and setting up there in and upon the said demised premises
of a howse structure or building used for Playhowse and Commonly called

---

[1] The whole sequence of lawsuits is cited and rather concisely summarized in *English Professional Theatre, 1530–1660*, ed. Glynne Wickham, Herbert Berry, William Ingram, Cambridge University Press,
2000, pp. 376–87.

the Globe the somme of One Thowsand pounds of lawfull English money at the leaste. (Court of Requests, 28 January 1632, Req. 2/706, quoted from Herbert Berry, *Shakespeare's Playhouses*, pp. 197–8)

12. Thomas Platter's diary, 21 September 1599
After dinner, at about two o'clock, I went with my party across the water; in the straw-thatched house we saw the tragedy of the first Emperor Julius Caesar, very pleasingly performed, with approximately fifteen characters; at the end of the play they danced together admirably and exceedingly gracefully, two in each group dressed in men's and two in women's apparel. (Translated by Ernest Schanzer, 'Thomas Platter's Observations on the English Stage', *Notes and Queries* 201, 1956, 466)

13. Privy Council Order, 22 June 1600
The Lordes and the rest of hir Majesties privie Councell, with one and full Consent, have ordered in manner and forme as followeth.
 – First, that there shall bee about the Cittie two howses and noe more allowed to serve for the use of the Common Stage plaies, of the which howses one shalbe in Surrey in that place which is Commonlie called the banckside or there abouts, and the other in Midlesex. And foras muche as there Lordshippes have bin enformed by Edmond Tylney Esquire, hir Majesties servant and Master of the Revells, that the howse now in hand to be builte by the said Edward Allen is not intended to encrease the number of the Plaiehowses, but to be in steed of an other, namelie the Curtaine, Which is either to be ruined and plucked downe or to be putt to some other good use, as also that the scituation thereof is meete and Convenient for that purpose. Yt is likewise ordered that the said howse of Allen shall be allowed to be one of the two howses, and namelie for the house to be alowed in Middlesex, soe as the house Called the Curtaine by (as yt is pretended) either ruinated or applied to some other good use. And for the other allowed to be on Surrey side, whereas [there Lordshipps are pleased to permitt] to the Companie of players that shall plaie there to make there owne Choice which they will have [of divers houses that are there], Choosinge one of them and noe more, [And the said Companie of Plaiers, being the Servantes of the L. Chamberlen, that are to plaie there have made choise of the house called the Globe, yt is ordered that the said house and none other shall be there allowed]. And especiallie yt is forbidden that anie stage plaies shalbe plaied (as sometimes they have bin) in any Common Inn for publique assembie in or neare about the Cittie.

– Secondlie, forasmuche as these stage plaies, by the multitude of houses and Companie of players, have bin too frequent, not serving for recreacion but inviting and Callinge the people daily from there trad and worke to mispend their time, It is likewise ordered that the two severall Companies of Plaiers assigned unto the two howses allowed maie play each of them in there severall howse twice a weeke and noe oftener, and especially that they shall refraine to play on the Sabboth daie, upon paine of imprisonment and further penaltie, and that they shall forbeare altogether in the time of Lent, and likewise at such time and times as anie extraordinarie sicknes or infeccion of disease shall appeare to be in and about the Cittie. (*Malone Society Collections* I.I, 1907, pp. 82–3; *Acts*, ed. Dasent, XXX.395)

14. Testimony at trial of Essex, 17 February 1601

Examination of Sir Gelly Merrick before Lord Chief Justice Popham and Edw. Fenner. On Saturday last was sevennight, dined at Gunter's in company with Lord Monteagle, Sir Christ. Blount, Sir Chas. Percy, Ellis Jones, Edw. Bushell and others. On the motion of Sir Chas. Percy, they went all together to the Globe over the water, where the Lord Chamberlain's men used to play, and were there somewhat before the play began, Sir Charles telling them that the play would be of Harry the Fourth. Cannot say whether Sir John Danvers was there or not, but he said he would be if he could; thinks it was Sir Chas. Percy who procured that play to be played at that time. The play was of King Henry the Fourth, and of the killing of Richard the Second, and played by the Lord Chamberlain's players. (*Calendar of State Papers, Domestic, 1598–1601*, 1869, p. 575)

15. Testimony at trial of Essex, 18 February 1601

Examination of Augustine Phillipps, servant to the Lord Chamberlain and one of his players, before Lord Chief Justice Popham and Edward Fenner. On Thursday or Friday sevennight, Sir Chas. Percy, Sir Josceline Percy, Lord Monteagle, and several others spoke to some of the players to play the deposing and killing of King Richard II, and promised to give them 40s. more than their ordinary, to do so. Examinate and his fellows had determined to play some other play, holding that of King Richard as being so old and so long out of use that they should have small company at it, but at this request they were content to play it. (*Calendar of State Papers, Domestic, 1598–1601*, 1869, p. 578)

16. Royal patent for King's Men, 19 May 1603

To all Justices Maiors Sheriffes Constables hedborowes and other our Officers and lovinge Subjectes greetinge knowe yee that Wee of our speciall grace certeine knowledge & mere motion have licenced and aucthorized and by theise presentes doe licence and aucthorize theise our Servauntes lawrence Fletcher William Shakespeare Richard Burbage Augustyne Phillippes John heninges henrie Condell William Sly Robert Armyn Richard Cowly and the rest of theire Assosiates freely to use and exercise the Arte and faculty of playinge Comedies Tragedies histories Enterludes moralls pastoralls Stageplaies, and Suche others like as theie have alreadie studied or hereafter shall use or studie aswell for the recreation of our lovinge Subjectes, as for our Solace and pleasure when wee shall thincke good to see them duringe our pleasure. And the said Commedies tragedies histories Enterludes Moralles Pastoralls Stageplayes and suche like to shewe and exercise publiquely to theire best Commoditie when the infection of the plague shall decrease aswell within theire nowe usual howse called the Globe within our County of Surrey as alsoe within anie towne halls or Moute halls or other conveniente places within the liberties and freedome of anie other Cittie universitie towne or Boroughe whatsoever within our said Realmes and dominions. (*Malone Society Collections* 1.3, 1909, p. 264)

17. Payment for attending the Spanish delegation, August 1604

To Augustine Phillippes and John Hemynges for thallowaunce of themselves and tenne of theire Fellowes his majesties groomes of the chamber, and Players for waytinge and attendinge on his majesties service by commaundemente uppon the Spanishe Embassador at Somersette howse the space of xviij dayes vizd from the ixth day of Auguste 1604 untill the xxvijth day of the same as appeareth by a bill thereof signed by the Lord Chamberlayne. xxjli. xijs. (Pipe Office, Declared Accounts 543. m.115–17)

18. A letter by Sir Walter Cope to Robert Cecil, December 1604

I have sent and bene all thys morning huntyng for players Juglers & Such kinde of Creaturs, but fynde them harde to finde, wherfore Leavinge notes for them to seeke me, Burbage ys come, & Sayes ther ys no new playe that the quene hath not seene, but they have Revyved an olde one, Cawled *Loves Labore lost*, which for wytt & mirthe he sayes will please her exceedingly. And Thys ys apointed to be playd to Morowe night at my Lord of Sowthamptons, unless yow send a wrytt to Remove the Corpus Cum Causa to your howse in Strande. Burbage ys my messenger Ready attendyng your pleasure.[2]

19. *Testimony by Odoardo Guatz at the trial of Ambassador Antonio Foscarini, Venice, 18 April 1617, about the period 1606–1608*
All the ambassadors, who have come to England have gone to the play more or less. Giustinian went with the French ambassador and his wife to a play called *Pericles*, which cost Giustinian more than 20 crowns. He also took the Secretary of Florence. (Quoted in Chambers, *William Shakespeare*, II.335)

20. *August 1608*
Now for the Blackfriers that is our inheritance, our father purchased it at extreame rates & made it into a play house with great charge & trouble, which after was leased out to one Evans that first sett up the Boyes commonly called the Queenes Majestes Children of the Chappell. In processe of time the boyes growing up to bee men which were Underwood, Field, Ostler, & were taken to strengthen the service, the boyes dayly wearing out, it was considered that house would bee as fitt for our selves, & soe purchased the lease remaining from Evans with our money & placed men Players, which were Hemings, Condall Shakspeare &c. (Testimony by Cuthbert Burbage, Appendix 3, Sharers' Papers)

21. *Compensation for the closure for plague, 26 April 1609*
John Hemynges one of his Majesties plaiers . . . by way of his majestes rewarde for their private practise in the time of infeccion that thereby they mighte be inhabled to performe their service before his Majestie in Christmas hollidaies 1609 . . . £40. (Pipe Office, Declared Accounts, Roll 543, m.214)

22. *A letter from Sir Henry Wotton to Sir Edmund Bacon, 29 June 1613*
I will entertain you at the present with what has happened this week at the Bank's side. The King's players had a new play, called *All is True*, representing some principal pieces of the reign of Henry VIII, which was set forth with many extraordinary circumstances of pomp and majesty, even

---

[2] Reprinted in E. K. Chambers, *William Shakespeare*, II.332, from the Hatfield MSS., and less accurately in *Elizabethan Stage*, IV.139. Its language and spelling make it look suspiciously like a nineteenth-century forgery. However, a letter of 15 January 1605 by Dudley Carleton to John Chamberlain about an earlier performance at Southampton's house authenticates it, if it did not give the occasion for the forgery.

to the matting of the stage; the Knights of the Order with their Georges and garters, the Guards with their embroidered coats, and the like: sufficient in truth within a while to make greatness very familiar, if not ridiculous. Now, King Henry making a masque at the Cardinal Wolsey's house, and certain chambers being shot off at his entry, some of the paper, or other stuff, wherewith one of them was stopped, did light on the thatch, where being thought at first but an idle smoke, and their eyes more attentive to the show, it kindled inwardly, and ran round like a train, consuming within less than a hour the whole house to the very grounds. This was the fatal period of that virtuous fabric, wherein yet nothing did perish but wood and straw, and a few forsaken cloaks; only one man had his breeches set on fire, that would perhaps have broiled him, if he had not by the benefit of a provident wit put it out with bottle ale. (Quoted in Chambers, *William Shakespeare*, II.343–4)

23. *Debate about rebuilding the Globe*

[John Witter, claimant to Augustine Phillips's share in the Globe] found that the reedifieing of the said playhowse would be a verie great charge & doubted what benefitt would arise thereby & for that the said originall Lease had then but a fewe yeeres to come he this defendant did geve away his said terme of yeeres & interest of & in the one Moitie of the said parte of the said Moitie of the said garden plottes & ground to the said other defendant Henry Condell gratis The reedifieing of which parte hath sithence Cost the said defendant about the somme of Cxx^{li} [£120]. (Deposition by Heminges and Condell against John Witter, 28 April 1619, quoted in Wallace, 'Shakespeare and his London Associates', 321)

24. *Petition of Blackfriars residents, 21 January 1619*

whereas in Novembr 1596 divers both honorable persons and others then inhabitinge the said precincte, made known to the Lordes and others of the privie Counsell, what inconveniences where likelie to fall upon them, by a common Playhouse which was then preparinge to bee erected there, whereupon their Honours then forbadd the use of the said howse, for playes, as by the peticion and endorsemente in aunswere thereof may appear.

Moreover whereas by orders of the Lordes and others of the privy Counsell, for many waightie reasons therein expressed beareing date the 22. Junii 1600, yt was lymitted their should bee only two Playhouses tollerated, whereof the one to bee the Banckside and the other att a place in or neere Gouldinge Lane, exemptinge thereby the Blackfryers, And whereas alsoe there was then a letter of the same date directed to the Lord Maior, and

Justices, strictlie requireinge of them to see these order put in execucion, and soe to bee continewed.

Nevertheles may it please your Lordship, and your brethren to bee advertised, that contrary to the said Orders, The owner of the said playhouse, doth under the name of a private howse (respectinge indeed private Comoditie only) convert the said howse to a publique playhouse; unto which there is daylie such resort of people, and such multitudes of Coaches (whereof many are Hackney Coaches, bringinge people of all sortes) That sometymes all our streetes cannott containe them, But that they Clogg upp Ludgate alsoe, in such sort, that both they endanger the one the other breake downe stalles, throwe downe mens goodes from their shopps, And the inhabitantes there cannott come to their howses, nor bringe in their necessary provisions of beere, wood, coale or haye, nor the Tradesmen or shopkeepers utter their wares, nor the passenger goe to the comon water staires without danger of ther lives and lymmes, whereby alsoe many times, quarrelles and effusion of blood hath followed; and what further danger may bee occacioned by the broyles plottes or practises of such an unrulie multitude of people yf they should gett head, your wisedomes cann conceave; Theise inconveniences fallinge out almost everie daie in the winter tyme (not forbearinge the tyme of Lent) from one or twoe of the clock till sixe att night, which beinge the tyme alsoe most usuall for Christeninges and burialls and afternoones service, wee cannot have passage to the Church for performance of those necessary duties, the ordinary passage for a great part of the precinct aforesaid beinge close by the play house dore.

Wherefore our humble suite to your Lordship, and your brethren is, That accordinge to the trust which the Lordes and the rest of the privy counsell repose in your wisedomes for the due execucion of the foresaid Orders, Course may bee taken in the premisses, And that the owner of the said play house may satisfie your Lordship and your brethren for his presumption in breakinge the same, and alsoe putt in good assurance for the tyme to come, that wee shall not bee thus endangered by such resort to this house. But that the kinges Majesties subjectes may have safe and quiett passage in the common streetes and the tradesmen for uttering their wares: wherein we doe the more earnestlie importune for preserving the peace, which is nowe often broken by reason of the inconveniences aforesaid; For preservinge whereof; yf wee shall either by Turnpikes, postes, chaines, or otherwise keepe theis Coaches without our gates, great inconvenience might thereby ensue, to Ludgate and the streates thereaboutes. Wherefore wee crave ayde and direccion from your Lordship and your brethren in all the premisses. (Petition of Blackfriars constables and officers to the Lord Mayor against the playhouse, *Malone Society Collections* i.i, 1907, pp. 90–1)

25. A funeral elegy for Richard Burbage, March 1619

> Hee's gone & with him what a world are dead,
> Which he revivd, to be revived soe.
> No more young Hamlett, ould Hieronymoe,
> Kind Leer, the greved Moore, and more beside,
> That lived in him, have now forever dy'de.
> (Quoted in Chambers, *Elizabethan Stage*, ii.309)

26. New company licence, following second petition from Blackfriars residents, 27 March 1619

To all Justices Maiors, Sheriffes Constables, Headborowes, and other our officers and loving Subjectes greeting. Knowe ye that wee of our speciall grace, certaine knowledge and meere mocion have licensed and authorized, and by these presentes do license and authorize theis our welbeloved servantes John Heminges, Richard Burbadge, Henry Condall, John Lowen, Nicholas Tooley, John Underwood, Nathan field, Robert Benfield, Robert Gough, William Ecclestone, Richard Robinson and John Shanckes and the rest of their associates freely to use and exercise the Art and facultie of playing Comedies, tragedies, Histories, Enterludes, Morralles, Pastoralles, Stage plaies, and such other like as they have alreadie studied, or herafter shall use or studie, aswell for ye recreacion of our lovinge Subjectes, as for our solace and pleasure when wee shall thinke good to see them, duringe our pleasure. And the said Comedies, Tragedies, Histories, Enterludes, Moralles, Pastoralls, Stage Plaies, and suche like to shew and exercise publiquely or otherwise to theire best commoditie when the infeccion of the Plague shall not weekely exceed the number of forty by the certificate of the Lord Maior of london for the time being aswell within their two their nowe usual houses called the Globe within our County of Surrey and their private house scituate in the precinctes of the Blackfriers within our City of london, as alsoe within any Towne halles or Mootehalles or other conveniente places within the liberties and freedome of any other City, University, Towne or Burrough whatsoever within our said Realmes and Dominions. (*Malone Society Collections* i.i, 1907, pp. 280–2)

27. A letter from Sir Gerard Herbert to Sir Dudley Carleton, 20 May 1619

The Marquise La Tremoile on Thursday last tooke leave of the Kinge . . . In the kinges great Chamber they went to see the play of Pirrocles, Priunce of

Tyre, which lasted till 2 aclocke. After two actes, the players ceased till the French all refreshed them with sweetmeates brought on Chinay voiders, & wyne & ale in bottells, after the players begann anewe. (Quoted in Chambers, *William Shakespeare*, II.346)

28. A letter from Thomas Locke to Sir Dudley Carleton, 14 August 1619
The Players heere were bringing of Barnavelt upon the stage, and had bestowed a great deale of money to prepare all things for the purpose, but at th'instant were prohibited by my Lord of London . . .

27 August 1619
Our players have fownd the meanes to goe through with the play of Barnavelt, and it hath had many spectators and receaved applause. (Sidney Lee, *Athenaeum*, 19 January 1884, p. 89)

29. Heminges and Condell, Dedication of the First Folio of Shakespeare to the Earls of Pembroke and Montgomery, 1623
But since your Lordships have beene pleas'd to thinke these trifles some-thing, heeretofore; and have prosequuted both them, and their Authour living, with so much favour: we hope, that (they out-living him, and he not having the fate, common with some, to be exequutor to his owne writing) you will use the like indulgence toward them, you have done unto their parent. There is great difference, whether any Booke choose his Patrones, or finde them: This hath done both. For, so much were your Lordships likings of the severall parts, when they were acted, as before they were published, the Volume ask'd to be yours. (First Folio, sig. A2r–v)

30. John Holles to the Earl of Somerset about 'A Game at Chess',
11 August 1624
My Lo. though from Mr Whittakers, or others, this vulgar pasquin may cum to your eares, yet whether he, or thei saw it, I know not, muche beeing the difference between ey-sight, & hear-say: when I returned from your Lordship hither uppon munday, I was saluted with a report of a facetious comedy, allreddy thryce acted with extraordinary applause: a representation of all our spannishe traffike, where Gundomar his litter, his open chayre for the ease of that fistulated part, Spalato &ca. appeared uppon the stage. I was invited by the reporter Sr Edward Gorge (whose balance gives all things waight to the advantage) to be allso an auditor therof, & accordingly yesterday to the globe I rowed, which hows I found so thronged, that by scores thei came away for want of space, though as yet little past one;

nevertheless lothe to check the appetite, which came so seldome to me (not having been in a playhouse thes 10. years) & suche a daynty not every day to be found, I marched on, & heard the pasquin, for no other it was which had been the more complete, had the poet been a better states-man: the descant was built uppon the popular opinion, that the Jesuits mark is to bring all the christian world under Rome for the spirituality, & under Spayn for the temporalty: heeruppon, as a precept, or legacy left those disciples from their first founder Ignatius Loyola, this their father serves for the prologue, who admiring no speedier operation of his drugg, is inraged, & desperate, till cumforted by one of his disciples, the plott is revealed him, prosperously advanced by their designe uppon England: with this he vanisheth, leaving his benediction over the work. The whole play is a chess board, England the whyt hows, Spayn the black: one of the white pawns, wth an under black dubblett, signifying a Spanish hart, betrays his party to their advantage, advanceth Gundomars propositions, works under hand the Princes cumming into Spayn: which pawn so discovered, the whyt King revyles him, objects his raising him in wealth, in honor, from meane condition, next classis to a labouring man: this by the character is supposed Bristow: yet it is hard, players should judge him in jest, before the State in ernest. Gundomar makes a large account of all his great feates heer, descrybes in scorne our vanities in dyet, in apparell, in every other excess, (the symptomes of a falling state) how many Ladyes brybed him to be groome of the stoole to the Infanta, how many to be mother of the mayds, with muche suche trashe, letters. from the nunnry in Drury Lane, from those in Bloomsbury &ca. how many Jesuites, & priests he loosed out of prison, & putt agayn into their necessary work of seducing how he sett the Kings affayrs as a clock, backward & forward, made him believe, & unbelieve as stood best with his busines, be the caws never so cleere: how he covered the roguery of the Jesuits in abusing wemen licensiously: how he befooled Spalato with a counterfeit lettre. from the Cardinall Paolo his kinsman, promising to leave his Cardinals hatt to him, himself then being elected Pope: with muche suche like stuff, more wittily penned, then wysely staged: but at last the Prince making a full discovery of all their knaveries, Olivares, Gundomar, Spalato, Iesuite, spannish bishop, & a spannish evenuke ar by the Prince putt into the bagg, & so the play ends . . . surely thes gamsters must have a good retrayte, else dared thei not to charge thus Princes actions, & ministers, nay their intents: a foule injury to Spayn, no great honor to England, rebus sic stantibus: every particular will beare a large paraphrase, which I submit to your better judgment. (Holles Letter Book, Nottingham University Library, Ne C 15,405, quoted in *A Game at Chess*, ed. T. H. Howard-Hill, Manchester University Press, 1993, pp. 198–200)

31. Privy Council letter to the King's secretary, 21 August 1624
Touching the suppression of a Scandalous Comedie, Acted by the Kings Players, We have called before us some of the principall Actors & demanded of them by what lycence and Authoritie, they have presumed to Act the same, in answere whereunto they produced a Booke being an Orriginall and perfect Coppie thereof (as they affirmed) seene and allowed by Sir Henry Herbert knight Master of the Revells under his owne hand, and subscribed in the last page of the said Booke, they confidently protested, they added or varied from the same nothing at all The Poett they tell us is one Middleton who shifting out of the way, and not attending the Board with the rest, as was expected We have given warrant to a Messenger for the Apprehending of him. To those that were before us, we gave a sound and sharpe reprooff making them sensible of his Majesties high displeasure herein, giving them straight Charg and Command, that they presume not to Act the said Comedie any more, nor that they suffer any Plaie or Enterlude whatsoever to be acted by them or any of their Company, untill his Majesties pleasure be furder knowne. We have Caused them lykewise to enter into Bond for their Attendance ypon the Board, whensoever they shalbe called, As for our Certifying to his Majestie (as was intimated by your lettre) what passages in the said Comedie we should fynd to be Offensive ansd Scandalous, we have thought it in our duties for his Majesties Clearer informacion, to send herewith all the Booke it selfe subscribed as afforesaid by thc Master of the Revells, that soe ither your selfe, or some other whom his Majestie shall appoint to peruse the same, may see the passages themselves out of the Orriginall, and call Sir Henry Herbert before you to know the reason of his lycensing thereof. (*Malone Society Collections* 1.4–5, 1911, pp. 380–1)

32. A letter of apology from the company to Henry Herbert, 20 December 1624
After our humble servise remembered unto your good worship, Whereas not long since we acted a play called The Spanishe Viceroy, not being licensed under your worships hande, nor allowd of: wee doe confess and herby acknowledge that wee have offended, and that it is in your power to punishe this offense, and are very sorry for it; and doe likewise promise herby that wee will not act any play without your hand or substituts hereafter, nor doe any thinge that may prejudice the authority of your office: So hoping that this humble submission of ours may bee

accepted, wee have therunto sett our hands. This twentieth of Decemb.
1624.

Joseph Taylor.	John Lowen.
Richard Robinson.	John Shancke.
Elyard Swanston	John Rice.
Thomas Pollard.	Will. Rowley.
Robert Benfeilde.	Richard Sharpe.
George Burght.	

(N. W. Bawcutt, *The Control and Censorship of Caroline Drama*, Oxford,
1966, p. 183)

*33. A warrant from the Master of the Revels ordering that the named people
should not be arrested or pressed for military service, 27 December 1624*
Theise are to Certefie you. That Edward Knight, William Pattrick, William
Chambers, Ambrose Byland, Henry Wilson, Jeffery Collins, William
Sanders, Nicholas Underhill Henry Clay, George Vernon, Roberte Pallant,
Thomas Tuckfeild, Roberte Clarke, [George Rickner,] John Rhodes,
William Mago, [and] Anthony Knight <(*in left margin*) and Edw.
Ashbourne, Will: Carver, Allexander Bullard, William Toyer, William
Gascoyne.> are all imployed by the Kinges Majesties servantes in their
quallity of Playeinge as Musitions and other necessary attendantes [Separate
warrants for Edward Shackerly and Richard Sharpe were attached]. (Quoted
by Bawcutt, *The Control and Censorship of Caroline Drama*, p. 158)

34. A licence from King Charles to his players, 24 June 1625
To all Justices Maiors Sheriffes Constables, headboroughes, and other our
Officers and lovinge Subjectes greeting knowe ye that we of our espe-
ciall grace certayne knowledge and meere mocion have licenced and authorised, and by these presentes do licence and authorise, these our welbeloved Servantes John heminges, henry Condall, John lowen, Richard
Robinson, Robert Benfeild, John Shanck, William Rowley, John Rice,
Elliart Swanston, George Birch, Richard Sharpe and Thomas Pollard, and
the rest of their associates, freely to use and exercise, the Art and facultye
of Playing Comedies, Tragedies, histories, Enterludes Morralles Pastoralles,
Stageplayes and such other like as they have alreadie Studied or hereafter
shall use or Studdy, aswell for the Recreacion of our lovinge Subjectes as for
our sollace and pleasure when we shall thinke good to see them duringe our

pleasure. And the saide Comedies Tragedies histories Enterludes Moralles Pastoralls, Stageplayes, and suche like to showe and exercise publiquely, or otherwise to theire best commodity, when the Infeccion of the plague shall not weekely exceede the nomber of Forty by the Certificate of the lord Maior of london for the tyme being, aswell within these two their most usuall houses called the Globe within our County of Surrey and theire private house scituate within the Precinct of the Blacke Friers within our Citty of london As alsoe within any Townehalles or Moutehalles or other convenient places within the liberties and freedome of any other Citty university Towne or Burrough whatsoever within our said Realmes and Domynions. (*Malone Society Collections* 1.3, 1909, pp. 282–3)

35. A letter from Robert Gell to Sir Martyn Stuteville, 29 July 1628

On Teusday his Grace [the Duke of Buckingham] was present at ye acting of K. Hen. the 8 at ye Globe, a play bespoken of purpose by himself; whereat he stayd till ye Duke of Buckingham was beheaded, & then departed. Some say, he should rather have seen ye fall of Cardinall Wolsey, who was a more lively type of himself, having governed this kingdom 18 yeares, as he hath done 14. (Quoted in Chambers, *William Shakespeare*, II.348)

36. John Pory, letter to Viscount Scudamore, 4 February 1632

Their lordships made my lord Thurles of Ireland also to doe the like satisfaction to Captaine Essex. The occasion was this. This Captaine attending and accompanying my Lady of Essex in a boxe in the playhouse at the black fryers, the said lord coming upon the stage, stood before them and hindred their sight. Captain Essex told his lordship they had payd for their places as well as hee, and therfore intreated him not to deprive them of the benefitt of it. Whereupon the lord stood up yet higher and hindred more their sight. Then Capt. Essex with his hand putt him a little by. The lord then drewe his sword and ran full butt at him, though hee missed him, and might have slaine the Countess as well as him. (William S. Powell, *John Pory / 1572–1636, The Life and Letters of a Man of Many Parts*, University of North Carolina Press, Chapel Hill, 1977, p. 128)

37. Lord Chamberlain's Office accounts, 16 March 1633

A Warraunt for payment of £270 unto John Lowen Joseph Taylor & Ellyard Swanston his Majesties Comaedians for Playes by them Acted before his Majestye. vizt. £20 for the rehersall of one at the Cockpitt by which meanes they lost their afternoone at the House & £20 apeece for two at Hampton Court in consideration of their charge of lodge & dyet for the Company &

£10 a peece for 21 more at Whitehall and Denmarke house Acted betweene
the 3d of May 1632 & ye 3d of March following. (*Malone Society Collections*
II.3, p. 360).

38. *Livery warrant, 15 April 1633*

A warraunt for Liveryes for 14 of his Majesties Players vizt fower yardes of
basterd Skarlet to each of them & a quarter of a yard of crimson velvet for
Capes to bee donated to John Lowen. Due at Easter 1633. (*Malone Society
Collections* II.3, 1931, p. 360)

39. *The Lord Chamberlain's warrant to the King's Men to take up players,*
6 May 1633

Wheras the late decease, infirmity & sicknes of diverse principall Actors
of his Majesties Company of Players hath much decayed & weakened
them, soe that they are disabled to doe his Majesty service in their quality,
unlesse there bee some speedy order taken to supply & furnish them with a
convenient number of new Actors. His Majestye having taken notice thereof
& signifyed his royall pleasure unto mee therin, Theis are to will & require
you & in his Majesties name straitly to charge, commaund & Authorize
you & either of you to choose, receave & take into your Company any
such Actor or Actors belonging to any of the lycensed Companyes within
& about the Citty of London as you shall thinke fitt & able to doe his
Majesty service in that kinde. Heerin you may not fayle And This shall bee
your sufficient Warrant & discharge in that behalfe. Court at Whitehall
the 6th of May. 1633

> To John Lowen and Joseph
> Taylor two of the Company of
> His Majestes Players.
> (*Malone Society Collections* II.3, 1931, p. 361)

40. *An Order of Privy Council in Star Chamber, 22 November 1633,*
acknowledging a further petition by the Blackfriars residents in 1631, and
subsequent protests about the trouble caused by coach traffic

Whereas the Board hath taken into consideracion the greate inconveniences
that growe by reason of the resort to the Playhowse of the BlackFryers in
Coaches, whereby the Streetes neere thereunto are at the Playtime soe
stopped, that his Majesties Subjectes goeing about theire necessarie affaires
can hardly finde passage, and are sometimes endangered: Their Lordships
remembring that there is an easie passage by water unto that Playhouse
without troubling the Streetes, and that it is much more fitt & reasonable

that those which goe thither should goe by water, or els on foote, rather then the necessary businesses of all others & the publique Commerce should bee disturbed by their pleasure, Doe therefore order, that if any persons, men or women, of what condicion soever, repaire to the aforesaid Playhowse in Coach, soe soone as they are gone out of their Coaches, the Coachmen shall depart thence, and not returne till the end of the Play, nor shall stay or retourne to fetch those, whome they carried, any neerer with their Coaches, then the farther part of St Paules Church yard on the one side, and Fleet conduit on the other side, and in the meane time betweene their departure & retourne shall either retourne home, or else abide in some other Streetes less frequented with Passengers, and so raunge their coaches in those places, that the waie bee not stopped . . . copies of this order shalbe sett up by direccion from the Lord Maior at Paules chaine, the west end of St Paules Church, Ludgate, the BlackFriers and Fleet Conduit. (*Malone Society Collections* 1.1, 1907, pp. 98–9. Further documents about the problem are in Malone Society Collections 1.4–5, 1911, pp. 386–9)

41. A note by the Master of the Revels, 9 January 1634
the kinge was pleasd to call mee into his withdrawinge chamber to the window, wher he went over all that I had croste in Davenants play-booke, and allowing of *faith* and *slight* to bee asserverations only, and no oathes, markte them to stande, and some few other things, but in the greater part allowed of my reformations. This was done upon a complaint of Mr Endymion Porters in December.

The kinge is pleasd to take *faith, death, slight*, for asserverations and no oaths, to which I doe humbly submit as my masters judgment; but under favour conceive them to be oaths, and enter them here, to declare my opinion and submission. (Quoted in Bawcutt, *The Control and Censorship of Caroline Drama*, p. 186)

42. A letter by Nathaniel Tomkyns to Sir Robert Phelips, 16 August 1634
Here hath bin lately a newe comedie at the globe called *The Witches of Lancashier*, acted by reason of the great concourse of people 3 dayes togither: the 3d day I went with a friend to see it, and found a greater appearance of fine folke gentmen and gentwoemen then I thought had bin in town in the vacation: The subject was of the slights and passages done or supposed to be done by these witches sent from thence hither and other witches and their familiars; Of ther nightly meetings in several places: their banqueting with all sorts of meat and drinke conveyed unto them by their familiars upon the pulling of a cord: the walking of pailes of milke by themselvers and (as they say of children) a highlone: the transforming of men and weomen

into the shapes of severall creatures and especially of horses by putting an inchaunted bridle into ther mouths: their posting to and from places farre distant in an incredible short time: the cutting off a witch-gentwoman's hand in the forme of a catt, by a soldier turned miller, known to her husband by a ring thereon, (the onely tragicall part of the storie:) the representing of wrong and putative fathers in the shape of meane persons to gentmen by way of derision: the tying of a knott at a mariage (after the French manner) to cassate masculine abilitie, and the conveying away of the good cheere and bringing in a mock feast of bones and stones steed thereof and the filling of pies with living birds and yong catts &c: And though there be not in it (to my understanding) any poeticall Genius, or art, or language, or judgement to state our tenet of witches (which I expected,) or application to vertue but full of ribaldrie and of things improbable and impossible; yet in respect of the newnesse of the subject (the witches being still visible and in prison here) and in regard it consisteth from the beginning to the ende of odd passages and fopperies to provoke laughter, and is mixed with divers songs and dances, it passeth for a merrie and excellent new play. (Quoted by Herbert Berry, *Shakespeare's Playhouses*, pp. 123–4)

43. August 1635

Then, to shew your Honour against these sayinges that wee eat the fruit of their Labours. Wee referre it to your honours judgement to consider their profittes, which wee may safely maintaine, for it appeareth by their owne Accomptes for one whole yeere last past beginning from Whitson-Munday 1634 to Whitson Munday 1635 how each of these complainantes gained severally as hee was a Player and noe Howskepper £180, Besides Mr Swanston hath receaved from the Blackfriers this yeere as hee is there a Houskeeper above £30, all which beeing accompted together may very well keepe him from starving. (From the counterpetition by Cuthbert Burbage and others, 1635. See Appendix 3, Sharers' Papers)

44. Strafforde's Letters, 25 January 1636

A little Pique happened betwixt the Duke of Lenox and the Lord Chamberlain about a Box at a new Play in the *Black Fryars*, of which the Duke had got the Key; Which if it had come to be debated betwixt them as it was intended, some Heat or other Inconvenience might have happen'd. His Majesty hearing of it, sent the Earl of *Holland* to commend them both not to dispute it, but before him, so he heard it and made them Friends. (Wiliam Knowler, ed., *The Earl of Strafford's Letters and Dispatches*, 2 vols., London, 1739, II.151)

45. A 'Players Passe', 17 May 1636

Wheras William Pen, Thomas Hobbes, William Trig, William Patrick Richard Baxter, Alexander Gough William Hart & Richard Hauley together with Tenne more or theraboutes of their fellowes his Majesties Comaedians & of the peculiar Company of Players in the Blackfryers London, are commaunded to attend his Majestye, and bee nigh about the Court this summer Progresse, in readines when they shall bee called upon to act before his Majestye: for the better inabling & incourageing them whereunto: His Majesty setting forth on his maine Progresse, as in all that time & after, till they have occasion to retourne homewardes, have all freedome & liberty to repayre unto all Townes Corporate, mercate Townes & other, where they shall thinke fitt & there in their Common Halles, moothalles, schoole houses or other convenient roomes Act Playes Comaedyes & interludes, without any lett, hinderance or molestation whatsoever (behaveing them selves civilly). Wherin it is his Majesties pleasure, and hee doth expect that in all places where they come, they bee treated & intertained with such due respect & courtesie, as may become his Majesties loyall & loveing subjectes towardes his servantes. In testimony wherof I have heerunto sett my hand & seale at Armes. Dated at Whitehall the 17th day of May 1636.

P& M.

To all Mayors Sheriffes, Bayliffes
Justices of peace, Constables Head –
boroughes & to all other his Majesties
Officers & Loveing Subjectes what –
soever whome this may concerne.

(*Malone Society Collections* II.3, 1931, pp. 378–9)

46. A letter from the Lord Chamberlain to the Stationers' Company,
10 June 1637

Wheras complaint was heeretofore presented to my Deare brother & predecessor by his Majesties servantes the Players, that some of the Company of Printers & Stationers had procured, published & printed diverse of their bookes of Comaedyes, Tragedyes Cronicle Historyes, and the like which they had (for the speciall service of his Majestye & for their owne use) bought and provided at very Deare and high rates. By meanes wherof not onely they themselves had much prejudice, but the bookes much corruption to the injury and disgrace of the Authors, And therupon the Masters and Wardens of the company of printers & stationers were advised by my Brother to take notice therof & to take Order for the stay of any further

Impression of any of the Playes or Interludes of his Majestes servantes without their consentes.

I am informed that some Coppyes of Playes belonging to ye King & Queenes servantes the Players, & purchased by them at Deare rates, haveing beene lately stollen or gotten from them by indirect meanes are now attempted to bee printed & that some of them are at ye Presse & ready to bee printed, which if it should be suffered, would directly tend to their apparent Detriment & great prejudice & to the disenabling of them to doe their Majesties service. (*Malone Society Collections* II.3, 1931, pp. 384–5)

47. Privy Council Register, 17 September 1637

His Majesties Servants ye Players having, by reason of the Infeccion of the Plague in and neare London, been for a long time restrained and having now spent what they got in many yeares before and soe not able any longer to subsist & mainteine their families did by their Peticion to his Majestie most humbly desire leave to bee now at libertie to use their quallity. It was thereupon this day Ordered (his Majestie present in Councell) that ye said Players should bee at liberty to play at Michaelmas next, if, by that time there bee noe considerable encrease of the Sicknesse nor that there dye not of ye infeccion in and about London more then there died this last weeke. (*Malone Society Collections* I.4–5, 1911, p. 394)

48. A letter from George Garrard to Lord Strafford, 7 February 1638

Two of the king's Servants, Privy-Chamber Men both, have writ each of them a Play, Sir *John Sutlin* and *Will. Barclay*, which have been acted in Court, and at the *Black Friars*, with much Applause. *Sutlin's* Play cost three or four hundred Pounds setting out, eight or ten Suits of new Cloaths he gave the Players; an unheard of prodigality. (*The Earl of Strafford's Letters and Dispatches*, II.150)

49. James Shirley, Prologue, 'The Doubtful Heir', 1639

> No shewes, no frisk, and what you most delight in
> (Grave understanders) here's no Target fighting
> Upon the Stage, all work for cutlers barrd,
> No Bawd'ry, nor no Ballads; this goes hard.
> The wit is clean, and (what affects you not)
> Without impossibilities the plot;
> No Clown, no squibs, no Divells in't; oh now
> you Squirrels that want nuts, what will ye do?
> (James Shirley, *Six New Plays*, 1653, sig. A3)

50. The Lord Chamberlain's protection of King's Men's plays, 7 August 1641
The Players which are his Majesties Servantes have addressed them selves
unto mee as formerly to my predecessors in Office, complaining that some
Printers are about to Print & publish some of their Playes which hetherto
they have beene usually restrained from by the Authority of the Lord Chamberlain. Their Request seemes both just and reasonable, as onely tending
to preserve them Masters of their proper Goodes which in justice ought
not to bee made common for another mannes profitt to their disadvantage.
Upon this Ground therfore I am induced to require your care (as formerly
my Predecessors have done) that noe Playes belonging to them bee put
into Print without their knowledge & consent The particulars to which
they now lay claime are contained in a List inclosed, and if any of those
Playes shall bee offered to ye Presse under another name then is in the
List expressed, I shall desire your care that they may not be defrauded by
that meanes but that they may bee made acquainted with it, before they
bee recorded in ye Hall & soe have Opportunity to shew their right unto
them.

A List of ye Playes followes

The wild goose chase	The humerous Lieuetennt	The Country Captaine
The litle french Lawyer	Bunduca	The discontented Colonell
The Loyall subject	The inconstant Lady	The Brothers
The spanish Curat	Chances	Minervae's sacrifice
The Custom o'th Country	The maid of the Mill	The Judge.
The double marriage.	The Bridegroome & ye Madman	The Citty Madam.
A wife for a moneth	The Queen of Corinth	The Corporall.
The Island Princess	The Coxcombe	Alfonso Emperor of Germany
The mad Lover	The noble gentleman	The Nobleman.
The Pilgrim	Beggars	The bashfull Lover
The Maior of Quinborow &	The honest mans fortune	Love & honor.
The womans Plott	The martiall maide	The 1st & 2nd pt of ye Passionat lover
The womans prize &c	Beauty in a trance	

The Switzar

More dissemblers
beside women

The widow

The Knight of Malta

The Novella

The lovesick maid

The Captaine

The for'c Lady

Alexius

The unfortunate
Lovers

The fair favourite

The Emperour
Valentinian

The Goblins

The distresses

The doubtfull heire

The Imposture

The Guardian.

The Duke of Lerma or
ye spanish Duke.

The Prophetesse

The Lovers Pilgrimage

The Lovers Progress

News from Plimouth.

(*Malone Society Collections*, II.3, 1931, pp. 398–9)

APPENDIX 3

The Sharers' Papers

This is a transcript of the testimonies made in the 1635 dispute over shares in the King's Men's playhouses. These testimonies, usually now known as the 'Sharers' Papers', are transcribed from *Malone Society Collections* II.3, 1931, pp. 362–4, 365–70, 370–3, and checked against the originals, which are in the Public Record Office at Kew in London, L.C. 5/133, pp. 50–1. A version in modernized spelling is available in *English Professional Theatre, 1530–1660*, ed. Glynne Wickham, Herbert Berry, William Ingram, Cambridge University Press, 2000, pp. 221–8.

(a) A petition by 'Robert Benefield, Heliard Swanston & Thomas Pollard' to 'Philip Earle of Pembroke & Montgomery, Lorde Chamberlaine of his Majesties Houshold.'[1]

– That the petitioners have a long time with much patience expected to bee admitted Sharers in ye Play houses of the Globe and Blackfriers; wherby they might reape some better fruit of their labours then hitherto they have done, & bee incouraged to proceed therin with cheerfulnes.

 – That those few interested in ye Houses have (without any defalcacion or abatement at all) a full moyety of the whole gaines ariseing therby exccpting the outer dores, And such of the sayd Housekeepers as bee Actors, doe likewise equally share with all the rest of the Actors, both in the other moiety, & in the sayd outer dores also.

 – That out of the Actors moicty, there is notwithstanding defrayed all wages to hired men, Apparell, Poetes, lightes, & other charges of the Houses

---

[1] The original text has been retained here, except that the standard manuscript abbreviations are expanded, and as in other quotations in this book 'j' is used for initial and medial 'i' where necessary, and initial 'v' becomes u and medial 'u' becomes v where appropriate. In addition, the modern £ sign is used in place of the original 'li'. On the other hand, 'ye', still in use as a common form of transcription for 'the', has been retained here. One accidentally repeated phrase has been silently deleted.

whatsoever, soe that, betweene the Gaynes of the Actors, & of those few interested as Housekeepers, there is an unreasonable inequality.

– That the House of the Globe was formerly divided into 16 partes wherof Mr Cutbert Burbidge and his sisters had 8, Mrs Condall 4 and Mr Hemings 4.

– That Mr Tailor and Mr Lowen were long since admitted to purchase 4 partes betwixt them from the rest (vizt) 1 part from Mr Hemings 2 partes from Mrs Condall, & halfe a part a peece from Mr Burbidge and his sister.

– That the 3 partes remaining to Mr Hemings were afterwardes by Mr Shankes surreptitiously purchased from him, contrary to the petitioners expectation; who hoped that when any partes had beene to bee sold, they should have beene admitted to have bought & divided the same amongst themselves, for their better livelyhood.

– That the petitioners Desire not to purchase or diminish any part of Mr Taylors or Mr Lowens shares (whose deserveings they must acknowledge to bee well worthy of their gaines) But in regard the petitioners labours (according to their severall wayes & abilityes) are equall to some of the rest, and for that others of the said Housekeepers are neither Actors, nor his Majesties servantes, & yet the petitioners profit & meanes of Livelyhood, soe much inferior & unequall to theires, as appears before They therefore desire that they may bee admitted to purchase for their moneys, at such rates as have been formerly given single partes a peece onely from those that have the greatest shares & may best share them (vizt) that Mr Burbadge and his sister having 3 partes & a halfe a peece may sell them two partes & reserve two and a halfe a peece to themselves. And that Mr Shankes having three may sell them one & reserve two; wherin they hope your Lordship will conceave their desires to bee just and modest; The rather for that the petitioners not doubting of beeing admitted sharers in the sayd house the Globe suffered lately the sayd Housekeepers in the name of his Majesties servantes, to sue & obtaine a Decree in the Court of Requestes against Sir Mathew Brand, for confirmation unto them of a lease paroll for about 9 or 10 yeeres yet to come, which they could other wise have prevented, untill themselves had beene made parties.

– That for the House in ye Blackfriers, it beeing divided into 8 partes amongst the aforenamed Housekeepers & Mr Shankes having two partes therof, Mr Lowen, Mr Taylor and each of the rest having but one part a peece, which two partes were by the sayd Mr Shankes purchased of Mr Heming, together with those 3 of the Globe as before, The petitioners desire & hope that your Lordship will conceave it likewise reasonable, that the sayd Mr Shankes may assigne over one of the sayd partes amongest them three, they giving him such satisfaccion for the same as that hee bee noe looser therby.

– Lastly that your Lordship would to that purpose bee nobly pleased, as their onely gracious refuge & protector, to call all the sayd housekeepers before you & to use your Lordships power with them to conforme themselves therunto: the rather considering that some of the sayd Housekeepers who have the greatest shares, are neither Actors nor his Majesties servantes as aforesayd, & yet reape most or the chiefest benefitt of the sweat of their browes, & live upon the bread of their Labours, without takeing any paynes themselves.

– For which your petitioners shall have just cause to blesse your Lordship, as however they are dayly bound to doe with the devotions of most humble & obliged Beadsmen.

(b) Reply from Pembroke, 'Court at Theoballes 12. July 1635'

Having considered this petition & the severall answeres & replyes of ye parties the merites of the petitioners & the disproportion of their shares & the interest of his Majesties service, I have thought fitt & doe accordingly order that the petitioners Robert Benefield, Eyllaerdt Swanston & Thomas Pollard bee each of them admitted to ye purchase of the shares desired of the severall persons mentioned in ye petition for the fower yeeres remayning of the lease of the House in Blackfriers & for five yeeres in that of the Globe at the usuall & accustomed rates & according to ye proportion of the time & benefitt they are to injoy. And heerof I Desire the Housekeepers & all others whome it may concerne to take notice & to conforme themselves therin accordingly. The which if they or any of them refuse or delay to performe, if they are Actors & his Majesties servantes I doe suspend them from the Stage & all the benefitt therof & if they are onely interested in ye Houses, I desire my Lord privy seale to take order that they may bee left out of the lease, which is to bee made upon the decree in ye Court of Requestes.

(c) Robert Benefield, Eyllardt Swanston & Thomas Pollard doe further humbly represent unto your Lordship

– That the Houskeepers beeing but 6 in number, vizt Mr Cutbert Burbage, Mrs Condall, Mr Shankes, Mr Taylor, Mr Lowen & Mr Robinson (in ye right of his wife) have amongst them, the full moyety of all the Galleries & Boxes in both Houses & of the tireing house dore at ye Globe.

– That the Actors have the other moyety with the outer dores but in regard the Actors are halfe as many more (vizt) nine in number their shares fall shorter & are a great deale lesse then the Housekeepers, And yet notwithstanding out of those lesser shares the sayd Actors defray all Charges of the House whatsoever (vizt) wages to hired men & boyes musicke lightes &c amounting to 900 or £1000 per annum or thereaboutes beeing £3 a day one day with another, besides the extraordinary Charge which the sayd Actors are wholly at for apparell & Poetes &c.

– Wheras the sayd Housekeepers out of all their gaines have not till our Lady day Last payd above £65 per annum rent for both Houses, towardes which they rayse betweene 20 & £30 per annum from the Taphowses & a Tenemt & a Garden belonging to the premisses &c and are at noe other charges whatsoever excepting the ordinary reparations of the Houses.

– Soe that upon a Medium made of the Gaynes of the Howskeepers & those of the Actors one day with another throughout the yeere, the petitioners will make it apparent that when some of the Houskeepers share the 12s^2 a day at ye Globe the Actors share not above 3s. And then what those gaine that are both Actors and Houskeepers & have their shares in both your Lordship will easily judge, & therby finde the modesty of the petitioners suite, who desire onely to buy for their money one part apeece from such three of the sayd Houskeepers as are fittest to spare them, both in respect of Desert and other wise (vizt) Mr Shankes, one part of his three, Mr Robinson & his wife, one part of their three & a halfe, And Mr Cutbert Burbidge the like.

– And for the House of the Blackfriers, that Mr Shankes who now injoyes two partes there, may sell them likewise one, to bee divided amongst them three.

– Humbly beseeching your Lordship to consider their long sufferings & not to permit the sayd Howskeepers any Longer to delay them but to put an end to & settle the sayd busines, that ye petitioners may not bee any further troublesome or importunate to your Lordship, but may proceed to doe their duty with cheerfullnes & alacritye.

– Or otherwise in case of their refusall to conforme themselves, that your Lordship would bee pleased to consider whether it bee not reasonable & equitable that the Actors in generall may injoy the benefitt of both Houses to themselves paying the sayd Howskeepers such a valuable rent for the same as your Lordship shall thinke just and indifferent.

---

^{2} i.e., twelve shillings, three-fifths of a pound.

(d) 'The answere of John Shankes to ye Peticion of Robert Benefield Eyllardt Swanston & Thomas Pollard Lately exhibited to the Right Honorable Philip Earle of Pembroke & Montgomery Lord Chamberlin of his Majesties Houshold

Humbly sheweth

– That about allmost 2 yeeres since, your supplicant upon offer to him made by William Hemings did buy of him one part hee had in the Blackfriers for about 6 yeeres then to come at the yeerely rent of £6 5s. & another part hee then had in ye Globe for about two yeeres to come & payd him for the same two partes in ready moneys £156 which sayd partes were offered to your supplicant, & were as free then for any other to buy as for your supplicant.

– That about 11 months since the sayd William Hemings offering to sell unto your supplicant the remaining partes hee then had (viz) one in the Blackfriers, wherin hee had then about 5 yeeres to come & two in ye Globe wherin hee had then but one yeere to come, your supplicant likewise bought the same & payd for them in ready moneys more £350, All which moneys soe disbursed by your supplicant amount to £506, the greatest part of which your supplicant was constrained to take up at interest & your supplicant hath besides disbursed to the said William Heminges diverse other small summes of money, since Hee was in prison.

– That your supplicant did neither fraudulently nor surreptitiously defeat any of the petitioners in their hope of buying the sayd partes, neither would the sayd William Hemings have sold the same to any of the petitioners for that they would not have given him any such price for the same but would (as now they endeavour to doe), have had the same against his will, & at what rates they pleased.

– That your supplicant bceing an old man in this quality, who in his youth first served your noble father & after that, the late Queene Eliz, then King James & now his royall Majestye, & having in this long time made noe provision for him selfe in his age, nor for his wife, Children & grandchild, for his and their better livelyhood, having this oportunity, did at deere rates purchase these partes, & hath for a very small time as yet receaved the profites therof & hath but a short time in them, & is without any hope to renew the same, when the Termes bee out, hee therfore hopeth hee shall not bee hindered in ye injoying the profitt therof, especially whenas the same are thinges very casuall & subject to bee discontinued & lost by sicknes & diverse other wayes & to yield noe proffitt at all.

– That wheras the petitioners in their complaint say that they have not meanes to subsist, it shall be by oath (if need bee) bee made apparent that

every one of the three petitioners for his own particular hath gotten &
receaved this yeere last past of the summe of £180 which, as your supplicant
conceaveth is a very sufficient meanes to satisfie & answere their long &
patient expectation & is more by above the one halfe then any of them
ever gott or were capable of elsewhere, besides what Mr Swanston, one of
them who is most violent in this busines, who hath further had & receaved
this last yeere above £34 for the profitt of a third part of one part in the
blackfriers which hee bought for £20 & yet hath injoyed the same 2 or 3
yeeres allready & hath still as long time in ye same as your supplicant hath
in his, who for soe much as Mr Swanston bought for £20 your supplicant
payd £60.

– That when your supplicant purchased his partes hee had noe certainty
therof more then for one yeere in the Globe & there was a chargeable
suit then depending in the Court of Requestes between Sir Mathew Brend
knight & the Lessees of the Globe & their assignes for the adding of nine
yeeres to their lease in consideration that they and their predecessors had
formerly been at the Charge of £1400 in building of the sayd House upon
the burning downe of the former, wherin, if they should miscarry, for as
yet they have not the assurance perfected by Sir Mathew Brend)[3] your
supplicant shall lay out his money to such a losse as the petitioners will
never bee partners with him therin.

– That your supplicant & other lessees in ye Globe & in the blackfriers
are chargeable with the payment of £100 yeerely Rent besides Reparacions,
which is dayly very chargeable unto them, all which they must pay and
beare, whether they make any proffitt or nott & soe reckoning their charge
in building & fitting the sayd Houses, yeerly Rent & Reparations, noe wise
man will adventure his Estate in such a course, considering their dealing,
with whome they have to doe, & the many casualtyes & dayly troubles
therwith.

– That in all the affayres & dealinges in this world betweene man &
man it was & is ever held an inviolable principle, that in what thing soever any man hath a lawfull interest & property Hee is not to bee com-
pelled to depart with the same against his will which the complainantes
endeavour.

– And wheras John Heminges the father of William Hemings of whome
your supplicant made purchase of the sayd partes injoyed the same 30 yeeres
without any molestacion beeing the most of the sayd yeeres both Player &

---

[3] The scribe began the parenthesis with a comma but ended it with a bracket. His marks have been
retained here.

Houskeeper, and after Hee gave over playing diverse yeeres, & his sonne William Hemings fower yeers after, though he never had any thing to doe with the sayd Stage, injoyed the same without any trouble, notwithstanding the complainantes would violently take from your petitioner the sayd partes who hath still of his owne purse supplyed the company for the service of his Majesty with boyes as Thomas Pollard, John Thompson deceased (for whome Hee payd £40) your supplicant having payd his part of £200 for other boyes since his coming to ye Company, John Honiman, Thomas Holcome and diverse others & at this time maintaines 3 more for the sayd service. Neither lyeth it in ye power of your supplicant to satisfie the unreasonable demandes of the complainantes. Hee beeing forced to make over the sayd partes for security of moneyes taken up as aforesayd of Robert Morecroft of Lincolne his wifes uncle for the purchase of the sayd partes untill hee hath made payment of the sayd moneys which hee is not able to doe unlesse Hee bee suffered to injoye the sayd partes during the small time of his Lease & is like to bee undone if they are taken from him.

– All which, beeing considered your supplicant hopeth that your Lordship will not inforce your supplicant against his will to depart with what is his owne & what hee hath deerly payd for unto them that can claime noe lawfull interest therunto And your supplicant (under your Lordships favour) doth conceave that if the petitioners by those their violent courses may obtaine their desires your Lordship will never bee at quiet for their dayly complaintes & it will bee such a president to all young men that shall follow heerafter, that they shall allwayes refuse to doe his Majesty service, unless they may have whatsoever they will though it bee other mens estates. And soe that which they pretend shall tend to the better government of the company & inabling them to doe his Majesty service, the same will bee rather to the destruccion of the Company & disabling of them to doe service to his Majestye, And besides the benefitt & profitt which the petitioners doe yeerely make without any charge at all, is soe good, that they may account them selves to bee well recompenced for their labour & paines & yet when any partes are to bee sold, they may buy the same, if they can gett the bargaine therof paying for the same as others doe.

The humble suit of your supplicant is that your honour will bee pleased that hee may injoy that which hee hath deerly bought & truly payd for.

(e) Counter-petition by Cuthbert Burbage, Winifred Burbage and William Burbage.

– Right Honorable & our singular good Lord. Wee your humble supplicantes Cutbert Burbage & Winifrid his Brothers wife & William his sonne
doe tender to your honorable consideration for what respectes & good reasons wee ought not in all charity to bee disabled of our livelyhoodes by men
soe soone shott up, since it hath beene the custome that they should come
to it by farre more antiquity and desert, then those can justly attribute to
them selves.

– And first humbly shewing to your honor the infinite Charges, the
manifold law suites, the leases expiration by the restraintes in sicknes time
& other accidentes that did cutt from them the best part of the gaines that
your honour is informed they have receaved.

– The father of us Cutbert & Richard Burbage was the first builder of
Playhowses & was himselfe in his younger yeeres a Player. The Theater hee
built with many Hundred poundes taken up at interest. The Players that
lived in those first times had onely the profitts arising from the dores, but
now the players receave all the commings in at the dores to them selves &
halfe the Galleries from the Houskeepers. Hee built this house upon leased
ground, by which meanes the Landlord & Hee had a great suite in law & by
his death, the like troubles fell on us, his sonnes; wee then bethought us of
altering from thence, & at like expence built the Globe with more summes
of money taken up at interest, which lay heavy on us many yeeres, & to
our selves wee joyned those deserving men, Shakspere Hemings, Condall,
Philips and others partners in ye profittes of that they call the House, but
making the Leases for 21 yeares hath beene the destruction of our selves &
others, for they dyeing at the expiration of 3 or 4 yeeres of their lease, the
subsequent yeeres became dissolved to strangers as by marrying with their
widdowes & the like by their Children.

– Thus Right Honorable, as concerning the Globe, where wee our selves
are but Lessees. Now for the Blackfriers that is our inheritance, our father
purchased it at extreame rates & made it into a play house with great charge
& trouble, which after was leased out to one Evans that first sett up the
Boyes commonly called the Queenes Majestes Children of the Chappell.
In processe of time the boyes growing up to bee men which were Underwood, Field, Ostler, & were taken to strengthen the service, the boyes dayly
wearing out, it was considered that house would bee as fitt for our selves,
& soe purchased the lease remaining from Evans with our money & placed
men Players, which were Hemings, Condall Shakspeare &c. And Richard
Burbage, who for 35 yeeres paines, cost, and Labour made meanes to leave
his wife and Children, some estate (& out of whose estates, soe many of
other Players and their families have beene mayntained) these new men

that were never bred from Children in the kings service, would take away with Oathes & menaces that wee shall bee forced, & that they will not thanke us for it, soe that it seemes they would not pay us for what they would have or wee can spare which, more to satisfie your honour then their threatning pride, wee are for our selves willing to part with a part betweene us, they paying according as ever hath beene ye custome & ye number of yeeres the lease is made for.

– Then, to shew your Honour against these sayinges that wee eat the fruit of their Labours. Wee referre it to your honours judgement to consider their profittes, which wee may safely maintaine, for it appeareth by their owne Accomptes for one whole yeere last past beginning from Whitson-Munday 1634 to Whitson Munday 1635 how each of these complainantes gained severally as hee was a Player and noe Howskepper £180, Besides Mr Swanston hath receaved from the Blackfriers this yeere as hee is there a Houskeeper above £30, all which beeing accompted together may very well keepe him from starving.

– Wherfore your honours most humble supplicantes intreates they may not further bee trampled upon then their estates can beare seeing, how deerly it hath beene purchased by the infinite cost & paynes of the family of the Burbages, & the great desert of Richard Burbage for his quality of playing that his wife should not sterve in hir old age, submitting our selves to part with one part to them for valuable consideration & let them seeke further satisfaccion else where (that is) of the Heires or assignes of Mr Hemings & Mr Condall who had theirs of the blackfriers of us for nothing, it is onely wee that suffer continually.

– Therefore humbly relyeing upon your honorable Charity in discussing their clamour against us wee shall, as wee are in duty bound, still pray for the dayly increase of your honours health & happines.

(f) A peticion of John Shankes to my Lord Chamberlaine shewing that according to his Lordships order hee did make a proposition to his fellowes for satisfaccion upon his assigening of his partes in ye severall houses unto them but they not onely refused to give satisfaccion but restrained him from the Stage, that therfore his lordship would order them to give satisfaccion according to his propositions & computation.

(g) Answered (vizt) I desire Sir H. Herbert & Sir John Finett & my sollicitor Daniell Bedingfield to take this petition & the severall papers heerunto annexed into their serious considerations & to speake with the severall parties interested, & therupon, & upon the whole matter to sett downe a proportionable & equitable summe of money to bee payd unto Shankes for the two partes which hee is to passe unto Benfield, Swanston & Pollard & to cause a finall agreement & convayances to bee settled accordingly & to give mee an account of their whole proceedinges in writing. Aug. 1. 1635.

APPENDIX 4

The repertory

This is an attempt at establishing a dating for the plays known to have been written for the Chamberlain's/King's Men and staged by them between 1594 and 1642.[1] This list includes the total of 211 plays known or strongly suspected to have been played in the company's repertoire between 1594 and 1642. Several exist only as titles. The 168 texts that survive in print or manuscript are listed in Appendix 5. Largely for practical reasons, the dates for the company's acquisition and staging of these plays are set in three-year periods, with some overlap between the dates. Few of the plays can be ascribed to an exact date, either of composition or of their sale to the company, and even fewer to a precise date of performance. The best evidence for first performances is in Henry Herbert's licensing records, which are noted as 'Herbert', as reproduced in N. W. Bawcutt's edition. Other evidence is taken from G. E. Bentley's list in *The Jacobean and Caroline Stage* (1.109–34), supplemented by evidence from individual play editions and the diaries of Simon Forman, Humphrey Mildmay, and John Greene. Known revivals are identified either from references by playgoers or from the court records, although not many of the court entries note the titles of the plays performed. The record of any court performance, here chiefly based on John Astington, *English Court Theatre, 1558–1642*, Appendix, 'Performances at Court, 1558–1642', presupposes a revival on the public stage in the year preceding the court's Christmas season of plays.

---

[1] Thanks for help in establishing this rough dating are due to Stanley Wells, Gary Taylor, and others from the Oxford Shakespeare for their analysis of the Shakespeare dates, and to Andrew Hickman for his ascription of the Beaumont and Fletcher plays, plus Gordon McMullan's chronology in Appendix 2 of *The Politics of Unease in the Plays of John Fletcher*, University of Masachusetts Press, Boston, 1994, pp. 267–9. For the period up to 1613, my chief debt is of course to Roslyn Lander Knutson. For plays post-1616, vols. III–V of G. E. Bentley, *The Jacobean and Caroline Stage*, 1956, were essential, as was the edition of Massinger by Philip Edwards and Colin Gibson (*The Plays and Poems of Philip Massinger*, 1.xxx–xxxi, lists Massinger's plays with co-authors, dates, and company).

27. Henry Peacham's drawing, probably from 1594, of a company playing *Titus Andronicus*, the Longleat manuscript. It was probably based on Peacham's view of the play performed by Sussex's Men at the Rose in late 1593 or early 1594, though it might equally have been a Chamberlain's performance later in 1594. For views on the date see Herbert Berry in *Shakespeare Bulletin* 17, and on the likelihood that it represents Shakespeare's play, see June Schlueter and Richard Levin in *Shakespeare Quarterly* 50 and 53.

Plays given to the company in 1594
The Two Gentlemen of Verona, *The Taming of the Shrew* (revived 1594, at court 26 Nov. 1633), *The Comedy of Errors* (1594, 1597, at court 28 Dec. 1604), *Love's Labours Lost* (at court 9 Jan. 1605), *1 Henry VI*, *2 Henry VI*, *3 Henry VI*, *Richard III* (at court 16 Nov. 1633), *Titus Andronicus* (revived 1594, 1596),[2] *Romeo and Juliet?* (revived 1598) [? + Queen's *Hester and Ahasuerus*, *Hamlet*, *King Leir*, *Troublesome Reign of King John*, *Famous Victories of Henry V*; and *Fair Em*, *Arden of Faversham*, *Edward III?*].[3]

Plays acquired 1594–1597
Richard II (revived 7 Feb. 1601, 12 June 1631), *King John* (revived 1610?), *A Warning for Fair Women*, *A Midsummer Night's Dream* (revived 1603, at court 1 Jan. 1604, 17 Oct. 1630), *The Merchant of Venice* (at court 10 and

[2] I am inclined to accept Gustav Ungerer's view (*Shakespeare Survey* 14, 1961, 106) that the *Titus* played for the new Lord Harington at Rutland on 1 January 1596 was by the Chamberlain's Men.
[3] Roslyn Lander Knutson, in 'Shakespeare's Repertory', *A Companion to Shakespeare*, ed. David Scott Kastan, Basil Blackwell, Oxford, 1999, pp. 346–61, argues as additional possibilities *Fair Em*, performed at the Rose by Sussex's along with *Titus Andronicus* in January 1594, *Arden of Faversham*, *Edward II* possibly *Edward III*, and *The Tartarian Cripple* (pp. 349–50), mostly on the grounds that they were Pembroke's plays, and some of Shakespeare's own plays did move from Pembroke's to the Lord Chamberlain's.

12 Feb. 1605), *1 Henry IV* (at court 1612–13, 1 Jan. 1625, as *Oldcastle* 1601, 6 Jan. 1631, 29 May 1638).

Plays acquired 1597–1600
The Merry Wives of Windsor (at court 4 Nov. 1604, 1612–13, 15 Nov. 1638, Greene[4] April 1635), *Much Ado about Nothing* (at court twice 1612–13), *2 Henry IV*, *Every Man in his Humour* (at court 2 Feb. 1605, 17 Feb. 1631, revived 18 Feb. 1630), *Every Man out of his Humour*[5] (at court 8 Jan. 1605), *As You Like It* (at court 2 Dec. 1603?), *Henry V* (revived 1602, at court 7 Jan. 1605), *Julius Caesar* (at court 1612–13, 31 Jan. 1637, 13 Nov. 1638), *A Larum for London*, *Cloth Breeches and Velvet Hose* (lost), *The Freeman's Honour* (lost).

Plays acquired 1600–1603
Hamlet (at court 24 Jan. 1637), *Satiromastix*, *Twelfth Night* (revived 1602,[6] at court 20 April 1618, 2 Feb. 1623), *Thomas Lord Cromwell*, *The Fair Maid of Bristow* (at court 26 Dec. 1603), *Sejanus*, *The London Prodigal*, *The Merry Devil of Edmonton* (at court 1612–13, 3 May 1618, 15 Feb. 1631, 6 Nov. 1638), *Troilus and Cressida* (revived 1609?), *Jeronimo* (? lost).

Plays acquired 1603–1606
The Malcontent (revived 1635), *Measure for Measure* (at court 26 Dec. 1604), *Othello* (at court 1 Nov. 1604, 1612–13, 8 Dec. 1636, revived 30 April 1610, 22 Nov. 1629,[7] Mildmay[8] 6 May 1635), *The Miseries of Enforced Marriage*, *All's Well that Ends Well*, *King Lear* (at court 26 Dec. 1606, revived 1610), *Volpone* (at court 27 Dec. 1624, 19 Nov. 1630, 8 Nov. 1638, Mildmay 27 Oct.

---

[4] i.e., John Greene, whose diary recorded visits to plays in the 1630s. He saw a play he called 'Falstaffe' in April 1635. Bentley reckoned this was a *Henry IV*, but it is more likely to have been the solo play.

[5] James P. Bednarz, in the 'Chronological Appendix' to his *Shakespeare and the Poets' War*, pp. 265–76, provides a careful analysis of the cross-referencing in the plays of the so-called Poets' War of 1600–2 to date the composition and staging of the plays in the War with some precision. He places *Every Man Out* in the autumn of 1599 (although the quarto has additions made later), *As You Like It* in the first three months of 1600, *Hamlet* later in 1600, *Twelfth Night* between January and September 1601, *Satiromastix* in mid-1601 (after *Poetaster* but before 24 October), *Troilus and Cressida* in the same period as *Satiromastix*, and the 'little eyases' addition to *Hamlet* in 1601 soon after *Satiromastix* and *Troilus* were staged.

[6] John Manningham recorded in his diary a performance at the Middle Temple Hall on 2 February 1602.

[7] On 30 April 1610 Prince Lewis of Wurtemberg saw it at the Globe. On 22 November in 1629 Herbert took 'the benefit of the winters day from the kinges company' a payment just four shillings short of ten pounds. We do not know what proportion of the total take such a payment was that day at Blackfriars.

[8] i.e., Sir Humphrey Mildmay, whose diary recorded his visits to plays between 1632 and 1640.

1638), *A Yorkshire Tragedy*, *The Revenger's Tragedy*, *The Tragedy of Gowrie* (lost), *The Spanish Maze* (at court 11 Feb. 1605; lost).

Plays acquired 1606–1609
The Devil's Charter (at court 2 Feb. 1607), *Macbeth* (Forman[9] 20 April 1611), *Pericles* (at court 20 May 1619, revived 10 June 1631), *Timon of Athens*, *Coriolanus*, *Antony and Cleopatra*, *Cymbeline* (Forman April 1611, at court 1 Jan. 1634), *Philaster* (at court twice 1612–13, 14 Dec. 1630, 21 Feb. 1637), *Richard the 2* (Forman, 30 April 1611; lost).

Plays acquired 1609–1612
The Winter's Tale (Forman 15 May 1611, at court 5 Nov. 1611, 1612–13, 21 April 1618, 18 Jan. 1624, 16 Jan. 1634, Herbert 19 Aug. 1623), *Mucedorus* (revised 1609, at court 3 Feb. 1611), *The Alchemist* (at court 1612–13, 1 Jan. 1623, revived 1 Dec. 1631, Mildmay 18 May 1639),[10] *The Tempest* (at court 1 Nov. 1611, 1612–13), *The Maid's Tragedy* (at court 1612–13, 9 Dec. 1630, 29 Nov. 1636), *Catiline* (Mildmay 9 Nov. 1634; at court 9 Nov. 1635), *A King and No King* (at court 26 Dec. 1611, 1612–13, 10 Feb. 1631, 10 Jan. 1637), *The Woman's Prize/The Tamer Tamed* (revived and blocked 18 Oct. 1633, at court 28 Nov. 1633), *Bonduca*, *Valentinian*, *The Second Maiden's Tragedy*, *A Bad Beginning makes a Good Ending* (at court 1612–13; lost), *The Twins' Tragedy* (at court 1 Jan. 1612, 1612–13; lost), *The Nobleman* (at court 23 Feb. 1612, 1612–13; lost).[11]

Plays acquired 1612–1615
The Two Noble Kinsmen, *The Captain* (at court 1612–13), *The Scornful Lady* (revived 18 Oct. 1633, at court 27 Dec. 1630, 6 Jan. 1642), *Henry VIII* (revived Aug. 1628), *The Duchess of Malfi* (at court 26 Dec. 1630), *Love's Pilgrimage* (Herbert renewed licence 16 Sept. 1635, at court 16 Dec. 1636), *The Honest Man's Fortune* (Herbert 8 Feb. 1625 'the originall being lost'), *Monsieur*

---

[9] Simon Forman's diary (Bentley, *Jacobean and Caroline Stage*, VI.16 n.1) records four visits to the Globe in April–May 1611, where he saw *Macbeth*, *Cymbeline*, *The Winter's Tale*, and a non-Shakespeare play about Richard II. It includes the death of Jack Straw, and Gloucester and Arundel's confrontation with Richard and their execution. John of Gaunt is the chief villain. Forman's account is reproduced in E. K. Chambers, *William Shakespeare*, 2 vols., Clarendon Press, Oxford, 1930, II.339–40.

[10] Ann Merricke, in a letter recorded in *Calendar of State Papers, Domestic*, 13.342 dated 21 January 1639, said she would have liked to be in town to see *The Alchemist*, 'which I heare this tearme is revis'd'.

[11] Possibly *The Atheist's Tragedy* should be included in this period of the company's acquisitions. Certainly Tourneur's *The Nobleman* of about the same time is registered as a company property in 1641. But the play was entered in the Stationers' Register and printed in 1611 with the title-page note '*as in divers places it hath often beene Acted*', which makes it unique among King's Men's plays of the time in omitting their name.

Thomas, The Laws of Candy, Cardenio (at court 1612–13, 8 June 1613; lost), *The Knot of Fools* (at court 1612–13; lost).

Plays acquired 1615–1618
The Beggar's Bush (at court 27 Dec. 1622, 30 Nov. 1630, 19 Nov. 1636, 1 Jan. 1639), *The Loyal Subject* (relicensed Herbert 23 Nov. 1633, at court 10 Dec. 1633, 6 Dec. 1636), *The Queen of Corinth, Thierry and Theodoret, The Devil is an Ass* (1616), *The Mad Lover* (at court 5 Jan. 1617, 5 Nov. 1630, revived 1630, 1639), *The Knight of Malta, The Widow, The Witch, The Fatal Dowry* (at court 3 Feb. 1631), *The Custom of the Country* (revived 22 Nov. 1628, at court 24 Oct. 1630, 27 Nov. 1638), *The Chances* (revived 1627, 1630, at court 30 Dec. 1630, 22 Nov. 1638).

Plays acquired 1618–1621
The Humorous Lieutenant, Epicene/The Silent Woman (at court 18 Feb., 21 April 1636), *The False One, Sir John van Olden Barnavelt* (Aug. 1619), *The Double Marriage, The Island Princess* (at court 26 Dec. 1621), *The Little French Lawyer, Anything for a Quiet Life, The Duke of Milan, Women Pleased, Hengist or The Mayor of Quinborough, The Bridegroom and the Madman* (lost) *The Woman's Plot* (at court 5 Nov. 1621; lost), *The Woman is too Hard for Him* (at court 26 Nov. 1621; lost).

Plays acquired 1621–1624
The Coxcomb (at court 5 Feb. 1622, 17 Nov. 1636), *The Prophetess* (Herbert 14 May 1622; revived 21 July 1629), *The Sea Voyage* (Herbert 22 June 1622 at Globe), *Osmond the Great Turk* (Herbert 6 Sept. 1622),[12] *The Spanish Curate* (Herbert 24 Oct. 1622 at Blackfriars; at court 26 Dec. 1622, 6 Dec. 1638, 7 Jan. 1639), *The Pilgrim* (at court 1 Jan., 29 Dec. 1622), *The Maid in the Mill* (Herbert 29 Aug. 1623, at court 29 Sept., 1 Nov. 'with reformations', 26 Dec. 1623), *The Wild Goose Chase* (at court 24 Jan. 1622, revived 6 Nov. 1632),[13] *The Nice Valour, More Dissemblers Besides Women* (1605? Herbert relicensed 17 Oct. 1623,[14] at court 6 Jan. 1624), *The Lovers' Progress/The Wandering*

---

[12] A play with this title, licensed by Herbert on 6 September on appeal by Heminges and Rice, was printed in 1657 as Carlell's, but the title-page declares that it was played by the Queen's company. All Carlell's other plays were for the King's, and Bentley, *Jacobean and Caroline Stage*, III.120–2, considers the 1657 attribution a mistake.

[13] In *Hengist*, written c. 1618–20 one of the plays purchased in print at Canterbury for sixpence and offered by the travelling players is said to be 'The Wildgoose chase'. All of their other play-titles are joke names, unlikely to be real. Conceivably Fletcher took the name for his play from *Hengist's* list.

[14] Bentley ran two of Herbert's entries into one, making *More Dissemblers besides Women*, which Herbert noted as 'old', the same play as Fletcher's lost *Devil of Dowgate*, which Herbert marked as 'new' in

Lovers (Herbert 6 Dec. 1623, at court 1 Jan. 1634, relicensed 7 May 1634 as *Cleander*; Queen saw it at Blackfriars 13 May 1634), *The Devil of Dowgate* (Herbert 17 Oct. 1623; lost), *The Buck is a Thief* (at court 28 Dec. 1623; lost), *Shankes Ordinary* (Herbert 16 March 1624; lost), *The Foolish Ambassador* (Herbert 18 Oct. 1623; lost), *The Bee* (Herbert 6 Sept. 1624; lost).

Plays acquired 1624–1628
Cupid's Revenge (at court 28 Dec. 1624), *A Wife for a Month* (Herbert 27 May 1624, at court 9 Feb. 1637), *A Game at Chess* (Herbert 12 June 1624), *Rule a Wife and Have a Wife* (Herbert 19 Oct. 1624, at court 2 Nov., 26 Dec. 1624, revived 1635), *The Staple of News* (1625), *The Fair Maid of the Inn* (Herbert 22 Jan. 1626 at Blackfriars), *The Noble Gentleman* (Herbert 3 Feb. 1626 at Blackfriars), *The Roman Actor* (Herbert 11 Oct. 1626), *The Cruel Brother* (Herbert 12 Jan. 1627), *Love's Cure* (Fletcher 1605, revised Shirley 1625), *The Elder Brother* (Greene Feb. 1635, Mildmay 25 April 1635, at court 5 Jan. 1637), *The Unnatural Combat, Rollo/The Bloody Brother* (at court 7 Nov. 1630, 21 Feb. 1631, 17 Jan. 1637, Mildmay 23 May 1633 at Globe, revived 1635), *The Woman Hater, Henry I* (Herbert 10 April 1624; lost), *The Spanish Viceroy* (1624; lost), *The Judge* (Herbert 6 June 1627; lost), *The Dumb Bawd of Venice* (at court 15 April 1628; lost).

Plays acquired 1628–1631
The Lover's Melancholy (Herbert 24 Nov. 1628), *The Deserving Favourite, The New Inn* (Herbert 19 Jan. 1629, at court 29 Nov., 28 Dec. 1638), *The Picture* (Herbert 8 June 1629), *The Soddered Citizen*,[15] *The Northern Lass* (Herbert 29 July 1629, at court 28 Dec. 1638), *The Just Italian* (Herbert 2 Oct. 1629), *The Fatal Dowry* (at court 3 Feb. 1631), *The Inconstant Lady* (at court 30 Sept. 1630, Greene March 1635), *Alphonsus Emperor of Germany* (written 1605? At court 3 Oct. 1630, 5 May 1636), *The Lovesick Maid* (Herbert 9 Feb. 1629, at court 6 April 1629; lost), *Minerva's Sacrifice* (Herbert 3 Nov. 1629; lost), *Beauty in a Trance* (at court 28 Nov. 1630; lost).

the next entry. He allowed *More Dissemblers* on the grounds that his predecessor Buc had allowed it, and it was 'free from alterations'. The second entry charges the usual fee for a new play. The two entries may refer to different plays, or to the original and a revision. They have been treated as two plays here.

15 Clavell's play in manuscript has inserts in the hand of the King's Men's book-keeper who revised *Believe As You List* and transcribed *Bonduca* and *The Honest Man's Fortune*. The list of 'Personae' in the manuscript names several King's players. Clavell's authorship is evident from a reference in the prologue to his having been a highwayman, a crime for which Clavell was given a royal pardon in 1627.

Plays acquired 1631–1634
Believe As You List (Herbert 11 Jan. 1631, 7 May 1631), *The Emperor of the East* (Herbert 11 Mar. 1631), *The Broken Heart, The Swisser* (1631),[16] *A Challenge for Beauty, The Novella* (1632), *The City Madam* (Herbert 25 May 1632), *The Magnetic Lady* (Herbert 12 Oct. 1632, revived 24 Oct. 1633), *The Queen's Exchange, The Guardian* (Herbert 31 Oct. 1633, at court 12 Jan. 1634), *The Wits* (Herbert 19 Jan. 1634, Mildmay 22 Jan. 1634, at court 28 Jan. 1634), *Bussy D'Ambois* (Paul's play revived; at court 7 April 1634, 27 March 1638), *A Very Woman* (Herbert 6 June 1634), *The Late Lancashire Witches* (Herbert 20 July 1634, Aug. 1634),[17] *Love and Honour* (Herbert 20 Nov. 1634, Mildmay 12 Dec. 1634, at court 1 Jan. 1637), *The Unfortunate Piety* (Herbert 13 June 1631; lost), *Love Yields to Honour* (Herbert, 25 April 1632: Queen saw it; lost), *The Corporal* (Herbert 14 Jan. 1633; lost),[18] *The Spartan Ladies* (Herbert April 1634, Mildmay 1 May 1634, Queen saw it at Blackfriars; lost).

Plays acquired 1634–1638
The Faithful Shepherdess (1609, revived 1633; at court 6 Jan., 18 Feb., 8 April 1634), *News from Plymouth* (Herbert 1 Aug. 1635), *The Conspiracy* (Greene 6 Nov. 1635), *The Platonic Lovers* (Herbert 16 Nov. 1635), *1* and *2 Arviragus and Philicia* (*2 Arviragus* at court 16 Feb., *1* and *2* on 18 and 19 April, 26 and 27 Dec. 1636), *The Bashful Lover* (Herbert 9 May 1636), *Aglaura* (Herbert 26 Jan. 1638, at court 3 April 1638), *The Royal Slave* (at court 12 Jan. 1637), *The Lost Lady* (at court 26 March 1638), *The Unfortunate Lovers* (Herbert 16 April 1638, at court 31 May, 30 Sept. 1638), *The Goblins, The Fair Favourite* (Herbert 17 Nov. 1638, at court 20 Nov., 11 Dec.1638), *1* and *2 The Passionate Lovers* (at court 26 and 28 July, 20 and 22 Dec. 1638), *Albertus Wallenstein* (Herbert 1639), *The Orator* (Herbert 10 Jan. 1635; lost), *The Governor* (at court 17 Feb. 1637; lost), *The King and the Subject* (Herbert 5 June 1638; lost), *The Apprentice's Prize* (lost), *The Duke of Lerma* (lost).

Plays acquired 1638–1642
The Distresses (*The Spanish Lovers?* Herbert 30 Nov. 1639), *The Doubtful Heir* (*Rosania*, Herbert 1 June 1640), *The City Match, The Imposture* (Herbert 10 Nov. 1640), *The Queen of Aragon* (Herbert 1640, at court 9 April 1640),

---

[16] *The Swisser* exists in a manuscript with a title page saying it was staged at the Blackfriars in 1631.
[17] Nathaniel Tomkyns described it at the Globe in a letter of 16 August. See Appendix 2.42.
[18] A title page of Wilson's play (Bodleian MS.Rawl. Poet.9) in his hand, says it was 'Acted at the Blackfriars'.

The Country Captain, Brennoralt, The Variety, The Brothers (The Politique Father? Herbert 26 May 1641), *The Cardinal* (Herbert 25 Nov. 1641), *The Sophy* (Herbert 1642), *The Sisters* (Herbert 26 April 1642), *Alexius* (Herbert 25 Sept. 1639; lost), *The Fair Anchoress of Pausilippo* (Herbert 26 Jan. 1640; lost), *The Fatal Friendship* (Herbert 1642; lost).

Jigs presumably played by the Chamberlain's/King's Men
Singing Simpkin (Kemp: 1594?),[19] *Phillips's jig of the slippers* (1595),[20] *Shankes Ordinary* (1624).[21]

---

[19] Kemp's only surviving jig, it is reprinted in C. R. Baskervill, *The Elizabethan Jig*, pp. 444–9.

[20] Entered in the Stationers' Register, 26 May 1595. No copy is extant.

[21] Not certainly a jig, it was licensed by Herbert on 16 March 1624 as 'written by Shankes himselfe'. Herbert charged the full pound that was the usual fee for licensing a play.

Surviving play-texts

This is a list, in chronological order of printing, of 160 plays that on the evidence of their title pages were staged by the Chamberlain's/King's Men. It includes any reprint editions up to 1642, together with a few notes of later and doubtful publications.[1] It includes the twelve plays that survive in print and also in manuscript form: *Bonduca, Hengist, A Game at Chess, The Humorous Lieutenant, The Honest Man's Fortune, The Beggar's Bush, The Elder Brother, The Tamer Tamed, The Court Secret, Aglaura, The Country Captain,* and *The Royal Slave.* It does not include the seven manuscript texts that were never printed in the seventeenth century: *The Second Maiden's Tragedy, The Witch, Sir John Van Olden Barnavelt, The Swisser, The Inconstant Lady, The Soddered Citizen,* and *Believe As You List.*[2] The list is set

---

[1] The list is compiled chiefly from W. W. Greg, *A Bibliography of the English Printed Drama to the Restoration,* London Bibliographical Society, Oxford, 1939, vols. I and II, supplemented by Bentley, *Jacobean and Caroline Stage,* vols. III–V. Reference has also been made to James P. Saeger and Christopher J. Fassler, 'The London Professional Theater, 1576–1642: a Catalogue and Analysis of the Extant Printed Plays', *Research Opportunities in Renaissance Drama* 34 (1995), 63–109, which, however, has a number of omissions.

[2] Copies of *Hengist, The Beggar's Bush,* and *The Tamer Tamed* are all Lambarde MSS. at the Folger Shakespeare Library; another copy of *Hengist* is in the Portland MS. at Nottingham University Library; *Bonduca* is in the British Library Add.MS.36758, and *The Elder Brother* in MS. Egerton 1994; *The Honest Man's Fortune* is Dyce MS.9 at the Victoria and Albert Museum; *The Humorous Lieutenant* is Brogynton MS.42 in Lord Harlech's Library; *The Court Secret* is Worcester College Oxford MS. 1200; *The Country Captain* is in British Library MS.Harl.7650; *Aglaura* is British Library MS.Royal 18c xxv, made for presentation to the king; *The Royal Slave* is in B.L. Add.MS.41616, Folger MS. 7044, Bodleian Arch.Seld.B26, and others. The six manuscripts of *A Game at Chess* are listed by T Howard Hill in his 1993 Revels Plays edition, p. xi. Three of these (Folger MS. v.a.231, British Library Lansdowne 690, and Bodleian Malone 25) are by Ralph Crane, one and part of another in the author's hand (Trinity College Cambridge MS. 0.2.66 and Huntingdon MS. EL34 B17), and another is a scribal copy (Folger MS. v.a.342). Of the unpublished manuscripts *The Second Maiden's Tragedy* is one of the three plays in Lansdowne 807 in the British Library, *The Witch* is in Malone 12 in the Bodleian Library, *Sir John Van Olden Barnavelt* is in B.L. Add.MS.18653, *The Swisser* is B.L.Add.MS.36759, *The Inconstant Lady* is a Lambarde MS. at the Folger Shakespeare Library and in Rawlinson Poet. 9, John Clavell's *The Soddered Citizen* was owned by Lt. Col. E. G. Troyte-Bullock when edited for the Malone Society in 1936, and *Believe As You List* is in Egerton 2828 in the British Library.

out in the order of each play's entry in the Stationers' Register (SR), or of its unregistered publication. Reprints of quartos published up to 1650 are included in the listings, and collected editions in square brackets. The one play misascribed to Queen Henrietta Maria's Men published in 1657, *Osmond the Great Turk*, is not included here. It takes the total of identifiable play-texts to 168.

1. Shakespeare, THE MOST Lamentable Romaine Tragedie of Titus Andronicus, SR 6 February 1594, Quarto 1594, 'As it was Plaide by the Right Honourable the Earle of *Darbie*, Earle of *Pembrooke*, and Earle of *Sussex* their Servants.' Further Qq 1600 ('As it hath sundry times beene playde by the Right Honourable the Earle of Pembrooke, the Earle of Darbie, the Earle of Sussex, and the Lord Chamberlaine theyr Servants'), 1611 [and F 1623, 1632].

2. Shakespeare, The First part of the Contention betwixt the two famous Houses of Yorke and Lancaster, with the death of the good Duke Humphrey: and the banishment and death of the Duke of *Suffolke*, and the tragicall ende of the proud Cardinall of *Winchester*, with the notable Rebellion of *Jacke Cade: and the Duke of Yorkes first claime unto the Crowne* [*2 Henry VI*], SR 12 March 1594, Q 1594. Further Qq 1600, 1619 [and F 1623, 1632].

3. Shakespeare, *The Taming of a Shrew*, SR 2 May 1594, Q 1594, 'As it was sundry times acted by the *Right honorable the Earle of* Pembrook his servants.' Further Qq 1596, 1607, 1623, 1631, 1632. [*Taming of the Shrew*, F 1623, 1632.]

4. Shakespeare, The True Tragedie of Richard *Duke of Yorke, and the death* of good King Henrie the Sixt, *with the whole contention betweene* the two houses Lancaster and Yorke, [*3 Henry VI*] Octavo 1595 'as it was sundrie times acted by the Right Honourable the Earle of Pembrooke his servants.' Further Qq 1600, 1619 [and F 1623, 1632].

5. Shakespeare, The Tragedie of King Richard the second, SR 29 August 1597, Q 1597, '*As it hath beene publikely acted by the right Honourable the Lorde Chamberlaine his Servants.*' Further Qq 1598 ('*By William Shakespeare*'), 1598, 1608 ('With new additions of the Parliament Sceane, and the deposing of King Richard, As it hath been lately acted by the Kinges Majesties servantes, at the Globe.'), 1615, 1634 [F 1623, 1632].

6. Shakespeare, The Tragedy of King Richard the third, SR 20 October 1597, Q 1597, 'As it hath beene lately Acted by the Right honourable the Lord Chamberlaine his servants.' Further Qq 1598 ('*By* William Shakespeare'), 1602, 1605, 1612, 1622, 1629, 1634 [F 1623, 1632].

7. Shakespeare, Romeo and Juliet, Q 1597, 'As it hath been often (with great applause) plaid publiquely, by the right Honourable the L. of *Hunsdon* his Servants.' Further Qq 1599 ('*Newly corrected, augmented, and amended*'), 1609, 1637 [F 1623, 1632].

8. Shakespeare, *The Hystorie of Henry the fourth* [*1 Henry IV*], SR 25 February 1598, Q 1598. Further Qq 1598, 1599 ('Newly corrected by *W. Shake-speare*'), 1604, 1608, 1613, 1622, 1639 [F 1623, 1632].

9. Shakespeare, Loves labors lost, Q 1598, 'As it was presented before her Highnes this last Christmas. Newly corrected and augmented *By W. Shakespere*.' Further Q 1631 [F 1623, 1632].

10. Anon., *Mucedorus . . . and Amandine*, Qq 1598, 1606. Q 1610, 'Amplified with new additions, as it was acted before the Kings Majestie at Whitehall on Shrove-sunday night. *By his Highnes Servantes usually playing at the Globe*.' Further Qq 1611, 1613, 1615, 1618, 1619, 1621, 1626, 1631, 1634, 1639.

11. Anon., A WARNING for Faire Women, SR 17 November 1599, Q 1599, 'As it hath beene lately diverse times acted by the right Honorable, the Lord Chamberlaine his Servantes.'

12. Jonson, EVERY MAN OUT OF HIS HUMOR, SR 8 April 1600, Q 1600, '*AS IT WAS FIRST COMPOSED* by the author B. J. *Containing more than hath been Publickely Spoken or Acted*.' [F 1616] 'First acted in the yeere 1599. By the then Lord CHAMBERLAINE his Servants,' 1640.

13. Shakespeare, THE CRONICLE History of Henry the fift, SR 4 August 1600 ('*To be staied*'), Q1600, '*As it hath bene sundry times playd by the Right honorable the Lord Chamberlaine his servants*.' Further Qq 1602, 1619 ('1608') [F 1623, 1632].

14. Shakespeare, THE Second part of Henrie the fourth [*2 Henry IV*], SR 23 August 1600, Q 1600, '*As it hath been sundrie times publikely* acted by the right honourable, the Lord Chamberlaine his servants. *Written by William Shakespeare*.' Further Qq 1600 [F 1623, 1632].

15. Shakespeare, Much adoe about Nothing, SR 23 August 1600, Q 1600, '*As it hath been sundrie times publikely acted, by the right honourable, the Lord Chamberlaine his servants. Written by William Shakespeare*.' [F 1623, 1632].

16. Shakespeare, A Midsommer nights dreame, SR 8 October 1600, Q1600, 'As it hath beene sundry times pub*likely acted, by the Right honourable, the Lord Chamberlaine his servants. Written by William Shakespeare*.' [F 1623, 1632].

17. Shakespeare, The most excellent Historie of the *Merchant of Venice*, SR 28 October 1600, Q 1600, '*As it hath beene divers times acted by the Lord Chamberlaine his Servants.* Written by William Shakespeare.' Further Qq 1619 ('1600'), 1637 [F 1623, 1632].

18. Jonson, EVERY MAN in his Humor, SR 14 August 1601, Q 1601, 'As it hath beene sundry times publickly acted by the right Honorable the Lord Chamber*laine his servants*. Written by BEN. JOHNSON.' [F 1616, 1640].

19. Shakespeare, A Most pleasaunt and excellent conceited Comedie, of Syr *John Falstaffe*, and the merrie Wives of *Windsor*, SR 18 January 1602, Q 1602, 'By *William Shakespeare*. As it hath bene divers times Acted by the right Honorable my Lord Chamberlaines servants.' Further Qq 1619, 1630 [F 1623, 1632].

20. Anon., *Thomas* Lord *Cromwell*, SR 11 August 1602, Q 1602, 'As it hath beene sundrie times pub-*likely Acted by the Right Hono*-rable the Lord Chamberlaine *his Servants*. Written by W. S.' Further Q 1613.

21. Anon., A LARUM *FOR* LONDON, OR *THE SIEDGE OF* ANTWERPE, SR 29 May 1602, Q 1602, 'As it hath been playde by the right Honorable the Lord Charberlaine his Servants.'

22. Dekker, Satiro–mastix, SR 11 November 1602, Q 1602, '*As it hath bin presented publikely*, by the right Honorable, the Lord Chamberlaine his Servants; and privately, by the Children of Paules.'

23. Shakespeare, THE Tragicall Historie of HAMLET *Prince of Denmarke*, SR 26 July 1602, Q 1603, 'As it hath beene diverse times acted by his Highnesse servants in the Cittie of London: as also in the two Universities of Cambridge and Oxford, and elsewhere.' Further Qq 1604–5 ('By William Shakespeare. Newly imprinted and enlarged to almost as much againe as it was, according to the true and perfect Coppie.'), 1611, n.d., 1637 [F 1623, 1632].

24. Marston, *THE* MALCONTENT, SR 5 July 1604, Q 1604, 'By John Marston.' Further Qq 1604, 1604 ('Augmented by *Marston*. With the Additions played by the Kings Majesties Servants. Written by *John Webster*').

25. Anon., THE FAIRE MAIDE of Bristow, SR 8 February 1605, '*played at Hampton Court by his Majesties players.*' Q1605, 'As it was plaide at Hampton, before the King and Queenes most excellent Majesties.'

26. Jonson, SEJANUS HIS FALL, SR 2 November 1604, 6 August 1605, Q 1605 'Written by BEN JONSON' (includes 'The names of the Actors.', A4v). [F 1616, 'Acted in the yeere 1603, By the K. MAJESTIES SERVANTS', 1640].

27. Anon., *THE* LONDON Prodigall, Q 1605, 'As it was plaide by the Kings Majesties servants. By *William Shakespeare.*'
28. Beaumont, *THE* WOMAN HATER, SR 20 May 1607, Q 1607, '*As it hath beene lately Acted by the Children of Paules*'. Further Q 1648 '*As it hath beene Acted by his Majesties Servants with great Applause*. Written by JOHN FLETCHER Gent.'
29. Wilkins, THE Miseries of Inforst MARIAGE, SR 31 July 1607, Q 1607, '*As it is now playd by his Majesties Servants.* By George Wilkins.' Further Qq 1611, 1629, 1637.
30. Middleton (Tourneur), THE REVENGERS TRAGEDIE, SR 7 October 1607, Q 1607, '*As it hath beene sundrie times Acted, by the Kings Majesties Servants.*'
31. Barnes, THE DIVILS CHARTER: A TRAGEDIE, SR 16 October 1607, Q 1607, 'As it was plaide before the Kings Majestie, upon Candlemasse night last: by his Majesties Servants. *But more exactly reveewed, corrected, and augmented since by the Author, for the more pleasure and profit of the Reader.*' Further Q 1607.
32. Jonson, VOLPONE Or THE FOXE, Q 1607. Further Q 1607 [F 1616, 'Acted in the yeere 1605. By the K. MAJESTIES SERVANTS. The Author B. J.', 1640].
33. Anon., THE MERRY DEVILL *OF* EDMONTON, SR 22 October 1607, Q 1608, '*As it hath beene sundry times Acted, by his Majesties Servants, at the Globe, on the banke-side.*' Further Qq 1612, 1617, 1626, 1631.
34. Shakespeare, King LEAR, SR 26 November 1607, Q 1608, '*As it was played before the Kings Majestie at Whitehall upon S. Stephans night in Christmas Holidayes.* By his Majesties servants playing usually at the Gloabe on the Bancke-side.' [F 1623, 1632].
35. Anon., A YORKSHIRE Tragedy, SR 2 May 1608, Q 1608, '*Acted by his Majesties Players at* the *Globe. Written by* W. Shakspeare.' Further Qq 1608 ('One of the foure Plaies in one, called a *York-shire* Tragedy: as it was plaid by the Kings Majesties Plaiers', 1619.
36. Shakespeare, The Historie of Troylus and Cressida, SR 7 February 1609 '*as yt is acted by my Lord Chamberlens men*', Q 1609, '*As it was acted by the Kings Majesties* servants at the Globe. *Written by* William Shakespeare.' Further Q 1609 [F 1623, 1632].
37. Shakespeare, Pericles, Prince of Tyre, SR 20 May 1608, Q 1609, 'As it hath been divers and sundry times acted by his Majesties Servants, at the Globe on the Banck-side. By William Shakespeare.' Further Qq 1609, 1611, 1619, 1630, 1635.

38. Fletcher, THE FAITHFULL Shepheardesse, Qq 1610, 1629, 1634 ('ACTED AT SOMERSET House before the KING and QUEENE on Twelfe night last, 1633. And divers times since with great applause at the Private House in Blacke-Friers, by his Majesties Servants. *Written by* JOHN FLETCHER. The third Edition, with Addition').

39. Jonson, THE ALCHEMIST, SR 3 October 1610, Q 1612, 'Written by BEN. JONSON.' [F 1616, 'Acted in the yeere 1610. By the Kings MAJESTIES Servants. The Author. B. J.'].

40. Jonson, CATILINE HIS CONSPIRACY, Q 1611, 'Written by BEN: JONSON.' Further Q 1635 'And now Acted by his MAJESTIES Servants with great applause'. [F 1616, 'Acted in the yeere 1611. By the Kings MAJESTIES Servants. The Author B. J.', 1640.]

41. Beaumont and Fletcher, THE SCORNFUL LADIE, SR 19 March 1616, Q 1616 'As it was Acted (with great applause) by *the Children of Her Majesties* Revels in the BLACKE FRYERS. Written by FRA. BEAUMONT and JO. FLETCHER, Gent.' Further Qq 1625 'As it was now lately Acted (with great applause) by the Kings Majesties servants, at the BLACKE FRYERS. Written by FRA. BEAUMONT, and JO. FLETCHER, Gentlemen', 1630, 1635, 1639.

42. Beaumont and Fletcher, The Maides Tragedy, SR 28 April 1619, Q 1619, 'AS IT HATH BEENE divers times Acted at the *Blacke-friers* by the Kings Majesties Servants.' Further Qq 1622 'Newly perused, augmented, and inlarged', 1630 'Written by *Francis Beaumont*, and *John Fletcher* Gentlemen', 1638, 1641.

43. Beaumont and Fletcher, A King and No King, SR 7 August 1618, Q 1619, 'Acted at the *Globe*, by his Maje-*sties Servants*. Written by *Francis Beamount*, and *John Fletcher.*' Further Qq 1625, 1631 'Acted at the *Blacke-Fryars*', 1639.

44. Beaumont and Fletcher, PHYLASTER. *OR*, Love lyes a Bleeding, SR 10 January 1620, Q 1620, '*Acted at the Globe by his Majesties Servants.*' Further Qq 1622 '*As it hath beene diverse times Acted*, at the Globe, and Blacke-Friers, by *his Majesties Servants. Written by Francis Beaumont* and *John Fletcher.* Gent. The second Impression, corrected, and amended.', 1628, 1634, 1639.

45. Fletcher, THE TRAGEDY OF THIERRY KING OF *France, and his Brother* Theodoret, Q 1621, 'As it was diverse times acted at the Blacke-*Friers by the Kings Majesties* Servants.' Further Qq 1648, 1649.

46. Shakespeare, THE Tragedy of Othello, The Moore of Venice, SR 6 October 1621, Q 1622, '*As it hath beene diverse times acted at the* Globe, and at the Black-Friers, by *his Majesties Servants. Written by* William Shakespeare.' Further Q 1630 (F 1623, 1632].

47. Massinger, THE DUKE OF MILLAINE. *A TRAGEDIE*, SR 20 January 1623, Q 1623, 'As it hath beene often acted by his Majesties servants, at the blacke Friers. *Written by* Philip Massinger.' Further Q 1638.

48. Webster, THE TRAGEDY *OF THE DUTCHESSE Of* Malfy, Q 1623, '*As it was Presented privatly, at the Black-Friers; and publiquely at the Globe, By the* Kings Majesties Servants. The perfect and exact Coppy, with diverse *things Printed, that the length of the Play would* not beare in the Presentment. Written by *John Webster.*' Further Q 1640.

49–64. Shakespeare, *The Tempest, The Two Gentlemen of Verona, Measure for Measure, The Comedy of Errors, As You Like It, All's Well that Ends Well, Twelfth Night or What You Will, The Winter's Tale, King John, I Henry VI, Henry VIII, Coriolanus, Timon of Athens, Julius Caesar, Macbeth, Antony and Cleopatra, Cymbeline,* [and 19 others published previously] SR 8 November 1623, F 1623, 1632.

65. Middleton, A Game at Chess, Q 1625 (?), 'As it was acted *nine days to gether at the Globe on the banks side.*' Further Q 1625.

66. Jonson, THE STAPLE OF NEWES. A COMEDIE, SR 14 April 1626, 7 September 1631, in *Second Volume of Works*, 1631, 'ACTED IN THE YEARE, 1625. *BY HIS MAJESTIES* SERVANTS. The Author Ben: Jonson.' Also in F 1640.

67. Ford, THE LOVERS Melancholy, SR 2 June 1629, Q 1629, '*ACTED* AT THE PRIVATE HOUSE IN THE BLACKE Friers, and publikely at the Globe by the Kings Majesties Servants.' [Dedicatory epistle signed 'John Ford'].

68. Carlell, The Deserving FAVORITE, Q 1629, 'As it was lately Acted, first before the Kings Majestie, and since publikely at the *BLACK-FRIERS*. By his MAJESTIES Servants. *Written by* LODOWICKE CARLELL, *Esquire.*'

69. Massinger, THE ROMAN ACTOR. *A TRAGEDIE,* Q 1629, 'As it hath divers times beene, with good allowance, Acted, at the private Play-house in the *Black-Friers*, by the Kings Majesties Servants. *WRITTEN By* Philip Massinger.'

70. Davenant, THE CRUELL BROTHER. A Tragedy, SR 10 January 1630, Q 1630, 'As it was presented, at the private house in the *Blacke-Fryers: By His Majesties Servants.*' [Dedicatory epistle signed 'William Davenant'].

71. Davenant, THE JUST ITALIAN, SR 10 January 1630, Q 1630, 'Lately presented in the private house at Blacke Friers, *By his Majesties Servants.*' [Epistle signed 'William D'avenant'].

72. Massinger, THE PICTURE *A TRAGAECOMEDIE*, Q 1630, 'As it was often presented with good allowance, at the *Globe*, and *Blackefriers* play-houses, by the Kings Majesties Servants. *Written by Philip Massinger.*'

73. Jonson, THE DIVELL IS AN ASSE: A COMEDIE, in *Second Volume of Works*, 1631, 'ACTED IN THE YEARE, 1616. *BY HIS MAJESTIES* SERVANTS. The Author BEN: JONSON.' Also in F 1640, Q 1641.

74. Jonson, THE NEW INNE. Or, *The light Heart. A COMOEDY*, SR 17 April 1631, Q 1631, 'As it was never acted, but most negligently play'd, by some, the Kings Servants. And more squeamishly beheld, and censured by others, the Kings Subjects. 1629. Now, at last, set at liberty to the Readers, his Majesties Servants, and Subjects, to be judg'd. 1631. By the Author, *B. Jonson.*'

75. Massinger, THE EMPEROUR OF THE EAST. A Trage-Comedie, SR 19 November 1631, Q 1632, 'As it hath bene divers times acted, at the *Black-friers*, and *Globe* Play-houses, by the *Kings Majesties Servants.* Written by PHILIP MASSINGER.'

76. Brome, THE NORTHERN LASSE, A COMEDIE, SR 24 March 1632, Q 1632, 'As it hath beene often Acted with good Applause, at the *Globe* and *Black-Fryers*. By his Majesties Servants. Written by RICHARD BROME.'

77. Massinger and Field, THE FATALL DOWRY: A TRAGEDY, SR 30 March 1632, Q 1632, '*As it hath beene often Acted at the Private House in Blackefryers, by his Majesties Servants. Written by P. M. and N. F.*'

78. Ford, THE BROKEN HEART. A Tragedy, SR 28 March 1633, Q 1633, '*ACTED* By the King's Majesties Servants at the private House in the BLACK-FRIERS.'

79. Fletcher and Shakespeare, THE TWO NOBLE KINSMEN, SR 8 April 1634, Q 1634, 'Presented at the Blackfriers by the Kings Majesties servants, with great applause: Written by the memorable Worthies of their time; Mr. *John Fletcher*, and Mr. *William Shakespeare.* Gent.'

80. Heywood and Brome, The Late Lancashire WITCHES, SR 28 October 1634, Q 1634, 'A well received Comedy, lately Acted at the *Globe* on the *Banke-side*, by the Kings Majesties Actors. WRITTEN, by THOM. HEYWOOD, AND RICHARD BROOME.'

81. Davenant, THE PLATONICK LOVERS. A Tragecomedy, SR 4 February 1636, Q 1636, 'Presented at the private House in the BLACK-FRYERS, *By his Majesties Servants.* The Authour WILLIAM D'AVENANT, Servant to her Majestie.'

82. Davenant, THE WITTS, A Comedie, SR 4 February 1636, Q 1636, 'PRESENTED AT THE Private House in Blacke Fryers, by his

Majesties Servants. *The Authour* WILLIAM D'AVENANT, *Servant to Her Majestie.*'

83. Heywood, A CHALLENGE FOR BEAUTIE, SR 17 June 1636, Q 1636, 'AS IT HATH BEENE SUN-dry times Acted, By the KINGS Majesties Servants: *At the* Blacke-friers, *and at the* Globe *on the* Banke-side. *Written by* THOMAS HEYWOOD.'

84. Fletcher, THE ELDER BROTHER A COMEDIE, SR 24 March 1637, Q 1637, 'Acted at the *Blacke Friers*, by his Majesties Servants.'

85. Berkeley, THE LOST LADY, A Tragy-COMEDY, SR 18 March 1638, Q 1638.[3]

86. Suckling, AGLAURA, SR 18 April 1638, Q 1638, 1646 'REPRESENTED At the Court, by his Majesties Servants.' Q 1648, 'PRESENTED At the Private House in *Black-Fryers,* by his Majesties Servants.'

87, 88. Carlell, ARVIRAGUS AND PHILICIA, SR 26 October 1638, Q 1639, 'As it was acted at the Private House in *Black-Fryers* by his Majesties Servants. *The first and second part.*'

89. Fletcher, MONSIEUR THOMAS. A COMEDY, SR 22 January 1639, Q 1639, 'Acted at the Private House in *Blacke Fryers.* The Author, JOHN FLETCHER. *Gent.*'

90. Massinger, THE UNNATURAL COMBAT. A Tragedie, SR 14 February 1639, Q 1639, 'Written by PHILP MASSINGER. As it was presented by the Kings Majesties Servants at the GLOBE.'

91. Glapthorne, THE TRAGEDY OF ALBERTUS WALLENSTEIN, SR 22 September 1639, Q 1639, 'Written by HENRY GLAPTHORNE . . . And Acted with good Allowance at the Globe on the Banke-side, by his Majesties Servants.'

92. Fletcher, THE BLOODY BROTHER. A Tragedy. By *B.J.F.* SR 4 October 1639, Q 1639, Further Q 1640 (Oxford), 'The Tragedy of ROLLO Duke of Normandy. ACTED BY HIS *Majesties Servants.* Written by JOHN FLETCHER *Gent.*'

93. Mayne, THE CITYE MATCH. *A* COMEDY, '*PRESENTED TO THE* KING and QUEENE *AT WHITE-HALL.* ACTED SINCE AT BLACK-FRIERS BY HIS Majesties *Servants.*'

94. Cartwright, THE ROYALL SLAVE. A Tragi-Comedy, Q 1639, 'Presented to the King and Queene by the Students of *Christ-Church*

---

[3] Sir William Berkeley's *The Lost Lady* was printed in 1638 without any ascription to the King's Men. But a note in *Strafforde's Letters*, II.150, states that 'Two of the King's Servants, Privy-Chamber Men both, have writ each of them a Play, Sir *John Sutlin* and *Will. Barclay,* which have been acted in Court, and at the *Black Friars*, with much Applause.'

in Oxford. *August* 30. 1636. Presented since to both their Majesties at *Hampton-Court* by the Kings Servants.' Further Qq 1640, 1651 ('Written by Mr WILLIAM CARTWRIGHT').

95. Habington, THE QUEENE OF ARRAGON. A Tragi-Comedie, SR 2 April 1640, Q 1640. Prologue and Epilogue 'at the Fryers.' [William Habington was related to Henry Herbert, Master of the Revels. The play was staged at court by Lord Chamberlain Pembroke's servants on 9 April 1640, and afterwards by the King's at Blackfriars].

96. Fletcher, RULE A WIFE And have a Wife, Q 1640, 'ACTED BY HIS *Majesties Servants.* Written by JOHN FLETCHER *Gent.*'

97. Jonson, THE MAGNETIC LADY: *OR,* HUMORS RECON-CIL'D. A COMEDY composed by BEN: JOHNSON. [F 1641].

98. Suckling, THE DISCONTENTED COLONELL (*Brennoralt*), SR 5 April 1642, Q 1642. [F 1646, 'Presented at the Private House in Black-Fryers, by His *Majesties* Servants. WRITTEN By Sir JOHN SUCKLING.']

99. Denham, THE SOPHY, SR 6 August 1642, Q 1642, 'As it was acted at the Private House in Black Friars by his Majesties Servants.'

100. Davenant, THE UNFORTUNATE LOVERS: A Tragedie, Q 1643, 'As it was lately Acted with great applause at the private House in *Black-Fryers*; By His Majesties Servants. The Author *William Davenaut*, Servant to Her Majestie.'

101. Suckling, THE GOBLINS A Comedy, SR 24 July 1646, Q 1646, 'Presented at the Private House in Black-Fryers, by His *Majesties* Servants. WRITTEN By Sir JOHN SUCKLING.'

102–34. Beaumont and Fletcher Folio, 1647 [the 34 collaboratively written plays not previously published in quarto], *The Mad Lover, The Spanish Curate, The Little French Lawyer, The Custom of the Country, The Noble Gentleman, The Captain, The Beggar's Bush, The Coxcomb, The False One, The Chances, The Loyal Subject, The Laws of Candy, The Lover's Progress, The Island Princess, The Humorous Lieutenant, The Nice Valour, The Maid in the Mill, The Prophetess, Bonduca, The Sea Voyage, The Double Marriage, The Pilgrim, The Knight of Malta, The Woman's Prize, Love's Cure, The Honest Man's Fortune, The Queen of Corinth, Women Pleased, A Wife for a Month, Wit at Several Weapons, Valentinian, The Fair Maid of the Inn, Love's Pilgrimage,* [the last of the 34, *Four Plays in One,* is excluded from the list of King's plays].

135. Cavendish, THE COUNTRY CAPTAINE, SR 4 September 1646, Q 1649, 'A COMEDYE LATELY PRESENTED By his Majesties Servants at the Blackfryers.'

136. Davenant, LOVE AND HONOUR, SR 4 September 1646, Q 1649, 'Written by W. DAVENANT Knight. Presented by His Majesties Servants at the *Black-Fryers*.'

137. Cavendish, THE VARIETY, A COMEDY, SR 4 September 1646, Q 1649, 'Lately presented by His Majesties Servants at the *Black-Friers*.'

138. Middleton, THE WIDDOW A COMEDIE, SR 12 April 1652, Q 1652, 'As it was Acted at the private House in *Black-Fryers*, with great Applause, by His late MAJESTIES Servants. Written by *BEN: JOHNSON. JOHN FLETCHER. THO: MIDDLETON*. Gent.'

139. Fletcher, THE Wild-Goose Chase. A COMEDIE, SR 4 September 1646, Q 1652, 'As it hath been Acted with singular Applause at the *Black-Friers*: Being the Noble, Last, and Onely *Remaines* of those Incomparable *Drammatists FRANCIS BEAUMONT, AND JOHN FLETCHER*, Gent. Retriv'd for the publick delight of all the Ingenious; And Private Benefit of *JOHN LOWIN* And *JOSEPH TAYLOR*, Servants to His late MAJESTIE.'

140. Brome, THE NOVELLA, A *COMEDIE*, SR 4 September 1646, in collection of Brome's plays, 1653, 'Acted at the Black-Friers, by his MAJESTIES Servants, *Anno* 1632. WRITTEN By RICHARD BROME.'

141. Shirley, THE DOUBTFUL HEIR. A Tragi-comedy, SR 4 September 1646, in collection of Shirley's plays, *Six New Playes*, 1653, 'AS It was Acted at the private House IN *BLACK FRYERS*. WRITTEN By JAMES SHIRLEY.'

142. Shirley, THE BROTHERS, A COMEDIE, SR 4 September 1646, in collection of Shirley's plays, *Six New Playes*, 1653, '*AS* It was Acted at the private House IN *BLACK FRYERS*. WRITTEN By JAMES SHIRLEY.'

143. Shirley, THE SISTERS, A COMEDIE, SR 4 September 1646, in collection of Shirley's plays, *Six New Playes*, 1653, 'AS It was acted at the private House IN *BLACK FRYERS*, WRITTEN By JAMES SHIRLEY.'

144. Shirley, THE CARDINAL, A TRAGEDIE, SR 4 September 1646, in collection of Shirley's plays, *Six New Playes*, 1653, 'AS It was acted at the private House IN *BLACK FRYERS*, WRITTEN By JAMES SHIRLEY.'

145. Shirley, THE IMPOSTURE A Tragi-Comedie, in Shirley collection, *Six New Playes*, 1653, '*AS* It was Acted at the private House In *BLACK FRYERS.* WRITTEN By JAMES SHIRLEY.'

146. Shirley, THE Court Secret, A TRAGI-COMEDY, in Shirley collection, *Six New Playes*, 1653, '*Never Acted*, But prepared for the Scene at *Black-Friers*. WRITTEN by JAMES SHIRLEY.'[4]

147. Middleton, THE MAYOR OF Quinborough: A COMEDY (*Hengist, King of Kent*), SR 4 September 1646, 13 February 1661, Q 1661, 'As it hath been often Acted with much Applause at *Black-Fryars*, By His Majesties Servants. *Written by* THO. MIDDLETON.'[5]

148. Chapman, THE TRAGEDY OF ALPHONSUS *EMPEROUR* OF GERMANY, SR 9 September 1653, Q 1654, 'As it hath been very often Acted (with great applause) at the Privat house in BLACK-FRIERS by his late MAJESTIES Servants. By *George Chapman* Gent.'

149–50. Carlell, THE PASSIONATE LOVERS, A *TRAGI-COMEDY. The First and Second Parts*, SR 4 September 1646, Q 1655, 'Twice presented before the KING and QUEENS Majesties at *Somerset-House*, and very often at the Private House in *Black-Friars*, with great Applause, *By his late* MAJESTIES *Servants. Written by LODOWICK CARLELL*, Gent.'

151. Davenant, *News from Plymouth*, SR 4 September 1646, in Davenant collection 1673 [licensed for acting on 1 August 1635; epilogue refers to King's Men].

152. Davenant, *The Distresses*, SR 4 September 1646, in Davenant collection 1673 [in list of King's plays 7 August 1641].

153. Davenant, *The Fair Favourite*, SR 4 September 1646, in Davenant collection 1673 [licensed for acting 17 November 1638].

154. Massinger, THE BASHFUL LOVER. A *TRAGI-COMEDY*, SR 9 September 1653, in Massinger collection 1655, 'As it hath been often Acted at the Private-House in *Black-Friers*, by His late MAJESTIES Servants, with great Applause. WRITTEN By *PHILIP MASSENGER*, Gent.'

155. Massinger, THE GUARDIAN, A *COMICAL-HISTORY*, SR 9 September 1653, in Massinger collection 1655, 'As it hath been often acted at the Private-House in *Black-Friers*, by his late

---

[4] A manuscript survives at Worcester College, Oxford, MS.1200.
[5] Two manuscripts contain scribal versions entitled *Hengist King of Kent*. The Lambarde MS. is at the Folger Shakespeare Library, the Portland copy at Nottingham University Library.

MAJESTIES Servants, with great Applause. *Written by PHILIP MAS-SENGER, Gent.*'

156. Massinger, A Very Woman, Or the PRINCE of TARENT. A *TRAGI-COMEDY,* SR 9 September 1653, in Massinger collection 1655, 'As it hath been often acted at the Private-House in *Black-Friars,* by his late MAJESTIES Servants, with great Applause. *Written by PHILIP MASSENGER, Gent.*'

157. Brome, THE QUEENS EXCHANGE, A COMEDY, SR 20 November 1656, Q 1657, 'Acted with generall applause at the *BLACK-FRIERS* BY *His* MAJESTIES *Servants.* WRITTEN BY Mr. RICHARD BROME.'

158. Middleton, MORE DISSEMBLERS BESIDE WOMEN. A COMEDY, SR 9 September 1653, in Middleton collection 1657.[6]

159. Massinger, The City-Madam, A COMEDIE, Q 1658, 'As it was acted at the private House in *Black-Friers* with great applause. Written by *Phillip Massinger* Gent.'

160. Middleton, ANY THING FOR A QUIET LIFE. A COMEDY, Q 1662, 'Formerly Acted at *Black-Fryers,* by His late Majesties Servants, *Never before Printed.* Written by *Tho. Middleton,* Gent.'

---

[6] The printing coupled it with *Women Beware Women,* which may also have been a King's play. It is listed here because it was included in the list of King's Men's plays of 7 August 1641 designed to check any unauthorized printing.

Court performances

This table gives the dates and where known the titles for all plays staged at court by the Lord Chamberlain's from the 1594–5 season until 1602–3, and the King's from late 1603 to 1642, in comparison with the total number by other companies, including the boy groups. The few plays recorded without any company being identified are included in the right-hand column. The figures are chiefly based on John Astington, *English Court Theatre 1558–1642*, Appendix, 'Performances at Court 1558–1642', pp. 234–67.

Chamberlain's/King's Men	Others
1594–5: 26 and 27 Dec., 26 Jan. = **3**	Admiral's 28 Dec., 1 and 6 Jan. = **3**
1595–6: 26, 27, 28 Dec., 6 Jan., 22 Feb. = **5**	Admiral's 1, 4 Jan., 22, 24 Feb. = **4**
1596–7: 26, 27 Dec., 1, 6 Jan., 6, 8 Feb. = **6**	None = **0**
1597–8: 26 Dec., 1, 6 Jan., 26 Feb. = **4**	Admiral's 27 Dec., 27 Feb.; Middle Temple (masque) 6 Jan. = **3**
1598–9: 26 Dec., 1 Jan., 20 Feb. = **3**	Admiral's 27 Dec., 6 Jan., 18 Feb. = **3**
1599–1600: 26 Dec., 6 Jan., 3 Feb. = **3**	Admiral's 27 Dec., 1 Jan., Derby's 5 Feb. = **3**
1600–1: 26 Dec., 6 Jan., 24 Feb. = **3**	Admiral's 28 Dec., 2 Feb., Derby's 1, 6 Jan., Paul's Boys 1 Jan., Blackfriars Boys 22 Feb. = **6**
1601–2: 26, 27 Dec., 1 Jan., 14 Feb. = **4**	Admiral's 27 Dec., Worcester's 3 Jan., Blackfriars Boys 6, 10 Jan., 14 Feb. = **5**
1602–3: 26 Dec., 2 Feb. = **2**	Italians 29 Aug., Admiral's 27 Dec., 6, 8 March, Paul's Boys 1 Jan., Worcester's 3 Jan., Hertford's 6 Jan. = **7**
1603–4: 26, 27, 28, 30 Dec., 1 Jan. (twice), 2, 19 Feb., (*The Fair Maid of Bristow*, *A Midsummer Night's Dream*) = **7**	1, 8 Jan. masques, 2, 13 Jan. Queen Anne's, 4, 15, 21, 22 Jan., 20 Feb. Prince's, 20 Feb. Paul's Boys, 21 Feb. Blackfriars Boys = **11**

Chamberlain's/King's Men	Others
1604–5: 1 Nov. (*Othello*), 4 Nov. (*Merry Wives*), 26 Dec. (*Measure for Measure*), 28 Dec. (*Comedy of Errors*), 7 Jan. (*Henry V*), 8 Jan. (*Every Man Out*), 2 Feb. (*Every Man In*), 10 Feb. (*Merchant of Venice*), 11 Feb. *The Spanish Maze*), 12 Feb. (*Merchant of Venice*) = **10**	23, 24 Nov., 14, 19 Dec., 15, 22 Jan., 5, 19 Feb. Prince's, 27 Dec. masque, 30 Dec. Queen Anne's, 1, 3 Jan. Blackfriars Boys, 6 Jan. *Masque of Blackness* = **13**
1605–6: King's undated = **10**	Paul's = 2 undated, 1, 30 Dec., 1, 4 Jan., 3, 4 March Prince's, 27 Dec. Queen Anne's, 5 Jan. masque = **10**
1606–7: July–Aug. 2 undated, 7 Aug., 26 Dec. (*King Lear*), 29 Dec., 4, 6, 8 Jan., 2 Feb. (*The Devil's Charter*), 5, 15, 27 Feb. = **12**	29 July, 1 Jan. Blackfriars Boys, 30 July Paul's Boys, 28 Dec., 13, 24, 30 Jan., 1, 11 Feb. Prince's, 6 Jan. masque = **10**
1607–8: 26, 27, 28 Dec., 2, 6 (2 plays), 7, 9, 17 (2 plays), 26 Jan., 2, 7 Feb. = **13**	19 Nov., 30 Dec., 3 Jan., 4 Jan. Prince's, 10 Jan. *Masque of Beauty*, 9 Feb. masque = **6**
1608–9: 12 undated = **12**	1, 4 Jan. Blackfriars Boys, 5 undated Queen Anne's, 3 undated Prince's, 1 undated Blackfriars Boys, 2 Feb. masque = **12**
1609–10: 13 undated = **13**	27 Dec. Queen Anne's, 28, 31 Dec., 7, 24 Jan. Prince's, 9 Feb. Charles's, 5 June masque, 5 undated Whitefriars Boys = **12**
1610–11: 15 undated = **15**	10 Dec. (3 plays), 27 Dec. Queen Anne's, 12, 20 Dec., 15 Jan. Charles's, 13 Dec., 2 Feb., 14 April Whitefriars Boys, 19, 28 Dec., 14, 16 Jan. Prince's, 5 June, 3 Feb. masques = **16**
1611–12: 31 Oct., 1 Nov. (*Tempest*), 5 Nov. (*Winter's Tale*), 9, 19 Nov., 16 Dec., 26 Dec. (*A King and No King*), 31 Dec., 1 Jan. (*The Twins' Tragedy*), 7, 12, 13, 15 Jan., 9, 19, 20, 23 Feb. (*The Nobleman*), 28 Feb., 28 March, 3, 16, 26 April = **22**	27 Dec., 12, 13, 21, 23 Jan., 2 Feb. Queen Anne's, 28, 29 Dec., 5, 29 Feb., 11 April Prince's, 5 Jan. Whitefriars Boys, 6 Jan. masque, 12, 28 Jan., 13, 24 Feb. Charles's, 19 Jan., 25 Feb., 11 March Lady Elizabeth's = **20**
1612–13: 19 undated (including *Alchemist, Cardenio, Bad Beginning, Much Ado, 1 Henry IV, Captain, Maid's Tragedy, King and No King, Philaster, Merry Devil, Much Ado, Winter's Tale, Julius Caesar, Tempest, 2 Henry IV, Twins' Tragedy, Nobleman*), 16 Feb., 8 June (*Cardenio*) = **21**	20 Oct., 25 Feb., 1 March Lady Elizabeth's, Nov., 1, 9 Jan., 27 Feb. Whitefriars Boys, 14, 15, 20 Feb. masques, 2, 5 March Prince's = **12**

Chamberlain's/King's Men	Others
1613–14: 1, 4, 5, 15, 16 Nov., 24, 27 Dec., 1, 4, 10 Jan., 2, 4, 8, 10, 18 Feb., 6, 8 March = **17**	12 Dec., 25 Jan. Lady Elizabeth's, 26, 29 Dec., 3 Jan. masques, 5 Jan. Queen Anne's = **6**
1614–15: 8 undated = **8**	1 Nov. Lady Elizabeth's, 6, 8 Jan. masques, 3 undated Queen Anne's, 6 undated Prince Charles's, 3 undated Palatine's = **15**
1615–16: 21 Dec., 13 undated = **14**	17 Dec., 6 undated Queen Anne's, 4 undated Charles's, 1, 6 Jan. masques = **13**
1616–17: 5 Jan. (*The Mad Lover*), 11 undated = **12**	28 Dec., 13 undated Charles's, 3 undated Queen Anne's, 6, 19 Jan., 4 May masques, 4 March, 1 undated French = **22**
1617–18: 6 April (*Twelfth Night*), 7 April (*Winter's Tale*), 3 May (*Merry Devil*), 15 undated = **18**	6 Sept. masque, 2 undated Queen Anne's, 6 Jan., 17, 19 Feb. masques = **6**
1618–19: 20 May (*Pericles*), 8 undated = **9**	3 unknown Sept., 1 Nov., 1 Jan. Charles's, 3 Jan. Prince's, 6 Jan., 8 Feb. masques = **8**
1619–20: 10 undated = **10**	2 Jan. Queen Anne's, 4 undated Charles's, 2 unknown, 6, 10 Jan., 29 Feb. masques = **10**
1620–1: 9 undated = **9**	29 Sept. unknown, 2 undated Prince's, 6 Jan., 11, 13 Feb. masques = **6**
1621–2: 5 Nov. (*The Woman's Plot*), 26 Nov. (*The Woman is too Hard for Him*), 26 Dec. (*The Island Princess*), 1 Jan. (*The Pilgrim*), 24 Jan. (*The Wild Goose Chase*), 5 Feb. (*The Coxcomb*) = **6**	26 Aug. Oxford students, 2 Sept. masque, 27, 29 Dec. Charles's, 30 Dec. Revels, 6 Jan., 6 May masque = **7**
1622–3: 26 Dec. (*The Spanish Curate*), 27 Dec. (*The Beggar's Bush*), 29 Dec. (*The Pilgrim*), 1 Jan. (*The Alchemist*), 2 Feb. (*Twelfth Night*), 4 undated = **9**	6 Jan. Charles's, 2 undated Lady Elizabeth's, 19 Jan. masque = **4**
1623–4: 29 Sept., 1 Nov., 26 Dec. (all *The Maid in the Mill*), 28 Dec. (*The Buck is a Thief*), 1 Jan. (*The Lovers' Progress*), 6 Jan. (*More Dissemblers Besides Women*), 18 Jan. (*The Winter's Tale*), 3–8 undated = **10–15**	5 Nov., 27 Dec., 4 Jan. Lady Elizabeth's = **3**
1624–5: 2 Nov., 26 Dec. (both *Rule a Wife and Have a Wife*), 27 Dec. (*Volpone*), 28 Dec. (*Cupid's Revenge*), 1 Jan. (*1 Henry IV*), 12 Jan., March = **7**	6 Jan. Lady Elizabeth's, 9 Jan. masque, 12 Feb. Cambridge students = **3**
1625–6: 10 undated = **10**	21 Feb. French play by Queen and ladies = **1**

Chamberlain's/King's Men	Others
1626–7: 12 undated = **12**	6 Nov. 'The Duke's Play', 19 Nov. 'The Queen's Play', 16 Nov., 14 Jan. masques, 2 unknown = **6**
1627–8: 15 April (*The Dumb Bawd of Venice*), 10 undated = **11**	2 Feb. unknown = **1**
1628–9: 6 April (*The Lovesick Maid*), 16 undated = **17**	1 unknown = **1**
1629–30: 12 undated = **12**	29 Sept. unknown, 10 undated Queen Henrietta's, 22 Feb. masque (?) = **12**
1630–1: 30 Sept. (*The Inconstant Lady*), 3 Oct. (*Alphonsus*), 17 Oct. (*Midsummer Night's Dream*), 24 Oct. (*Custom of the Country*), 5 Nov. (*The Mad Lover*), 7 Nov. (*Rollo*), 19 Nov. (*Volpone*), 28 Nov. (*Beauty in a Trance*), 9 Dec. (*The Maid's Tragedy*), 14 Dec. (*Philaster*), 26 Dec. (*Duchess of Malfi*), 27 Dec. (*Scornful Lady*), 30 Dec. (*Chances*), 6 Jan. (*Falstaff*),[1] 3 Feb. (*Fatal Dowry*), 15 Feb. (*Merry Devil*), 17 Feb. (*Every Man In*), 21 Feb. (*Rollo*) = **18**	9 Jan., 22 Feb. masques, 16 undated Queen Henrietta's = **18**
1631–2: 3 May, 11 undated = **12**	8 Jan., 14 Feb. masques, 9 undated Queen Henrietta's, 3 undated King's Revels = **14**
1632–3: 20 undated = **20**	9 Jan., 5 March masques, 14 undated Queen Henrietta's = **16**
1633–4: 16 Nov. (*Richard III*), 26 Nov. (*Taming of the Shrew*), 28 Nov. (*Tamer Tamed*), 10 Dec. (*Loyal Subject*), 1 Jan. (*Cymbeline*), 6 Jan. (*Faithful Shepherdess*), 12 Jan. (*Guardian*), 16 Jan. (*Winter's Tale*), 28 Jan. (*Wits*), 30 Jan. (*Night Walker*), 7 April (*Bussy D'Ambois*), 8 April (*Faithful Shepherdess*), 14 undated = **26**	19 Nov., 16 Dec., 14 Jan., 30 Jan., 6 Feb., 2 undated Queen Henrietta's, 3 undated Prince Charles's, 3, 18 Feb. masques = **12**
1634–5: 9 Nov. (*Catiline*), 27 undated = **28**	19, 20–6 Nov., 8 undated Queen Henrietta's, 17 Feb., 30 March, 15–16 April French, 6 undated Prince Charles's, 10–14 Feb. masque (3 repeats) = **23**
1635–6: 18 Feb. (*Epicene*), 18 April (*1 Arviragus and Philicia*), 19 April (*2 Arviragus and Philicia*), 21 April (*Epicene*), 12 undated = **16**	12 Aug., 19 Nov., 21 Dec. plays by Queen's ladies, Nov. Spanish play, Dec. French play, 24 Feb. King's Revels, 28 Feb. Beeston's Boys, 9 undated Queen Henrietta's, 2 undated King's Revels, 1 undated Beestons' Boys = **19**

[1] It is not clear which play this name fits, one of the *Henry IV* plays or *Merry Wives of Windsor*.

Chamberlain's/King's Men	Others
1636–7: 17 Nov. (*Coxcomb*), 19 Nov. (*The Beggar's Bush*), 29 Nov. (*Maid's Tragedy*), 6 Dec. (*Loyal Subject*), 26 Dec. (*1 Arviragus and Philicia*), 27 Dec. (*2 Arviragus and Philicia*), 1 Jan. (*Love and Honour*), 5 Jan. (*Elder Brother*), 10 Jan. (*King and No King*), 12 Jan. (*Royal Slave*), 17 Jan. (*Rollo*), 24 Jan. (*Hamlet*), 31 Jan. (*Julius Caesar*), 9 Feb. (*Wife for a Month*), 16 Feb. (*Governor*), 21 Feb. (*Philaster*) = **16**	12 Sept. masque, 7, 14 Feb. Beeston's Boys = **3**
1637–8: 30 Sept., 3 Feb., 26 March (*The Lost Lady*), 27 March (*Bussy D'Ambois*), 3 April (*Aglaura*), 29 May (Falstaff), 31 May (*Unfortunate Lovers*), 12 undated[2] = **19**	7 Jan., 6 Feb. masques, 3 undated Prince Charles's = **5**
1638–9: 26 July (*1 Passionate Lovers*), 28 July (*2 Passionate Lovers*), 30 Sept. (*Unfortunate Lovers*), Oct. 5 undated, 6 Nov. (*Merry Devil*), 8 Nov. (*Volpone*), 13 Nov. (*Julius Caesar*), 15 Nov. (*Merry Wives*), 20 Nov. (*Fair Favourite*), 22 Nov. (*Chances*), 27 Nov. (*Custom of the Country*), 29 Nov. (*Northern Lass*), 6 Dec. (*Spanish Curate*), 11 Dec.(*Fair Favourite*), 18 Dec., 20 Dec. (*1 Passionate Lovers*), 22 Dec. (*2 Passionate Lovers*), 27 Dec., 28 Dec. (*Northern Lass*), 1 Jan. (*The Beggar's Bush*), 7 Jan. (*Spanish Curate*) = **25**	7 undated Queen Henrietta's = **7**
1639–40: 11 Feb., 20 undated = **21**	14 Oct., 21 Jan., 18 Feb. masque, 9, 10 April Chamberlain's Servants,[3] 3 undated Prince Charles's, 7 undated Queen Henrietta's = **15**
1640–1: up to 16 undated = **16**	None = **0**
1641–2: 6 Jan. (*Scornful Lady*) = **1**	None = **0**
Total: 579 (or 583)	**Total: 412 (348 plays, 64 masques)**

[2] The twelve included possible repeats of Suckling's *Aglaura* and Berkeley's *The Lost Lady*.
[3] A special performance, repeated the following night, of Habington's *The Queen of Aragon*.

In the forty-eight years of their existence, the Chamberlain's/King's Men performed at court nearly twice as often as all other groups put together: they played more than 582 times, against 348 by other groups, including Italian, French, and Spanish visitors, Oxford and Cambridge students, and some groups of courtiers and masquers. They also delivered the speaking parts in a large proportion of the sixty-four masques, making an average for the number of their attendances at court at more than twelve nights each winter. In no year did they fail to appear at least twice. Their evenings spent entertaining the court ranged between two in their lowest season while Elizabeth was dying to twenty-eight at the height of Queen Henrietta's enthusiasm for plays in the 1634–5 festivities.

The Shakespeare company: a bibliography

No work relating to the Shakespeare industry and its many associated interests can presume to record every work, book, article, or manuscript that a scholar may have consulted in the years of preparing it for publication. This list of works consulted includes only those to which direct reference is made in this book and others which have supplied tangible help.

Aaron, Melissa D., 'The Globe and *Henry V* as business document', *Studies in English Literature* 40 (2000), 277–92.

Acts of the Privy Council of England, ed. J. R. Dasent, 32 vols., HMSO, London, 1890–1907.

Albright, Evelyn May, 'Shakespeare's *Richard II* and the Essex Conspiracy', *PMLA* 42 (1927), 686–720.

Altman, Joel B., *The Tudor Play of Mind: Rhetorical Inquiry and the Development of Elizabethan Drama*, University of California Press, Berkeley, 1978.

Archer, Ian, *The Pursuit of Stability: Social Relations in Elizabethan London*, Cambridge University Press, 1991.

Ashbee, Andrew, Lasocki, David, and Holman, Peter, *A Biographical Dictionary of English Court Musicians*, Ashgate, London, 1998.

Astington, John H., *English Court Theatre 1558–1642*, Cambridge University Press, 1999.

  'The Globe, the Court and *Measure for Measure*', *Shakespeare Survey* 52 (1999), 133–42.

Bald, R. C., *Bibliographical Studies in the Beaumont and Fletcher Folio of 1647*, Supplement to the Bibliographical Society's *Transactions* no. 13, Oxford University Press, 1938.

Baldwin, Thomas Whitfield, *The Organization and Personnel of the Shakespearean Company*, Princeton University Press, 1927.

Barish, Jonas, *The Anti-Theatrical Prejudice*, University of California Press, Berkeley, 1981.

  'Three Caroline "Defenses" of the Stage', in *Comedy from Shakespeare to Sheridan*, ed. A. R. Braunmuller and J. C. Bulman, University of Delaware Press, Newark, 1986, pp. 194–214.

Barroll, J. Leeds, 'A New History for Shakespeare and his Time', *Shakespeare Quarterly* 39 (1988), 441–64.

Politics, Plague, and Shakespeare's Theater: The Stuart Years, Cornell University Press, Ithaca, 1991.

Anna of Denmark, Queen of England: A Cultural Biography, University of Pennsylvania Press, Philadelphia, 2001.

Barton, Anne, *Ben Jonson Dramatist*, Cambridge University Press, 1984.

Baskervill, Charles Read, *The Elizabethan Jig and Related Song Drama*, University of Chicago Press, 1929.

Bate, Jonathan, *Shakespearean Constitutions – Politics, Theatre, Criticism 1730–1830*, Oxford University Press, 1989.

Bawcutt, N. W., *The Control and Censorship of Caroline Drama: The Records of Sir Henry Herbert, Master of the Revels 1623–73*, Oxford University Press, 1996.

Beal, Peter, 'Massinger at Bay: Unpublished Verses in a War of the Theatres', *Yearbook of English Studies* 10 (1980), 190–203.

'The Burning of the Globe', *Times Literary Supplement* 20 June 1986, 689–90.

Beaumont, Francis, and Fletcher, John, *The Dramatic Works of Beaumont and Fletcher*, General Ed. Fredson Bowers, 10 vols., Cambridge University Press, 1966–96.

Beckerman, Bernard, *Shakespeare at the Globe, 1599–1609*, Macmillan, New York, 1962.

'Philip Henslowe', in *The Theatrical Manager in England and America*, ed. Joseph W. Donohue, Jr, Princeton University Press, 1971, pp. 19–62.

Bednarz, James P., *Shakespeare and the Poets' War*, Columbia University Press, New York, 2001.

Bentley, Gerald Eades, *The Jacobean and Caroline Stage*, 7 vols., Clarendon Press, Oxford, 1941–68.

The Profession of Dramatist in Shakespeare's Time, Princeton University Press, 1971.

The Profession of Player in Shakespeare's Time, Princeton University Press, 1984.

Bergeron, David M., *Shakespeare's Romances and the Royal Family*, Kansas University Press, Lawrence, 1985.

'The King's Men's king's men: Shakespeare and folio patronage', in *Shakespeare and Theatrical Patronage in Early Modern England*, ed. Paul Whitfield White and Suzanne Westfall, Cambridge University Press, 2002, pp. 45–63.

Berry, Herbert, ed., *The First Public Playhouse: The Theater in Shoreditch 1576–1598*, McGill–Queen's University Press, Montreal, 1979.

'The Player's Apprentice', *Essays in Theatre* 1 (1983), 73–80.

'The Globe Bewitched and *El Hombre Fiel*', *Medieval and Renaissance Drama in England* 1 (1984), 211–30.

Shakespeare's Playhouses, AMS Press, New York, 1987.

'The Date on the "Peacham" Manuscript', *Shakespeare Bulletin* 17 (1999), 5–6.

Berry, Ralph, *Shakespeare and Social Class*, Humanities Press International, Atlantic Highlands, 1988.

Bevington, David, *Tudor Drama and Politics: A Critical Approach to Topical Meaning*, Harvard University Press, Cambridge, MA, 1968.

Bevington, David, and Holbrook, Peter, eds., *The Politics of the Stuart Court Masque*, Cambridge University Press, 1988.

Birch, Thomas, *The Court and Times of James I*, London, 1849.

Bland, Mark, 'The London Book-Trade in 1600', in *A Companion to Shakespeare*, ed. David Scott Kastan, Blackwell, Oxford, 1999, pp. 450–63.

Blayney, Peter W. M., 'The Publication of Playbooks', in *A New History of Early English Drama*, ed. John D. Cox and David Scott Kastan, Columbia University Press, New York, 1997, pp. 383–422.

Bliss, Lee, 'Tragicomic romance for the King's Men, 1609–1611: Shakespeare, Beaumont and Fletcher', in *Comedy from Shakespeare to Sheridan*, ed. A. R. Braunmuller, University of Delaware Press, Newark, 1986, pp. 148–64.

Bly, Mary, *Queer Virgins and Virgin Queans on the Early Modern Stage*, Oxford University Press, 2000.

Boehrer, Bruce Thomas, *Monarchy and Incest in Renaissance England*, University of Pennsylvania Press, Philadelphia, 1992.

Boose, Lynda E., 'The 1599 Bishops' Ban, Elizabethan Pornography, and the Sexualization of the Jacobean Stage', in *Enclosure Acts: Sexuality, Property, and Culture in Early Modern England*, ed. Richard Burt and John Archer, Cornell University Press, Ithaca, 1994, pp. 185–200.

Born, Hanspeter, 'The Date of *2, 3 Henry VI*', *Shakespeare Quarterly* 25 (1974), 323–34.

Bowers, Rick, 'John Lowin: Actor–Manager of the King's Company, 1630–1642', *Theatre Survey* 28 (1987), 15–35.

John Lowin and Conclusions upon Dances, Garland Publishing, New York, 1988.

Bradbrook, Muriel C., *The Rise of the Common Player*, Chatto & Windus, London, 1962.

Shakespeare the Craftsman, Chatto & Windus, London, 1969.

Bradley, David, *From Text to Performance in the Elizabethan Theatre: Preparing the Play for the Stage*, Cambridge University Press, 1992.

Briggs, Julia, *This Stage-Play World. English Literature and its Background 1580–1625*, Oxford University Press, 1983.

Brinkley, Roberta Florence, *Nathan Field, The Actor–Playwright*, Yale University Press, New Haven, 1928.

Bristol, Michael D., 'Theater and Popular Culture', in *A New History of Early English Drama*, ed. John D. Cox and David Scott Kastan, Columbia University Press, New York, 1997, pp. 231–48.

Brooks, Douglas A., *From Playhouse to Printing House. Drama and Authorship in Early Modern England*, Cambridge University Press, 2000.

Brownlow, F. J., *Shakespeare, Harsnett, and the Devils of Denham*, University of Delaware Press, Newark, 1993.

Bruster, Douglas, *Drama and the Market in the Age of Shakespeare*, Cambridge University Press, 1992.

Quoting Shakespeare: Form and Culture in Early Modern Drama, University of Nebraska Press, Lincoln, 2000.

Burt, Richard A., ' " 'Tis writ by me", Massinger's *The Roman Actor* and the Politics of Reception in the English Renaissance Theatre', *Theatre Journal* 40 (1988), 332–46.

    Licensed by Authority: Ben Jonson and the Discourses of Censorship, Cornell University Press, Ithaca, 1993.

Bushnell, Rebecca W., *Tragedies of Tyrants. Political Thought and Theater in the English Renaissance*, Cornell University Press, Ithaca, 1990.

Butler, Martin, *Theatre and Crisis, 1632–1642*, Cambridge University Press, 1984.

    'Massinger's *The City Madam* and the Caroline Audience', *Renaissance Drama* n.s. 13 (1982), 157–87.

    'Romans in Britain: *The Roman Actor* and the Early Stuart Classical Play', in *Phillip Massinger: A Critical Reassessment*, ed. Douglas Howard, Cambridge University Press, 1985, 139–70.

Calendar of State Papers, Domestic, HMSO, London; 1595–7, ed. Everett Green, 1869; 1598–1601, 1601–3, 1870.

Calendar of State Papers, Venetian, HMSO, London; 1615–17, ed. A. B. Hinds, 1908.

Campbell, Lily B., *Shakespeare's 'Histories': Mirrors of Elizabethan Policy*, Huntington Library, San Marino, 1947.

Cannon, Charles Dale, *'A Warning for Fair Women': A Critical Edition*. Mouton, The Hague, 1975.

Carleton, Sir Dudley, *Dudley Carleton to John Chamberlain, 1603–1624: Jacobean Letters*, ed. Maurice Lee, Jr, Rutgers University Press, New Brunswick, 1972.

Carnegie, David, ' "Malvolio Within": Performance Perspectives on the Dark House', *Shakespeare Quarterly* 52 (2001), 393–414.

Carroll, D. Allen, 'Greene, the Burbages, and Shakespeare', *Renaissance Papers 1980*, 45–51.

Carson, Neil, *A Companion to Henslowe's Diary*, Cambridge University Press, 1988.

Cartelli, Thomas, *Marlowe, Shakespeare and the Economy of Theatrical Experience*, University of Pennsylvania Press, Philadelphia, 1991.

Cercignani, Fausto, *Shakespeare's Works and Elizabethan Pronunciation*, Clarendon Press, Oxford, 1981.

Cerasano, S. P., 'The Chamberlain's–King's Men', in *A Companion to Shakespeare*, ed. David Scott Kastan, Blackwell Publishers, Oxford, 1999, pp. 328–45.

Chalfant, Fran C., *Ben Jonson's London: A Jacobean Placename Dictionary*, University of Georgia Press, Athens, GA, 1978.

Chamberlain, John, *The Letters of John Chamberlain*, ed. Norman Egbert McClure, 2 vols., American Philosophical Society, Philadelphia, 1939.

Chambers, E. K., *The Elizabethan Stage*, 4 vols., Clarendon Press, Oxford, 1923.

    William Shakespeare: A Study of Facts and Problems, 2 vols., Clarendon Press, Oxford, 1930.

Chan, Mary, *Music in the Theatre of Ben Jonson*, Clarendon Press, Oxford, 1980.

Clare, Janet, *'Art Made Tongue-tied by Authority': Elizabethan and Jacobean Censorship*, Manchester University Press, 1990.

Clark, Sandra, *The Plays of Beaumont and Fletcher: Sexual Themes and Dramatic Representation*, Harvester Press, New York, 1994.

Clegg, Cyndia Susan, *Press Censorship in Elizabethan England*, Cambridge University Press, 1997.

Cogswell, Thomas, 'Thomas Middleton and the Court, 1624: *A Game at Chess* in Context', *Huntington Library Quarterly* 47 (1984), 273–88.

Cohen, Walter, 'Prerevolutionary Drama', in *The Politics of Tragicomedy: Shakespeare and After*, ed. Gordon McMullan and Jonathan Hope, Routledge, London, 1992, pp. 122–50.

Coman, Alan C., 'The Congleton Accounts: Further Evidence of Elizabethan and Jacobean Drama in Cheshire', *Records of Early English Drama Newsletter* 14 (1989), 3–18.

Cook, David, and Wilson, F. P., *Dramatic Records in the Declared Accounts of the Treasurer of the Chamber 1558–1642*, Collections VI, The Malone Society, Oxford, 1961.

Cox, John D., 'Stage Devilry in Two King's Men Plays of 1606', *Modern Language Review* 93 (1998), 934–47.

The Devil and the Sacred in English Drama, 1350–1642, Cambridge University Press, 2000.

Crosfield, Thomas, *The Diary of Thomas Crosfield*, ed. Frederick S. Boas, Oxford University Press, London, 1935.

Cutts, John P., 'William Lawes' Writing for the Theatre and the Court', *The Library*, 5th series 7 (1952), 225–34.

La Musique de la troupe de Shakespeare: The King's Men sous la regne de Jacques Iier, Editions du centre national de la recherche scientifique, Paris, 1959.

Danby, John F., *Poets on Fortune's Hill: Studies in Sidney, Shakespeare, and Beaumont and Fletcher*, Faber, London, 1952.

Davies, H. Neville, 'Beaumont and Fletcher's Hamlet', in *Shakespeare, Man of the Theater*, ed. Kenneth Muir, Jay L. Halio, and D. J. Palmer, University of Delaware Press, Newark, 1983, pp. 173–81.

Davies, Sir John, *The Poems of Sir John Davies*, ed. Robert Krueger, Clarendon Press, Oxford, 1975.

Davison, Peter, 'Commerce and Patronage: the Lord Chamberlain's Men's Tour of 1597', in *Shakespeare Performed: Essays in Honor of R. A. Foakes*, University of Delaware Press, Newark, 2000, pp. 56–71.

Dekker, Thomas, *The Dramatic Works of Thomas Dekker*, ed. Fredson Bowers, 4 vols., Cambridge University Press, 1953–61.

Non-Dramatic Works, ed. A. B. Grosart, 5 vols., London, 1884–6.

Dessen, Alan C., *Elizabethan Stage Conventions and Modern Interpreters*, Cambridge University Press, 1984.

Dessen, Alan C., and Thomson, Leslie, *A Dictionary of Stage Directions in English Drama, 1580–1642*, Cambridge University Press, 1999.

Diehl, Huston, *Staging Reform, Reforming the Stage: Protestantism and Popular Theater in Early Modern England*, Cornell University Press, Ithaca, 1997.

Dillon, Janette, *Language and Stage in Medieval and Renaissance England*, Cambridge University Press, 1998.

Theatre, Court and City, 1595–1610: Drama and Social Space in London, Cambridge University Press, 2000.

Dobson, E. J., *English Pronunciation 1500–1700*, 2 vols., Clarendon Press, Oxford, 1957.

Dolan, F. E., *Dangerous Familiars: Representations of domestic crime in England, 1550–1700*, Cornell University Press, Ithaca, 1994.

Donaldson, Ian, ' "Misconstruing Everything": *Julius Caesar* and *Sejanus*', in *Shakespeare Performed: Essays in Honor of R. A. Foakes*, University of Delaware Press, Newark, 2000, pp. 88–107.

Downes, John, *Roscius Anglicanus*, ed. Judith Milhous and Robert D. Hume, Society for Theatre Research, London, 1987.

Duncan-Jones, Katherine, *Ungentle Shakespeare: Scenes from his Life*, Arden Shakespeare (Thomson Learning, London), 2001.

Dutton, Richard, '*Hamlet, An Apology for Actors*, and the Sign of the Globe', *Shakespeare Survey* 41 (1989), 35–43.

Mastering the Revels: The Regulation and Censorship of English Renaissance Drama, Routledge, London, University of Iowa Press, 1991.

'The Birth of an Author', in *Texts and Cultural Change in Early Modern England*, ed. Cedric C. Brown and Arthur Marotti, St Martin's Press, New York, 1993, pp. 153–78.

Licensing, Censorship and Authorship in Early Modern England: Buggeswords, Palgrave, Basingstoke, 2000.

Eccles, Mark, *Shakespeare in Warwickshire*, University of Wisconsin Press, Madison, 1961.

'Elizabethan Actors i: A–D', *Notes and Queries* 236 (1991), 38–49.

'Elizabethan Actors ii: E–K', *Notes and Queries* 236 (1991), 454–61.

'Elizabethan Actors iii: K–R', *Notes and Queries* 237 (1992), 293 303.

'Elizabethan Actors iv: S to End', *Notes and Queries* 238 (1993), 165–76.

Edmond, Mary, *Rare Sir William Davenant*, Revels Plays Companion Library, Manchester University Press, 1987.

'On Licensing Playhouses', *Review of English Studies* 46 (1995), 373–4.

'Yeomen, Citizens, Gentlemen and Players: the Burbages and their Connections', in *Elizabethan Theater: Essays in Honor of S. Schoenbaum*, ed. R. B. Parker and S. P. Zitner, University of Delaware Press, Newark, 1996, pp. 30–49.

Edwards, Philip, 'The Danger not the Death: the Art of John Fletcher', in *Jacobean Theatre*, Stratford-upon-Avon Studies 1, 1960, ed. John Russell Brown and Bernard Harris, Edward Arnold, London 1960, pp. 159–78.

Egan, Gabriel, 'John Heminges's Tap-House at the Globe', *Theatre Notebook* 55 (2001), 72–7.

Engle, Lars, *Shakespeare's Pragmatism: Market of his Time*, Chicago University Press, 1993.

Erne, Lukas, 'Shakespeare and the Publication of His Plays', *Shakespeare Quarterly* 53 (2002), 1–20.

Evans, Robert, *Ben Jonson and the Poetics of Patronage*, Bucknell University Press, Lewisburg, 1989.

Farmer, Alan B., and Lesser, Zachary, 'Vile Arts: the Marketing of English Printed Drama, 1512–1660', *Research Opportunities in Renaissance Drama* 39 (2000), 77–165.

Feather, John, 'Robert Armin and the Chamberlain's Men', *Notes and Queries* 19 (1972), 448–50.

Fehrenbach, Robert J., 'When Lord Cobham and Edmund Tilney "Were att Odds": Oldcastle, Falstaff, and the Date of *1 Henry IV*', *Shakespeare Studies* 18 (1986), 87–102.

Felver, Charles S., *Robert Armin, Shakespeare's Fool*, Kent State University Press, Ohio, 1961.

Feuillerat, Albert, ed., *Documents Relating to the Office of the Revels in the Time of Queen Elizabeth*, A. Uystpruyst, Louvain, 1908.

Finkelpearl, Philip J., '"The Comedians' Liberty": Censorship of the Jacobean Stage Reconsidered', *English Literary Renaissance* 16 (1986), 123–38.
  Court and Country Politics in the Plays of Beaumont and Fletcher, Princeton University Press, 1990.

Fisher, F. J., *London and the English Economy, 1500–1700*, Hambledon, London, 1990.

Flint, Laura, *Shakespeare's Third Keyboard: The Significance of Rime in Shakespeare's Plays*, University of Delaware Press, Newark, 2000.

Foakes, R. A., *Illustrations of the English Stage, 1580–1642*, Stanford University Press, 1985.

Foakes, R. A., and Rickert, R. T., *Henslowe's Diary*, Cambridge University Press, 1961, second edition, 2002.

Friedenreich, Kenneth, ed., *'Accompaninge the Players': Essays Celebrating Thomas Middleton, 1580–1980*, AMS Press, New York, 1983.

Frost, David L., *The School of Shakespeare: The Influence of Shakespeare on English Drama 1600–42*, Cambridge University Press, 1968.

Frye, Roland Mushat, *The Renaissance Hamlet: Issues and Responses in 1600*, Princeton University Press, 1984.

Fuller, David, 'Ben Jonson's Plays and their Contemporary Music', *Music and Letters* 58 (1977), 60.

Gaw, Allison, 'John Sincklo as one of Shakespeare's Actors', *Anglia* 49 (1925), 289–303.

George, David, 'Early Cast Lists for Two Beaumont and Fletcher Plays', *Theatre Notebook* 28 (1974), 9–11.
  'Shakespeare and Pembroke's Men', *Shakespeare Quarterly* 32 (1981), 305–23.

Gerschow, Frederic, 'Diary of the Journey of Philip Julius, Duke of Stettin-Pomerania through England in the year 1602', *Transactions of the Royal Historical Society* n.s. 6 (1892), 1–35.

Gibbs, A. M., ed., *Sir William Davenant: The Shorter Poems, and Songs from the Plays and Masques*, Clarendon Press, Oxford, 1972.

Gibson, Colin A., 'Another Shot in the War of the Theatres (1630)', *Notes and Queries* 232 (1987), 308–9.

Goldberg, Jonathan, *James I and the Politics of Literature*, Stanford University Press, 1983.

Gowan, Juliet Mary, ed., *An Edition of Edward Pudsey's Commonplace Book (c.1600–1615) from the Manuscript in the Bodleian Library*, University of London, 1967.

Grantley, Darryll, *Wit's Pilgrimage: Drama and the Social Impact of Education in Early Modern England*, Ashgate, Aldershot, 2000.

Graves, R. B., *Lighting the Shakespearean Stage, 1567–1642*, Southern Illinois University Press, Carbondale, 1999.

Gray, Austin K., 'Robert Armine, The Foole', *PMLA* 42 (1927), 673–85.

Gray, H. D., 'The Roles of William Kemp', *Modern Language Review* 25 (1930), 261–73.

Greenblatt, Stephen, ed., *The Power of Forms in the English Renaissance*, Pilgrim Books, Oklahoma, 1982.

   Shakespearean Negotiations: The Circulation of Social Energy in Renaissance England, University of California Press, Berkeley, 1988.

Greg, W. W., *Dramatic Documents from the Elizabethan Playhouses*, 2 vols., Clarendon Press, Oxford, 1931.

Gurr, Andrew, 'Who Strutted and Bellowed?', *Shakespeare Survey* 16 (1963), 95–102.

   'Intertextuality at Windsor', *Shakespeare Quarterly* 38 (1987), 189–200.

   'Singing through the Chatter: Ford and Contemporary Theatrical Fashion', in *John Ford: Critical Re-Visions*, ed. Michael Neill, Cambridge University Press, 1988.

   'Money or Audiences: the Impact of Shakespeare's Globe', *Theatre Notebook* 42 (1988), 3–14.

   'Playing in Amphitheatres and Playing in Hall Theatres', *Elizabethan Theatre* 13 (1993), 27–62.

   Playgoing in Shakespeare's London, second edition, Cambridge University Press, 1996.

   The Shakespearian Playing Companies, Clarendon Press, Oxford, 1996.

   '*Measure for Measure*'s Hoods and Masks: the Duke, Isabella, and Liberty', *English Literary Renaissance* 27 (1997), 89–105.

   'Who is Lovewit? What is he?' in *Ben Jonson and Theatre*, ed. Richard Allen Cave and Brian Woolland, Routledge, London, 1999, pp. 5–19.

   'Privy Councilors as Theatre Patrons', in *Shakespeare and Theatrical Patronage in Early Modern England*, ed. Paul Whitfield White and Suzanne Westfall, Cambridge University Press, 2002, pp. 221–45.

Haaker, Ann, 'The Plague, the Theater, and the Poet', *Renaissance Drama* 1 (1968), 283–305.

Hamilton, Donna, *Shakespeare and the Politics of Protestant England*, University of Kentucky Press, Lexington, 1992.

Hamline, William M., 'Scepticism in Shakespeare's England', *The Shakespearean International Yearbook* 2 (2002), 290–304.

Harbage, Alfred B., *Annals of English Drama, 975–1700*, third edition by Sylvia Stoler Wagenheim, Methuen, London, 1989.

Harp, Richard, and Stewart, Stanley, eds., *The Cambridge Companion to Jonson*, Cambridge University Press, 2000.

Harris, Jonathan Gill, and Korda, Natasha, eds., *Staged Properties in Early Modern Drama*, Cambridge University Press, 2002.

Harrison, William, *The Description of England*, ed. Georges Edelen, Folger Shakespeare Library/Dover Publications, Washington, DC, 1994.

Hayes, Tom, *The Birth of Popular Culture: Ben Jonson, Maid Marian and Robin Hood*, Duquesne University Press, Pittsburgh, 1992.

Haynes, Jonathan, *The Social Relations of Jonson's Theater*, Cambridge University Press, 1992.

Heinemann, Margot, *Puritanism and Theatre: Thomas Middleton and Opposition Drama under the Early Stuarts*, Cambridge University Press, 1980.

Helgerson, Richard, *Forms of Nationhood: The Elizabethan Writing of England*, University of Chicago Press, 1992.

Hillman, Richard, *Intertextuality and Romance in Renaissance Drama: The Staging of Nostalgia*, Macmillan, Basingstoke, 1992.

Hodgdon, Barbara, *The End Crowns All: Closure and Contradiction in Shakespeare's History*, Princeton University Press, 1991.

Honan, Park, *Shakespeare: A Life*, Oxford University Press, 2000.

Honigmann, E. A. J., and Brock, Susan, eds., *Playhouse Wills, 1558–1642: An Edition of Wills by Shakespeare and His Contemporaries in the London Theatre*, Manchester University Press, 1993.

Honneyman, David, 'The Family Origins of Henry Condell', *Notes and Queries* 230 (1985), 467–8.

Hopkins, Lisa, *John Ford's Political Theatre*, Manchester University Press, 1994.

Hotson, Leslie, *The Commonwealth and Restoration Stage*, Harvard University Press, Cambridge, MA, 1928.

Howard, Jean E., *The Stage and Social Struggle in Early Modern England*, Routledge, London, 1994.

Howard, Skiles, 'A Re-Examination of Baldwin's Theory of Acting Lines', *Theatre Survey* 26 (1985), 1–20.

Howard-Hill, T. H., 'Buc and the Censorship of *Sir John Van Olden Barnavelt* in 1619', *Review of English Studies* 39 (1988), 39–63.

'Political Interpretations of Middleton's *A Game at Chess* (1624)', *Yearbook of English Studies* 21 (1991), 274–85.

Middleton's 'Vulgar Pasquin': Essays on A Game at Chess, University of Delaware Press, Newark, 1995.

'Ralph Crane: the Life and Works of a Jacobean Scribe in the Next Millennium', *The Shakespearean International Yearbook* 2 (2002), 150–7.

Hoy, Cyrus, *Introductions, Notes and Commentaries to Texts in 'The Dramatic Works of Thomas Dekker'*, ed. Fredson Bowers, 4 vols., Cambridge University Press, 1980.

Ingram, William, 'The Globe Playhouse and its Neighbours in 1600', *Essays in Theatre* 2 (1984), 63–72.

'The Early Career of James Burbage', *Elizabethan Theatre* 10 (1988), 18–36.

The Business of Playing: The Beginnings of the Adult Professional Theater in Elizabethan England, Cornell University Press, Ithaca, 1992.

'The Cost of Touring', *Medieval and Renaissance Drama in England* 6 (1993), 57–62.

'The Economics of Playing', in *A Companion to Shakespeare*, ed. David Scott Kastan, Blackwell Publishers, Oxford, 1999, pp. 313–27.

Jackson, MacD. P., 'Shakespeare's *Richard II* and the Anonymous *Thomas of Woodstock*', *Medieval and Renaissance Drama in England* 14 (2001), 17–65.

Jackson, William A., *Records of the Court of the Stationers' Company 1602 to 1640*, The Bibliographical Society, London, 1957.

Jonson, Ben, *Works*, ed. P. and H. Simpson and C. H. Herford, 11 vols., Clarendon Press, Oxford, 1925–52.

Jowett, John, 'The Audacity of *Measure for Measure*', *Ben Jonson Journal* 8 (2001), 229–47.

Jump, J. D., ed., *Rollo Duke of Normandy*, University Press of Liverpool, London, 1948.

Kahn, Maura Slattery, 'Much Virtue in "If" ', *Shakespeare Quarterly* 28 (1977), 40–50.

Kamps, Ivo, *Historiography and Ideology in Stuart Drama*, Cambridge University Press, 1996.

Kastan, David Scott, 'Proud Majesty Made a Subject: Shakespeare and the Spectacle of Rule', *Shakespeare Quarterly* 37 (1986), 458–75.

Kathman, David, 'Reconsidering *The Seven Deadly Sins*', *Early Theatre* 7 (2004).

'Freemen and apprentices in the Elizabethan Theatre', *Shakespeare Quarterly* 55 (2004).

Kay, W. David, *Ben Jonson: A Literary Life*, Macmillan, Basingstoke, 1995.

Kernan, Alvin, *Shakespeare, the King's Playwright: Theater in the Stuart Court 1603–1613*, Yale University Press, New Haven, 1995.

King, T. J., *Casting Shakespeare's Plays: London Actors and their Roles, 1590–1642*, Cambridge University Press, 1992.

Kinney, Arthur, 'Essex and Shakespeare vs. Hayward', *Shakespeare Quarterly* 44 (1993), 464–6.

Lies Like Truth: Shakespeare, Macbeth, and the Cultural Moment, Wayne State University Press, Detroit, 2000.

Kirkland, Stuart M., '*Henry VIII* and James I: Shakespeare and Jacobean Politics', *Shakespeare Studies* 19 (1987), 203–17.

Knapp, Jeffrey, *Shakespeare's Tribe: Church, Nation, and Theater in Renaissance England*. University of Chicago Press, 2002.

Knapp, Margaret, and Kobialka, Michal, 'Shakespeare and the Prince of Purpoole: the 1594 Production of *The Comedy of Errors*', *Theatre History Studies* 4 (1984), 70–81.

Knutson, Roslyn Lander, *The Repertory of Shakespeare's Company 1594–1613*, The University of Arkansas Press, Fayetteville, 1991.

'Telling the Story of Shakespeare's Playhouse World', *Shakespeare Survey* 44 (1992), 145–56.

'Shakespeare's Repertory', in *A Companion to Shakespeare*, ed. David Scott Kastan, Blackwell Publishers, Oxford, 1999, pp. 346–61.

Playing Companies and Commerce in Shakespeare's Time, Cambridge University Press, 2001.

'Two Playhouses, Both Alike in Dignity', *Shakespeare Studies* 30 (2002), 111–17.

'Filling Fare: the Appetite for Current Issues and Traditional Forms in the Repertory of the Chamberlain's Men', *Medieval and Renaissance Drama in England* 15 (2003), 57–76.

Latham, Jacqueline E. M., 'Machiavelli, Policy and *The Devil's Charter*', *Medieval and Renaissance Drama in England* 1 (1984), 97–108.

Lavin, J. A., 'Shakespeare and the Second Blackfriars', *Elizabethan Theatre* 3 (1973), 66–81.

Law, Ernest, *Shakespeare as a Groom of the Chamber*, G. Bell & Sons, London, 1910.

Lawless, Donald S., 'The Parents of Philip Massinger', *Notes and Queries* 213 (1968), 256–8.

Leech, Clifford, *The John Fletcher Plays*, Chatto, London, 1962.

Leinwand, Theodore, *Theatre, Finance and Society in Early Modern England*, Cambridge University Press, 1999.

Lennam, T. N. S., 'Sir Edward Dering's Collection of Playbooks, 1619–1624', *Shakespeare Quarterly* 16 (1965), 145–51.

Lesser, Zachary, 'Mixed Government and Mixed Marriage in *A King and No King*: Sir Henry Neville Reads Beaumont and Fletcher', *ELH* 69 (2002), 947–77.

Levin, Harry, 'Two Magian Comedies: *The Tempest* and *The Alchemist*', *Shakespeare Survey* 22 (1971), 47–58.

Levin, Richard, 'The Longleat Manuscript and *Titus Andronicus*', *Shakespeare Quarterly* 53 (2002), 323–40.

Lieblein, Leanore, 'The Context of Murder in English Domestic Plays', *Studies in English Literature* 23 (1983), 181–96.

Limon, Jerzy, *Dangerous Matter: English Drama and Politics in 1624*, Cambridge University Press, 1989.

Lopez, Jeremy, *Theatrical Convention and Audience Response in Early Modern Drama*, Cambridge University Press, 2003.

Loughlin, Marie H., *Hymeneutics. Interpreting Virginity on the Early Modern Stage*, Bucknell University Press, Lewisburg, 1997.

McCabe, Richard, 'Elizabethan Satire and the Bishops' Ban of 1599', *Yearbook of English Studies* 11 (1981), 188–94.

MacIntyre, Jean, *Costumes and Scripts in the Elizabethan Theatres*, University of Alberta Press, Edmonton, 1992.

MacIntyre, Jean, and Epp, Garrett P. J., ' "Cloathes Worth All the Rest": Costumes and Properties', in *A New History of Early English Drama*, ed. John D.

Cox and David Scott Kastan, Columbia University Press, New York, 1997, pp. 269–86.

McDonald, Russ, *Shakespeare and the Arts of Language*, Oxford University Press, 2001.

McKeithan, D. M., *The Debt to Shakespeare in the Beaumont-and-Fletcher Plays*, privately printed, Austin, Texas, 1938.

MacKenzie, Ann L., 'A Study in Dramatic Contrasts: the Siege of Antwerp in *A Larum for London* and *El saco de Ameres*', *Bulletin of Hispanic Studies* 59 (1982), 283–300.

MacLean, Sally-Beth, 'Tour Routes: "Provincial Wanderings" or Traditional Circuits?', *Medieval and Renaissance Drama in England* 6 (1993), 1–14.

McLuskie, Kathleen, 'The Plays and the Playwrights: 1613–42', in *The Revels History of Drama in English Volume IV: 1613–1660*, Philip Edwards, Gerald Eades Bentley, Kathleen McLuskie and Lois Potter, Methuen, London, 1981.

Renaissance Dramatists: Feminist Readings, Harvester Wheatsheaf, London, 1989.

McMillin, Scott, 'Casting for Pembroke's Men: the *Henry VI* Quartos and *The Taming of A Shrew*', *Shakespeare Quarterly* 23 (1972), 141–59.

'Sussex's Men in 1594: the Evidence of *Titus Andronicus* and *The Jew of Malta*', *Theatre Survey* 32 (1991), 214–23.

'Professional Playwrighting', in *A Companion to Shakespeare*, ed. David Scott Kastan, Blackwell Publishers, Oxford, 1999, pp. 225–38.

McMillin, Scott, and MacLean, Sally-Beth, *The Queen's Men and their Plays*, Cambridge University Press, 1998.

McMullan, Gordon, *The Politics of Unease in the Plays of John Fletcher*, University of Massachusetts Press, Amherst, 1994.

Maguire, Laurie E., 'A Stage Property in *A Larum for London*', *Notes and Queries* 231 (1986), 371–3.

Shakespearean Suspect Texts: The 'Bad' Quartos and their Contexts, Cambridge University Press, 1996.

Maguire, Nancy Klein, ed., *Renaissance Tragicomedy: Explorations in Genre and Politics*, AMS Press, New York, 1987.

Manningham, John, *The Diary of John Manningham, of the Middle Temple, 1602–1603*, ed. R. Parker Sorlien, University Press of New England, Hanover, NH, 1976.

Marcus, Leah S., *Puzzling Shakespeare: Local Reading and its Discontents*, University of California Press, Berkeley, 1988.

Marlowe, Christopher, *The Complete Works of Christopher Marlowe*, ed. Fredson Bowers, 4 vols., second edition, Cambridge University Press, 1981.

Massinger, Philip, *The Plays and Poems*, ed. Philip Edwards and Colin Gibson, 5 vols., Clarendon Press, Oxford, 1976.

Masten, Jeffrey A., 'Beaumont and/or Fletcher: Collaboration and the Interpretation of Renaissance Drama', *ELH* 59 (1992), 337–56.

Maurer, Margaret, 'Constering Bianca: *The Taming of the Shrew* and *The Woman's Prize, or The Tamer Tamed*', *Medieval and Renaissance Drama in England* 14 (2001), 186–206.

Meads, Chris, *Banquets Set Forth: Banqueting in English Renaissance Drama*, Manchester University Press, 2001.

Melchiori, Giorgio, *Shakespeare's Garter Plays: 'Edward III' to 'Merry Wives of Windsor'*, University of Delaware Press, Newark, 1994.

Middleton, Thomas, *The Works of Thomas Middleton*, ed. A. H. Bullen, 8 vols., London, 1885–7.

  A Game at Chess, ed. T. H. Howard Hill, Revels Plays, Manchester University Press, 1993.

Milhous, Judith, and Hume, Robert D., 'New Light on English Acting Companies', *Review of English Studies* 42 (1991), 487–509.

Montrose, Louis A., *The Purposes of Playing: Shakespeare and the Elizabethan Theatre*, Chicago University Press, 1996.

Mowat, Barbara A., 'The Theater and Literary Culture', in *A New History of Early English Drama*, ed. John D. Cox and David Scott Kastan, Columbia University Press, New York, 1997, pp. 213–30.

Mulryne, J. R., and Shewring, Margaret, eds., *Theatre and Government under the Early Stuarts*, Cambridge University Press, 1993.

Munro, Ian, 'Secrecy and Publication in *A Game at Chess*', *Medieval and Renaissance Drama in England* 14 (2001), 207–26.

Murray, John Tucker, *English Dramatic Companies, 1558–1642*, 2 vols., Constable, London, 1910.

Norbrook, David, *Poetry and Politics in the English Renaissance*, Routledge, London, 1984.

Nosworthy, J. M., 'A Note on John Heminge', *The Library* 3 (1948), 287–8.

Nungezer, E., *A Dictionary of Actors and Other Persons Associated with the Public Representation of Plays in England before 1642*, Yale University Press, New Haven, 1929.

Orgel, Stephen, 'Making Greatness Familiar', in *The Forms of Power and the Power of Forms in the Renaissance*, ed. Stephen Greenblatt, University of Oklahoma Press, Norman, 1984, pp. 41–8.

  'What is a Text?', in *Staging the Renaissance: Reinterpretations of Elizabethan and Jacobean Drama*, ed. David Scott Kastan and Peter Stallybrass, Routledge, New York, 1991, pp. 83–7.

  Impersonations: The Performance of Gender in Shakespeare's England, Cambridge University Press, 1996.

Parry, Graham, *The Golden Age Restor'd: The Culture of the Stuart Court, 1603–42*, Manchester University Press, 1981.

Patterson, Annabel, *Shakespeare and the Popular Voice*, Basil Blackwell, Oxford, 1989.

  Reading Holinshed's Chronicles, Chicago University Press, 1994.

Patterson, W. B., *King James VI and I and the Reunion of Christendom*, Cambridge University Press, 1997.

Pearson, Jacqueline, *Tragedy and Tragicomedy in the Plays of John Webster*, Manchester University Press, 1980.

Pechter, Edward, ed., *Textual and Theatrical Shakespeare: Questions of Evidence*, University of Iowa Press, 1996.

Peck, Linda Levy, 'The Caroline Audience: Evidence from Hatfield House', *Shakespeare Quarterly* 51 (2000), 474–7.

Pepys, Samuel, *The Diary of Samuel Pepys*, transcribed and edited by Robert Latham and William Matthews, 9 vols., HarperCollins, London, 1983.

Pettet, E. C., '*Coriolanus* and the Midlands Insurrection of 1607', *Shakespeare Survey* 3 (1950), 34–42.

Pettit, Thomas, 'The Seasons of the Globe: Two New Studies of Elizabethan Drama and Festival', *Connotations* 2 (1992), 234–56.

Pinciss, G. M., 'Shakespeare, Her Majesty's Players, and Pembroke's Men', *Shakespeare Survey* 27 (1974), 129–36.

Pollard, Tanya, 'Beauty's Poisonous Properties', *Shakespeare Studies* 27 (1999), pp. 187–210.

Poole, Kristen, 'Saints Alive! Falstaff, Martin Marprelate, and the Staging of Puritanism', *Shakespeare Quarterly* 46 (1995), 47–75.

Powell, William S., *John Pory / 1572–1636: The Life and Letters of a Man of Many Parts*, Microfiche Supplement: Letters and Other Minor Writings, The University of North Carolina Press, Chapel Hill, 1977.

Pugliatti, Paola, *Shakespeare the Historian*, St Martin's Press, New York, 1996.

Puttenham, George, *The Arte of English Poesie*, ed. Gladys Doidge Willcock and Alice Walker, Cambridge University Press, 1936.

Pye, Christopher, *The Royal Phantasm: Shakespeare and the Politics of Spectacle*, Routledge, London, 1990.

Rackin, Phyllis, *Stages of History: Shakespeare's English Chronicles*, Cornell University Press, Ithaca, 1990.

Randall, Dale B. J., *Winter Fruit: English Drama, 1642–1660*, University Press of Kentucky, Lexington, 1995.

Rapaport, Stephen, *Worlds within Worlds: Structures of Life in Sixteenth-century London*, Cambridge University Press, 1989.

Rasmussen, Eric, 'Shakespeare's Hand in *The Second Maiden's Tragedy*', *Shakespeare Quarterly* 40 (1989), 1–26.

Riddell, James A., 'Some Actors in Ben Jonson's Plays', *Shakespeare Studies* 5 (1969), 285–98.

Riggs, David, *Ben Jonson: A Life*, Harvard University Press, Cambridge, MA, 1987.

Rollins, Hyder E., ed., *A Pepysian Garland: Black-letter Broadside Ballads of the Years 1595–1639*, Cambridge University Press, 1922.

Rutter, Carol Chillington, ed., *Documents of the Rose Playhouse*, Revels Plays Companion Library, Manchester University Press, 1984, revised edition 2001.

Sadie, Stanley, ed., *The New Grove Dictionary of Music and Musicians*, second edition, 29 vols., Macmillan, London, 2001, vol. VI.

Saeger, James P., and Fassler, Christopher J., 'The London Professional Theater, 1576–1642: a Catalogue and Analysis of the Extant Printed Plays', *Research Opportunities in Renaissance Drama* 34 (1995), 63–109.

Salingar, Leo 'Jacobean Playwrights and "Judicious" Spectators', *Renaissance Drama* n.s. 22 (1991), 209–34.

Salzman, Paul, *Literary Culture in Jacobean England: Reading 1621*, Palgrave, Basingstoke, 2002.

Sams, Eric, 'The Timing of the Shrews', *Notes and Queries* 230 (1986), 33–45.

Sanders, Julie, *Ben Jonson's Theatrical Republics*, Macmillan Press, Basingstoke, 1998.

    'Caroline Salon Culture and Female Agency: the Countess of Carlisle, Henrietta Maria, and Public Theatre', *Theatre Journal* 52 (2000), 449–64.

Schlueter, June, 'Rereading the Peacham Drawing', *Shakespeare Quarterly* 50 (1999), 171–84.

Schoenbaum, William, *William Shakespeare: A Compact Documentary Life*, Clarendon Press, Oxford, 1977.

Shakespeare, William, *The Complete Works*, The Norton Shakespeare, New York, 1997.

Sharpe, Kevin, *Criticism and Compliment: The Politics of Literature in the England of Charles I*, Cambridge University Press, 1987.

    The Personal Rule of Charles I, Yale University Press, New Haven, 1992.

Sheen, Erica, ' "The Agent for his Master": Political Service and Professional Liberty in *Cymbeline*', in *The Politics of Tragicomedy: Shakespeare and After*, ed. Gordon McMullan and Jonathan Hope, Routledge, London, 1992, pp. 55–76.

Shepherd, Simon, and Womack, Peter, *English Drama: A Cultural History*, Blackwell, Oxford, 1996.

Shirley, Frances Ann, *Shakespeare's Use of Off-stage Sounds*, University of Nebraska Press, Lincoln, NA, 1963.

Simpson, P., 'King Charles the First as Dramatic Critic', *Bodleian Library Record* 8 (1935–7), 257–62.

Skura, Meredith Ann, *Shakespeare the Actor and the Purposes of Playing*, University of Chicago Press, 1993.

Smith, Bruce R., *The Acoustic World of Early Modern England*, University of Chicago Press, 1999.

Smith, Emma, 'Studying Shakespeare and his Contemporaries', in *Talking Shakespeare: Shakespeare into the Millenium*, ed. Deborah Cartmell and Michael Scott, Palgrave, Basingstoke, 2001, pp. 55–69.

Smith, Irwin, *Shakespeare's Blackfriars Theater: Its History and Its Design*, New York University Press, 1964.

Somerset, J. A. B., ''How Chances it They Travel?': Provincial Touring, Playing Places, and the King's Men', *Shakespeare Survey* 47 (1994), 45–60.

Southworth, John, *Fools and Jesters at the English Court*, Sutton Publishing, Stroud, 1998.

Spiekerman, Tim, *Shakespeare's Political Realism: The English History Plays*, State University of New York Press, Albany, 2001.

Stallybrass, Peter, and Jones, Annie, *Renaissance Clothing and the Materials of Memory*, Cambridge University Press, 2000.

Steen, Sara Jayne, *Ambrosia in an Earthen Vessel: Three Centuries of Audience and Reader Response to the Works of Thomas Middleton*, AMS Press, New York, 1993.

Steggle, Matthew, *Wars of the Theatres: The Poetics of Personation in the Age of Jonson*, English Literary Studies 78, Victoria, BC, 1998.

Stern, Tiffany, ' "On each Wall / And Corner Poast": Playbills, Title-pages, and Advertising in Early Modern London', *English Literary Renaissance*, forthcoming.

Stone Peters, Julie, *Theatre of the Book, 1480–1880: Print, Text, and Performance in Europe*, Clarendon Press, Oxford, 2000.

Streitberger, W. R., ed., *Jacobean and Caroline Revels Accounts, 1603–1642*, Collections XIII, The Malone Society, Oxford, 1986.

'Personnel and Professionalization', in *A New History of Early English Drama*, ed. John D. Cox and David Scott Kastan, Columbia University Press, New York, 1997, pp. 337–56.

Suckling, John, *The Works of Sir John Suckling: The Plays*, ed. L. A. Beaurline, Clarendon Press, Oxford, 1971.

The Works of Sir John Suckling. The Non-Dramatic Works, ed. Thomas Clayton, Clarendon Press, Oxford, 1971.

Taunton, Nina, 'Did John Fletcher the Playwright go to University?', *Notes and Queries* 235 (1990), 170–2.

Taylor, Gary, 'The Fortunes of Oldcastle', *Shakespeare Survey* 38 (1985), 85–100.

'William Shakespeare, Richard James, and the House of Cobham', *Review of English Studies* 38 (1987), 334–54.

Taylor, Gary, and Jowett, John, *Shakespeare Reshaped*, Clarendon Press, Oxford, 1993.

Teague, Frances, *Shakespeare's Speaking Properties*, Bucknell University Press, Lewisburg, 1991.

Tomlinson, Sophie, ' "She that Plays the King": Henrietta Maria and the Threat of the Actress in Caroline Culture', in *The Politics of Tragicomedy: Shakespeare and After*, ed. Gordon McMullan and Jonathan Hope, Routledge, London, 1992, pp. 189–207.

Thomson, Peter, *Shakespeare's Theatre*, second edition, Routledge, London, 1992.

Shakespeare's Professional Career, Cambridge University Press, 1992.

'Rogues and Rhetoricians: Acting Styles in Early English Drama', in *A New History of Early English Drama*, ed. John D. Cox and David Scott Kastan, Columbia University Press, New York, 1997, pp. 321–36.

Traister, Barbara, *The Notorious Astrological Physician of London: Works and Days of Simon Forman*, Chicago University Press, 2001.

Tricomi, Albert H., *Anti-court Drama in England, 1603–1642*, University Press of Virginia, Charlottesville, 1989.

Trousdale, Marion, '*Coriolanus* and the Playgoer in 1609', in *The Arts of Performance*, ed. Murray Biggs, Edinburgh University Press, 1991, pp. 124–34.

Turner, Robert Kean, 'Collaborators at Work: *The Queen of Corinth* and *The Knight of Malta*', in *Shakespeare, Text, Language, Criticism: Essays in Honour of Marvin Spevack*, ed. Bernhard Fabian and Kurt Tetzeli von Rosador, Olms-Weidmann, Hildesheim, 1987, pp. 315–33.

Ungerer, Gustav, 'Shakespeare in Rutland', *Rutland Record* 7 (1987), 242–8.

Veevers, Erica, *Images of Love and Religion: Queen Henrietta Maria and Court Entertainment*, Cambridge University Press, 1989.

Wallace, Charles William, 'Shakespeare and his London Associates as Revealed in Recently Discovered Documents', *University of Nebraska Studies* 10 (1910), 261–360.

'The First London Theatre: Materials for a History', *University of Nebraska Studies* 13 (1913), 1–297.

Weimann, Robert, *Author's Pen and Actor's Voice: Playing and Writing in Shakespeare's Theatre*, Cambridge University Press, 2000.

Wells, Robin Headlam, *Shakespeare on Masculinity*, Cambridge University Press, 2000.

Wentersdorf, Karl P., 'The Origin and Personnel of the Pembroke Company', *Theatre Research International* 5 (1979), 45–68.

Wentworth, Thomas, *The Earl of Strafforde's Letters and Dispatches*, ed. William Knowler, 2 vols., London, 1739.

West, Anthony James, *The Shakespeare 'First Folio': The History of the Book, vol. I, An Account of the First Folio Based on its Sales and Prices, 1623–2000*, Oxford University Press, 2001.

White, Paul Whitfield, 'Shakespeare, the Cobhams, and the Dynamics of Theatrical Patronage', in *Shakespeare and Theatrical Patronage in Early Modern England*, ed. Paul Whitfield White and Suzanne Westfall, Cambridge University Press, 2002, pp. 64–89.

Whitney, Charles, 'The Devil his Due: Mayor John Spencer, Elizabethan Civic Antitheatricalism, and *The Shoemaker's Holiday*', *Medieval and Renaissance Drama in England* 14 (2001), 168–85.

Wickham, Glynne, Berry, Herbert, and Ingram, William, *English Professional Theatre, 1530–1660, A Documentary History*, Cambridge University Press, 2000.

Wiggins, Martin, *Shakespeare and the Drama of his Time*, Oxford University Press, 2000.

Wikander, Matthew K., *Princes to Act: Royal Audience and Royal Performance, 1578–1792*, Johns Hopkins University Press, Baltimore, 1993.

Wiles, David, *Shakespeare's Clown: Actor and Text in the Elizabethan Playhouse*, Cambridge University Press, 1987.

Shakespeare's Almanac: A Midsummer Night's Dream, Marriage, and the Elizabethan Calendar, D. S. Brewer, Woodbridge, 1993.

Williams, Clare, *Thomas Platter's Travels in England 1599*, Jonathan Cape, London, 1937.

Williams, Gary Jay, *Our Moonlight Revels: 'A Midsummer Night's Dream' in the Theatre*, University of Iowa Press, 1997.

Wills, Gary, *Witches and Jesuits: Shakespeare's 'Macbeth'*, Oxford University Press, New York, 1995.

Wilson, Arthur, *The Swisser*, ed. Linda V. Itzoe, Garland Publishing, New York, 1984.

Wilson, F. P., *The Plague in Shakespeare's London*, Oxford University Press, 1927.

Wilson, Luke, *Theaters of Intention: Drama and the Law in Early Modern England*, Stanford University Press, 2000.

Wilson, Richard, ' "A Mingled Yarn": Shakespeare and the Cloth Workers', *Literature and History* 12 (1986), 164–80.

Winstanley, Lilian, *Hamlet and the Scottish Succession*, Edinburgh, 1920.

   'Hamlet and the Essex Conspiracy. Part I', *Aberystwyth Studies* 6 (1924), 47–66.

   'Hamlet and the Essex Conspiracy. Part II', *Aberystwyth Studies* 7 (1925), 37–50.

Womack, Peter, 'Imagining Communities: Theatres and the English Nation in the Sixteenth Century', in *Culture and History 1350–1600: Essays on English Communities, Identities, and Writing*, Wayne State University Press, Detroit, 1992, pp. 91–146.

Wright, James, *Historia Histrionica*, London, 1699.

Yachnin, Paul, 'The Powerless Theatre', *English Literary Renaissance* 21 (1991), 49–74.

Zimmer, Ruth K., *James Shirley: A Reference Guide*, G. K. Hall, Boston, 1980.

Index